Preachers ought to focus major atter
seem to be a firm grasp of the obv
preachers focus on everything else ex
welcome Donald Hamilton's profound
perceptive book, *Preaching with Balance*. This book by the man
who holds the Stephen F. Olford chair of Biblical Preaching at
Columbia Biblical Seminary makes a genuine contribution to the
important study of this noble art.

Paige Patterson, President
Southwestern Baptist Theological Seminary
Fort Worth, Texas

Week by week we take up the Scriptures and mount the homiletical
high wire. In the study and in the pulpit swirling winds and
trends threaten to send us plummeting from our divinely appointed
calling. Extremes beckon us from either side. Balance alone keeps us
on the thin line of God's calling to faithfully proclaim God's Word.
Now, through *Preaching with Balance*, a firm hand reaches out to
steady preachers both neophyte and veteran. Through seven wisely
placed steps Dr. Donald Hamilton enables us to firmly plant our feet,
steadily keep our balance, humbly move ahead—all while faithfully
declaring, "Thus saith the Lord!"

John Kitchen, Senior Pastor
Stow Alliance Fellowship, Stow, Ohio

"For too long homileticians have camped out on the practical "how
to" while blatantly neglecting foundational matters in preaching. Don
Hamilton has brought a corrective to the work. *Preaching with
Balance* truly is a balanced approach to preaching, addressing theology
and philosophy as well as practical application. To top it off, Hamilton
weds hermeneutical integrity, homiletical ingenuity and healthy sermon
delivery into one volume—a much-needed feature in books on
preaching. It's got it all! And all of us who preach will do a better job
of handling God's Word rightly as a result of reading this book."

Jim Shaddix, Teaching Pastor
Riverside Baptist Church – Denver, CO

Don Hamilton, my seminary professor and mentor in my doctoral studies is well acquainted with the terrain of preaching and homiletics. He brings to this book four decades of preaching experience and two decades of teaching on the subject. "Preaching With Balance" covers all the bases for a preacher to maintain balance in the preaching task. The author is insightful and incisive when handling issues of balance. He cautions the preacher of the possibility of getting into a rut. This book is a plumbline for all preachers. It is an invaluable contribution to the preaching fraternity. A must for the preacher's shelf.

George Sumadraji (Rajoo)
Academic Dean: Durban Bible College - Durban, South Africa

My colleague at Columbia International University Seminary and School of Missions (we have very large sweatshirts) has produced for us an enormously practical work on all the critical issues of preaching in today's world. I commend Preaching with Balance without reservation.

Someone has said that balance may be just another word for deadness, but that is certainly not true with this very helpful discussion of faithfully and fruitfully proclaiming God's Word. The topics covered are balance in theological and personal perspective, in preaching purpose, in homiletical variety, and in sermon content and delivery.

Dr. Hamilton makes the point that most congregations would be pleased to hear better preaching, and most preachers would be pleased to be more effective in the pulpit. This text, carefully studied and applied, will greatly help to fulfill both desires.

Larry Dixon, Ph.D.
Professor of Theology
Columbia International University Seminary and School of Missions
Columbia, South Carolina

Preaching With Balance

ACHIEVING AND MAINTAINING BIBLICAL PRIORITIES IN PREACHING

Donald L. Hamilton

MENTOR

Copyright © Donald L Hamilton 2007

ISBN (10) 1-84550-265-5
ISBN (13) 978-1-84550-265-2

Published in 2007 by
Christian Focus Publications, Geanies House,
Fearn, Ross-shire, IV20 1TW, Scotland

www.christianfocus.com

Cover design by www.moose77.com

Printed and bound by CPD, Wales

Contents

Introduction

Fulcrum (fool'kram, ful'-) n.,pl. -crums or -cra (kra) [Lat.,
bedpost, from fulcire, to support.] 1. The point or support
on which a lever turns. 2. A centralized means of exerting
influence or pressure.[1]

In all likelihood, you've had the experience, though probably not very recently. Your body was thrust upward for a few feet, stopped for a split second, and then almost immediately began to fall toward the earth. Another almost instantaneous stop took place and then you were headed skyward again. You were not alone. A second, very necessary person was involved. While you were going up, he or she was going down; as you made your way downward, that person was on the way up. Up and down the two of you went until one or the other crawled off. Then, gravity took over and the person remaining was stranded in the down position.

We called them see-saws when I was a child. They were also called teeter-totters. It didn't take much to make one. A board eight or ten feet in length and a sawhorse usually did the job. Fancier ones, of course, could be found in public parks and playgrounds. There, the boards were thicker and usually included a handle. The sawhorse was replaced by a sturdy pipe or bar. But the principle and the results were the same.

You may recall that this equipment worked best if the children on each end weighed about the same. If there was much of a difference in weight, a remedy could sometimes be had by sliding the board in one direction or the other. The person who weighed less required a longer portion of the board, or *lever*, on his or her side of the pivot point, the *fulcrum*. The heavier person needed less. The principle at stake was that of balance. Without it, this toy wasn't much fun because it didn't accomplish what it was designed to do. Instead,

7

the riders either ended up suspended in mid-air, or sat stranded on the ground. Either way, you went nowhere fast!

I sometimes think of see-saws in regard to preaching. If preaching is to be effective in *exerting influence or pressure*, a fair amount of balance is required. Achieving this balance is no simple matter, however, for there are many more factors to consider than physical weight.

This volume is an attempt to offer some practical steps on how to pursue, achieve, and maintain balance in one's preaching ministry. It is intended primarily for those who preach to the same congregation on a regular basis, for this is where the issue of imbalance most frequently becomes an actual problem. It is also aimed in large part at those who are relatively new to the preaching task, for those persons still tend to be finding their way in developing both a theory and practice of preaching. Others – those who are experienced in the pulpit as well as those whose preaching is less frequent or perhaps itinerate – hopefully will find suggestions and perspectives in these pages which are useful in motivating them toward a more effective pulpit ministry. I will be gratified if this is the case.

While this book deals with preaching from the broader perspective of balance, it is also by necessity a discussion of preaching philosophy. In fact, the two subjects are related so closely that it is virtually impossible to separate them.

Every preacher has a philosophy of preaching. In some instances, it may be unarticulated; it may be inconsistently or haphazardly conceived; it may be poorly informed theologically; or it may lack a good foundation in homiletical and communication studies. In other instances, one's preaching philosophy may have been carefully formulated and refined over a significant period of time. It may be integrally related to theological and exegetical foundations and well informed in matters of communication theory, homiletical arrangement, and audience analysis. But regardless of which situation is true – or if the truth lies somewhere in the middle, which is generally the case – each time a sermon is conceived, planned, prepared, and delivered, the preacher's philosophy of preaching is most assuredly informing the finished product.

Furthermore, this finished product, the sermon, along with all the others which constitute one's preaching ministry, will produce results of one kind or another. The point is simply this: developing a philosophy of preaching is not an extra-curricular or extraneous activity for the one called to preach. This philosophy will directly impact the overall effectiveness, or lack thereof, of pulpit ministry. This is not to say that a carefully thought out philosophy of preaching will assure success, however one may attempt to define it. Other factors and competencies are certainly involved as well. But a sound overall philosophy of the preaching task is foundational, for it informs and challenges everything else associated with pulpit ministry.

This volume is meant, then, to assist preachers who desire to review and refine their philosophy of preaching. This will be done from the perspective of achieving and maintaining balance in one's preaching ministry.

The plan of the book is to focus on seven broad areas related to preaching: the theological perspective, the personal perspective, biblical foundations, preaching purpose, homiletical variety, sermon content, and delivery. These in turn will be broken down into smaller categories which represent many of the basic issues faced by a person desiring to be effective in the pulpit. There are also some appendixes which may prove helpful.

It is impossible to consider every facet of preaching in a single volume. It is hoped, however, that a sufficient number will come under scrutiny so that the reader will review his own existing ideas about the subject and be motivated to consider changes where that might seem necessary or wise. While perfection in preaching is an illusive dream, improvement is within the grasp of virtually everyone. Perhaps considering the matter of balance in preaching will serve as a catalyst in moving us toward this improvement.

Step One

Maintain a Balance in Theological Perspective

'In preaching, finite, frail, and fault-ridden human beings bear
bold witness to the infinite, all-powerful, and perfect Lord.
Such an endeavor would smack of unmitigated arrogance and
over-reaching were it not for the fact that God Himself has
set us to the task. In this light, preaching is not an act of
arrogance, but of humility. True preaching is not an exhibition
of the brilliance or intellect of the preacher, but an exposition
of the wisdom and power of God' (R. Albert Mohler).[1]

There is no responsibility in the world quite like it, this business of
being the pastoral leader of a congregation! Who else is expected
to prepare and present from one to three relatively lengthy public
speeches each week, week in and week out with few exceptions,
year after year, throughout one's entire career? The deadlines never
stop! Ernest T. Campbell, a former minister at New York's Riverside
Church, said that 'Sundays come toward the preacher like telephone
poles by the window of a moving train'.[2] And so it seems.

But preaching is only one aspect of pastoral ministry. A pastor is
expected to fulfill numerous other responsibilities during the course
of a week. These tasks may range from intense private counseling
to organizational administration; from uniting a couple in marriage to
officiating at a funeral and burial; from participating in a community
event to offering comfort and hope to a hospital patient; from
attending or leading a committee meeting to teaching a class of
teenagers or children; from visiting new church members in their
homes to writing a column for the church newsletter; from engaging
in evangelism to planning corporate worship. All of these and more
are separate from sermon preparation and delivery, though not
unrelated.

The preaching task alone would be quite formidable even if the other responsibilities were not present. Sermons are expected to be relevant, original, scholarly, properly organized, varied, accurate, rooted in tradition, contemporary, challenging, inspiring, enthusiastically presented and comforting. And this is to specify only a few of the standard requirements!

The pastor is expected to be generally available to his constituents for all matter of concerns, but still spend adequate time alone in the study in order to achieve an acceptable level of competence in the skill of preaching. And, as is the case with everyone else, there are personal and family concerns which require attention. It should not be a surprise, therefore, that the typical workweek of the minister involves full days, several evenings, and even weekend time in addition to the scheduled Sunday services.

In the midst of these considerations, however, two basic assumptions seem to be true: most congregations would be pleased to hear better preaching, and most preachers would be pleased to be more effective in the pulpit. How, then, can these desires be realized? The place

to begin is to consider certain theological perspectives as foundational to the preacher's total philosophy of ministry including, of course, a corollary philosophy of preaching. It is vitally important to put first things first!

Understand Theological Foundations

Make no mistake about it, preachers are expected to preach. This is attested formally in church constitutions and books of church order across denominational and theological boundaries. It is also attested by virtually any job description prepared for a senior or 'solo' pastor. Even those called to staff positions other than 'senior pastor' are occasionally asked to present sermons to their own congregations or in other settings. Preaching goes with the territory.

Why in the world is this the case? In an age of cable television networks, wide-spread accessibility to audio and video tapes, compact discs, multi-media computers, communications satellites, and cyber-space technology, isn't this preaching business a little archaic? Isn't there a better way to deal with religious information? Isn't there a more efficient means of reaching the unchurched with the gospel? Aren't there better ways of teaching and inspiring those who have previously responded positively to the message of Christ? Shouldn't this part of the pastor's job description be changed?

From a human perspective alone, the answers to these questions would probably be 'yes' each time. In fact, even from a Christian viewpoint, the questions should be answered with a partial affirmation. It is true that preaching is indeed an old, old method of presenting the truth of God, and that special effort is required to retain freshness and vigor. It is also necessary to affirm that modern technologies should be employed whenever possible to reach the unreached and minister to the reached.

Technology should never be viewed as a threat *per se*, but as a potential asset in the spreading of Christian truth. The Protestant Reformation was assisted on its way because of the prior invention of the printing press. It may be that no one capitalized on this more than the nineteenth century 'Prince of Preachers', C. H. Spurgeon. From his early ministry onward, his sermons were recorded stenographically and then almost immediately put into print in order to be distributed on both sides of the Atlantic. In the twentieth century, Charles Fuller pioneered Christian radio through *The Old Fashioned Revival Hour*. Missionary Joy Ridderhof was instrumental in taking the gospel to numerous unreached tribal peoples by means of portable wind-up phonographs and battery-operated tape players. Fifty years ago, Roman Catholic Bishop Fulton J. Sheen was one of the first to recognize the potential usefulness of television as a means to spread the Christian message. The Billy Graham Evangelistic Association and other organizations have made extensive use of motion pictures. The widespread availability of video recorders and DVD players has led to the production of numerous Christian-oriented videos for the home and church. The Internet and other on-line computer services offer accessibility to numerous Christian organizations which can use this means to share ministry-related information. Satellites have been used to reach multiple millions with the gospel simultaneously as well as for instructional purposes in the classroom. Technology has its rightful place in the work of the church and we should be grateful for it.

None of these advances either negates or legitimizes the role of preaching in our day because preaching, like all Christian concerns, depends on other standards. If the practice of preaching is to be either questioned or justified, this must be done on the basis of biblical theology. Where do we begin, then, with our consideration of theological concerns?

The Nature of God
The rightful starting point is with God himself. We must remember that he is not the absentee god of the Deists, but a God who is both transcendent and immanent. His greatness and 'total otherness' not withstanding, God is actively involved in the affairs of our world. He is not a passive bystander. Further, he is a communicative Being who has chosen to make his presence known.

Paul's ministry at Athens (Acts 17:16-34) is a great illustration of this truth. The apostle informed the learned philosophers of that polytheistic culture that their unknown god was actually the one-and-only God of the universe and that he had revealed himself through general and special revelation. Further, this self-disclosure of God has made necessary a response by all persons.

The idea that God has spoken should not surprise us. Instead, we should be utterly flabbergasted had he not done so. If a personal God capable of creation exists, it is reasonable to assume that he would make himself known to his creation by some means. This would be both possible and probable. Otherwise, his personal nature would not be known for certain. At best, human beings would be able to theorize or guess about his nature, but little could be known for certain. Thankfully, God has spoken and we too can now speak intelligently about him.

General Revelation
God has revealed general things about himself in the natural world and by other means. Through nature, for example, God has informed

humanity that he exists, that he has divine power, and that the human race is somehow responsible to him. Furthermore, we cannot claim ignorance of his existence. As the apostle Paul argues, we are without excuse (Rom 1:20).

This kind of revelation is helpful, but incomplete. It tells us relatively little about the personal nature of God. It does not inform us of his Trinitarian nature. It does not tell us about most of his attributes. It does not explain how we are to worship him. It does not clarify the nature of sin, atonement, and salvation. It offers little hope of an individual's ongoing existence after death. In short, it raises more questions than it answers.

Special Revelation

Thankfully, God has revealed specific truths about himself in two noteworthy ways. In the Scriptures, we have the written Word of God. In Christ, God is wonderfully revealed in the incarnate Word. Making himself known is evidently a high priority with him. While he might have chosen to remain the 'great unknown', God has disclosed himself and his will for mankind sufficiently so that we can know what he expects of us.

Scripture. We find numerous instances in Scripture – far too many to discuss here – of God making himself known. From Genesis to Revelation, he has spoken in specific ways about himself, his relationship with people, and his will for their lives. Not only has that communication record been preserved in the Bible, but the Bible itself has traditionally (and correctly) been regarded as the very Word of God. Scripture is the primary means by which God has chosen to communicate verbally with the human race.

The Incarnation. The primacy of the written revelation is not to minimize the role of Christ in revealing God. In fact, it may be reasonably argued that the incarnation revealed God in the most precise way possible. Paul stated in Colossians, 'For in Christ all the fullness of the Deity lives in bodily form' (Col 2:9). In the same letter (1:15), Paul stated that Christ is 'the image of the invisible God'. The Greek *eikon* means *likeness* or *manifestation* and we should remember that 'In Gk. thought an image shares in the reality

of what it represents. The essence of the thing appears in the image.'[3]
Thus, Jesus could explain to Philip and the other disciples, 'Anyone
who has seen me has seen the Father.... Don't you believe that I am
in the Father, and that the Father is in me?... Believe me when I say
that I am in the Father and the Father is in me' (John 14:9-11).

Christ is both the very essence of God and a chief means by
which God has revealed himself. An unknown writer to early Jewish
Christians reminds them that 'In the past God spoke to our forefathers
through the prophets at many times and in various ways, but in these
last days he has spoken to us by his Son' (Heb 1:1-2).

In his teachings and actions, Jesus was communicating God.
Everything about him was a means by which the Almighty was
disclosing himself to the human race. Why, then, was the statement
made previously that Scripture is the *primary* means by which God
has chosen to communicate verbally with people? It is because the
incarnation, though an utterly precise revelation of God, was limited
by time and space. Only those who were in the right place at the
right time experienced that revelation of God firsthand. Others have
subsequently heard of it secondhand, but only those who were in
Palestine during a particular brief period of history – indeed, even at
the right place and time there and then – actually saw and heard
God in the flesh. For most of humankind, the written Scriptures
themselves, or the communication of the written Scriptures by means
such as preaching, have been the means by which the incarnation of
Jesus Christ itself, as well as the other truths about God, is known.

Preaching and Revelation. Without this twofold special
revelation, humanity would be ignorant of numerous important truths
about God and his expectations for us. We could never be certain
of how to communicate with him or please him. We would have
little in the way of moral guidance to guide us through life. We could
only guess about eternal matters such as life, death, heaven, and
hell. This is why the function of preaching is so vitally important. Its
theological basis is the communication of truth about God which he
has previously made known in the written and incarnate Word.

The Scriptures, both Old and New Testaments, confirm this.
The prophets of old spoke only because God spoke to them and

subsequently through them. Isaiah, for example, is instructed by God to "Go and tell this people . . ." (Isa 6:9). In Jeremiah, there is a frequent formula such as the statement in 17:19-21:

> This is what the LORD said to me: 'Go and stand at the gate of the people, through which the kings of Judah go in and out; stand also at the other gates of Jerusalem. Say to them, "Hear the word of the LORD, O kings of Judah and all people of Judah and everyone living in Jerusalem who come through these gates. This is what the LORD says..." '

What is true of Isaiah and Jeremiah is true of the other Old Testament prophets as well. Time after time these spokesmen for God urged their audiences to 'hear the word of the Lord'. Their messages were not their own, but God's.

In the New Testament, it is again the revelation of God that is central to preaching and teaching. Paul explained that although some sought miraculous signs and others desired wisdom, 'We preach Christ crucified' (1 Cor 1:23). It was the message of the incarnation, the gospel, that was the focal point of his public ministry. But Paul was also aware of that special revelation of God which is written. He states that 'All Scripture is God-breathed and is useful for teaching, rebuking, correcting and training in righteousness, so that the man of God may be thoroughly equipped for every good work' (2 Tim 3:16-17). Paul, along with the other leaders of the early church, desired to bring people to faith in Christ and to encourage them toward an increasingly deep faith-walk. They were convinced that the Scriptures must be a central focus in this because 'faith comes from hearing the message, and the message is heard through the word of Christ'(Rom 10:17).

Human Nature

As we consider the theological foundations of preaching, we must also recall that God created us in his image. As such, we are intelligent, emotional, volitional, communicative beings. We have the ability to process information received, make value judgments concerning it, and then make decisions as to how to respond. This is true of information received through any of the senses, including the ears and eyes. Thus, we are capable of interacting with verbal information received audibly and reinforced visually, including preaching.

Again, this is not to discredit other methods of communicating the Christian message. Let us never fall into the 'either/or trap' and claim that preaching is the only means of declaring the gospel that is worthwhile. At the same time, let us not deprecate the traditional sermon as being hopelessly archaic. Nothing could be further from the truth. God has blessed biblical preaching throughout the centuries, and he continues to do so.

Biblical Authority
Another theological truth to remember is that of the authority of Scripture. If it is true that 'all Scripture is God-breathed', then today's preacher can declare the truths of the Bible with complete boldness and conviction. God honors and blesses the preaching of his Word.

If preaching is worthy of being called Christian, it will consist of sermons that set forth biblical truth without apology. And it will call people to rethink and redirect their lives in accordance to the truth set forth. This can be done only because of the inherent authority of Scripture. It is indeed *God's Word* and it carries *his* authority.

The Holy Spirit
It is impossible to consider the ministry of preaching without considering the role of the Holy Spirit. He is involved in the declaration of God's Word in several ways, all of which are extremely important. It might be said that he is involved in the process prior to the first thought given to preaching, during the preparation process, during the preaching event, and even after the preaching itself has been concluded.

Inspiring Scripture. First, it must be recalled that the Scriptures themselves claim to have come to us through the agency of the Holy Spirit. This is implied in 2 Timothy 3:16 in the term 'God-breathed' (*theopneustos*). It is explicitly stated in 2 Peter 1:21 where the apostle states, 'For prophecy never had its origin in the will of man, but men spoke from God as they were carried along by the Holy

Spirit.' Earlier, Peter, in his first speech following the Lord's ascension, said that 'the Scripture had to be fulfilled which the Holy Spirit spoke long ago through the mouth of David' (Acts 1:16). Likewise, the author of Hebrews ascribes 3:7-11, a direct quotation from Psalm 95:7-11, to the Holy Spirit. He does the same thing with the text about the new covenant in Jeremiah 31:33-34 when it is quoted in Hebrews 10:16-17. He specifically says that 'The Holy Spirit also testifies to us about this' (Heb 10:15).

Illumination. The Holy Spirit is active also in the work of illumination. This means that the pastor-teacher is not alone in his attempts to handle the Scripture. Jesus promised:

> When he, the Spirit of truth, comes, he will guide you into all truth. He will not speak on his own; he will speak only what he hears, and he will tell you what is yet to come. He will bring glory to me by taking what is mine and making it known to you. All that belongs to the Father is mine. That is why I said the Spirit will take from what is mine and make it known to you (John 16:13-14).

While we must guard against abuse by preachers who claim infallibility in their interpretation of Scripture, we must remember that God's Spirit assists the finite interpreter in understanding this special revelation of the infinite God. He is called the "Spirit of truth" for one of his works is that of guiding the believer into the truth of God.

Furthermore, not only does the Spirit of God assist the preacher in the work of under-standing the meaning of a text, he assists the listeners also as the truth of the authoritative Word of God is persuasively rooted in the heart. Referring to this seeming tension between the objectivity of Scripture and the subjectivity of the work of the Spirit, Erickson states:

> Actually, it is the combination of these two factors that constitutes authority. Both are needed. The written word, correctly interpreted, is the objective basis for authority. The inward illuminating and persuading work of the Holy Spirit is the subjective dimension. This dual dimension prevents sterile, cold, dry truth on one hand, and over-excitability and ill-advised fervor on the other. Together, the two yield a maturity that is necessary in the Christian life – a

cool head and warm heart (not a cold heart and hot head). As one pastor put it in a rather crude fashion: 'If you have the Bible without the Spirit you will dry up. If you have the Spirit without the Bible, you will blow up. But if you have both the Bible and the Spirit together, you will grow up.'[4]

Conviction. The Holy Spirit is also actively involved in the work of spiritual conviction. Jesus said that when the Spirit comes, 'he will convict the world of guilt in regard to sin and righteousness and judgment' (John 16:8). The preacher's job is not to make converts, but to state the truth in a compelling way. It is the work of the Spirit to seize the heart of the listener, convincing the person that truth has been spoken and a response is required. It is he who begins the process that leads to great change in a person's life.

Conversion and sanctification. The appropriate response to the Word is always change, change brought about by a faith response to the truth of the Word. The initial change is that of spiritual conversion. This consists of repentance, a change in the heart and mind of a sinner in which the person turns from sin; and faith, in which the person turns to Christ and his work on the cross. Conversion – both repentance and faith – involves a person's intellect, emotion, and will. The Holy Spirit actively convinces the intellect of spiritual truth, changes the emotional response from fear to grateful acceptance, and motivates the seeker to surrender the will in obedience.[5]

When a Christian believer hears the Word of God, the appropriate response is to receive it as instruction for the soul to be lived out by faith. The result of this is an ever-deepening walk with Christ and a desire to be conformed to his image. This change toward Christ-likeness is called sanctification. It is informed and motivated by the truth of Scripture and enabled by the indwelling of the Spirit in a Christian's life. The result is that the believer experiences a growing distancing of one's self from sin and its influences, and at the same time experiences a growing affinity toward the holiness of God.

Empowerment. Finally, it must be noted that the Holy Spirit empowers the Christian communicator to minister the Word with power. In writing to the Corinthian church, Paul confesses that his earlier preaching in Corinth was characterized not by 'eloquence or superior wisdom', but by 'weakness and fear, and with much trembling'. Nevertheless, the message was delivered 'with a demonstration of the Spirit's power' (see 1 Cor 2:1-5.). In the same way, Paul reminds his readers at Thessalonica that 'our gospel came to you not simply with words, but also with power, with the Holy Spirit and with deep conviction' (1 Thess 1:5). Without the presence and involvement of the Holy Spirit in our preaching, empty words will fall on deaf ears, and the result will be of no lasting value.

The Church
Another theological truth needing to be mentioned relates to the nature of the church. The Christian community is both the product and instrument of the spreading of Christian truth. The church exists because the Word of God has been repeatedly proclaimed, bringing people to faith and helping mature them in Christ. Sometimes this proclamation takes place as the believing community gathers for corporate worship, edification, or evangelism. On other occasions the Word goes forth while the saints are scattered. In either case, the church itself is part of this ongoing proclamation process.

Thomas Long speaks of preaching as 'witness'. He discusses the preacher's image as herald, pastor, and storyteller (he might well have included other images such as teacher and steward) but settles on the concept of witness because 'this new image is more suited than any of the others to disclose the true character of Christian preaching'.[6]

I concur with Long and find his insights to be quite instructive and helpful. It must be remembered, and Long affirms this as well, that preaching is not a solitary witness. The church is a collaborating witness and her collective testimony strengthens and enhances the witness of preaching. The preacher does not speak in a vacuum. While the sermon is *witness* to those who hear, the church is also *witness* to the preacher's right to speak and the truthfulness of what is being said. The church's very existence as a transformed and transforming community gives credibility to pulpit ministry.

The Preacher

Finally, our brief discussion of the various factors related to a theology of preaching must include the person who assumes the responsibility for preaching. This is, perhaps, the area of greatest surprise. Who would assume or imagine that the eternal, all resourceful God would allow finite, weak persons to speak for him? Yet, that is what he has chosen to do!

One need only review the sorts of individuals called by God in Old Testament times to get the picture! None of them is perfect and only a few – Daniel, for example – stand out as spiritual giants, yet each is used by God to carry out a unique and needed ministry. Elisha was prone to depression. Hosea had a broken marriage. Amos declared that he was not a prophet or even from a line of prophets. Isaiah was warned of failure even before he began to preach. Jeremiah was given to fits of melancholy and great mood swings. How many would be high on the list of most pastor search committees today?

The preachers in the New Testament aren't any more impressive than those in the Old Testament. Some apostles are scarcely known. Their reputations depend on a smattering of church traditions which are sketchy at best. Those who are well known are seen as imperfect persons, each bringing one or more liabilities to the task. Peter was impulsive and had a habit of speaking and acting before thinking. Paul, by his own admission, did not have great abilities in public speaking and, in fact, was prone to stage fright (1 Cor 2:1-3). Others apparently concurred with his self-assessment (2 Cor 10:10). Timothy was young and timid, needing encouragement as he served as pastor of the church at Ephesus.

Yet all of these preachers – prophets and apostles alike – had something in common. They were all chosen, called, and empowered by God. Strange as it may seem, it has been God's intention all along to use weak, imperfect people to declare his Word among the nations.

There is an old legend told of the Lord Jesus returning to heaven following his earthly ministry. He was greeted by Moses who asked how things had gone.

'All went well,' replied Jesus.

'Wonderful,' exclaimed Moses. 'Now everyone is a Christian.'

'No, there are only a few,' Jesus said.

Moses, completely baffled, responded: 'Lord, I don't understand. You've returned to heaven and yet most of the people on earth are not believers. How will they hear of you and become followers?'

Jesus paused and then gestured earthward toward the little band of Christians there and said, 'Now it depends upon them. I have no other plan.'

It has always been this way. With the exception of a few theophanies and angelic announcements, God has always chosen to use human beings to communicate his truth to others.

What a privilege to realize that despite our own imperfections and liabilities, God selects some from among us to serve as preachers.

Summary

It is unlikely that what has been said here is new to the reader. Still, it is easy to lose sight of the theological foundations of preaching and even a familiar word can help remind us of the preacher's unique calling. We are not simply to be about the business of giving public speeches on the state of current affairs. Nor are we to consider ourselves to be one voice among many giving advice on the various themes and fads of the day. Rather, we have been entrusted with the gospel, the truth about God's plan and provision for His creation.

While we preach because we are expected to – both congregational expectation and our job description reminds us of this – let us preach because we must! Our sense of calling and our understanding of how God is made known should not allow us to do otherwise. Paul's charge to 'Preach the Word; be prepared in season and out of season; correct, rebuke and encourage – with great patience and careful instruction' (2 Tim 4:2) is as appropriate today as it was when directed to Pastor Timothy.

Consider Ecclesiological Purposes

A philosophy of ministry, including a philosophy of preaching, has tremendously practical ramifications. It is much more than a statement printed on a piece of paper or an explanation given to a search committee looking for a new pastor. Instead, assuming it is believed to the point of conviction, it is a personally imposed description of beliefs, priorities, and activities pertaining to one's ministry which will guide and govern the way ministry is planned and executed.

It is sometimes said that a person's philosophy of life can be known by examining his check book. How are financial resources expended? What really seems to be most important in view of monies spent for various commodities and services? Because of circumstances beyond the control of some, this may not be completely accurate. Yet, there is probably an element of truth in this that many folks would be wise to heed.

Similarly, it is usually true that a pastor's philosophy of ministry can be known by looking at his weekly schedule. How are the resources of time and effort utilized? What seems to take priority week after week? Some activities, of course, will be beyond the control of the pastor. But there is also much discretionary time at the pastor's disposal. How this time is used is quite informative as to one's ministry philosophy.

A pastoral leader, for example, may say something like this: 'My ministry philosophy places great importance on the nurturing and discipling of congregational lay leaders so they in turn can care for and disciple others in the church family.' Now this may well be an extremely valid and important part of one's perspective on pastoral ministry, but it is one thing to say this and quite another to carry it out. How much time is actually carved out of one's schedule to meet regularly with leaders in small groups or even individually? Are the leaders catching the vision to spend similar time with those in the church over whom they have responsibility or with whom they have good relationships? Or, is this part of ministry philosophy simply a pipedream? If there is ownership of such a philosophy, it will be implemented. If one's philosophy is not put into practice, then it may rightly be called into question. This is true whether we speak of discipleship, prayer, evangelism, preaching, or any of the ministry functions conceivably carried on by a pastor.

The New Testament Church

A study of the New Testament readily shows that a proper philosophy of pastoral ministry can never be one-sided or even double-sided. It must be multi-faceted for that is the picture of the church that is found there. The New Testament church functioned with certain emphases in the forefront of all she did. If our philosophy of ministry is to reflect biblical ecclesiology – and it must if ministry is truly Christian – then our philosophy must reflect the importance of those functions given greatest emphasis in Scripture.

The New Testament does not contain a systematic treatise on the church. Most of what we know about the nature of the church we know inductively. We read the Book of Acts and see the early church in action. We see her beginning to grow quite rapidly and we note some of the steps taken by early leaders to ensure that she would be all that God intended. We read statements that summarize the repeated activities of the church: 'They devoted themselves to the apostles' teaching and to the fellowship, to the breaking of bread and to prayer' (Acts 2:42). We note those things that characterized that body such as selling possessions and sharing the proceeds with one another, meeting daily in the temple and in homes where they constantly praised God, and continuing in their numerical growth. We see the early church proclaiming her faith in public places, in church gatherings, and in hostile surroundings. We observe her leaders dealing with problems such as persecution, church discipline, doctrinal issues, organizational matters, and evangelistic outreach to other lands and peoples.

We move beyond Acts into the epistles and again discover that there is nothing resembling a constitution or by-laws document. Instead, we see local churches struggling with specific issues of doctrine or practice. At other times we find churches whose members are struggling through problems and need encouragement. We also see church leaders being taught and guided by a Paul or Peter.

Wouldn't it have been helpful if Acts or one of the epistles included some clearly arranged statements on church government and church ministry? But such is not the case. Instead, the portrait of the church is painted with broad strokes and a somewhat impressionistic style. This is the leading factor contributing to diversity of thought in these areas. Thus, we have those who are convinced that the New Testament model of church government is episcopal in nature, while others are equally convinced it is congregational or presbyterian. Likewise, there is no single philosophy of ministry articulated, although there are emphases which are extremely instructive. What are these emphases related to ministry philosophy which seem to get special attention in the New Testament? At the risk of over-looking other important ones, I will briefly discuss seven.

They Carefully Set Ministry Priorities
As the early church grew rapidly – literally by the thousands – complaints were voiced that the physical needs of all were not being met. Some widows were not receiving their daily food shares. This is what happened:

> So the Twelve gathered all the disciples together and said, 'It would not be right for us to neglect the ministry of the word of God in order to wait on tables. Brothers, choose seven men from among you who are known to be full of the Spirit and wisdom. We will turn this responsibility over to them and will give our attention to prayer and the ministry of the word' (Acts 6:2-4).

When the early church was small, the Apostles probably took responsibility for some of the more mundane needs of the body. As the church grew, it increasingly became necessary to set priorities; namely, to devote their energies to praying and preaching. In effect, this became the over-arching principle of ministry philosophy on the part of the leadership of the young church.

By the time the apostle Paul wrote Ephesians, arguably the definitive book in the New Testament regarding the nature and purpose of the church, there was a conviction that ministry was to be shared by all of the members of the body. Those who were gifted for leadership were not solely responsible for carrying out all of the ministries needing done. The leadership gifts mentioned in Ephesians 4:11 (apostles, prophets, evangelists, pastor-teachers) were given to take the gospel into new geographical areas, proclaim the truth of God, and *train and prepare everyone in the church to do the work of ministry*. It was this latter function of church leadership on the local level that made it possible for prayer and the ministry of the Word to be prioritized in the lives of church leaders.

They Recognized the Spiritual Gifts of All
In five different passages in the New Testament (Rom 12:3-8, 1 Cor 12, 1 Cor 14, Eph 4:7-13, and 1 Pet 4:10-11), the concept of spiritual gifts is discussed. While there is disagreement over some issues related to spiritual gifts, one thing is certain: the Spirit of God wondrously gifted the members of the body with a wonderful diversity in ministry functions. Some gifts were "up-front" in nature, while others were exercised behind the scenes. Some served the whole body directly, while others ministered to only one person at a time. Some appeared to be extremely practical in nature, while others were supernaturally manifested.

Yes, there were abuses and problems associated with spiritual gifts. Paul addressed some of these in 1 Corinthians 12–14. While he stated that spiritual gifting apart from Christ-like love is empty and worthless, he still affirmed the importance of the gifts. When he discussed the subject in Romans 12, there was no direct word of rebuke or correction. He simply taught that all persons in the church were to exercise their gifts with spiritual commitment.

The purpose of the gifts was to serve the many and varied needs of those in the body and beyond. One gift was not more important than another. All were seen as necessary if the body was to function properly. The early church recognized this and her ministry was enriched.

They Emphasized Worship
The Jewish people of the Old Testament were a worshiping people. This was done individually and in family settings even before the Tabernacle and the Temple came into existence.

The worship of God was seen as the primary duty of people. Both in private and public settings it consisted of praise, prayer, instruction, and sacrifice. While this appears to have happened informally during the age of the Patriarchs, the building of the Tabernacle brought about a more systematic way of carrying out public worship. This continued with even more regulations after the Temple was erected.

Even when they were in exile following the destruction of the Temple, the believing remnant of Jews carried out worship activities such as prayer and meditation. Some of their worship activities were curtailed because of a lack of a Temple altar. Yet, deep spiritual devotion is seen in the lives of people like Daniel, Nehemiah, and Ezra. It is probable that synagogues, an extremely important part of Jewish spiritual life in the time of the New Testament and up to the present, came into existence during the Babylonian exile. Praise, worship, prayer, and the reading and explanation of Scripture were the dominant aspects of synagogue liturgies – these were very detailed in their arrangement of prayers, blessings, and readings – and those New Testament Christians from Jewish backgrounds were well acquainted with them. Jesus himself customarily attended synagogue on the Sabbath.

While the earliest Jewish converts to Christianity continued for a time to worship in the Temple, at least for praise and prayer, this appears to have lasted only a few years. The last mention of active Christian participation in Temple worship is found in Acts 21 where Paul was arrested during a time of ritual purification apparently done to appease some newly converted Jewish-Christians.

The participation of early Jewish-Christians in synagogue worship was a different matter. Synagogues were quite numerous in Palestine – it is thought that there were about five hundred in Jerusalem alone – and therefore quite small. New synagogues could be established in any place where ten Jewish men resided. Because of the relative numerical smallness of synagogues as compared to the single large Temple, Christians tended to be more obvious in synagogues and disputes over doctrinal matters were easily provoked. Gradually, therefore, Christians began to assemble and meet regularly apart from either the Temple or local synagogues, although the latter were often used as starting points for evangelistic outreach in new places. Worship in the New Testament church appears to have been modeled somewhat after the synagogue pattern, although there is no direct evidence of a precise liturgy being followed. The early chapters of Acts mentions gatherings in which meals – perhaps common meals or the Lord's Supper – were shared, prayer was offered, and teaching took place. Paul spoke of meetings in which the attendees might contribute 'a hymn, a word of instruction, a revelation, a tongue or an interpretation' (1 Cor 14:26). The context, however, has more to do with orderliness in worship than precise instructions regarding the content of worship. In the pastoral epistles instruction regarding public worship emphasized prayer and the teaching of the Word.

They Practiced Evangelism

The early church took seriously the final instructions of Jesus to disciple the peoples of the world (Matt 28:19-20). This occurred initially as the Good News of salvation in Christ was shared, faith was evidenced, and people were baptized into the fellowship of believers. While this did not constitute the end of disciple-making, but only the beginning, it was a very necessary beginning that was vigorously pursued in the early church.

A simple study of the Book of Acts shows that evangelism was considered to be a major priority among the early Christians. From the Day of Pentecost onward the small band of believers began to grow numerically as the gospel was preached. Those Christians were not passive in their outreach, but intentional, as both individuals and specially designated outreach groups took on that responsibility.

Philip is often recalled because of his encounter with the eunuch, an individual with an important position in the court of the Ethiopian Queen, Candace (Acts 8:26ff). He is less often remembered for his evangelistic activity prior to that as he spearheaded the gospel initiative into Samaria prior to the arrival there of Peter and John (Acts 8:4-8). He is one example among several of individuals declaring the gospel from place to place.

Although Peter and John went to Samaria in response to the successful ministry of Philip, they were also a part of the evangelistic effort there. This is seen primarily as they returned to Jerusalem in an indirect way, preaching the gospel in many Samaritan towns as they journeyed. Paul and Barnabas, and later Paul and Silas, are the prime examples of those thrust out by the early church to take the gospel to far places. This was a collective effort as the apostolic band was sent out by the local church and accountable to it. (See Acts 13:1-3 and Acts 14:26-28.)

While the New Testament epistles are primarily edificational and corrective in nature, being addressed for the most part to established churches, the reader still catches the importance of evangelism. The Faith is not something to horde to oneself, but it is the 'power of God for the salvation of everyone who believes' (Rom 1:16). In addition to explanations and clarifications of the gospel, as in Romans, Galatians and Hebrews, there are repeated encouragements to readers to make an evangelistic impact on the world.

Paul's relatively mild correctives to the Philippian church, for example, addresses both the matter of right living in the church and right living in society so that the gospel will receive a good hearing.

> Do everything without complaining or arguing, so that you may become blameless and pure, children of God without fault in a crooked and depraved generation, in which you shine as stars in the universe as you hold out the word of life (Phil 2:14-16).

Similarly, Peter, using Old Testament language that is extremely descriptive, reminds his readers of both their privilege and responsibility:

> But you are a chosen people, a royal priesthood, a holy nation, a people belonging to God, that you may declare the praises of him who called you out of darkness into his wonderful light. Once you were not a people, but now you are the people of God; once you had not received mercy, but now you have received mercy (1 Pet 2:9-10).

While passages such as these are somewhat rare in the epistles, there should be no doubt that holy living and a right relationship with God are not seen to be ends in themselves. Rather, they bring glory to God and influence others toward Him.

They Emphasized Edification

The second part of the great commission to make disciples is building believers up toward maturity in Christ. Jesus said that the church, as it is going into the world, should be involved in both *baptizing* (winning converts) and *teaching*: 'Therefore go and make disciples of all nations, baptizing them in the name of the Father and of the Son and of the Holy Spirit, and teaching them to obey everything I have commanded you' (Matt 28:19-20).

We find this modeled in the earliest church. As we read in Acts 2:42, the early church was devoting 'themselves to the apostles' teaching and to the fellowship, to the breaking of bread and to prayer.' The majority of the New Testament literature deals with Jesus' teaching and the subsequent teaching of the apostles.

One of the richest texts in Scripture regarding the functioning of the church is found in the fourth chapter of Ephesians. We find there both a summary statement of how the church is to operate as well as the ultimate purpose of the process. Paul states that gifted leaders have been given to the church – specifically apostles, prophets, evangelists, and pastor-teachers. These leaders have the responsibility of preparing the people of God (i.e. the so-called laity) for works of ministry so that the entire church will be 'built up' (edified) toward 'unity in the faith and in the knowledge of the Son of God' for the ultimate purpose of 'attaining to the whole measure of the fullness of Christ' (Eph 4:11-13).

Elsewhere, Paul speaks of his personal desire to 'know Christ and the power of his resurrection and the fellowship of sharing in his sufferings' (Phil 3:10). He continues:

Not that I have already obtained all this, or have already been made perfect, but I press on to take hold of that for which Christ Jesus took hold of me. Brothers, I do not consider myself yet to have taken hold of it. But one thing I do: Forgetting what is behind and straining toward what is ahead, I press on toward the goal to win the prize for which God has called me heavenward in Christ Jesus. All of us who are mature should take such a view of things (Phil 3:12-15).

The early church took very seriously the matter of spiritual growth toward Christlikeness for each person in the body.

They Valued Christian Fellowship
In a societal setting where the early Christians were often a despised and even persecuted minority, the need for spiritual support and encouragement was great. Thus, when those believers spoke of fellowship they were not referring to casual relationships or an occasional meal shared. They were speaking of a new entity – a new community – one in which citizenship came by virtue of spiritual rebirth and participation by spiritual need and desire. The Book of Acts tells us that the very earliest believers were 'devoted ... to the fellowship' (Acts 2:42).

The noun *koinonia*, used some twenty times in the New Testament, can be traced from classical Mycenean Greek (the oldest form of the language known) onward. Meanings include the concepts of 'association, communion, fellowship, participation'.[7] In ancient Greek culture the word was used to speak of 'the evident, unbroken fellowship between the gods and men'. Interestingly, however, the Septuagint never uses the word to speak of the relationship between God and man. *Koinonia* was also used to describe an ideal kind of relationship between men, much as we might use the term 'brotherhood'.

The term is used in both ways in the New Testament. The apostle John wrote of both kinds of fellowship as being integrally related: 'We proclaim to you what we have seen and heard, so that you also may have fellowship with us. And our fellowship is with the Father and with his Son, Jesus Christ' (1 John 1:3). The horizontal and vertical dimensions of fellowship cannot be separated from one another. Christian fellowship is not simply an association of persons joined by a common purpose or value. Rather, it is based on spiritual oneness that is supernaturally originated. It is not the work of man as much as it is the work of God. As Schattenmann states, 'But *koinonia* expresses something new and independent. It denotes the unanimity and unity brought about by the Spirit.'[8]

An example of the blending of the spiritual and human dimensions of fellowship is seen in Philippians 2, a text often seen as dealing primarily with matters of humility.

> If you have any encouragement from being united with Christ, if any comfort from his love, if any fellowship with the Spirit, if any tenderness and compassion, then make my joy complete by being like-minded, having the same love, being one in spirit and purpose (Phil 2:1-2).

Clearly, unity on the human level is rooted in our spiritual oneness with Christ and the Spirit.

Even the communal sharing of goods or money in the early church is related to the concept of *koinonia*. The term root of the term *koinos* means, among other things, 'common property.' When we read in Acts 2:44 that 'All the believers were together and had everything *in common*,' and in Acts 4:32 that 'No one claimed that any of his possessions was his own, but they *shared* everything they had' (italics mine), the word used is *koinos*. Similarly, the giving of offerings by the Macedonian believers to the needs of the Jerusalem church is said by Paul in 2 Corinthians 8:4 to be 'the fellowship of the ministry' (*ten koinonian tes diakonias*).

It must be remembered that the sharing of possessions was entirely voluntary, being prompted by a strong sense of spiritual unity.

> Experientially, the spiritual oneness the believers found to be a living reality through their common allegiance to Jesus must, they realized, be expressed in caring for the physical needs of their Christian brothers and sisters. Indeed, their integrity as a community of faith depended on their doing this.[9]

The importance of the biblical concept of fellowship – spiritual community—must not be overlooked as we consider the formulation of philosophies of ministry and preaching.

They Exemplified God's Care for People

The early church continued on in the tradition of their master, Jesus Christ. Just as Jesus cared for the problems of others – whether physical, emotional, or spiritual – so the early Christians showed love and compassion on those outside the church as well as those within.

The Old Testament, of course, shows that the pattern for this benevolent behavior is rooted in the very character of God.

> For the LORD your God is God of gods and Lord of lords, the great God, mighty and awesome, who shows no partiality and accepts no bribes. He defends the cause of the fatherless and the widow, and loves the alien, giving him food and clothing. And you are to love those who are aliens, for you yourselves were aliens in Egypt (Deut 10:17-19).

The New Testament too shows that this is an ongoing expectation. James gives a very practical explanation of true religion: 'Religion that God our Father accepts as pure and faultless is this: to look after orphans and widows in their distress and to keep oneself from being polluted by the world' (Jas 1:27). And again:

> What good is it, my brothers, if a man claims to have faith but has no deeds? Can such faith save him? Suppose a brother or sister is without clothes and daily food. If one of you says to him, 'Go, I wish you well; keep warm and well fed,' but does nothing about his physical needs, what good is it? In the same way, faith by itself, if it is not accompanied by action, is dead (Jas 2:14-17).

John goes so far as to suggest that we cannot prove our love for God apart from lovingly helping those in need:

> This is how we know what love is: Jesus Christ laid down his life for us. And we ought to lay down our lives for our brothers. If anyone has material possessions and sees his brother in need but

has no pity on him, how can the love of God be in him? Dear children, let us not love with words or tongue but with actions and in truth (1 John 3:16-18).

The early church rightly assumed that it had a benevolent role to play in human society. While those believers were wrongfully accused of many evils, they were never accused of being uncaring toward those in need.

The Contemporary Church

Having examined these seven important emphases in the New Testament church, we must necessarily make comparisons between the values and practices of that church and those of the church today. This will be quite helpful as we give serious attention to this matter of ministry and preaching philosophy. The point here is not to attempt to duplicate all of the actions and concerns of the New Testament church. Rather, we must be aware of the transferable principles and deal with how they should be implemented in the body of Christ today.

We Must Re-evaluate Our Ministry Priorities

Almost every preacher is inundated with a never-ending list of possible activities, almost all of which are good or even excellent. Some of these are regularly scheduled responsibilities. Others are unexpected, though perhaps important, intrusions which demand someone's attention. What's a preacher to do?

The setting of right ministry priorities is done much more easily apart from busyness and intrusion than in response to them. No person can keep an unrealistic schedule continuously and keep his health and sanity at the same time. Preachers cannot and should not be expected to be responsible for all that takes place in the church.

Unfortunately, preachers are often their own worst enemy in this regard. We often act as though the success of the local church depends solely on us, not to mention the success of the Kingdom itself! We insist that we must have a place at every committee meeting, play a key role in every decision made (regardless of its mundaneness), and grace the flock with our presence every time the church is open for any kind of activity. And then we wonder why fatigue and stress take their toll.

To act in such an irresponsible manner is to ignore the realities of who we are and what the church is. It is to ignore the concepts of the priesthood and ministry of all believers. It is to ignore the models given to us in Scripture which demonstrate how the body is to function.

The apostles, when confronted with the demands of serving a rapidly growing church, did not experience ministerial burn-out, though they might have if suitable measures had not been taken. There were, after all, important needs to be met. Factions were developing because one group, the Grecian Jews, were being overlooked by the Aramaic-speaking Jews in the matter of caring for the daily distribution of foods. Now the apostles, in good twenty-first-century practice, could have simply increased their own workloads in order to give firsthand supervision. They didn't. Instead, they followed the principle of delegation. They called a church meeting and stated their case. While caring for the needy was an important ministry, it could readily be done by other persons. These persons would need to be spiritually qualified and suitably skilled ('seven men ... who are known to be full of the Spirit and wisdom'). The apostles, in turn, would give their 'attention to prayer and the ministry of the word' (see Acts 6:1-4).

I wonder what might happen if today's church leaders would try this. One might hope that the membership would be duly impressed with the pastor's desire to set lofty priorities. On the other hand, there might be an outcry to the effect that all of these secondary demands are equally important and 'that's why we pay the preacher'. If the latter is the expected and probable result, then preachers have no one to blame but themselves. We have allowed culture to dictate ministry practice and philosophy rather than insist on the biblical norm. Instead of working to be counter-cultural in this regard, we have allowed the status quo to exist. Indeed, we have endorsed it by remaining silent on the matter.

The narrative of Acts 6 is only one example of biblical teaching regarding the priorities of church leadership. Another text, mentioned previously, is Ephesians 4. As in Acts 6, this text teaches the important truth that pastors should not – indeed, must not – be the only persons who do church ministry. Ministry is the responsibility of *everyone* in the church.

It was very early in the history of the early church that the dichotomy between the so-called 'clergy' and 'laity' arose. The church has never quite recovered! The usual result has been that 'doing ministry' has been seen as the responsibility of the professional clergy, while non-clergy have generally assumed maintenance-type tasks.

This kind of thinking runs more deeply than we like to admit. I recall a conversation some years ago in which I was asked by a church member about a certain individual we had met at a denominational conference. 'Is he a pastor?' I was asked. 'No,' I replied, 'he's just a layman.' *Just* a layman! My conscience was immediately pricked as I realized what I had said. It was not a comfortable moment, nor should it have been.

There are no tiers of status in Christ's church, only differences in ministries. The ministry assignment given to some in the church – those who have been identified as apostles, prophets, evangelists, and pastor-teachers (Eph 4:11) – is to equip others in the body so they in turn can minister effectively. A careful exegetical study of Ephesians 4:11-16, unfortunately beyond the scope of this book, will confirm this is so. Today's pastor must prioritize ministry efforts to emphasize what Scripture emphasizes: the ministry of the word, prayer, training, and spiritual oversight. It is highly likely that others in the body are gifted and willing to share in these priorities and to care for other important ministries needing done if the pastoral leadership will patiently but firmly instruct them accordingly.

The attitude of a pastor in a small, rural community in Montana is worthy of emulation in regard to this extremely important matter.

When I came to this church, I was told not so subtly, 'Pastor, you do the marrying, burying, evangelizing, praying, and counseling. That's what we pay you for.' I've done all that with joy. But along the line, folks have learned that I'm committed to Ephesians 4:11-13, 'to equip the saints to do the work of ministry.' Because of the example I've set, even long-time members are beginning to catch that vision. Rather than grow unhappy, change my role, or look for the perfect church, I set out to train people in what the scriptural role of the pastor and the flock ought to be. That takes time. It meant I had to commit to a long-term ministry.[10]

We Must Deal with the Issue of Spiritual Gifts

Closely related to this matter of setting right ministry priorities is that of recognizing and dealing with the issue of spiritual gifts. The past five decades or so have seen the subject of spiritual gifts become increasingly important for a much wider spectrum of Christians than was previously the case. This is doubtless true because ecclesiology, the doctrine of the church, became one of the primary theological foci of the late twentieth century. Many, perhaps most, evangelicals today – not just pentecostals and charismatics – would affirm the following regarding spiritual gifts:

1. Every believer has been given one or more spiritual gifts; (see 1 Corinthians 12:7: 'Now to each one the manifestation of the Spirit is given for the common good,' and 1 Corinthians 12:11: 'All these are the work of one and the same Spirit, and he gives them to each man, just as he determines').

2. These gifts are given by God according to His sovereign wisdom; (1 Corinthians 12:18: 'But in fact God has arranged the parts in the body, every one of them, just as he wanted them to be').

3. Particular gifts are not to be regarded as either inferior or superior. All are important if the body is to function properly; (Romans 12:3-6: 'For by the grace given me I say to every one of you: Do not think of yourself more highly than you ought, but rather think of yourself with sober judgment, in accordance with the measure of faith God has given you. Just as each of us has one body with many members, and these members do not all have the same function, so in Christ we who are many form one body, and each member belongs to all the others. We have different gifts,

according to the grace given us.' See also, 1 Corinthians 12:12-26).

While there may be general agreement about these statements, there are other issues related to spiritual gifts which are not held by all. The reasons for these disagreements are encountered when one examines the activities of the church in Acts along with the five passages in Scripture in which spiritual gifts are discussed. These texts are Romans 12, 1 Corinthians 12, 1 Corinthians 14, Ephesians 4, and 1 Peter 4.

When these lists are studied one discovers around eighteen or nineteen different gifts being mentioned, allowing for duplication. This leads to the first issue that prompts disagreement: are these lists intended to be exhaustive or suggestive? Are these the only spiritual gifts given to the church by God, or are there others, perhaps many others, of which these are merely examples? This is an issue about which devout believers disagree.

The second issue relates to the character and purpose of some of the gifts listed. It is easily seen that the nature of spiritual gifts vary widely, ranging from those which appear to be fairly ordinary (serving, teaching, liberality, leadership, administration) to those which appear to be more remarkably supernatural (glossolalia, interpretation, healings, miracles). While most evangelicals would affirm the necessity of the first category of gifts, there is disagreement in some circles as to the intended perpetuity of the latter category.

While it is beyond my present purpose to attempt a resolution of these disagreements, it is my desire to encourage the reader to wrestle with them if this hasn't been done previously. We must recognize that the implications of the issue of spiritual gifts for Christian living and ministry in and beyond the church are important. From the perspective of the preaching pastor, beliefs about spiritual gifts affect one's philosophy of ministry and this in turn impacts one's philosophy of preaching as well as its content.

We Must Reinvigorate Worship

As we continue to examine our own ministry practices with those of the early church, we must briefly discuss a third necessary emphasis, that of worship. This too is an area of vital concern in the contemporary church for it directly relates both to what the body does when it meets together as well as to the role of preaching.

Worship practice – I'm using the term 'worship' rather broadly in this context – varies considerably from church to church and even within many denominations. While it is usually difficult to pigeon-hole churches into precise categories of worship styles, the following are some models of worship services which at least suggest some ways in which worship is conducted.

1. Liturgical and sacramental: Churches which worship in this style may be referred to as those which follow a 'high church' tradition, emphasizing the Eucharist as the high point of corporate worship. Music may include stately anthems and chanting. Vestments and other aids such as candles and crosses are utilized. Sermons are often in the form of brief homilies based on a lectionary text.

2. Orderly and formal: Many churches in the so-called mainline denominations follow fairly rigid orders of service without much deviation. Worship leaders are often robed, creeds recited, and traditional-style choral and congregational music used. Preaching is often based on the designated lectionary text.

3. Orderly and informal: This is a worship style found in many 'free' or independent church traditions, as well as some mainline churches and smaller evangelical denominations. The common ingredient is that an order of service is carefully planned, though the order may vary from time to time. In fact, within a given service, liberty may be exercised to alter the original plan. Music may be traditional, it may be somewhat contemporary, or it may be a mixture, referred to as 'blended'. Sermons vary widely, both in style and purpose.

4. Pentecostal/charismatic: Services of this type may include a great deal of lively singing, audience participation (some unplanned), and energetic preaching, often punctuated with encouragements

and expressions of agreement from the audience. The public use of spiritual gifts, especially glossolalia, interpretations, words of knowledge, and healings, may be a regular part of gathered worship, though not necessarily so.

5. Teaching emphasis: Some churches in the evangelical tradition place such a great deal of emphasis on the edification of believers that public worship is similar to a classroom experience. That which happens before the message – congregational singing, special music, drama, testimony – is often seen as preliminary to the all-important business of preaching. Sermons are almost always 'expository' and are often presented in long series stretching over many weeks or even many months. Attendees avidly take notes on written materials provided.

6. Seeker-sensitive model: A growing number of North American churches are carefully differentiating between those meetings planned for maximal evangelistic effectiveness and those planned with the committed believer in mind. In many instances, Sunday gatherings are carefully geared toward unbelievers and include contemporary music, drama, and preaching designed to answer the spiritual questions and concerns of the unchurched. Worship emphases are not directly included in seeker services because worship is seen to be the prerogative of the Christian. Seeker-sensitive churches often have an additional gathering designed with worship, edification, and fellowship in mind.

Again, these worship models are not precisely separate categories. There is inevitable overlapping that takes place. A liturgical church may have a charismatic theology that influences the way it worships. Those in the category labeled as 'orderly and informal' may emphasize biblical exposition or may, on the other hand, emphasize preaching that is more topical in nature. Pentecostal and charismatic churches may hold services which are fairly rigid in their structure and some churches in this category have a strong emphasis on biblical exposition. Culture and ethnicity also influence the way worship is conducted.

Regardless of worship style employed, the early church

emphasized worship and so must the contemporary church. Worshiping God, giving the glory, honor, praise, and adoration that is due him, is never out of date. In fact, everything we do as individuals and as the church must be done with the worship of God in mind. He exists to be worshiped!

Corporate worship is too often an afterthought among Christians, especially those of us in the evangelical tradition. We tend to plan public services with the needs and expectations of the anticipated audience of men, women, teens, and children in mind. But we fail to realize that true worship involves an audience of one – God himself! Whether or not what we do is really worship, and whether or not our worship pleases him, are crucial matters with which we must diligently wrestle.

This is obviously an important issue for the pastor-preacher. It impacts both the way we superintend the planning of public services and the way we preach. In regard to preaching, do we preach simply to offer our insights and opinions on current events? Do we preach simply to transfer knowledge into the heads of listeners? Do we preach simply to offer psychological or even spiritual solutions to the problems our constituents face? Do we preach simply to motivate people toward more faithful performance of their Christian duties, especially their responsibilities to the church? While these purposes for preaching all have merit, should it not be our chief desire to preach in order to remind people of the greatness of God, strengthening their faith in him, so that they may grow in their desire and ability to worship him in spirit and in truth? In reality, those purposes for preaching stated above should all properly relate to our understanding of worship.

We Must Carry Out Effective Evangelism

It wasn't long ago – thirty or forty years, perhaps – that many local churches in the evangelical tradition focused their evangelistic efforts almost exclusively in a specially designed Sunday evening service. There was lively congregational singing of gospel hymns and choruses, special music, testimonies, an evangelistic sermon, and an invitation extended to profess Christ in that public gathering. Many came to Christ in that kind of setting as others had for a hundred years or so.

It is my understanding that this type of service began with the spread of gas lighting in public places when most private homes still used candles or oil lamps. Innovative pastors saw this as an opportunity to draw crowds of curious onlookers to see the evening darkness dispelled. As a result of this creative thinking, many people experienced the dispelling of spiritual darkness as well, as the light of Christ was made known to them.

One would be hard pressed today to find many churches that emphasize evangelism through Sunday evening services. Indeed, when they are held, most Sunday evening services tend to duplicate traditional morning services, take the direction of small group studies, or focus on praise and fellowship. The reason is simple: very few unconverted persons will attend a church service on Sunday evening. Because of this, other methods of outreach have been introduced in the place of this one.

This relatively sudden change of evangelistic strategy shouldn't surprise us. It may be that nothing else in the history of the church has taken on as many different shapes as her efforts to reach others with the gospel. Methods as diverse as the sending out of Jesuit priests with the Spanish conquistadors, the open air crusades of Wesley and Whitefield, the revivalism of Finney and Moody, the mass crusades of Billy Graham, local church 'revivals' lasting a week or so, friendship evangelism, tracts, neighborhood evangelistic Bible studies, seeker services, various humanitarian efforts, and regular evangelistic preaching by local church pastors have all been used as evangelistic strategies by the church at large.

Evangelism is not an optional ministry. Christ has mandated that we do this in our own local 'worlds' as well as in the world at large. While the issue may seem to be the best way of carrying out evangelism, the fact is that there is no best way. People unreached with the gospel cannot be thought of in monolithic terms. They are extremely diverse in terms of culture, lifestyle, religious background, spiritual understanding, and spiritual hunger. No single method will reach them all.

A carefully articulated philosophy of ministry will acknowledge the need to be involved in evangelism and suggest suitable approaches. The contemporary church, like her New Testament counterparts, must include outreach on her "to do" list and devise appropriate methods to carry out the task. The pastor must be an active leader and participant in this effort. As in other areas of ministry philosophy, decisions made regarding evangelistic outreach will have direct bearing on one's preaching philosophy. Should evangelism be carried out primarily in the gathered church or in the scattered church? To what extent should pulpit ministry be evangelistic? Can preaching in the context of public worship be effectively evangelistic and edificational at the same time? These are some of the questions with which we must deal.

We Must Help People toward Spiritual Maturity
The preacher must have not only a concern for evangelism, but for edification as well. Coming to Christ in saving faith is not the end of a process, but the beginning of a new life. This life must be nourished and cared for in the nurturing environment of the church. Like a new born infant left to fend for itself, it is tragic for a new born believer to be deprived of spiritual care and sustenance.

I grew up in a church noted for its evangelism. The pastor preached evangelistic sermons predominantly throughout his thirty-four years of ministry there. He was extremely effective as a pulpit evangelist and literally hundreds and hundreds came to Christ through the years. From humble beginnings with a core group of barely a dozen adults, the church grew at a good pace and peaked at an attendance of over 800 within twenty years. Yet, at the end of the pastor's term of ministry some fourteen years later, the church numbered only a little over two hundred in attendance, though many more were still on the roles.

What went wrong? A few folks had relocated to other localities and others had died. Most, however, were still in the community. The vast majority had either become members of other churches or had simply dropped out of church altogether except, perhaps, for an occasional visit on Christmas, Easter, or some other special occasion. While there were doubtless several factors that contributed to this attrition, the primary reason appears to have been a lack of long term follow-up and assimilation of new believers into the life and ministry of the church. People were not being nurtured toward spiritual maturity but were hearing the same basic truths over and over again. They were not being equipped for ministry themselves and thus became mere spectators.

It is sometimes forgotten that the mission of the church as articulated by Jesus in Matthew 28:16-20 is not simply to win converts, but to *make disciples*. In verse 19 and the first part of verse 20, Jesus said:

> Therefore, as you are going forth, *make disciples* of all nations. Do this by baptizing them in the name of the Father and of the Son and of the Holy Spirit, and by teaching them to obey everything I have commanded you (author's paraphrase).

Of the four verbs in this sentence, three are participles. Only *matheteusate* ('make disciples') is an imperative as the preceding paraphrase attempts to communicate. This does not minimize the importance of the first participle, *poreuthentes* ('going'), for the importance of going cannot be ignored in the context itself. The church must be a 'going church' if the peoples of the nations are to become followers of Christ. Having said this, however, it is important to emphasize what the text emphasizes: the church is to follow the instructions of her Lord to make disciples by evangelizing and teaching.[11]

While making disciples begins with the winning of converts – bringing people into the family of God through effective evangelism – this is only the beginning. Making disciples continues with the nourishing, strengthening, and encouraging of new believers toward Christlikeness by feeding them the milk of the word initially, and later the meat of the word.

The implications for preaching should be clear. Our preaching – as with everything we do as a church – must be preaching that makes disciples. This will include some measure of pulpit evangelism in the local church setting, and it will assuredly include a large measure of edificational preaching there. Jesus said that we are not only to be involved in *baptizing* (evangelism), but in *teaching* (edification).

We Must Re-emphasize Spiritual Fellowship

Pot-lucks, brotherhood meetings, and ladies' socials sometime seem to be the part and whole of the efforts of many churches in this matter of fellowship. We seem to assume that if a few people get together in the same room that fellowship will automatically happen. That is simply not the case. Spiritual fellowship is more than 'two guys in the same boat'.

The New Testament church saw itself as a new community. This is seen, for example, in the letter to the Ephesians where the theme of 'God's new people' is prominent. The Apostle Paul reminds us that two peoples formerly at opposition, Jews and Gentiles, have now been brought into one spiritual community through the work of Jesus Christ.

> For he himself is our peace, who has made the two one and has destroyed the barrier, the dividing wall of hostility.... His purpose was to create in himself one new man out of the two.... Consequently, you are no longer foreigners and aliens, but fellow citizens with God's people and members of God's household, built on the foundation of the apostles and prophets, with Christ Jesus himself as the chief cornerstone (Eph 2:14-20).

While the concept of community, *koinonia*, is common in the New Testament church, it is not always easy to realize in today's church. One problem is that a sense of community tends to stand in opposition to Western culture's proclivity toward increasing isolationism. In spite of technology that enables us to be in touch almost instantly with anyone anywhere, our contacts with others tend to be superficial. We carry on our necessary business, but we choose not to become deeply involved in the affairs of others. Even families become more and more fragmented as siblings go their own directions, often living hundreds or thousands of miles apart and maintaining relatively little contact in comparison to former generations. Children often barely know grandparents, let alone aunts, uncles, and cousins.

For the church, this reality is both a problem and an opportunity. It is a problem because many people are becoming more reclusive, apparently enjoying (or at least enduring) their privacy and seemingly not being in any great hurry to change this aspect of their lifestyles. As in other areas of life, many who are connected to a church will maintain a somewhat distant relationship.

On the other hand, the church can view this social phenomenon as a great opportunity. Humanity was created to be social beings, both in relation to God and in relation to one another. The creation account in Genesis 1 and 2 is indicative of the fact that God created man to fellowship with him. Further, God said that it was not a good thing for Adam to live alone, and Eve was created to be his companion. These basic social principles have not been revoked. Humanity still needs to relate to God and to one another.

There is no better place for these relationships to exist than in the genuine fellowship experienced in the church. The importance of our fellowship with God is seen in an amazing statement concerning Christ made by the apostle Paul: 'And God placed all things under his feet and appointed him to be head over everything for the church, which is his body, the fullness of him who fills everything in every way' (Eph 1:22-23).

While it seems almost unthinkable, the most obvious meaning of this statement is that apart from the church, Christ would somehow be incomplete. Some commentators have tried to sidestep this meaning, but I remain unconvinced. Wood, for example, discusses four exegetical possibilities but ignores the one that is most obvious. He asks:

> But is Christ in any sense incomplete? To make the church essential to the full being of Christ is to reverse the true relationship. The NT regards Christ as essential to the full being of the church, not vice versa...[12]

While Wood correctly raises the central issue, he attempts to answer it on the basis of theological presupposition rather than exegesis. I concur that in an ontological sense Christ is not dependent on the church for his completeness. The text, however, is not dealing with *being* but with *relationship*.

It is more plausible, in my opinion, to take the verse at face value: apart from the body, Jesus, the head of the church—and the one who himself makes all things complete—is somehow incomplete. As is stated in the *New Bible Commentary*:

> In the further description of the church, *the fulness of him that filleth all in all* (23), it is seen as something without which Christ is not complete. This is true, not from any defect in the Godhead which the church makes up, but simply by the will of the Father who *gave him to be the head over all things to the church* (22). As He is Head of the church, so the church is His fulness.[13]

Similarly, Charles Hodge states that the preferred understanding is that 'the church is the fullness of Christ, because it fills him, i.e. completes his mystical person. He is the head, the church is the body. It is the complement, or that which completes, or renders whole.'[14]

The venerable Matthew Henry, writing in the early eighteenth century, explains the matter quite simply, but accurately:

> And yet the church is said to be his fulness, because Christ as Mediator would not be complete if he had not a church. How could he be a king if he had not a kingdom? This therefore comes in to the honour of Christ, as Mediator, that the church is his fulness.[15]

Surely the significance of the church's relationship with God through Christ is seen in an astounding way in Ephesians 1:22-23.

It must be remembered, however, that in addition to this marvelous relationship that the church has with God, those within the church have a special relationship with one another. While it may be that this relationship operates more in the realm of the *potential* than the *actual*, those who have been entrusted with the well-being of the body need to facilitate the realization of this *koinonia.* The concepts of community (Acts 2), unity (John 17), body-life (1 Cor 12), partnering (Gal 6:1-6), and mutual participation in the things of Christ (1 Cor 10:16-17) are important New Testament themes. We must work diligently to bring about these realities in the life of the local church.

Christian fellowship is first and foremost a spiritual matter. It is developed as persons grow in their understanding of the things of God, their commitment to the Lordship of Christ, and their maintenance of a holy life. The apostle John reminds us:

> We proclaim to you what we have seen and heard, so that you also may have fellowship with us. And our fellowship is with the Father and with his Son, Jesus Christ. We write this to make our joy complete. This is the message we have heard from him and declare to you: God is light; in him there is no darkness at all. If we claim to have fellowship with him yet walk in the darkness, we lie and do not live by the truth. But if we walk in the light, as he is in the light, we have fellowship with one another, and the blood of Jesus, his Son, purifies us from all sin (1 John 1:3-7).

Beyond these basic spiritual realities, congregational leaders can be actively committed to enhance opportunities for genuine fellowship to occur. In spite of societal trends that tend to encourage isolation, many people would welcome the opportunity to be a part of a *genuine* community.

We Must Exemplify God's Care for People

The matter of social concern was not easily handled by Christians during the twentieth century, especially in America. There was, in fact, a rather large division of opinion throughout most of that period. Some groups minimized the individuality of redemption and substituted in place of the biblical gospel that which became known as the 'social gospel'. On the other hand, those who emphasized personal salvation often did little or nothing for people's temporal needs.

Neither of these extremes reflects the biblical perspective. In addition to coming into the world to resolve the sin problem, Jesus went about doing good. These truths need not be set in opposition. He fed hungry people. He healed the sightless and restored withered limbs. He showed love toward the unlovely. He comforted the grieving. Should the church be doing less than following her Lord's example?

Historically, prior to the twentieth century, the church's record was fairly credible in this regard. For example, England was socially revolutionized primarily through the efforts of two giants of the Faith, John Wesley in the eighteenth century and William Wilberforce in the nineteenth. The former was a great catalyst in the reform of labor laws and the penal system. The latter worked longer than a quarter century urging parliament to abolish slavery. Unfortunately, the modernist-fundamentalist debate during the first part of the twentieth century was a major factor in the abandonment of social ministries by many who were part of the conservative movement. Their theology may have been preferable to that offered by the opposition, but their practice of a full-orbed ministry was sadly lacking.

Our motivation in seeking social justice and caring for the needs of the hurting should be the same as our motivation for all that we do – the glory of God. Jesus said:

> You are the salt of the earth. But if the salt loses its saltiness, how can it be made salty again? It is no longer good for anything, except to be thrown out and trampled by men. You are the light of the world. A city on a hill cannot be hidden. Neither do people light a lamp and put it under a bowl. Instead they put it on its stand, and it gives light to everyone in the house. In the same way, let your light shine before men, that they may see your good deeds and praise your Father in heaven (Matt 5:12-16).

Our philosophy of ministry as well as our philosophy of preaching must be impacted by a correct view of exemplifying God's loving concern for people. Those in the church as well as those outside the church should never suffer from a sense of lonely despair when problems become too great to handle. The church must be there for them.

Summation

This chapter has attempted to set forth some important theological foundations upon which a solid understanding of preaching might be built. The starting point, of course, is with God himself. He is a self-disclosing Being who has revealed himself in a variety of ways, but most importantly in Scripture, the written word, and in the person of Jesus Christ, the incarnate Word. Obviously, God wants to be known. He desires to have fellowship with his creation and has gone to great lengths to see this take place.

The preacher has the unique function of participating in the disclosure of God to his creation. Through preaching we have the privilege of re-communicating what God has previously revealed. We do that without any inherent authority, simply serving in the role of ambassador. (See 2 Corinthians 5:20 and the surrounding context.)

Since preaching is only one part of pastoral ministry, however, it is first necessary to consider the matter of ministry philosophy in a broader sense. Thus, the matter of ecclesiology is crucial, for it is in and through the church that ministry is carried out. In this regard, seven distinct emphases of the early church were discussed including the setting of priorities, spiritual gifts, worship, evangelism, edification, fellowship, and meeting people's temporal needs. Finally, these seven emphases were discussed in relation to the contemporary church. As we grapple with these issues, our own philosophy of ministry should begin to take shape.

Our philosophy of preaching is one part of our larger philosophy of ministry. Our view of preaching must not dictate the nature of the church; rather, the biblical view of the church must inform and guide the nature of all of our ministry, including our preaching ministry.

Points to Ponder

1. How does preaching compare to other forms of public speaking? What are some similarities? What are some differences?

2. What qualifies some persons to be preachers? Are there certain character traits, talents, gifts, aptitudes, intellectual abilities, or educational experiences that are necessary? Which of these are crucial and which, while possibly helpful, are not?

3. The term *ambassador* is used to speak of the role of the preacher. What are some of the other biblical terms or images used to describe the preacher's role?

4. Should we expect ministry priorities to change from era to era? How do we determine the constants as well as the variables?

5. How does preaching, which is primarily proclamatory and response-evoking, fit into the context of corporate worship in the local church setting?

Step Two

Maintain a Balance in Personal Perspective

'If preaching be, in sober fact, the communication of a Person through a person to a company of persons, then it follows naturally and by an inescapable logic that the kind of personality requisite in the preacher is the type through which Christ can be transmitted to mankind. Nothing less will suffice. Let me not hesitate to say it. A man may be veritably glittering with oratorical gifts, he may seem above most 'to have what it takes' to be a minister, but if his character be such that he is not fitted to discharge homiletically the function fulfilled physically by Mary long ago, he can never be a true preacher' (Ian Macpherson).[1]

Joseph Parker, the English Congregational preacher of the nineteenth century whose sermons were collected in a twenty-five volume work titled *The Preacher's Bible*, reportedly said that the most important thing about a sermon is the man behind it. While this is an obvious over-statement – the most important thing about a sermon is the truth about the Godhead being told – the hyperbole of Parker is understandable. The importance of the role of the preacher is indeed awesome!

It is a rarity to find a book on preaching that does not have a chapter, or at least part of a chapter, devoted to the preacher as a person. This is as it should be. Can the Christian message be separated from the Christian messenger? Does not the veracity of the former depend on the integrity of the latter? If the message of the Christian preacher is to be heard and believed, the preacher must give strong evidence of complete trustworthiness, of being an individual of personal and professional integrity. The preacher will also need to be a person who recognizes the importance of hard work and devotion to the task while at the same time being fully aware that preaching is a spiritual enterprise depending entirely on the grace of God for any success that may accompany the proclamation of biblical truth.

Exemplify Personal and Professional Integrity

When we consider the concept of integrity, our minds tend to move immediately to issues like sex, money, and power. These seem to be the areas which cause the most serious problems for those in ministry. While there is no way to exaggerate the severity of those issues and the personal and professional shipwreck they may bring about, there are other issues which are possibly even more serious, not because of their depth but because of their breadth. For every pastor who 'falls' as a result of pilfering funds, becoming a tyrant, or having a sexual affair, dozens more wrestle with other integrity issues in their lives.

Our English word 'integrity' comes from the Latin *integritas*, referring initially to soundness, completeness, or wholeness. In reference to ethical issues, it came to mean 'firm adherence to a code or standard of values'.[2] Pastoral ministry is worthy of the very highest of standards, both in those well known areas of sex, money, and power, but also in every other area of life. There are important standards that must be sought and maintained in personal matters and there are also standards for adherence in what might be called the professional matters, though it is admittedly impossible to distinguish the two neatly.

The Preacher's Personal Integrity
It is important to look in some detail at the subject of the preacher's personal integrity. As Jones stated so well, 'Sermons cannot be detached from the person who preaches them. They are conditioned by what he is, what he does, what he thinks, and what he feels.'[3] Our discussion of this all-important subject of personal integrity will include the matters of spirituality, character, and reputation.

Spirituality

Unlike many topics addressed by public speakers, the gospel message is more than an interesting subject to research and discuss. It is about redemption and spiritual transformation. It is about experiencing truth. The gospel is not merely cerebral in nature, or only subjectively experiential. It is concerned with ultimate Truth, Jesus, the Son of God, being embedded into the life of any person who will trust him with his or her eternal soul. The gospel is spiritual reality in a very narrow and specific way. Jesus said, 'I am the way and the truth and the life. No one comes to the Father except through me' (John 14:6).

Because of this, the one who would dare proclaim the gospel must know and be certain both intellectually and experientially whereof he speaks. It is reported that Thomas Carlyle, the nineteenth century Scottish writer, when asked his opinion regarding the kind of minister needed in a certain church without a pastor, replied: 'What this parish needs is a man who knows God otherwise than by hearsay.'[4] Isn't this the kind of preacher needed by every church?

Since the preaching of the gospel is redemptive and transformational, the preacher must be one who has a personal knowledge of spiritual redemption and transformation. Without an intimate knowledge of Christ – knowledge in the fullest sense – a person cannot hope to draw others to the Savior. George Whitefield spoke about this in a sermon titled *The Duty of a Gospel Minister*, in which he said:

> You will never preach with power feelingly, while you deal in a false commerce with truths unfelt. It will be but poor, dry, sapless stuff – your people will go away out of the church as cold as they came in. For my part, I would not preach an unknown Christ for ten thousand worlds. Such offer God strange fire, and their sermons will but increase their own damnation.[5]

At the beginning of his letters, the apostle Paul always reminds his readers of his own relationship with Christ. While his salutations serve as a formal greeting, they also serve as a statement of his right to speak and write on behalf of the gospel, for it is *his* gospel as well as theirsChe had received it as *his own* (cf. 2 Cor 4:3; 1 Thess 1:5).

An example of the depth of Paul's appropriation of the gospel for himself is seen in his second letter to the young pastor, Timothy. Paul states:

> Remember Jesus Christ, raised from the dead, descended from David. This is my gospel, for which I am suffering even to the point of being chained like a criminal. But God's word is not chained. Therefore I endure everything for the sake of the elect, that they too may obtain the salvation that is in Christ Jesus, with eternal glory (2 Tim 2:8-10).

For Paul, the gospel was not an abstract truth that may lead to interesting discussion on religion. The gospel was a matter of life and death. He had come to experience its saving power for himself and was committed to share it with as many others as possible regardless of the personal price he might have to pay (see 2 Cor 6:3-10).

It is absolutely imperative that the preacher *owns* the gospel as his very own, even as Paul did, having enjoyed the spiritual redemption and transformation it alone brings. Apart from this personal encounter with the Christ of the gospel, the preacher is at best an aloof viewer of spiritual reality without any hope of convincing others of its wonder and necessity.

In addition to being a person who has been brought into union with Christ, the preacher must be an individual who maintains an intimate relationship with him. This is a relationship nurtured by spiritual disciplines like Scripture reading, meditation, and prayer. This relationship, like all personal relationships, requires effort. It will require that we devote time and energy to Divine matters. Martyn Lloyd-Jones, in a sermon preached at Westminster Chapel as part of his Romans series, encouraged his listeners to build this relationship with God by consciously and consistently pursuing it in such a manner that they might indeed encounter the Living God in life-changing ways.

... give Him opportunities of telling you. He will meet you in the Scriptures, and He will tell you. Give time, give place, give opportunity. Set other things aside, and say to other people, 'I cannot do what you ask me to do; I have another appointment, I know He is coming and I am waiting for Him.'[6]

It is important to realize that spirituality has to do with our relationship to God, not with our relationship to the things of God such as the church and ministry. One might conceivably love Christian things without being very spiritual.

Is it possible to love ministry more than we love God? For some, to speak of loving the ministry is an exaggeration at best. Feelings toward the ministry are sometimes ambivalent; a kind of love/hate relationship. I felt that way until I left pastoral ministry to teach in a seminary. Then I discovered that I had indeed loved pastoral ministry more than I ever suspected. I actually went through a grieving process that lasted around two years. This was how long it took before I could attend church without a sense of longing or even envy. Thus I can understand the confession of Martin Copenhaver, a Congregational pastor who said:

> I am in danger of falling in love with the ministry.... I'm falling for this whole crazy jumble that is parish ministry. I always knew I would like the staples: worship, calling, teaching, counseling, preaching, study, dreaming. But I'm beginning to love the rest as well: coffee hour chit-chat; temperamental choir directors and dirt-blind sextons; holding the hand of grief; slapping the hand of greed; the kids with disarming questions; the silver-haired ladies who insist upon calling you 'young man'; appointment calendars that look as thickly settled as the *New York Times*; confirmation class giggles. I know this may be hard to believe, but sometimes I even enjoy board and committee meetings.[7]

Now there is nothing too alarming about loving pastoral ministry. In fact, the pastor who doesn't like what he's doing is in for a tough time. The danger is that we can easily confuse love for the ministry with love for God! The two are not synonymous at all.

Ministry is a means to an end. That end is God himself. It is God who is to be loved supremely, not the means which take us to him. To love ministry more than we love God is a form of idolatry and it should be alarming to consider that we might come to the point of committing idolatry in the Name of the God whom we profess to serve.

When Christ was asked about the essence of piety, he quoted Deuteronomy 6:5 and said it was to be found in loving God with all that we have: our heart, soul, mind, and strength (Mark 12:30). This was true in Moses' day, in Jesus' day, and it is true in our day. It is true for all people including the pastor. It is a standard that has not changed, nor will it. Even the very best things in life such as one's spouse, one's children, or one's calling as a pastor-teacher must not be allowed to interfere with our relationship with the Lord. He should be the focal point of our affections. Our deepest love must be directed to him.

Love for God does not develop automatically. It does not come by virtue of seminary training or even ecclesiastical credentialling. Nor does it ordinarily come in a sudden surge of emotion, a kind of spiritual 'love at first sight'. Rather, it develops gradually as we get to know him better through his words and his works. It develops as we spend time with him, not just his business, in meditation and prayer. Richard Baxter wrote:

> O, brethren, watch, therefore over your own hearts! Keep out sinful passions, and worldly inclinations: keep up the life of faith and love; be much at home: and be much with God.... More particularly, a minister should take some special pains with his heart before he is to go to the congregation. If it be then cold, how is it likely to warm the hearts of his hearers. Go, therefore, then specially to God for life....[8]

If our love for God becomes genuine and deep-rooted, our attitude toward ministry will be affected. Since loving God is now our primary concern, struggles or disappointments in ministry will not be nearly as earth-shattering as they might have been formerly. Why? Because ministry is correctly seen as a means to an end, not the end itself. Things are seen in proper perspective and relative values are more easily understood.

Learning to love our ministry less while striving to love God more will actually strengthen our ministry. We will be serving with integrity. Our personal lives will model our message. Our purposes in serving will be primarily spiritual instead of the maintenance of an organization.

Of all the matters related to preaching – exegesis, hermeneutics, homiletics, voice, presentation, persuasion, and the like – nothing is more important than the spiritual condition of the preacher. I concur with Lloyd-Jones who said that the preacher's 'most important task is to prepare himself, not his sermon.'[9] And again,

> What then is the chief thing?... What matters? The chief thing is the love of God, the love of souls, a knowledge of the Truth, and the Holy Spirit within you. These are the things that make the preacher. If he has the love of God in his heart, and if he has a love for God; if he has a love for the souls of men, and a concern about them; if he knows the truth of the Scriptures; and has the Spirit of God within him, that man will preach. That is the big thing. The other things can be helpful; but keep them in their right place, and never allow them to usurp any other position.[10]

The preacher's personal integrity must be rooted in a devout spirituality. This must take precedence over everything else.

Character
Spirituality and character cannot be separated. The result of genuine spirituality is a life that increasingly emulates the character of God. It is a life that pursues holiness, for this is arguably the quintessential attribute of God.[11] Peter writes, 'But just as he who called you is holy, so be holy in all you do; for it is written: "Be holy, because I am holy" ' (1 Pet 1:15-16).

God's holiness has to do with his uniqueness. He is totally separate and distinct from his creation both in his personhood and in his moral values. The Hebrew *qadosh* has as its basic meaning, 'separation.'

In reference to God, the term tells us that he is fully apart from his creation in terms of being. He is completely different and distinct. Isaiah expresses it like this: 'For this is what the high and lofty One says – he who lives forever, whose name is holy: "I live in a high and holy place .."' (Isa 57:15). Following their deliverance at the Red Sea, Moses and the Israelites sang to the Lord extolling his virtues. They sang in Exodus 15:11: 'Who among the gods is like you, O LORD? Who is like you – majestic in holiness, awesome in glory, working wonders?'

God is also separate from moral evil of any kind. His moral purity is without limit. He is the standard by which all morality is measured. In the book of Habbakuk, we find that prophet questioning God about some important moral issues of his day. Following the Lord's response regarding how he will handle these matters, God himself states: 'But the LORD is in his holy temple; let all the earth be silent before him' (Hab 2:20). Habakkuk questions God no further, instead only affirming trust and reliance in his prayer-song in chapter 3.

God is indeed the standard of holiness. Furthermore, he fully expects his followers to press after this standard. Jesus said, 'Be perfect, therefore, as your heavenly Father is perfect' (Matt 5:48).

Biblical ministry must never lose sight of God's holiness and our appropriate response to it. When Moses was called by God through the episode of the burning bush to be God's instrument of deliverance, he was admonished to 'Take off your sandals, for the place where you are standing is holy ground' (Ex 3:5). Moses responded by hiding his face lest he gaze upon the glory of God. A generation later, Joshua, the man who succeeded Moses as leader of Israel, was given the same instruction. An angelic being known as 'the commander of the Lord's army' confronted Joshua prior to the decisive battle at Jericho (Josh 5:13-15). Joshua was quick to remove his shoes as instructed. In both instances, the appropriate response was to revere with great awe that which was holy.

Similarly, the temple vision of the prophet Isaiah that led to his call emphasized the holiness of God. Isaiah saw six-winged heavenly beings hovering around the throne of God calling out to one another in ceaseless praise: 'Holy, holy, holy is the LORD Almighty; the whole earth is full of his glory' (Isa 6:3). In view of the majesty and holiness of God, he cried out, 'Woe to me... I am ruined! I am a man of unclean lips, and I live among a people of unclean lips, and my eyes have seen the King, the LORD Almighty' (Isa 6:5). Before being commissioned by God, Isaiah received forgiveness and cleansing. Is it coincidental that Isaiah refers to God as 'the holy one of Israel' some thirty times?

I fear that the concept of holiness has fallen upon hard times in our day, even among some evangelicals. It somehow seems out-of-date in a culture that values little that is eternal and most everything that is temporal. But holiness is completely integral to the Christian life. A statement that caught the attention of J. Hudson Taylor was included in a letter to him from a fellow missionary in China, John McCarthy: 'The Lord Jesus received is holiness begun; the Lord Jesus cherished is holiness advancing; the Lord Jesus counted upon as never absent would be holiness complete....'[12]

God expects all of his people to reflect his holiness, especially those who are in leadership positions. James, the half brother of our Lord, reminds us: 'Not many of you should presume to be teachers, my brothers, because you know that we who teach will be judged more strictly' (Jas 3:1).

Robert Murray McCheyne was a minister in the Church of Scotland in the nineteenth century. He served only about seven years, dying at the age of thirty. One of the best known ministers in Scotland during his day, he remains an admired model of pastoral piety. He gave this advice in a charge to a young man being ordained into the gospel ministry:

> Study universal holiness of life. Your whole usefulness depends on this. Your sermon on Sabbath lasts but an hour or twoyour life preaches all the week. Remember, ministers are standard-bearers. Satan aims his fiery darts at them. If he can only make you a covetous minister, or a lover of pleasure, or a lover of praise, or a lover of good eating, then he has ruined your ministry for ever.... cast yourself at the feet of Christ, implore His Spirit to make you a holy man.[13]

And again, in a letter to a pastoral colleague, McCheyne states: '... according to the purity and perfections of the instrument, will be the success. It is not great talents God blesses so much as great likeness to Jesus. A holy minister is an awful weapon in the hand of God.'[14]

E. M. Bounds, known for his writing on prayer, also spoke of the importance of the pursuit of holiness by those in ministry:

> The preacher's sharpest and strongest preaching should be to himself. His most difficult, delicate, laborious, and thorough work must be with himself.... Preachers are not sermon makers, but men makers and saint makers, and he only is well-trained for this business who has made himself a man and a saint. It is not great talents or great learning or great preachers that God needs, but men great in holiness, great in faith, great in love, great in fidelity, great for God – men always preaching by holy sermons in the pulpit, by holy lives out of it. These can mold a generation for God.[15]

An example of this is seen in the life of D. L Moody during his first visit to England. The account is taken from the biography of Moody written by his son, William, about a year after the great evangelist's death.

> Among other meetings he attended the Mildmay Conference, and thus records his impression of the Rev. William Pennefather, the founder of Mildmay: 'I well remember sitting in yonder seat looking up at the platform and seeing the beloved Mr. Pennefather's face illuminated as it were with heaven's light. I don't think I can recall a word that he said, but the whole atmosphere of the man breathed holiness, and I got then a lift and impetus in the Christian life that I have never lost, and I believe the impression will remain with me to my dying day. I thank God that I saw and spoke with that holy man; no one could see him without the consciousness that he lived in the presence of God.'[16]

Should not every preacher desire to radiate the presence of God in such a way that he and his glory will be remembered long after our words are forgotten?

Practically, it should be remembered that the primary instrument of God in causing us to become increasingly conformed to his holiness is the Scriptures. In his high priestly prayer for his followers, Jesus prayed, 'Sanctify them by the truth; your word is truth' (John 17:17). It is in the Bible that we encounter God's own holiness and the standards and principles by which we are to live to become holy ourselves. Yet, it is at this very point that danger lurks.

Every preacher is susceptible to the danger of loving to preach the Word of God more than loving to live the Word of God. The Bible itself says that we are to 'be doers of the word, and not hearers only' (Jas 1:22). We sometimes like to quote this verse and encourage our people to follow it, as well we should. But do we take the instruction of this little verse as seriously for ourselves as we do for our flocks?

Most of my seminary teaching load is in the area of preaching, so I have a vested interest in its importance. I believe that the pulpit sets the pace for the life of the church. I would argue that while preaching is certainly not the only worthwhile activity of the pastor, more can probably be accomplished with the time invested in the preparation and delivery of biblical sermons than in any other pastoral function. Yet, in this very ministry the pastor encounters this danger that might well undermine personal integrity.

I'm convinced that one of the occupational hazards of pastoral ministry is that of being unable to think about Scripture except in a sermon or lesson context. How often do we look at the Word of God and study it for ourselves without a sermon or lesson deadline fast approaching? How easy is it to pick up the Scripture and contemplate its teaching without thinking of sermon propositions or homiletical approaches? If you're like me in this regard – and I suspect many preachers are – it is not easy at all!

While I was a seminary student, Dr. Malcom Cronk, then pastor of the Wheaton Bible Church, was an adjunct professor under whom I studied. He deeply impressed upon me that the one thing that ought to distinguish the pastor from everyone else is that the pastor should be known as 'a person of the Book'. He meant that the Scriptures, more than anything else, should be our area of expertise.

While I'm in basic agreement with this, I want to clarify the issue a bit. You see, it's not enough to be a person of the Book in an analytical sense only. Even if you're able to locate easily every event recorded in Scripture, or to discuss intelligently the important introductory matters of each book, or to work competently in the biblical languages of Hebrew, Aramaic, and Greek, or to outline clearly from memory the issues and arguments of each book of the Bible, that's not enough.

It's also not enough to be a person of the Book in a theological sense only. Even if you're able to trace the various issues in systematic theology throughout the Old and New Testaments, or even if you're able to offer appropriate proof texts in any theological discussion, that's not really enough.

It's also not enough to be a person of the Book in a homiletics sense. Even if there is no text in Scripture above your sermonic abilities, that's not really enough.

To be a person of the Book in the best sense means that in addition to the abilities above, there is no area of your life, professional or private, that is apart from the scrutiny of Scripture. It means that you are unsatisfied with even a superior ability to deal with Scripture unless Scripture first deals with you. It means that you will fight to resist the temptation to represent God in the proclamation of his Word without first having taken that Word seriously for yourself. If that Word has not first taught, rebuked, corrected, and trained you in righteousness, then how can you think it will have an effect on others? In context, these words from 2 Timothy 3:16 are directed first to Pastor Timothy, and then to his flock. Likewise, we must be 'doers of the Word' before we can rightly expect others to be either hearers or doers.

Howard Snyder, in his book *Liberating the Church*, says,

> The purpose of the Bible is to create and sustain a faithful people. And the fundamental concern of the church should be to live in fidelity to God's covenant as revealed in Scripture. This means searching the Scriptures to know, understand, and live out God's Kingdom plan for the church. The proof of understanding Scripture is living the lifestyle of the Kingdom.[17]

The lifestyle of the kingdom is first and foremost that of holiness. The pastor who fails to be a 'doer' of the Word in this regard demonstrates the lack of an experiential understanding of the Word that leads to God-likeness. Calvin instructs us well:

'...rule is, that in reading the Scriptures we should constantly direct our inquiries and meditations to those things which tend to edification, not indulge in curiosity, or in studying things of no use. And since the Lord has been pleased to instruct us, not in frivolous questions, but in solid piety, in the fear of his name, in true faith, and the duties of holiness, let us rest satisfied with such knowledge.[18]

We preachers need to dedicate ourselves wholeheartedly to the never-ending pursuit of holiness. This will please God and strengthen his people. It will also become a well-spring of satisfaction and spiritual fulfillment for us as we become more and more conformed to the image of God's dear Son, the Lord Jesus Christ.

Reputation

Spirituality and character together form the foundation of personal integrity. A positive reputation in personal integrity – an absolute necessity for a productive preaching ministry – will be the result. While it may be possible to build a seemingly positive reputation apart from this foundation, such an effort will eventually self-destruct. God will not bless such a ministry, and people will eventually see its pretense. While the concept of character speaks of what we really are, reputation has to do with what people perceive us to be. While the two will probably never be identical, they should be very close if true integrity is present.

Public speaking, including homiletics, owes a great deal to the thinking of the Greek philosopher Aristotle. Writing during the fourth century before Christ, Aristotle produced a work on the subject of rhetoric, the discipline of writing and speaking for persuasive communication. He identified three primary elements in rhetoric: *ethos, pathos, and logos*.

Of the means of persuasion supplied by the speech itself there are three kinds. The first kind reside in the character (*ethos*) of the speaker; the second consist in producing a certain (the right) attitude in the hearer; the third appertain to the argument proper, in so far as it actually or seemingly demonstrates.[19]

According to Aristotle, then, persuasion is effected primarily by the audience's perception of the speaker's character, i.e. reputation (*ethos*), the emotion that is aroused in the hearer (*pathos*), and the verbal content of the speech (*logos*).

Now *ethos* refers to more than reputation in the moral sense of the word only. It refers also to professional competence (Does the speaker know what he's talking about?), and to the manner of the presentation (Is the speaker personally excited about the message that is being shared?). In this section, however, the matter of moral reputation is our focus.

As one who is a long-time observer of speeches, especially sermons, it is my opinion that speakers give far more attention to *pathos* and *logos* than to *ethos*. On the one hand, sermons often emphasize various emotions at the expense of sound argumentation based on a solid exegesis of the Scriptures and careful homiletical arrangement. Listeners deserve more than an assortment of emotional stimuli used to manipulate them toward response. On the other hand, sermons may contain rich content but be almost completely void of the necessary emotional element. Why should we expect the hearer to be stirred if the preacher isn't? In either case, relatively little attention is given to the personal element of the preacher himself.

It is noteworthy, therefore, that Aristotle viewed *ethos* as the most important of the three elements of persuasion.

It is not true, as some writers on the art maintain, that the probity of the speaker contributes nothing to his persuasiveness; on the contrary, we might affirm that his character (*ethos*) is the most potent of all the means of persuasion.[20]

If the ancient philosopher is correct, and I believe he is, then today's preacher needs to be concerned with the matter of reputation, the perception of the audience regarding his character. Is the speaker to be believed?

This is a concern of Paul as he writes to Timothy, the young pastor at Ephesus. As Paul states the qualifications of an overseer (this term is used interchangeably in the epistles with 'pastor' and 'elder'), he emphasizes issues of character more so than issues of ability (1 Tim 3:1-7). He says that the church leader must be 'above reproach,... temperate, self-controlled, respectable,... not given to much wine, not violent but gentle, not quarrelsome, not a lover of money' (vss 2-4). Paul says too that this person 'must also have a good reputation with outsiders' (vs 7). Later in this same letter, Paul instructs the young pastor to 'set an example for the believers in speech, in life, in love, in faith and in purity' (1 Tim 4:12). And again, 'Watch your life and doctrine closely' (1 Tim 4:16).

The importance of *ethos* is seen also in Paul's first letter to the church at Thessalonica. Here, Paul appeals repeatedly to his reputation, gained while he labored among them. Following are some excerpts from 1 Thessalonians 1 and 2 which are examples of this:

> You know how we lived among you for your sake (1:5).... We speak as men approved by God to be entrusted with the gospel. We are not trying to please men but God, who tests our hearts. You know we never used flattery, nor did we put on a mask to cover up greed – God is our witness (2:4-5).... Surely you remember, brothers, our toil and hardship; we worked night and day in order not to be a burden to anyone while we preached the gospel of God to you. You are witnesses, and so is God, of how holy, righteous and blameless we were among you who believed (2:9-10).

I'm not suggesting that preachers constantly justify their reputations to their audiences. Paul, in this instance, was facing a situation in which the integrity of the gospel was in question, and the gospel was inseparably linked to the apostle. Thankfully, his reputation was such that no one could rightly question his personal integrity and as a result, the gospel was not slandered.

It is crucial that preachers of the gospel live beyond criticism, as much as is humanly possible, in this matter of personal reputation.

As Paul Cedar explains, this means more than simply doing what we know to be proper on a personal level.

> Most pastors and Christian leaders want to do what is right. As we serve Christ and his church, we want to live above reproach. Yet despite our best efforts, people frequently misinterpret, although not always maliciously, our actions and words.
>
> So I've found it isn't enough to be true to myself and God alone. I must go the second mile, not only that others might not be confused but that ministry might effectively continue.[21]

This matter of reputation – *ethos*, as Aristotle called it – is vitally important in matters pertaining to preaching. Communication of any kind cannot be fully processed and understood without some knowledge of the sender. For example, an individual may be seated at a computer 'surfing the net' as a means of doing research. Information on the subject is abundant, but is it all to be believed? It helps to have some understanding of the source of the information including issues like the sender's qualifications to speak on the subject, as well as his credibility, honesty, and motivation.

What is true of the internet is also true of the marketplace, the classroom, the political arena, the home, and the pulpit. In fact, the importance of the person speaking forth the Christian message is even more important than the sender of other kinds of communication. Christianity claims to change lives. Spiritual transformation is a large part of the gospel. Can the gospel be believed if notable spiritual transformation has not taken place in the life of the person talking about it? Yes, the gospel remains *true* regardless of the spiritual condition of its spokespersons. But is it likely to be *believed*?

Suppose an individual claims to have found the secret to living an utterly peaceful, tranquil life regardless of outward circumstances. Books are written and a lecture itinerary planned. In the meanwhile, it becomes widely known that this person is tottering on the edge of a complete nervous breakdown because of some relatively insignificant happenings that have taken place. Would you stand in line to buy this person's books or lecture tickets? I would hope not!

Listeners must be convinced that the speaker can be believed. They have this right.

> Preachers, however, need to understand how persuasive their moral characters are. They also need to realize how destructive their lives can be if they are immoral or lacking in those positive elements of *ethos*. We all have seen the sad spectacle of ministers who have failed because they surrendered to impure passions, quarrelsomeness, impatience, unkindness, and ineptness in teaching and preaching. We are also aware of the winsomeness of preachers who are pure, consecrated, prepared, righteous, faithful, loving, peaceful, not quarrelsome, kind, patient, tolerant, and gentle. The conscientious Christian would be foolish to ignore or avoid such ethical considerations.[22]

Having looked at the matter of the preacher's personal integrity in terms of spirituality, character, and reputation, we conclude that it is impossible to exaggerate the importance of this matter. As we continue to develop a philosophy of preaching, this issue of personal integrity must be at the forefront. Our people deserve nothing less from us than an ever-deepening relationship with God that results in the pursuit of holiness accompanied by an unblemished reputation. Our Savior demands this!

The Preacher's Professional Integrity
In addition to personal integrity being a necessary part of one's philosophy of preaching, there is also the matter of professional integrity. The preacher must understand and take seriously several matters which are foundational to the whole endeavor of preaching. These include the matter of call, the issue of gifting, one's viewpoint concerning the importance of preaching, proper motivation, and personal discipline in the task.

Called to Preach
The notion of the importance of a preacher's divine call is not nearly as pervasive as it once was. There was a time when ordination councils quizzed the ordinand extensively on this issue. More recently,

however, this subject is not often addressed in any detail. This is regrettable.

There are those in preaching ministry today, perhaps many, who would be hard pressed to explain their sense of call. Some, in fact, may not even consider it important. This is not to say that these individuals necessarily have ulterior motives. Some choose the ministry as a vocation because they sincerely believe they can make an important difference in people's lives. They care about people individually and collectively. They see the Christian message as having great potential for good in society and they want to be directly involved in sharing it. It is difficult to be critical of such reasoning. Yet, there seems to be one thing lacking – a conviction regarding the will of God for one's life.

Taking upon oneself the role of preacher is no small thing. It is a vocation which a person should readily avoid without an unshakeable conviction that this is indeed God's will and it must be followed. Sangster offers this wise counsel:

> It is a high and awful task from which any man might well shrink. That is why the Church in its wisest hours has always insisted that a man must have a divine call to it. The work cannot be sustained on anything less. Men have begun the work just as an occupation, a way of earning their bread. A man may, indeed, enjoy it in his early days... he may, for a while, be content. But only for a while! He cannot sustain a ministry that way.[23]

The call to ministry is not a matter of human desire or human ingenuity. It is not simply a matter of vocational aptitude or ecclesiastical needs. It is a matter of divine compulsion and human obedience. Macpherson states it this way:

> No real minister ever merely drifts into the work. Nor does he enter it simply because someone in a position of influence has, as we commonly say, 'pulled the strings' for him. The only strings that are pulled in all genuine calls to the preacher's office are the heartstrings. And it is God who pulls them![24]

And again, John Henry Jowett says:

> I would affirm my own conviction that in all genuine callings to the ministry there is a sense of the divine initiative, a solemn communication of the divine will, a mysterious commission, which leaves a man no alternative, but which sets him in the road of this vocation bearing the ambassage of a servant and instrument of the eternal God.[25]

Frank Pollard, writing in the *Handbook of Contemporary Preaching*, recalls something about his sense of call that he wrote as a young man.

> I am a preacher for the same reason that Moby Dick was a whale. I can't help it. It is what I was born to and created for. My only ambition is to be a communicator of God's truths found in His Word. My one goal is to state the great, old truths of the Bible in simple, fresh ways. My only tools are words, short, simple words born in the love of God. It is as impossible for me to see preaching as dull, tedious work as it is for a bird to dread to fly.[26]

There is an apostolic ring in this kind of statement not unlike the declaration of Paul: 'Yet when I preach the gospel, I cannot boast, for I am compelled to preach. Woe to me if I do not preach the gospel!' (1 Cor. 9:16).

The nature of the call to preaching ministry is somewhat unique in each case. There is no usual way that it takes place. For some, the call may come as a definite inward impression at a time of spiritual seeking or even during a time of spiritual crisis. For others, it may occur in a sudden, unexpected way as with Paul on the highway to Damascus. For still others it may grow as a developing awareness that this is what God expects of this person. While some have testified of an overwhelming and consuming sense of God's presence, most probably receive the call through the 'still small voice of God' breathed deep within.

The call to preaching ministry ordinarily is impressed first upon the individual being called and later confirmed by the church. There is, of course, biblical precedent for this. As I stated elsewhere,

> In the New Testament, the call to ministry leadership seems to be both internal and external. The called ones have a strong sense that this is what they must be doing. At the same time, the church confirms the call. We see this happening throughout the Book of Acts. Those who are called never act in a 'lone ranger' manner but are always accountable to the larger body.[27]

A notable example of this is seen in the experience of Barnabas and Saul (later Paul) as recorded in the first part of Acts 13. While Paul was aware of his own call to ministry and often testifies of it in his letters, it is the church in Antioch that validates the call to missionary service and commissions them to go. This did not in any way minimize Paul's own sense of calling, but rather strengthened it.

Sometimes, the events of the call take place in an opposite fashion with the church sensing the calling of God upon a person's life before the person does. There are some notable examples of this throughout the centuries. Schaff, the historian, mentions several.

> On a visit to his parents' house, Gregory against his will, and even without his previous knowledge, was ordained presbyter by his father before the assembled congregation on a feast day of the year 361. Such forced elections and ordinations, though very offensive to our taste, were at that time frequent, especially upon the urgent wish of the people, whose voice in many instances proved to be indeed the voice of God. Basil also, and Augustine, were ordained presbyters, Athanasius and Ambrose bishops, against their will. Gregory fled soon after, it is true, to his friend in Pontus, but out of regard to his aged parents and the pressing call of the church, he returned to Nazianzum towards Easter in 362, and delivered his first pulpit discourse, in which he justified himself in his conduct, and said: 'It has its advantage to hold back a little from the call of God, as Moses, and after him Jeremiah, did on account of their age; but it has also its advantage to come forward readily, when God calls, like Aaron and Isaiah; provided both be done with a devout spirit, the one on account of inherent weakness, the other in John of Antioch, known as Chrysostom, the "golden

mouth," was also put upon by the church to enter into a ministry of preaching. reliance upon the strength of him who calls.'[28]

It has been said, incidentally, of Augustine: 'Ordained in spite of his "protests and weeping" while visiting Hippo in 391, he began to preach at his bishop's request and to study the Scriptures.[29]

Chrysostom was reluctant to become a priest. In fact, he had avoided ordination on more than one occasion. Finally, in 386, he was made a presbyter and designated as the chief preacher in Antioch. The church called him to be a preacher – he did not volunteer for the task. Chrysostom did not experience so much an inner call of God to preach as he experienced a call from the church.[30]

This kind of experience appears to have been the case with the Scottish reformer, John Knox. A learned man in the Scriptures, theology, and fluent in speech, Knox had been ordained in the Roman Catholic Church about 1530. He never felt called to be a priest or monk, however, and instead had become a schoolmaster. Later, at the age of 42, he became acquainted with a preacher named John Rough. This relatively unknown preacher followed the teachings of the reformers and was pleased to find a kindred spirit in Knox, who had gradually changed his views during the fifteen years or so following his ordination. Macpherson briefly tells the story.

> There was a memorable May Sunday in a church at St. Andrews when John Rough, formerly chaplain to the Earl of Arran, preached on the right of a Christian congregation to elect its own minister. John Knox was there. Breaking off dramatically in the midst of his sermon, Rough appealed directly to Knox in the hearing of the people. 'Take upon you the public office and charge of preaching,' he adjured him, 'even as you look to avoid God's heavy displeasure.' The congregation ratified the call. Rough was, indeed, only voicing their collective vote. 'Whereat,' says the chronicler quaintly, 'the said John, abashed, burst forth in most abundant tears and withdrew himself to his chamber.' The call may come through congregational constraint.[31]

The initiative of the local church in 'announcing the call' seems also to have been the case with John Bunyon as he explains in his autobiography.[32] Bunyon was an uneducated man who, in fact, was illiterate prior to his marriage. Still, the little Baptist church in Bedford saw in him a man intended by God to preach. A more recent example of this is seen in the unusual experience of George W. Truett (1867–1944). Truett received his education at Baylor University in Waco, Texas. He then returned east and established a high school in Georgia, becoming its principle. In 1889 he returned to Texas where he entered Grayson Junior College, planning eventually to study law. He became involved in the Baptist church in Whitewright, Texas. Truett was astounded one Saturday evening in 1890 when a church business meeting resulted in his being called into the ministry. The account is recorded in his biography written by Powhatan W. James:

> And when they got through with all the rest of the church conference, at the close of the minister's sermon, the oldest deacon, then quite frail in health, rose up and began to talk deliberately and very solemnly. . . .
>   'There is such a thing as a church duty when the whole church must act. There is such a thing as an individual duty, when the individual, detached from every other individual, must face duty for himself; but it is my deep conviction, as it is yours – for we have talked much with one another – that this church has a church duty to perform, and that we have waited late and long to get about it. I move, therefore, that this church call a presbytery to ordain Brother George W. Truett to the full work of the gospel ministry.'[33]

After the motion was seconded, Truett strongly protested, insisting that he wanted to be a lawyer. The will of the people prevailed, however, and he was ordained later that year and began a ministry that soon took him to the First Baptist Church of Dallas, Texas. There he served with great distinction for a period of 47 years, during which the church became the largest in the Southern Baptist Convention with a membership that exceeded 7000.

Whether the call of God is first impressed upon the one being called, or becomes the collective sense of a congregation, the importance of a call to ministry is not to be minimized. Knowing that we have been called by God to preach will be a great help in those darker times that inevitably come to cloud the preacher's ministry.

> Called to preach! That is the basic thing at the last. Let a man be sure of that, and he will keep his certitude by obedience, and he will have the answer to all the doubts that dog the steps of a preacher regarding his vocation.[34]

Gifted to Preach

The call of God to a preaching ministry, regardless of the attending circumstances, will not occur without complimentary gifting. This is in keeping with numerous biblical examples such as Moses, Samuel, Isaiah, Jeremiah, Paul, Timothy, and Titus. It is also in keeping with direct biblical teachings such as: 'Each of us should use whatever gift he has received to serve others, faithfully administering God's grace in its various forms. If anyone speaks, he should do it as one speaking the very words of God' (1 Pet 4:10-11), and 'It was he who gave some to be apostles, some to be prophets, some to be evangelists, and some to be pastors and teachers' (Eph 4:11).

Calling and gifting are somewhat like the two wheels of a bicycle. One should not presume calling without the accompanying gifting, nor should one view gifting alone as tantamount to a call to preach. Note the wise counsel of Charles Bridges in his classic work, *The Christian Ministry*.

> So important, however, is the combination of desire and capacity, that neither, separated from the other, can be deemed sufficient. The desire ... does not of itself attest a Divine vocation. We cannot suppose the Lord to send unqualified labourers, *however willing*, into his vineyard: and none but he can qualify them....
>
> Nor will the richest furniture of Ministerial gifts, without a special desire and interest in the work, (though it may qualify the Christian for important usefulness as a helper of the church) evidence a movement by the Holy Ghost for this high and important service.[35]

As Bridges states, it is necessary to recognize a balance in the two.

While the concept of calling relates specifically to a life being devoted to serving God and His people, gifting speaks of the kind of service that is to be rendered. It is noteworthy that the gifted leaders affirmed in Ephesians 4:11 are all gifted in various ministries of the Word of God. The apostles were those who were taught the Word by Christ and then subsequently took the Word into virgin territory. The New Testament prophets were recipients of special revelation prior to the writing of the books of the New Testament and 'forth tellers' of that word like their Old Testament counterparts. Evangelists are those who are especially gifted to present the gospel of salvation to those who have never heard or responded favorably. Pastor-teachers minister the Word to those in the local church context.

This is not to say that the so-called *laity* have no responsibility in handling and presenting the Word of God. It is to say, rather, that those called by God into leadership positions in the church will be gifted by Him to handle the Word effectively for the salvation of the lost and the edification of the church. Walvoord comments:

> The gift of evangelism mentioned in Ephesians 4:11 refers to unusual capacity to preach the gospel of salvation and to win the lost to Christ. While all Christians should be a channel of information to others and should do the work of an evangelist as Timothy was instructed to do (2 Tim 4:5), nevertheless, some will be more effective in preaching the gospel than others.
>
> The gift of being a pastor or shepherd of the flock also calls for special abilities. In Ephesians 4:11, pastors and teachers are linked, indicating that a true shepherd will also be able to teach or feed his flock, and that a true teacher should have some pastoral abilities. While these qualities may be found in various degrees in different individuals, the link between teaching and shepherding the flock is inevitable for one who wants to be effective in preaching the Word of God.[36]

Writing with the subject of foreign missions in mind, though certainly applicable to all who struggle with the concepts of calling and gifting, Peters offers a helpful summary of the nature of the ministry of the Word.

Principally there are three ministries of the Word to be performed today: (1) The ministry of evangelism which definitely majors in the gospel expansion and church planting ministry at home and abroad. It principally refers to all pioneer work whether on the home front or on the foreign field. Thus Timothy is charged to 'do the work of an evangelist.' The evangelist is the herald of the gospel to the people without the gospel. This is the ministry of the 'general missionary.' (2) The ministry of shepherding the flock which embraces the various ministries in the local congregation. This is the service of the pastor and the spiritual overseer and guide. (3) The ministry of teaching. Though Ephesians 4:11 does not strictly separate the teaching ministry from the pastoral assignment, the mentioning of the teacher in a specific and separate way in 1 Corinthians 12:28-29 justifies our distinction of the two ministries. It is also noteworthy that Paul speaks of himself several times as teacher, but never as pastor (1 Tim 2:7; 2 Tim 1:11; cf. 2 Tim 4:3; Heb 5:12; Jas 3:1).

Though we readily acknowledge the sovereignty of the Holy Spirit who is relevant in His operations and ministry to the needs and demands of the time, it seems to us that in general the call to the ministry of the Word is with reference to one of the foregoing three areas for which the Holy Spirit qualifies the individual in a special way.[37]

Our philosophy of ministry, including our philosophy of preaching, must necessarily cause us to reflect on a personal assessment, as well as an assessment by others, of our gifting to preach. In both 1 Timothy and Titus, Paul includes ability in the ministry of the Word as qualifications for overseers (1 Tim 3:2 and Tit 1:9). Has God given us a special ability to study, understand, articulate, and apply the Word of God to ourselves and to others? This is more than a human talent for public speaking, though such a talent may be a wonderful asset in ministry. It is a God-bequeathed grace-gift given to the preacher by the risen Christ through the work of the Holy Spirit.

I can't help but reflect on my own experience, doubtless duplicated in the lives of many others who have answered the Lord's call to preach the Word. I am not, by natural endowment, talented in public speaking. While in high school, for example, some of my most terrifying experiences were preparing and giving brief speeches in a public speaking class. Similarly, I was often quite ill-at-ease raising questions or offering comments in various classes throughout high school and college. Even today, though I have four decades of preaching experience, I can be quite uncomfortable sometimes when speaking to groups in situations other than preaching. Yet, I have been generally comfortable in my role as a preacher from college onward! Further, those to whom I have ministered the Word in pastoral and other settings have repeatedly affirmed my gifting to do so. I attribute this to the pleasure received by God in using the weak things of this world to accomplish His ends.

Convinced of Preaching's Importance

A third issue to consider under the heading of professional integrity is that of our attitude toward the importance of preaching. We will never do well at this task unless we're genuinely convinced that preaching is a valid and crucial means of communicating the truth of God's Word to people today.

Not everyone believes that preaching is important. I recall an article I read in *Time* magazine during the 1960s while I was in seminary preparing for a preaching ministry. It was about a priest in Canada who was experimenting with new ways to present his homilies. He was specifically interested in using multi-media approaches such as slides, overhead projection, sound equipment, and film. He predicted that the future of the traditional spoken sermon would be short-lived. This was not a particular encouragement to my fellow students and me!

As I began to teach preaching in a seminary setting in the early eighties, I was appalled to discover that a large minority of my students (about one-fourth) had doubts about the validity of preaching. Many had come to Christ during their college years through campus ministries that used other approaches of presenting the Word such as small group inductive Bible studies and one-on-one discipleship training. I found it to be a challenging and helpful process to affirm traditional preaching along with other ministry approaches.

Another concern that sometimes seems to denigrate the importance of preaching is the increasing complexity of pastoral ministry. There are so many worthwhile needed ministries in the contemporary church that it is only natural for the pastor to wonder about the wisdom of devoting a large block of time each week to sermon preparation and delivery. It is not difficult to make a list of 12 to 15 (or more) functions – counseling, administration, visitation, mentoring, worship planning, vision-casting, etc. – in which a pastor is involved on a regular basis. It is sometimes argued, therefore, that relatively little time remains for sermon preparation.

While I understand that the various ministries in the church must be undertaken by *someone*, I'm not convinced that everything needs to be done by the pastor. As we discussed previously, one of the roles of the pastor is to 'prepare God's people for works of service' (Eph 4:12). To state it a bit differently, pastors are to 'train church folks to do ministry!' While there may well be certain matters that require the expertise of the pastor, many others can be handled by church members who have been adequately trained. Some pastors have turned over matters such as administration, some kinds of visitation, worship planning and leading, and some kinds of counseling to gifted and trained people in the local church. Not everything needs to be done by a 'professional'.

It is necessary to deal with this issue because preaching is an extremely important priority in the life and well-being of the church. This is seen in the pastoral epistles, for example, where Paul tells Timothy,

> Don't let anyone look down on you because you are young, but set an example for the believers in speech, in life, in love, in faith and in purity. Until I come devote yourself to the public reading of Scripture, to preaching and to teaching. Do not neglect your gift, which was given you through a prophetic message when the body of elders laid their hands on you (1 Tim 4:12-14).

In his second letter to the young pastor, Paul emphatically charged Timothy to 'Preach the Word; be prepared in season and out of season; correct, rebuke and encourage – with great patience and careful instruction' (2 Tim 4:2). Much of the book of Titus deals with the teaching of sound doctrine and ethics (cf. Tit 1:1:9; 2:1ff).

The earliest church leaders understood that the ministry of the Word was to be a priority. The apostles chose seven men to serve in some other necessary ministries so that they, the apostles, could give their 'attention to prayer and the ministry of the word' (Acts 6:4).

In addition to the emphasis of Scripture, there are also some pragmatic reasons to view preaching as important. While one or more weekly sermons may require a great deal of time expenditure, it is time well spent. Preaching enables the pastor to address the entire congregation in a single setting, bringing the Word of God to bear on a topic of mutual importance. No other ministry in the church does this with the possible exception of the printed page. It is thus a very economical use of the pastor's time in comparison to one-on-one encounters or small group ministries, both of which are important.

Further, much good can happen in an effective pulpit ministry if it is balanced according to the varied needs of attenders. It is a ministry through which doctrinal instruction, evangelism, counseling, personal Christian living, and issues dealing with personal and societal ethics can all be addressed in a forum in which a high percentage of people in attendance come to listen expectantly. It is also a ministry that can help create a strong sense of *esprit de corps* among those in the church's constituency. It is highly doubtful that any other ministry in the church can accomplish all of this and more!

All preachers are not equally gifted, nor will all see similar results from their pulpit ministries. Yet, all should be excited about the importance of preaching and its potential for great good among the body of Christ and those who yet need to know Him.

Commissioned of God to teach the Word! A herald of the great King! A witness of the eternal gospel! Could any work be more high and holy? To this supreme task God sent his only begotten Son. In all the frustration and confusion of the times, is it possible to imagine a work comparable in importance with that of proclaiming the will of God to wayward men?[38]

Faithful preaching of the Word of God is an extremely important ministry in the church in every generation. Our day is not an exception to this. If a pastor is to serve with professional integrity, the importance of preaching will be understood well.

Properly Motivated to Preach

In view of what has been discussed, it shouldn't be necessary to belabor the importance of proper motivation. Yet, frail creatures that we are, it is easy to make ourselves believe that our reasons for preaching are pure, when in actuality they may be a bit tainted. In addition to those who serve with lofty motives, the ministry also attracts self-centered individuals more interested in personal kingdom building than in building the Kingdom of God; more interested in temporal self-advancement than the eternal advancement of others; more dedicated to self-glory than the glory of God. Such impure motives bring great harm to the cause of Christ and his church.

Preaching for the right reasons means to serve with simple, godly motivations like obedience, humility, and self-sacrifice. The issues of success or failure are seen to be beyond our own abilities, belonging only to God. Our job is to plant, cultivate, and water. His responsibility is to give the harvest. And when the harvest comes – make no mistake about it – it is he who must receive the credit and the glory.

One is struck by the example of proper motivation in the journals of John Wesley. While there were not horrible ulterior motives prior to his Aldersgate experience, Wesley struggled with ministry and its failures and attributed it to his own inner failings. In a well-known statement, he wrote:

> I went to America, to convert the Indians; but O! who shall convert me? who, what is he that will deliver me from this evil heart of unbelief? I have a fair summer religion. I can talk well; nay, and believe myself, while no danger is near: But let death look me in the face, and my spirit is troubled. Nor can I say, 'To die is gain!'[39]

Yet, when Wesley became utterly convinced of the validity of his own relationship with Christ, ministry took on new meaning. He became a man almost obsessed as he traveled endlessly and with great hardship. His message, however, is an indication of his motivation. On one occasion he traveled a few miles from the town of Bath to preach, but was received rather coldly by an individual whom he thought would welcome him. He wrote in his journal this simple description of his ministry there:

> However, some persons who were not of his mind, having pitched on a convenient place, (called Bear Field, or Bury-Field) on the top of the hill under which the town lies; I there offered Christ to about a thousand people, for 'wisdom, righteousness, sanctification, and redemption.'[40]

He 'offered Christ' to his hearers: what a simple, but elegant motivation! There is no trace of Wesley's preoccupation with self, simply a desire to preach the gospel.

We can learn much regarding proper motivation from the pages of Scripture. In Paul's letters particularly, we catch a vision of what it means to preach in such a way so as to render loving and humble service both to God and to people. Note the following:

> When I came to you, brothers, I did not come with eloquence or superior wisdom as I proclaimed to you the testimony about God. For I resolved to know nothing while I was with you except Jesus Christ and him crucified. I came to you in weakness and fear, and with much trembling. My message and my preaching were not with wise and persuasive words, but with a demonstration of the Spirit's power, so that your faith might not rest on men's wisdom, but on God's power (1 Cor 2:1-5).

> Now I want you to know, brothers, that what has happened to me has really served to advance the gospel. As a result, it has become clear throughout the whole palace guard and to everyone else that I am in chains for Christ. Because of my chains, most of the brothers in the Lord have been encouraged to speak the word of God more courageously and fearlessly. It is true that some preach Christ out of envy and rivalry, but others out of goodwill. The latter do so in love, knowing that I am put here for the defense of the gospel.

The former preach Christ out of selfish ambition, not sincerely, supposing that they can stir up trouble for me while I am in chains. But what does it matter? The important thing is that in every way, whether from false motives or true, Christ is preached. And because of this I rejoice (Phil 1:12-18).

You know, brothers, that our visit to you was not a failure. We had previously suffered and been insulted in Philippi, as you know, but with the help of our God we dared to tell you his gospel in spite of strong opposition. For the appeal we make does not spring from error or impure motives, nor are we trying to trick you. On the contrary, we speak as men approved by God to be entrusted with the gospel. We are not trying to please men but God, who tests our hearts. You know we never used flattery, nor did we put on a mask to cover up greed – God is our witness. We were not looking for praise from men, not from you or anyone else. As apostles of Christ we could have been a burden to you, but we were gentle among you, like a mother caring for her little children. We loved you so much that we were delighted to share with you not only the gospel of God but our lives as well, because you had become so dear to us. Surely you remember, brothers, our toil and hardship; we worked night and day in order not to be a burden to anyone while we preached the gospel of God to you (1 Thess 2:1-9).

The pure motivation of the great apostle is clearly seen in these texts and others also. The preacher today would do well to study and meditate on passages like these regularly, prayerfully examining one's own heart for tell-tale signs of questionable stimuli. Are we compelled to preach for the right reasons?

It may be that the most prevalent faulty motivations for preaching – whether a desire for power, attention, flattery, or something similar – are based on the sin of self-love, narcissism. This is not a very pretty word, is it? It seems to run blatantly counter to the concept of the ministry of the gospel.

In Greek mythology, Narcissus was an extremely handsome young man who was loved by a young maiden named Echo. He paid her very little attention and she eventually died of a broken heart. Nemesis, the goddess of retribution, decided to pay back Narcissus for his neglect of Echo. She punished him by causing him to fall in love with his own image which he saw mirrored in a pool of water. He became so much in love with his own image that he was unable to tend to basic human needs, so he too eventually died. Nemesis turned him into a flower which we know today as the narcissus.

That's the mythological background of what we know as narcissism. It has to do with those who are so infatuated with themselves that they are virtually worthless to anyone or anything else. In fact, they even bring themselves to ruin! From a theological perspective, I would see narcissism as a manifestation or illustration of sin. Sin, among other things, is grounded in self-centeredness.

Wayne Oates, well known as a scholar in the discipline of Christian counseling and a professor of behavioral psychology at the University of Louisville School of Medicine, listed some characteristics of narcissistic persons.

1. They have a grandiose sense of self-importance. They expect to be noticed as 'special.'

2. They take advantage of others to achieve their own ends. They are interpersonally exploitative.

3. They have a sense of entitlement, i.e., they assume unreasonable expectations of especially favorable treatment and attention on all occasions.

4. They react to criticism with feelings of rage, shame, or humiliation.

5. They routinely lack empathy for others.

6. They are preoccupied with feelings of envy.[41]

When we relate some of these characteristics to narcissism, it is a little easier to see that self-love is not the distant danger we first thought it to be. We probably know pastors who periodically exhibit some of these traits. Perhaps, we're guilty on occasion ourselves!

Love of self can creep into our ministries in unexpected ways. For example, the pastor who almost always insists on getting his own way when church decisions are being made is flirting with this pitfall. So is the pastor who plays the game of 'one-up-man-ship', always comparing the achievements of his ministry with the efforts of his pastoral peers. Or, have you ever tried to have a conversation with someone who is able to take every idea you advance and turn it into a comment about himself or his work? This too is a sign of self-love.

The tendency toward narcissism is ever so different from the kind of selfless attitude required by Jesus. He said that the person following him would need to deny self, not augment self! He said that his follower would need to take up the cross and carry that burden with him on his spiritual pilgrimage. Are Christian leaders somehow exempt from these basic requirements of Christian discipleship?

Instead of loving self, the Scriptures strongly teach that the humility of a servant's heart is a basic requirement for ministry. Jesus said that the greatest among us will be those who serve and that those who insist on elevation will instead be brought down (Matt. 23:11-12).

Paul used the very mystery of the incarnation to illustrate the kind of humble heart that should characterize every believer, pastor-teachers included (Phil. 2:1-8). Peter likewise, in speaking directly to elders, tells them that they should be motivated to serve, and not to lord it over the flock. Their leadership is not to be based on authoritarianism, but rather on being godly examples (1 Pet. 5:2-3).

Christian leadership must be characterized by a willingness to deny self for the good of the people for whom we are responsible. Charles Bridges wrote, 'Unless our work exhibit the self-denying character of the cross of Christ, it is the Christian Ministry in the letter only, not in the spirit; it is not the work that God has engaged to bless.'[42]

It is crucial that all of our ministry, including our preaching, be done with the proper motivation. The diary of McCheyne reveals a poignant illustration of this extremely important matter:

Today missed some fine opportunities of speaking a word for Christ. The Lord saw I would have spoken as much for my own honor as His, and therefore shut my mouth. I see a man cannot be a faithful minister until he preaches Christ for Christ's sake – until he gives up striving to attract people to himself, and seeks only to attract them to Christ. Lord, give me this![43]

May God grant this kind of proper motivation to every preacher!

The concept of integrity seems to have fallen on hard times in recent days. Descriptions like efficient, capable, and results-producing seem to have moved to the foreground of desirable personal traits not only in government and the business world, but in the church as well. But Christian ministry deserves to be carried out by people of Christian integrity. This is true at both the personal level and the professional level. In regard to the latter, a sound philosophy of preaching requires that a person's entrance into preaching ministry be based on a firm conviction of God's calling, and this call must be confirmed by the church. Further, it must be recognized that spiritual gifting will accompany a genuine Divine call. The preacher must also be utterly convinced of the unique importance of preaching. This is not to deprecate other giftings and ministries in any way, but to affirm resolutely that God continues to choose the preaching of the Word to bring people to Himself and mature them into the likeness of His Son, Jesus Christ. Finally, professional integrity requires the preacher to be both highly and properly motivated, assuring that it is God alone who will be honored. To fall short of integrity at the professional level is to assert that our own will and capabilities are of higher importance in the scheme of things than is God's perspective. This is sure to lead to disaster. Lloyd-Jones said it well: 'To me there is nothing more terrible for a preacher, than to be in the pulpit alone, without the conscious smile of God.'[44]

Practice Hard Work and Simple Faith

As we continue to examine the importance of maintaining a balance in our personal perspective toward preaching, we must also come to understand a proper balance between our own efforts in preaching and the gracious work of God in the preaching task. God does not call and gift us and then cast us to the wind to manage for ourselves. In preaching, as in all of the Christian life, God enters into an arrangement with us wherein he entrusts to us various responsibilities, gives to us the needed resources, and blesses our efforts as we exercise faithfulness in the task. This arrangement has the effect, then, of giving us great responsibility in the work of God without taking credit for anything that is accomplished. This is the way it should be. We are instruments. Some plant. Some water. God gives the increase. And he alone rightly receives the glory for what is done faithfully in his name.

For God's ministry arrangement to work effectively, three commitments are needed by those who are involved in the task of preaching. There is a need for the preacher to be committed to work, to prayer, and to faith.

A Commitment to Work

Right Priorities
In some of the preaching classes I teach, I ask students to help me list all the responsibilities faced by a contemporary pastor. It is not unusual for this list to grow to 25 or 30 items. The list is usually very realistic in terms of the expectations placed upon pastors by present-day congregations. Few items on the list would be seen as negotiable by most. This can be confirmed by examining a few job descriptions! When I suggest that such a long list may not have much of a biblical basis, looks of concern and uncertainty sweep across the faces of most of the students.

In chapter one, the priorities of the church were discussed. It may have surprised some to learn that the number of biblical priorities for the church is relatively small, numbering only five or six. The same is true of the preacher. The number of primary tasks found in the New Testament for preachers is also fairly small. (The term 'preacher' in this context is used interchangeably with other words used to identify local church leaders in the New Testament. These words are pastor, elder, and overseer. That these words are used interchangeably is seen in passages like Acts 20:17-28 and 1 Peter 5:1-4.)

When the primary ministry tasks of these church leaders are

discovered, the list looks something like this: 1) declaring the truth of God; 2) praying; 3) equipping all others in the church to do ministry; 4) warning of error; 5) exercising church discipline; 6) and helping others in the church to recognize and utilize their spiritual gifts. It may be granted that other activities were sometimes undertaken by pastoral leaders in the New Testament, but these appear to be the primary responsibilities they were expected to fulfill.

There is quite a difference between the biblical expectations in this regard and those on most job descriptions. Is it any wonder that many pastors are exhausted, frustrated, and stressed out to the point of questioning their call, or even resigning?

As was emphasized in chapter one, the church must re-evaluate all it is trying to do and accomplish in view of the biblical teachings on the subject. Likewise, preachers must constantly be on guard against misplaced busyness. As Gordon MacDonald stated, 'Ministry produces activities, programs, conversations. If our choices of time-use are not disciplined by call and purpose, our energies become like a lazy, shallow river.'[45]

What are the right ministry priorities for the preacher? The right priorities are those emphasized in Scripture. Those are the activities to which time and energy must be devoted. W. E. Sangster wisely said it like this:

> But being a shepherd isn't the same as being a sheep dog! Caring for people doesn't mean fussing around them in the morning hours when a man should be in his study and on his knees. Collecting a congregation by assiduous visiting, but having no sure word from God when they come together in worship, is only to disappoint the expectations one has aroused, and to fail in a task so solemn and exalted that no part of our duty can exceed its importance.[46]

To consistently focus attention elsewhere is to run the risk of practicing a kind of ministry that God never intended.

Proper Discipline

In addition to making certain that 'the main thing is the main thing' in our ministries, preachers must also practice self-discipline in the development and ongoing maintenance of good work habits. The fact is that in most cases, preachers can lead relatively lazy lives if they choose to do so. They can show up to a few board or committee meetings each month, visit a few folks who need special attention, be available for emergencies, conduct weddings and funerals, preach once or twice a week, and lead a Bible study or two. In small churches, emergencies, hospital and shut-in ministry, and weddings and funerals tend not to be very numerous. In large churches, there are usually staff persons who help with many of these responsibilities. In both instances, complete sermons and Bible studies are readily available from numerous sources. It can be quite tempting to subscribe to a sermon service or borrow the bulk of one's sermon material from others. So I repeat, in many situations preachers can lead relatively lazy lives if they choose to do so. Stuart Briscoe offers this insight from his own experience:

> When I entered the pastorate, I talked to Hal Brooks, a dear pastor friend in Fort Worth, now deceased, who cautioned me that pastors can work extremes and get away with it. You can labor from dawn to midnight, or you can become bone idle.
>
> When I pressed him, he said, 'It's easy for a pastor to do nothing much, as long as he shows up and keeps the wheels turning. People's expectations aren't all that high, so normally it isn't too difficult to meet them. And if anybody in authority questions him about what he's doing, or more specifically what he's not doing, he can offer a spiritual answer to a practical question. That usually makes the lay person feel stupid and humiliated.'
>
> Our preaching can also become lazy. We can keep carting out golden oldies. If people get restless, we can always rejoin, 'But this is the simple gospel!'[47]

The body of Christ most certainly deserves better than half-hearted efforts on the part of its shepherds? An excellent sermon diligently prepared by another preacher for an entirely different congregation will probably not be excellent when recycled. It will not reflect the passion of the preacher's own heart because his heart has never been passionate about this sermon. Similarly, spending an hour or two in a text and throwing together a slightly prepared outline to be extemporized upon neither exemplifies passion nor provides the kind of meaty biblical teaching and application that each listener has the right to expect.

Excellent sermons don't grow on trees, waft down from heaven, or magically materialize when we step into the pulpit. They are the product of disciplined study and labor. It used to be said that the preacher should spend one hour in the study for every minute in the pulpit. This standard seldom seems to be followed in our day. The great Baptist preacher Alexander Maclaren, who ministered to two English congregations for a total of more than fifty-seven years, often spent sixty hours in the preparation of his two Sunday sermons. Perhaps this is why they are still in print today nearly a century after his death.

It may be argued that all preachers do not possess the same skills and abilities in matters of study and scholarship. This is true. But the same argument can be made regarding medical doctors. Not all doctors have equal intelligence or the same desire to do reading and research. Still, when our life is on the line most of us will not settle for a slipshod practice of medicine. We demand the best. Should not the same principle hold true for the care of souls?

When the Apostle Paul wrote his final letter to Pastor Timothy, a young man somewhat intimidated by the demands of pastoral ministry in Ephesus, this is the advice he gave: 'Do your best to present yourself to God as one approved, a workman who does not need to be ashamed and who correctly handles the word of truth' (2 Tim 2:15). While this translation is accurate, it seems to diminish slightly the strength of the unique words found in the Greek text, words like *spoudason* ('diligence, eagerness, zeal'), *anepaischunton* ('not to be put to shame), and *orthotomounta* ('holding a straight course').[48] The following is an attempt to reflect the fuller meaning of this verse:

Be eagerly zealous, making every effort to demonstrate that you are worthy of God's own approval as a laborer who will never be put to shame when his work is inspected, one who studies and teaches God's truthful word with straightforward accuracy. (author's own expanded paraphrase)

Every preacher should examine his own work habits with this text in mind.

A strong but needed word of rebuke is given by James S. Stewart in his classic work, *Heralds of God*. This applies both to the need of right priorities discussed earlier as well as to the need for proper discipline.

> What right... have we to speak to the labouring and the heavy-laden, if we are not ourselves as busy as the hardest toiler amongst them? Common decency ought to tell us that to stand in a pulpit on Sunday, and presume to instruct in the things of God men and women who all the week before have been beating us in simple faithfulness to duty, is a mockery and a sham.... Beware the professional busyness which is but slackness in disguise! The trouble is that we may even succeed in deceiving ourselves. Our diary is crowded. Meetings, discussions, interviews, committees throng the hectic page.... Laziness? The word, we protest, is not in our vocabulary.... But God, who searches the heart, knows how much of our outward strenuousness is but a rationalization of a latent slackness.[49]

A Commitment to Prayer

In addition to a strong commitment to work, as seen in the matters of setting proper priorities and exercising self-discipline, the preacher must also be committed to prayer. It is in prayer, perhaps more than anywhere else, that we acknowledge our complete dependence on God to use our efforts to bring about spiritual good.

Prayer is much talked about, but too seldom done. This is true of preacher and layperson alike. There are, thankfully, exceptions to this somewhat cynical assessment. There are those who labor long and hard at prayer, but they appear to be a small minority.

Prayer is at the very heart of the Christian Faith! It is the means by which we can communicate with God regarding everything in our lives. Communication is often regarded as the key component of human relationships such as marriage or parenting. If this is true, and I believe it is, how much more is communication the key to an ongoing vital relationship with God? Lloyd-Jones made a challenging statement in this regard:

> When a man is speaking to God, he is at his very acme. It is the highest activity of the human soul, and therefore it is at the same time the ultimate test of a man's true spiritual condition. There is nothing that tells the truth about us as Christian people so much as our prayer life. Everything we do in the Christian life is easier than prayer.[50]

Yet, prayer is often treated as an add-on or something to be kept in reserve for future needs or crises.

In his Beecher Lectures on preaching at Yale Divinity School in 1943, Paul Scherer tells of a friend who during months of spiritual struggle sought help from sermons and pastoral counseling. He seldom if ever heard that prayer might be of help. Scherer says, 'To this day he wonders if there is anything in prayer, if clergymen themselves believe in it.'[51] This friend of Scherer then went on to say:

> Have the brilliant liberals of the church,... the intelligentsia, a new revelation of God which they hesitate to disclose for fear that the laity cannot bear the truth? Perhaps laymen do not need to pray except vicariously, en masse, Sundays, or when about to die. Perhaps modernity has outmoded prayer. Perhaps the clergy are convinced they can make the world Christian by preaching, by education and reason, rather than by faith.... Why isn't he taught by the church what he has a right to expect through prayer?[52]

Scherer comments on prayer by stating, 'There is nothing that lies nearer the center of the Christian ministry than this. Our poverties here cannot long be concealed.'[53]

While Scherer was admittedly speaking from the perspective of theological liberalism, the same issues need to be addressed among evangelicals. Whereas liberals may not speak much about prayer, evangelicals tend to talk about it regularly but not practice it nearly as often. The result, prayerlessness, is the same.

Now prayer is not the exclusive privilege or responsibility of the preacher. It is to be a foundational stone in the life of each person who is in Christ. But prayer seems to be a special responsibility and need of the preacher. The weight of the preaching ministry can become oppressive and we preachers are in constant need of the help of God in bearing this load.

Furthermore, preaching, like the other facets of ministry – indeed, like everything in the Christian life – is predominantly a spiritual act. It is the communication of the truth of a Spirit-inspired book to persons who are spiritual beings and who are ministered to by the Holy Spirit as the truth is spoken. As a spiritual act, therefore, preaching is clearly dependent on the great spiritual resource of prayer.

> Prayer is vital to the life of the preacher. Read the biographies and the autobiographies of the greatest preachers throughout the centuries and you will find that this has always been the great characteristic of their lives. They were always great men of prayer, and they spent considerable time in prayer.... These men found that this was absolutely essential, and that it became increasingly so as they went on.[54]

It must be remembered also that preaching involves not only the communication of biblical truth, but the communication of the life of the messenger. What will be the substance of this part of the message? A consistent prayer life will help assure that the message being communicated and the messenger doing the communication will be so nearly alike that, for practical purposes, only one message is being proclaimed. It is a message declared in the pages of Scripture and exemplified in the life of the preacher.

Prayer must be a consistent part of the preacher's experience apart from the preaching task, but it must also permeate everything that is done in regard to preaching. The planning of one's preaching schedule for several months or longer should be saturated with prayer. Time spent doing exegetical study for specific sermons should not be thought of as merely scholarly or academic activity, but must be interspersed with prayer for clarity of thinking and spiritual understanding. The process of homiletics must likewise be done prayerfully so that the proper goal is maintained, namely, the clear communication of the truth of God rather than a clever outline. The final preparation of writing a manuscript or extensive outline and then thoroughly internalizing it for delivery must also be bathed in prayer. Throughout the process, the preacher should be praying not only for the sermon's preparation but also for his own personal preparation. The sermon must become a personal possession to be believed and appropriated. The congregation to which the message will be preached must also be brought before the Father in heaven so that the seed of the Word will take root in fertile ground. Finally, as the time for preaching approaches, the preacher can again pray, this time for the anointing of the Spirit of God on his effort to declare the Word of God powerfully, clearly, and convincingly.

We dare not underestimate the importance of prayer in the life of the preacher. James S. Stewart, in fact, asks:

> Is it too much to say that revival in the church depends upon the prayer-life of its ministers? Too often we take for granted that here at least all is well. But still today, as when the winds of Pentecost stirred the world, the first essential is the broken spirit and the contrite heart of those who preach the Word, the sense of dreadful inadequacy driving every apostle to his knees.[55]

When preachers fail to pray they fail to appropriate the power of God working for them and their people. The entire sermon process – from the conception of a preaching schedule weeks or months in advance, through the hard tasks of exegesis and homiletics, and on to the delivery of a completed sermon – should be saturated with prayer. It is not coincidental that the first preachers in the church said with determination that we 'will give our attention to prayer and the ministry of the word' (Acts 6:4). These ministry priorities are inseparable.

Paul concludes an important discussion of spiritual warfare by returning to the theme of ministry, reminding his readers that the effective ministry of the Word depends on an effective undergirding ministry of prayer.

> Pray also for me, that whenever I open my mouth, words may be given me so that I will fearlessly make known the mystery of the gospel, for which I am an ambassador in chains. Pray that I may declare it fearlessly, as I should (Eph 6:19-20).

Prayer and preaching must be seen as inseparably linked. Preaching will never accomplish its purposes without prayer.

When we preachers are prayerless, we commit the sin of idolatry. We replace the need of God with our own sense of adequacy. We set ourselves up as being self-sufficient, needing to rely only on our own intellects and skills. We need to flee from all forms of idolatry (1 Cor 10:14), including this rather insidious type.

A Commitment to Faith

This section of chapter 2 has discussed the importance of laboring hard at the preaching task while appropriating the help and blessing of God through prayer. These two seemingly opposite commitments are seen to be quite compatible when considered from the perspective of faith. It is faith that prompts us toward obediently exercising our calling and gifts. It is faith that requires us to look beyond ourselves to the One who alone must supernaturally attend the declaration of his Word in such a way that it accomplishes its intended purposes.

Preachers are not omniscient, though we sometimes act like we are. While we rightly try to keep in mind the listeners to whom we will be speaking and their burdens, problems, and longings, we can never know exactly who will be present on a given occasion, let alone the multitude of needs they bring. At best, our knowledge is surface-level. Yet we can prepare and pray in faith because God knows. And when we have done so, we will discover that people have been encouraged, burdens have been lightened, confessions have been offered, and problems have been resolved. The truth of God's Word has made a difference in people's lives because we have, by faith, allowed the Lord to work sovereignly through that Word. As Paul the apostle said, 'Consequently, faith comes from hearing the message, and the message is heard through the word of Christ' (Rom 10:17).

There is another aspect of our preaching ministry which relates to faith. This is the matter of our own relationship with God. While we may labor for the welfare of God's flock, we dare not forget that we are a part of that flock.

Just as others need to be challenged toward knowing God in his fulness, so do we. How does the flock, including ourselves, come to know God as he is? We do this by appropriating, by faith, the truth about him which is found in the Word. Both people and preacher equally need the truth of the Bible in this regard.

Just as others need to be confronted regarding the dangers of sin, so do we. We are not special 'holy persons' who live above temptation and sin. Like those to whom we minister, we often need the convicting presence of the Holy Spirit in our lives to remind us that 'God alone is good'. This often occurs as we see ourselves in the pages of holy writ as the Scriptures serve as a mirror, reflecting back to us our own shortcomings and proneness to sin. Thankfully, we are not only confronted by our sin, but by God's forgiveness and transformational power as well.

Just as others need to be encouraged by God's infinite love and grace, so do we. Faith continues to teach us that while we fall short of God's high standards, he does not abandon us to our foolish ways. Just as Hosea loved, forgave, and restored his estranged wife Gomer, so God continues his work of love and grace in us. We receive this by faith.

Just as others need to be brought before God in genuine worship, so do we. In fact, the sermon and its preparation should be considered an act of worship by the preacher. It is a gift of worship just as surely as any monetary or material gift. God deserves our best efforts at preaching for this is a stewardship he has entrusted to us. We must be faithful stewards who understand that genuine worship is a costly endeavor. Our attitude should reflect that of David. To one who generously offered to give the king oxen for a sacrifice and wood for the fire, David replied: 'I insist on paying you for it. I will not sacrifice to the LORD my God burnt offerings that cost me nothing' (2 Sam 24:24). What does our preaching cost us in terms of time and energy? Do we ever think of it as a sacrifice offered in worship to our worthy God?

> Aware that a sermon is a gift to God, preachers are challenged to give nothing less than their very best. Who can justify an ill-conceived, ill-prepared, barely understandable gift to God? All sermon preparation should begin, end, and be pervaded by prayer and praise, adoration and devotion to God. Preachers must bring to the pulpit the same qualities of thoroughness, excellence, and integrity that they wish to characterize the other gifts offered by people in worship.[56]

Just as others need to be growing in their faith-walk with the Lord, so do we. Jesus said in John 15:5, 'I am the vine; you are the branches. If a man remains in me and I in him, he will bear much fruit; apart from me you can do nothing.' This is true of all those in God's flock, people and pastor alike. We should not lose sight of the fact that most sermons have relevance for both the audience and the speaker. The faith of all should be strengthened.

Summation

There are two chief initial perspectives to be considered when sorting through all of the issues related to a philosophy of preaching. One is the theological perspective which was discussed in the first chapter. The other is the personal perspective which has been discussed in this second chapter. In this chapter, we have examined our personal and professional integrity, looking at topics like spirituality, character, reputation, calling, giftedness, attitude toward preaching, and motivation. We have also looked at the importance of hard work, earnest prayer, and faith.

Education and skills training are important components in the preparation of preachers. They must, however, never be allowed to substitute for matters of integrity and responsibility. Preachers are not just technicians, skilled to do something few others in the congregation are skilled to do. First and foremost, the biblical standard for preachers is that they be people of God who humbly attempt to follow his calling on their lives. *Who they are* as people is far more important than *what they do* as preachers.

Points to Ponder

1. What is at the heart of the meaning of integrity? What is the source of true integrity?

2. What is the proper role of formal education in the preparation of the preacher? What can education accomplish that piety alone does not? Is there biblical evidence for this?

3. What is the proper role of skills training (such as public speaking, communication, and homiletics) in the preparation of the preacher?

4. What is the relationship between calling and giftedness in the life of the preacher? Are they always found in tandem, or can one be found without the other?

5. It is a given in most congregations that the pastor is charged with a large variety of responsibilities ranging from preaching and counseling to committee meetings and social functions. What should/can a pastor who is committed to adhering to the biblical priorities for ministry do in terms of ordering his professional life?

Step Three

Maintain a Balance in Biblical Foundations

When they come to church, they expect *a message from God* in response to the needs of their hearts today. Few of them could put into words any theory about revelation and inspiration, but then the minister himself cannot begin to comprehend the spell that the Scriptures cast over the spirits of men and women. The lay friends feel themselves in the presence of a mystery they do not understand, but they can tell when the living Christ speaks through His servant in the pulpit. On the way home they say to one another: 'Did not our heart burn within us, while he talked with us by the way, and while he opened to us the Scriptures?' (Andrew Watterson Blackwood).[1]

It should be understood without saying that the basis for all Christian preaching is the Bible. Christian preaching must be biblical preaching!

This is not to say that all preaching will approach the Scriptures in the same way or at the same time. Ideas for sermons enter our minds in a variety of ways. We may be intentionally studying through a section of Scripture in order to discover its preaching possibilities and ideas continue to show themselves. We may be working on a particular sermon that heads off in a certain thematic direction only to discover that within this text there is another sermon idea that points in a somewhat different direction. We may be reading the Bible devotionally and the thought breaks through that this is a text needing to be preached. We may be speaking with someone in a ministry situation and a sermon idea comes to mind that fits the needs of the larger congregation. Or, our conversation might be quite informal and yet an idea materializes. Sometimes our minds are far away from preaching or the ministry and sermon ideas still come.

Television, radio, theater, casual reading, and even recreation may serve as catalysts for the planting of a sermon seed into our thinking.

Regardless of the origination of a sermon idea, the constant that gives validity to every sermon idea is the Bible. Unless Scripture has something significant to say about the idea, the seed should never be allowed to germinate into a sermon. Preaching that is not biblical preaching is not Christian preaching!

As we consider this matter of maintaining a balance in biblical foundations, we will examine four necessities for the truly biblical preacher. We must: 1) preach from both the Old and New Testaments; 2) include all kinds of biblical literature; 3) preach both familiar and unfamiliar texts; and 4) wrestle with both simple and difficult texts. Paying attention to these matters will greatly assist us as we strive to have a balanced preaching ministry.

Preach from the Old Testament
as well as the New Testament

Marcionism, at least a form of it, is alive and well in many segments of today's church. We may not want to admit it, but it's true. An early heretic, Marcion was excommunicated in about A.D. 144 primarily for his views regarding the total discontinuity between the Old and New Testaments. This included his opinion that the god of the Old Testament was not the same being as the one true God revealed by Jesus in the New Testament. Marcion set limits on the sacred canon as consisting of ten letters by Paul (the pastoral epistles were not included) and Luke's Gospel. These were edited to conform to his teachings with references to the Old Testament conveniently deleted.[2]

Some are probably crying 'foul' just now, and for some this may be justifiable. The fact remains that many evangelical preachers pay scant attention to the Old Testament. This can be verified by looking at their sermon records over an extended period of time. Sermons based on texts from the Gospels and the Epistles – even Acts and Revelation – are found in abundance, but sermons from the Old Testament are often very sparsely represented.

According to virtually all evangelical statements of faith, something akin to 'we believe the Scriptures, both Old and New Testaments, are the inspired word of God...' can be found. We say that we stake our lives on this. Perhaps so, but it would be good to stake some of our preaching there too.

Approximately three-fourths of the Protestant canon consists of the Hebrew Bible, as the Old Testament is sometimes called. Among most Protestant preachers, however, especially those who call themselves evangelical, probably less than ten percent of sermons are based on these older texts. This is admittedly an estimate on my part, but one based on over forty years of listening to sermons in a variety of churches and reading sermons from many more. Preaching from the Old Testament is not particular popular, at least not in the circles to which I've been exposed over the years. It is possible that an exception to this may be found in churches which make use of lectionary readings. Even when this is the case, however, the readings of the day emphasize the New Testament, both numerically and in terms of prominence.

Why should 'New Testament Christians' bother to preach from the Old Testament? Except for a few pertinent psalms, proverbs, and advent texts, isn't the Old Testament outdated? With relatively few preaching opportunities during the year, aren't we better stewards of our preaching ministry if we devote our attention almost exclusively to the New Testament? While our preaching may reflect this sentiment, I must suggest it's simply not true.

A Holistic View of Scripture

To begin, we need to consider Scripture as a whole – both Old and New Testaments. It is a truism that we cannot possibly understand the New Testament until we understand the Old. There is simply too much overlap, too much continuity. It is sometimes thought that because the Old Testament is a Jewish book, dealing with 'God's chosen people', and the New Testament is about God's 'new people', then the Old has been superseded by the New and the Old is no longer relevant. While there is an element of truth in the first part of this statement, it doesn't allow us to therefore discard the

Old. Both Testaments are intertwined in such a way that each is crucial to the other.

Consider, for instance, the Old Testament roots of New Testament descriptions of God's people. Believers are called 'children of Abraham' (Gal 3:7). The church is called the 'Israel of God' (Gal 6:16). We are also said to be have been 'grafted' into Israel's root (Rom 11:17) and we're called 'the true circumcision' (Phil 3:3). Christian believers are now, according to Paul, 'fellow citizens with God's people and members of God's household' (Eph 2:19). The New Testament picture of God's new people is grounded in Old Testament imagery. Peter, for example, uses the same language to describe Christians as was spoken at Mt. Sinai to Israel (1 Pet 2:9-10). Think too of the matter of the law. Jesus said that he did not come to destroy it, but to fulfill it (Matt 5:17). The new covenant promised in the Old Testament is fulfilled in the work of Christ (see Jer 31:31-34 and Heb 8:10-12). How can we ignore the Old Testament and do justice to the preaching of the New?

Consider also the Bible that was used by the early church. When Paul spoke of Scripture being 'God breathed and profitable', he was speaking of the Old Testament. When Paul told Timothy to 'preach the Word', he was again speaking, at least for the most part, of the Old Testament. *A number of years would pass before the New Testament writings would be accepted as inspired and authoritative, and therefore canonical.* Yet, much of the preaching found in the New Testament is based on these Old Testament Scriptures. They were adequate, when linked with the work of Christ, to establish the early Christian church. Should we ignore them today?

Crucial Themes in the Old Testament

In addition to the integrated nature of the Bible, it must be reaffirmed also that many of the important teachings in the New Testament find their genesis in the Hebrew Bible. There are many crucial subjects – both doctrinal and ethical – to be found there, sometimes in fuller detail than what we find in the New Testament. For example, the creation is described there in greater detail than in the New Testament.

Doctrinal Foundations. An important reason to include the Old Testament in our preaching plans relates to the doctrinal subject matter to be found there. In addition to teaching about creation in general, our knowledge of the creation and nature of the human race, including the Divine image in which we've been created, is found there. The ideas of 'man as steward' and man's responsibility to God are rooted there. Our understanding of the origin and problem of sin cannot be properly understood apart from Genesis. The concept of Divine covenant is discovered there along with the doctrine of grace. Subjects like spiritual rebellion, punishment, forgiveness, and restoration are established. It is in the Old Testament where we first see the awesome greatness of God and many of his attributes. And we see not only the greatness of God but his personableness, approachability, and tender care for his people as well.

As we move through the various sections of the Old Testament, we are reminded of many foundational concepts of Christianity. In the historical books we find a God who acts in history, knowing the end from the beginning. We see his story unfolding even as we read about the history of his chosen channel of revelation, Israel. We see how his plans take shape even when man is disobedient. In the wisdom literature, we discover how life is to be lived even in the midst of doubts and questions. In the Psalms, we see a sovereign God who is greatly to be praised, a God who faithfully cares for his people, and we learn to worship him appropriately with our whole beings. In the prophets, we see a God who does not forsake a wayward people but pleads for their return to his fellowship. We also see a God who is capable of punishment but more desirous of forgiveness and blessing.

Ethical Foundations. It is in the Old Testament that we initially find God's standards regarding righteousness, standards whose principles remain intact today. Sometimes these standards are presented as fiats, such as the ten commandments. At other times his standards are found in stories about people, both great and small. These biographical narratives alert us to the issue of how we ought to live. God's standards of righteousness do not change when we look in the New Testament. He is still holy and he expects us to pursue holiness as well. This is reiterated over and over again as the New Testament echoes the Old. Peter, for example, states: 'As obedient children, do not conform to the evil desires you had when you lived in ignorance. But just as he who called you is holy, so be holy in all you do; for it is written: "Be holy, because I am holy" ' (1 Pet 1:14-16).

Missions Theology. There is a theology of missions in the Old Testament in spite of the mistaken view that it is about the Jewish people only. But unlike the tribal deities of other ancient peoples, the God of the Old Testament is the God of all the peoples of the earth. For instance, we find the psalmist praying: 'May God be gracious to us and bless us and make his face shine upon us, that your ways may be known on earth, your salvation among all nations (Ps 67:1-2). We discover a young Moabite woman (Ruth) who becomes an integral part of the human lineage of Jesus. We read about a reluctant prophet, Jonah, commissioned by God to take a word of warning to the foreign terrorists of his day, and then becoming agitated when the people of Nineveh repent. He confesses that he suspected this might happen:

> But Jonah was greatly displeased and became angry. He prayed to the LORD, 'O LORD, is this not what I said when I was still at home? That is why I was so quick to flee to Tarshish. I knew that you are a gracious and compassionate God, slow to anger and abounding in love, a God who relents from sending calamity. Now, O LORD, take away my life, for it is better for me to die than to live' (Jon 4:1-3).

The message of God's concern for the Assyrian people is clear in spite of the gross nationalism of the messenger.

These and similar passages should not surprise us, however, for the Abrahamic covenant includes the nations.

> The LORD had said to Abram, 'Leave your country, your people and your father's household and go to the land I will show you. I will make you into a great nation and I will bless you; I will make

your name great, and you will be a blessing. I will bless those who bless you, and whoever curses you I will curse; and all peoples on earth will be blessed through you' (Gen 12:1-3).

The missionary endeavor of the church is but a recognition of God's longstanding and persistent desire to bring the nations of the earth to himself. We see the fulfillment of this in Revelation 7:9-10:

After this I looked and there before me was a great multitude that no one could count, from every nation, tribe, people and language, standing before the throne and in front of the Lamb. They were wearing white robes and were holding palm branches in their hands. And they cried out in a loud voice: 'Salvation belongs to our God, who sits on the throne, and to the Lamb.'

While we see the fulfillment of God's heart for the world in Revelation, we must not forget that this has always been his heart's desire. The Old Testament tells us so.

The Promise. How, then, was God's desire to be accomplished? It was to take place through the coming of a Messiah, a teaching that is firmly rooted in the Old Testament writings. We find messianic teachings in the historical books, in the Psalms, and in the prophets. Allusions to him are found in other books as well. While the precise number of such prophecies cannot be established because of scholarly disagreement regarding the precise messianic interpretation of some, to say there are scores of them is by no means an exaggeration. Further, we need to understand that our knowledge of Christology would be enormously incomplete if we paid no attention to these Old Testament passages.

Practical Issues Related to Preaching the Old Testament

The Frequency of Old Testament Preaching. As can be seen in this brief discussion, the Old Testament, like the New, is the very Word of God and contains information that is absolutely crucial to Christian theology and practice. It is not only important for preachers and scholars to know the Old Testament, but is mandatory for all Christians to understand the foundations of their faith. The Old

Testament must be preached with regularity if this is to happen.

What is meant by regularity? This is not an easy question to answer because the frequency of our preaching on the Old Testament will depend on what is happening in the total biblical education program in the church. Is the congregation exposed to sufficient Old Testament studies in adult Sunday School or other training classes? What percentage of the congregation participates in these other sessions? How deep are these studies? If exposure to the Old Testament is weak beyond the pulpit, then our preaching plans will need to consider this.

The bottom line is that our people need to be consistently exposed to both testaments. Even with favorable coverage in the church's educational programs, the pulpit must also model an attitude toward the Old Testament that communicates its importance. Perhaps basing about twenty to twenty-five percent of our preaching on the Old Testament would be a place to begin. This might involve two brief series each year as well as a couple of individual sermons. This number is admittedly arbitrary but I believe it could well be considered as minimal. In fact, Elizabeth Achtemeier suggests that ministers ought to preach from Old Testament texts at least half the time.[3]

Some may fear preaching from the Old Testament because it is far less familiar than the New and it seems to present hermeneutical challenges which are formidable. While these concerns may be real, the task of preaching well from the Old Testament can be accomplished. Lack of familiarity should not be a stumbling block. If we are unfamiliar with the various passages in the Old Testament it is simply because we spend relatively little time in them. We tend to spend considerably more time in the New Testament both in terms of choosing and studying main preaching texts and also in terms of cross-referencing and secondary support. As we make the deliberate choice to preach more often from the Hebrew Bible, we will become more knowledgeable cumulatively about this part of the canon.

As far as hermeneutical issues are concerned, many of the same principles followed in New Testament interpretation are valid in the Old Testament. Remember too that even in the New Testament, we find texts that are hermeneutically tricky. Parables, for instance, can be quite a challenge, as can apocalyptic literature. The New Testament contains long sections of narrative material, not unlike the Old Testament. It is true that genre like poetry, wisdom literature, and predictive prophecy require their own peculiar interpretational methods, but these can be learned and applied without insurmountable difficulty. Basic hermeneutics books such as those by Kaiser,[4] McQuilkin,[5] and Mickelsen[6] will prove to be very helpful. There are also several books written especially for preachers which deal with various literary genre in Scripture.[7]

The Method of Old Testament Preaching. A concern related to hermeneutics and faced by the Christian preacher is the matter of preaching from the Old Testament in a *Christian* way. In other words, how does the preacher adequately handle the Old Testament text in terms of the New Testament's completion of the Old in the person and work of Jesus Christ?

It is suggested that an Old Testament text be preached in conjunction with a New Testament text. This will demonstrate the fact that the Old Testament was the beginning of a story that was not completed until the New Testament Scriptures were written. Some times, a New Testament text will show how an Old Testament promise has been fulfilled. An obvious example would be the use of Isaiah 7:14 for an Advent text. When this passage is linked with Matthew 1:22-23, the sermon can clearly demonstrate how something prophesied more than seven centuries prior to the event came to pass. Another example might be the concept of the 'Day of the Lord', found in several of the prophets, including Joel. He spoke of that Day in terms of a locust plague, but also speaks of a future Day of the Lord (cf. Joel 1:15). In the New Testament, Paul speaks of the Day of the Lord in eschatological terms, tieing it in with the second coming of Jesus Christ:

> For the Lord himself will come down from heaven, with a loud command, with the voice of the archangel and with the trumpet call of God, and the dead in Christ will rise first. After that, we who are still alive and are left will be caught up together with them in the clouds to meet the Lord in the air. And so we will be with the Lord forever. Therefore encourage each other with these words.

Now, brothers, about times and dates we do not need to write to you, for you know very well that the day of the Lord will come like a thief in the night (1 Thess 4:16–5:2).

On other occasions, the use of the New Testament coupled with the Old will demonstrate how the teaching of the Old Testament has become complete in the New. This relates to the principle of progressive revelation. Clowney states: 'Biblical theology formulates the character and content of the progress of revelation in these periods, observing the expanding horizons from age to age.'[8] This concept is also advocated by Kaiser in introductory comments in his *The Old Testament in Contemporary Preaching*:

> Then how should the Old Testament text be regarded? These six chapters argue for a progressive march of revelation, from the first words and deeds in Genesis, on into the New Testament. This march not only accumulates newer and fuller revelatory data, but it has an epigenetic unity which relates the first truth of the Old Testament and the last truth of the New, even as a seed is related to the full-grown tree.[9]

For example, we would not know how the Abrahamic covenant will result in the blessing of all the peoples of the earth if we looked only at the Genesis texts. They are the right place to begin, but they are not the right place to end. They must be linked with a text such as the one found in Galatians if the covenant is to be fully understood:

> Understand, then, that those who believe are children of Abraham. The Scripture foresaw that God would justify the Gentiles by faith, and announced the gospel in advance to Abraham: 'All nations will be blessed through you.' So those who have faith are blessed along with Abraham, the man of faith (Gal 3:7-9).

Another example would be the statement in the law given in Leviticus 19:18: 'Do not seek revenge or bear a grudge against one of your people, but love your neighbor as yourself. I am the LORD.' While the preacher might preach on this individual text, it would make more sense to couple it with the 'Parable of the Good

Samaritan' in Luke 10. This parable, of course, was told in response to the self-serving question by the lawyer, 'Who is my neighbor?' Jesus then explains in concrete terms what the Leviticus text means as he defines who a neighbor is and the kind of action that shows love to a neighbor.

The Old Testament can also be utilized in our preaching by making use of examples or illustrations of New Testament truths. Negative examples of sinfulness abound in the Old Testament, and these reinforce and visualize our understanding of the New Testament's teaching of our utter depravity before a holy God. I recently heard a sermon based on an unlikely text from the Book of Judges, chapter 19, in which a Levite allows his concubine to be raped and murdered. Afterward, he cuts up her body into twelve pieces and sends them to the various areas of Israel. A strange text indeed for a sermon, but the preacher skillfully used this story to convince the audience of mankind's inherent sinfulness and capacity to do the unthinkable.

On the other hand, there are notable examples of virtue and godly living. Hebrews 11 uses many examples from the Old Testament of people who pleased God because they consistently lived by faith. Persons like David, Moses, Abraham, Gideon and countless others serve as examples of people who lived with God's blessing on their lives.

Typology is another way we can preach the Christian gospel from the Old Testament. This approach is not nearly as popular as it once was; a result, no doubt, of its misuse. Some commentators in the past seemed to see Old Testament types of Christ 'under every bush'. This was not always legitimate because typology was confused with allegorizing and the result was an interpretation of Scripture that often depended on the fancies and whims of the interpreter. (While there are some allegories in Scripture, they are few in number and easily recognized as such. The practice of using allegorizing as a hermeneutical method, emulating Origen and the early Alexandrian school, is to be avoided.)

Are there Old Testament texts that are typological in nature? Yes, but as with allegories, we ought to limit them to texts identified as such. A safe practice is to ask whether or not an Old Testament concept or person is identified as a type in the New Testament. For instance, I've heard some preachers speak of the patriarch Joseph as a type of Christ. He was sold for the price of a slave, was mistreated badly, but eventually brought deliverance to his people. While there are some obvious parallels between Joseph and Jesus, there are no New Testament teachings that link the two typologically. On the other hand, Paul uses the word *tupos* to describe the events of the exodus and apply them to Christian teaching:

> For I do not want you to be ignorant of the fact, brothers, that our forefathers were all under the cloud and that they all passed through the sea. They were all baptized into Moses in the cloud and in the sea. They all ate the same spiritual food and drank the same spiritual drink; for they drank from the spiritual rock that accompanied them, and that rock was Christ. Nevertheless, God was not pleased with most of them; their bodies were scattered over the desert. Now these things occurred as examples to keep us from setting our hearts on evil things as they did (1 Cor 10:1-6).

The word translated in the NIV as 'examples' is *tupos*.

There are typological overtones in the Book of Hebrews regarding the sacrificial work of Christ. There is also a discussion of the tabernacle which views it typologically. Some have gone into great detail regarding the way the tabernacle structure and services prefigured the atoning work of Christ. There is obviously some validity in this but it must be remembered, as some unknown person has said, that some of the tent stakes were there just to hold up the tent! In other words, don't exaggerate the type beyond what is affirmed in the text.

These are some of the ways in which the Old Testament Scriptures can be used with great profit in a Christian context. Regardless of the exegetical/hermeneutical methods used, the preacher must exercise great caution to avoid whimsical interpretations not validated in the text of Scripture itself. It should be remembered that preaching not only communicates a message, but a method as well.

Every preacher has heard horror stories of gross interpretational errors being taught in Bible classes. I recall as a seminarian sitting in a Sunday School class taught by a well-meaning church member on the subject of salt – 'You are the salt of the earth.' In one particular lesson, the teacher was attempting to establish some deep spiritual truth – exactly what it was has long since been forgotten – by demonstrating that salt crystals are shaped like cubes. He mentioned that if we were to look at salt under a microscope, we would see beautiful cubes. He was right, for I've looked. They are indeed nicely shaped cubes, but to draw spiritual truths from this is an example of gross eisogesis.

Where do these fanciful interpretations come from? In part, I suggest, they come from poor hermeneutical modeling in the pulpit. As stated above: when we preach we not only communicate a message, but a hermeneutical method as well. If preachers handle the Word carefully in the pulpit, folks in the pew will be less likely to go off in wrong directions.

Maintaining a balance in regard to the biblical foundations of our preaching means that we will be committed to preach the Old Testament as well as the New. We will do this regularly and conscientiously, handling the Old Testament Word as carefully as we do the New Testament Scriptures. 'All Scripture is God-breathed and profitable...'

Preach From All Kinds of Biblical Literature

The Bible is a wondrous book indeed in terms of the breadth of its literature. This has become increasingly recognized by preachers in the last few years as they have seen that a 'one-method-fits-all' approach doesn't work in terms of applying homiletics to the many kinds of literature found in Scripture. The rising popularity of 'expository' preaching has also contributed to the need to be able to deal exegetically and hermeneutically with a variety of literary genre. While it is beyond the scope of this volume to deal in great detail with all of the kinds of literature found in Scripture, we will look briefly at several including historical narrative, poetry, wisdom, prophecy, apocalyptic, the teachings of Jesus, miracles, parables, and epistles.

Preaching from Historical Narrative

It is probable that over fifty percent of the Bible is narrative. The seventeen books known as the Historical Books (Genesis through Esther) are primarily narrative, although they also contain other materials such as poetry, genealogies, prophecies, and law codes. There are narrative passages, sometimes extended, in the Old Testament prophetic books. In the New Testament, the Gospels and Acts are a mixture of event and discourse. It is easy to see, then, that at least fifty percent of Scripture – probably closer to sixty percent – consists of descriptions of historical persons and events.

Approaching Biblical Narrative. It must be remembered that narrative texts are much more than passages that tell stories. They are also texts of theological and ethical importance, though the preacher will have to work a little differently and perhaps a little harder to get at the essence of these matters. Whether a text is biographical or event-centered (can we really separate the two?), there is always a deeper message, a Divine revelation to instruct and guide us. Every narrative, regardless of length, has some point to be made that can be helpful today. It may present the stories of people with whom the reader can identify. Or, it may tell us something about the nature of human existence that we need to know.

Not all stories (or all other texts for that matter) are equally important. But 'all Scripture is inspired and profitable' and even seemingly insignificant events should not be arbitrarily discarded. If they are not useful for an entire sermon, they might be useful in other ways, such as an illustration or cross-reference.

Getting 'Inside' A Narrative Text. Understanding the plot of a narrative passage is just part of the sermon process. The preacher must also gain an understanding of the text from a theological and ethical perspective. To do this, a series of closely related questions should be asked of the text. This will almost always generate a sufficient amount of information and insight to lead to the development of a worthwhile sermon. Following are some questions which can be applied to narrative passages:

1. Where does the story begin and where does it end? (It is important to work with a complete story, not just a part of one, for

the entire story is necessary both to understand the plot and to grasp its theology.)

2. What are the various parts of the story and what seems to be their function? (Identify and summarize the various scenes, actions, and settings.)

3. Are there any statements or speeches in the story? (Who makes them? To whom? About what? What is their significance?)

4. What do we know about each of the persons in the story? (Describe how these characters are developed in each part of the story. What do we know about them from elsewhere?)

5. What is God doing throughout the story? (Describe his direct and indirect actions or allusions to him.)

6. What are the details in the story, even those which may seem insignificant? (Biblical details almost always have a purpose other than being mere adornment.)

7. Are there any rhetorical devices included in the narrative? (Things like repetition, figures of speech, or a play on words may be important.)

8. What is the purpose of this story? (What would we miss if it was not in the Bible?)

9. What is the theological/Christological dimension in the story? (Does the story teach us something about the ways of God? If in the Old Testament, what is the Christian meaning or application?)

By posing questions like these, the preacher is on his way to formulating a subject and theme which are in keeping with God's purpose for including this account in Scripture in the first place. At the same time, a sermon structure suitable to both the text and the preaching setting will begin to emerge.

Sermonizing. Preaching on narrative texts presents special challenges not encountered when preaching on direct statements such as those found in the prophets, Epistles, or the sayings of Jesus. With narrative, it is necessary to work with the text holistically and inductively in order to understand what it is saying and how best to communicate this truth.

With some texts, we can speak of a person who lived a life which made contributions of a positive nature toward the purposes and people of God. These contributions might be developed sermonically by tracking his character traits, standards, principles, convictions, qualities, actions, or strengths to describe the means by which a person lived. For example, a sermon dealing with the example of Jehoshaphat in 2 Chronicles 20:1-30 might look at the *actions* he took when the Moabites and Ammonites made war against Judah. When the odds were against him, he determined, with the help of God, to be an overcomer. We can likewise be an overcomer.

1. We must turn to God first (1-4).
2. We must talk to God about our situation (5-13).
3. We must confess our own lack of ability to cope (12).
4. We must trust God to help us in our need (14-15).
5. We must thank God in advance for his response to our need (20ff).

This kind of approach will sometimes work with biographical texts when the person in the text clearly models the godly life. Conversely, God's people can sometimes learn how to live rightly by observing the bad behavior of others. A sermon might examine the mistakes, weaknesses, flaws, or bad choices a person has made and contrast these with right behavior.

When preaching on biographical texts, the preacher should remember that the Scriptures present these people in a very objective way (unlike much secular literature) which includes 'warts and all', as the saying goes. Their faults, failures, and short-comings should not be ignored. The Spirit of God can use these negatives, as well as the positives, to instruct and build up his people.

Another approach, somewhat predictable, would be to tell the story and then discuss the lessons to be learned. It might be outlined something like the following:

Introduction: A brief hook introducing the general subject and why it is important.
1. The telling of the story. (Sermonizing, theologizing, and application would not be included here.)

2. The presentation of two or more lessons (or truths, or warnings, or encouragements, or implications, etc.).

Conclusion: Application and challenge.

This approach is quite useful although, as with any approach, a steady diet will become tedious and too repetitious.[10]

A narrative sermon approach – one in which the entire sermon is presented as a story, either in the first person or in the third person – might be used on a rare special occasion or with an audience especially open to this approach. This method is most useful when the person whose life is being used as the sermon subject did an unusual thing or experienced an unusual turn of events – something of a surprising nature. The plot of the narrative can be built around this surprise. For example, why would Adam and Eve disobey God when they had a paradise to lose? This 'twist' in the biblical account can then be applied to today. Why do people today deliberately disobey God when there is so much to lose?

Some Precautions. There are several precautions we need to take when dealing with narrative texts. While these are applicable to all kinds of texts, they are particularly relevant here.

1. Consider the original hearers or readers. What would they have thought the point of the text to be? Sensing the text as they would have will help the preacher avoid straying far off course.

2. Identify the particular kind of narrative encountered in the text. Is it 'event narrative', 'heroic narrative', or 'tragic narrative'?

3. Are there other kinds of literary materials found in the narrative text being dealt with? This might include speeches, census records, genealogies, poems, and prophecies? The Gospels and Acts, though primarily narrative, have a great deal of other genre within the narrative.

4. Avoid drawing doctrinal or ethical norms from texts which are narrative. This can only be done inductively, and induction requires more than one 'particular' in order to arrive at a general truth.

5. Avoid normalizing the behavior of past people. Their behavior may serve as a worthy example for emulation, but not necessarily. What does the text itself say about this? What does it imply? Does

Scripture discuss this behavior at a later time? Principles for godly living implied in the text are more important than emphasizing specific behaviors.

6. Avoid presenting your personal conjectures as fact. Stories in Scripture often omit many details, and our minds want to fill these in. Allow your imagination to work on what might have been, but be careful to differentiate between conjectures and stated facts.

7. Avoid allegorizing. I once heard an evangelist preach a sermon in which he represented the seven locks of hair cut from Samson's head (Judg 16:19) as seven favorable traits lost by Samson. This is a gross misuse of the Scripture.

Preaching from Passages of Poetry

Large sections of Scripture, as well as occasional short quotations, take the form of Hebrew poetry. To preach on texts from Psalms, Proverbs, The Song of Songs, Lamentations, Obadiah, Micah, Habakkuk, and Zephaniah means that the preacher will be dealing exclusively with poetic texts. Other books that have extended sections of poetry include Job, Hosea, Ecclesiastes, Isaiah, Jeremiah, Joel, Amos, and Nahum. One can also find shorter sections of poetry in other books of both the Old and New Testaments.

The Peculiar Nature of Hebrew Poetry. Poetry is not like other forms of literature, and Hebrew poetry is dissimilar to much of the poetry in other languages and cultures.

Poetry, in many languages, is composed with a *balance of sound.* This may be done by rhyming words or utilizing distinct rhythms or meters. Hebrew poetry, however, is characterized by a *balance of thought.* Ideas are related to one another in various parallelistic ways.

In synonymous parallelism, for example, the idea expressed in the first line is repeated with different terminology a second and perhaps even a third time.

> Blessed is the man
> Who does not walk in the counsel of the wicked
> or stand in the way of sinners
> or sit in the seat of mockers (Ps 1:1)

In antithetic parallelism, the first line is followed by a statement of sharp contrast. This type is found throughout Scripture, but is especially common in the book of Proverbs.

> For the LORD watches over the way of the righteous,
> but the way of the wicked will perish (Ps 1:6)

In constructive (or synthetic) parallelism, the second line of a verse adds an idea to the thought of the first, building upon it.

> But his delight is in the law of the LORD,
> and on his law he meditates day and night (Ps 1:2).

Another type of poetry is called climactic parallelism. This is similar to the previous form except that part of the first line is repeated in the second as the idea is completed.

> Ascribe to the LORD, O mighty ones,
> ascribe to the LORD glory and strength.
> Ascribe to the LORD the glory due his name;
> worship the LORD in the splendor of his holiness (Ps 29:1-2).

With figurative parallelism, we see one line of the poem making a figurative statement and the other line making a literal one.

> Like a gold ring in a pig's snout
> is a beautiful woman who shows no discretion (Prov 11:22).

Some Hebrew poetry was written in an acrostic form. In this style, successive verses, half-verses, or sections begin with successive letters of the Hebrew alphabet. The best known is probably Psalm 119 which is written in 22 sections, each consisting of 8 verses. Each verse in each section begins with the same letter of the Hebrew alphabet, with the first eight verses beginning with *aleph*, the second eight with *beth*, and so it continues throughout the psalm. Other psalms written in the acrostic style include 9, 10, 25, 34, 37, 111, 112, and 145. The Book of Lamentations is also written in an acrostic style. There, chapters 1, 2, and 4 each consist of 22 verses. Each of these chapters forms an acrostic. The third chapter is 66 verses long and each three-verse stanza utilizes successive letters at the beginning of each verse. The fifth chapter is not an acrostic although there are 22 verses. The acrostic style was probably used as an aid to memory. In terms of beautiful literature, acrostic poems are outstanding.

Challenges for Preaching. The preacher should have a good understanding of the principles related to interpreting biblical poetry. It must be remembered that this *is* poetry and we should not treat it like prose. C. S. Lewis made an astute comment concerning the Psalms that is applicable to all Biblical poetry:

> The Psalms must be read as poems; as lyrics, with all the licenses and all the formalities, the hyperboles, the emotional rather than logical connections, which are proper to lyric poetry.[11]

In his book *Preaching and the Literary Forms of the Bible*, Thomas Long remarks:

> Poetry stretches the ordinary uses of words, and places them into unfamiliar relationships with each other, thereby cutting fresh paths across the well-worn grooves of everyday language. Poems change what we think and feel not by piling up facts we did not know or by persuading us through arguments, but by making finely tuned adjustments at deep and critical places in our imaginations.[12]

This means that we must not press the details of poetry too far. That which is being said often reflects many of the deepest emotions we humans have in common.

Another kind of difficulty has to do with particular kinds of passages. The Imprecatory Psalms, for example, are difficult to understand and even more difficult to preach. These psalms (35, 69, 83, 109, and 137, for example) consist of prayers for the defeat and overthrow of the wicked. When preaching these, the preacher must emphasize that the psalmist is expressing a strong hatred toward sin, an assignment of vengeance into God's hands, and he is also expressing his feelings in a language characterized by hyperbole.

Messianic Psalms represent another challenge. Some Christian preachers seem to think that every Old Testament text is somehow messianic, but this is not the case. It is best to treat texts as messianic only if the New Testament writers do. For example, Psalm 8:4b-8 is cited in Hebrews 2:5-10 and Psalm 22 is referred to in Matthew 27:35-46. There are many other examples that could be cited but their number isn't endless.

Another interesting challenge in Hebrew poetry is the mixing of metaphors. We see this in the first and last parts of Psalm 23. In an instance like this, we should treat these metaphors as means to an end. We should concentrate less on the figure and more on the truth it represents in this particular text.

General Suggestions for Preaching from Poetry. First, determine the kind of parallelism employed. How is this used to make the point being made? Paying attention to this initial step will prevent a sermonic disaster later.

Thematically, what is the primary single concept that drives this poem? This should become the central subject of the sermon. Along with this, ask yourself about the theology of the passage. What is it teaching about God, about man, about salvation, and other doctrinal themes?

As mentioned above, the uniqueness of poetic language should be respected. Do not attempt to establish fine points of doctrine on poetry. Instead, think in terms of the bigger picture. Ask questions like: 'As a whole, what is this entire passage about?' The historical occasion for the particular poem should be determined and studied for this will sometimes help with establishing the theme and the mood. Psalm titles, though not inspired, can help in this regard.

Try to get inside the *mood* of the poem. Remember that poetry is emotional in nature and speaks to the heart as well as the mind. The emotional breadth of the Hebrew poetry found in the Old Testament covers the entire scope of human experience. Calvin called the book of Psalms 'an anatomy of all the parts of the soul'. The psychological moods of the Song of Songs and the Book of Lamentations are obviously quite dissimilar. Our sermons should accurately reflect the mood of the text.

Pay attention to figures of speech but remember that they are not ends in themselves. They represent important concepts that must become integrated into our preaching.

Finally, pay attention to the perspective of the speaker or writer. The speeches of Job's friends, though truthfully recorded, are not necessarily truthful. Likewise, the viewpoint of the speaker in the book of Ecclesiastes is not always in agreement with the truth of God.

Preaching from Wisdom Literature

Which books of the Bible should be included in the category of wisdom literature? Other than Proverbs, included by all, there is disagreement among the biblical scholars. Some see the Song of Songs as a drama, rather than wisdom poetry. Job is also categorized as drama by some. The Book of Psalms does not seem to fit because it is primarily a hymn and prayer book, even though some of the psalms (1, 14, 36, 37, 49, 53, 73, 78, 112, 119, 127, 128, and 133) are considered to be wisdom literature. For the purposes of this section, I'll include, arbitrarily, the books of Job, Proverbs, Ecclesiastes, and the Song of Songs.[13]

Most of the wisdom literature in Scripture is written as poetry. Therefore, descriptions and guidelines regarding poetry, as discussed above, must be understood and applied to this category of Scripture as well.

Wisdom literature seeks to impart a proper, wise, and godly view of life ('The fear of the LORD is the beginning of wisdom' [Prov 1:7], and it often does this by means of short proverbial sayings. This is not always the case, however, as will be seen in the following discussion.

The Book of Job. Job, unlike Proverbs, is presented as a narrative. It relates the story of a person who suffered extreme loss, wondered why this had happened, evoked the same questions in the minds of others, heard God's point of view, and was then the recipient of material blessing once again. The first two chapters and the end of the last chapter are written as prose. The rest of this lengthy book is poetry of high literary quality. Samuel Schultz affirms this with certainty:

The Book of Job has been recognized as one of the greatest poetic productions of all times. Among the Hebrew writers the author of this book displays the most extensive vocabulary – he is at times referred to as the Shakespeare of Old Testament times. Exhibited in this book are vast resources of knowledge, a superb style of forceful expression, profundity of thought, excellent command of language, noble ideals, a high standard of ethics, and a genuine love for nature. The religious and philosophical ideas have claimed the consideration of the greatest theologians and philosophers down to the present day.[14]

It is very important to handle this book as a whole before attempts are made to preach on smaller sections. To preach on individual verses in the book, even if they are well known (e.g. 'I know that my redeemer lives...' Job 19:25), can be hazardous to one's hermeneutical health. The Book of Job is a classic case of untrue statements being truthfully recorded. The preacher must carefully distinguish between God's truth in the book, and the opinions of people including Job himself. Following the description of the devastation by Satan, the rest of the book consists of six spokesmen each stating his own opinions concerning the calamity that has come. These speakers are Job, Eliphaz, Bildad, Zophar, Elihu, and God. The first five express some notable ideas, but not everything said is the truth. This is why the larger context is so important.

This book discusses some of the most important questions man can ask. It is always contemporary because people still face evil and suffering. The most natural sermon approach, therefore, is to preach the book pastorally. We need to remember that the book does not give easy answers to the difficult question of evil and suffering. The answers that are given will be discovered on an implicational level.

Because of the mixture of false opinions and truthful statements in the book, it is preferable to preach the book as a whole or, at most, in a very brief series. The following is an example of how a sermon might be planned to cover the entire book, an admittedly difficult thing to do in view of its length.

Text: Job

Method: Analytical

Title: 'Why Do Bad Things Happen?'

Proposition: A study of the reality of evil in the book of Job will help us better understand why bad things happen.

    I. The root cause of all evil is seen in Job 1 and 2.

    II. The reality of evil's pain is seen in Job 3.

    III. The rationalizing of evil is seen in Job 4–37.

    IV. The Lord's response regarding evil is seen in Job 38–42.

It would be necessary, obviously, to be highly selective in the choice of texts to be covered in sub-pointing, especially under the third and fourth main points. Rather than numerous references being used, it would be best, in the third point, to present brief sample arguments from each of the speakers. Then, ample time can be given to God's responses.

Proverbs. Unlike Job, the Book of Proverbs is best preached in shorter sections. Much of its material consists of individual statements not linked with the surrounding context except in a general way. Generally, it is important to understand a text's background, but this is often difficult, if not impossible, with single proverbs.

A proverb is a statement of a general truth. It reflects a principle of truth, but we should not view them in a mechanical way that suggests that if certain behaviors are practiced, the results will be predictable. Proverbs 22:6, for example, states: 'Train a child in the way he should go, and when he is old he will not turn from it.' Assuming that this verse is speaking of child-rearing and not vocational training as suggested by some, should we view this proverb mechanistically, as expressing an absolute promise? Or, is it simply giving a principle by which parents should live? The latter is the case. a similar example is found in Proverbs 10:27, where we find: 'The fear of the LORD adds length to life, but the years of the wicked are cut short.' Again, this is a statement of general principle, not an absolute promise of longevity for every godly person.

When we consider each proverb to be an independent statement of a general principle, we are freed from the obligation of explaining the seeming contradictions found in the book. We read in Proverbs 26:4, 'Do not answer a fool according to his folly, or you will be like him yourself.' The very next verse says, however, 'Answer a fool according to his folly, or he will be wise in his own eyes.' In terms of the nature of proverbs, both statement are true.

While at first glance the Book of Proverbs seems to lack variety, this is not the case. The first nine chapters discuss wisdom and foolishness. a father-son or teacher-student kind of format is utilized, though it is not directly conversational. These chapters are more thematically arranged and therefore more unified than the chapters that follow. Because a theme may be discussed over several verses, a traditional homiletical approach can often be used.

Text: Proverbs 3:5-6 (This is a single, unified stanza)
Method: Keyword
Title: 'How to Have a Happy New Year'
Proposition: We can have a happy new year. (How?)
Transition: We can have a happy new year by following the steps given to us in Proverbs 3:5-6.

  I. The first step is to place your faith completely in the Lord (5a).
 II. The second step is to know and avoid personal inadequacies (5b).
III. The third step is to consider God at every juncture in life (6a).
IV. The fourth step is to follow the leading the Lord gives (6b).

This section of the book from 10:1 through 22:16 contains about 375 individual proverbs. Most of these, but not all, are written in the form of antithetic parallelism. They comment on many kinds of behavior and often relate to issues quite relevant to today's listeners. These proverbs can often be preached allowing the text itself (the single proverb) to serve as the sermon's proposition. This can be regarded as a proposition of impression in that the proposition can be restated numerous times during the course of the sermon. The body of the sermon might be developed by using a series of illustrations to exemplify the truth of the proposition. The body might also be developed by drawing inferences from the proverb, as seen in the following:

Text: Proverbs 18:21(This is a single, self-contained statement)
Method: Textual (Inferential)
Proposition: 'The tongue has the power of life and death and those who love it will eat its fruit.'
    I. We can infer from this statement that the tongue has power beyond its size.
    II. We can infer from this statement that the tongue can contribute to great good.
    III. We can infer from this statement that the tongue can cause great devastation.

The next section, chapters 22:17 through 24:34, is similar to the first nine chapters of the book as it assumes a teacher-student posture. Sometimes the sayings are found as couplets, but this is not always the case.

In chapters 25–29 we find an assortment of proverbs usually in the couplet form, but sometimes extending to three lines and even four. Many of these are similes stating that one thing is like another. Proverbs 25:28 is a typical example of the sayings found in this section: 'Like a city whose walls are broken down is a man who lacks self-control.' When the preacher deals with similes and metaphors, the approach I call the *Comparative Method* can be useful. The following outline uses Proverbs 25:11 as an example: 'a word aptly spoken is like apples of gold in settings of silver.'

Text: Proverbs 25:11
Method: Comparative
Title: 'Precious Indeed'
Proposition: A consideration of beautiful jewelry will teach us about the preciousness of well-timed words.
    I. Just as fine jewelry is rare, so is the well-timed word.
    II. Just as fine jewelry is valuable, so is the well-timed word.

The final chapters stand alone with chapter 30 attributed to Agur, an unknown writer, and chapter 31 to King Lemuel, also unknown. Chapter 30 speaks of the importance of God's guidance in view of man's limitations. The last chapter includes some instructions to the king himself and then ends with the ideal wife being described in an acrostic poem.

Ecclesiastes. This book is the most philosophically-oriented book in Scripture. While Job is about searching for answers in the midst of suffering, and Proverbs deals in principle with how to live, Ecclesiastes is a book of frustration and pessimism as it searches for meaning in life. This is a book that, at first glance, seems to contradict the rest of Scripture as well as to itself. It does, in fact, express contradictions within its own pages. And it is true that there are opinions expressed in the book that do not represent the traditional views of either Judaism or Christianity. Contrary to what seems to be the situation, the central message of this book is not unlike that found elsewhere in Scripture. One author says: 'This book espouses the most basic theme of biblical literature – that life lived by purely earthly or human values, without faith in God and supernatural values, is meaningless and futile.'[15]

Some are troubled by the pessimistic tone of the book. The reason this tone is present relates to the essential theme and methodology of the composition. The book follows what Ryken calls the quest motif. The writer is a wise person searching for the good life. He tries different avenues only to discover that most are dead-end streets. He examines all the main thoroughfares of man's existence: the city, fields, gardens, the temple, a house, a bedroom, courts of justice, seats of power, and even warfare. He ponders the meanings of wealth, power, religion, relationships, work, and play. He finally concludes that life has meaning only if people are in right relationship with God.[16]

When viewed as a whole, this book has a tremendously relevant message for today's thinking person. It is also another good example of a book that can be preached profitably in a single sermon designed to cover all of it thematically in one presentation. This might be done using an *Inductive Approach.*

Text: Ecclesiastes

Method: Inductive (This method will be discussed in the next chapter.)

Thematic Question: What is life all about anyway?

I. It's not about wisdom; wisdom alone is meaningless (1:12-18; 2:12-16).

II. It's not about pleasure; pleasure alone is meaningless (2:1-3, 10-11).

III. It's not about hard work; work alone is meaningless (2:4-9, 17-23).

IV. It's not about position; position alone is meaningless (4:13-16).

V. It's not about money; money alone is meaningless (5:8-17).

Proposition: The meaning of life is found only in a right relationship with the God who created us.

The preacher can deal with the book section by section as long as the overall message of the book is not forgotten. Both positive passages (truthful statements) and negative passages (pessimistic and inaccurate statements) can be preached. The latter type can be compared to the mistaken philosophies in today's world. The conclusion of each message can emphasize the meaning of life from God's perspective. Special caution should be used when isolated texts are chosen. Just as we saw with Job, not everything recorded in this book is true, though everything is truthfully recorded. Sermon should be based on single texts only when they accurately reflect the theme of the immediate context and the overall message of the book is not ignored.

A sermon based on chapters 4 and 5 might include a discussion of both the negative descriptions of 'life under the sun' in 4:1-16 and then move to 5:1-7 to find a positive response to the issue of life's meaning.

The Song of Songs. There has been much difference of opinion about the purpose and proper interpretation of the Song of Songs.

1. Some have seen the book as an allegory, expressing the loving relationship that exists between God and his people. (The early

church father Origen preached a long series on this book in which this position was taken.)

2. Others have seen the book as a drama or love story.

3. Still others understand the book to be a collection of love poems reflecting a single relationship, but not telling a story *per se*.

4. The book has also been viewed as a miscellaneous collection of love poems, but not about anyone in particular.

5. Finally, some hold that the book is both historical (reflecting the love of Solomon for his Shunammite bride) and typical (a type of God's love for his people, his bride).[17]

It is not an easy matter to preach on this book and the approach taken will be determined by which of these understandings of the book is held by the preacher. It is my opinion that extreme allegory should be avoided even if the typological view is maintained. The book does have a practical value in communicating the goodness of erotic love and this can be of value in marital counseling.

Preaching from Prophecy

Books of prophecy make up one-fourth of the books in the Bible. Altogether, they constitute approximately 22% of Scripture. These books include the longest book in the Bible (Jeremiah), as well as the shortest book in the Old Testament (Obadiah). They cover a period of about 500 years of Israel's history, dealing not only with God's people, but with the surrounding nations as well. They are books that are quite varied as they present a wide array of styles and topics. The prophetic literature is not a literary classification as such, but a combination of most of the literary genre found in Scripture

The Identity of the Writing Prophets. It seems that the prophets and prophetic literature are difficult parts of the Bible for some students and even preachers. This is probably due, at least partly, because some of these books (Isaiah, Jeremiah, and Ezekiel) are quite lengthy and sometimes without an obvious thematic or chronological story line. Our difficulty with the prophets may also be due to the fact that they highly unusual persons, even eccentric. Kaiser speaks of them as being both revolutionaries and conservatives.[18] Heschel speaks of them as 'disturbing people'.[19]

We can regard them as *revolutionaries* because they espoused radical ideas compared to the people to whom they spoke. Great change was their agenda both for people individually and for society as a whole. On the other hand, they were *conservatives*. They were calling the Jewish people back to the old ways, especially in terms of religion.

The Role of the Prophets. As discussed in an earlier chapter, these persons were primarily 'forthtellers' rather than 'foretellers'. Interestingly, when preachers propose to preach from one of the prophets, congregations immediately assume that the sermon will be about the future. Most folks think automatically of predictive prophecy. The prophets, however, were preachers. Sometimes their messages were about the future, but this was not the case much (most?) of the time. They were largely concerned about how people to whom they spoke were living. They desired to see God's people give up their idolatry, false worship, and godless behavior and recommit themselves to living for God. They desired to see a people characterized unwaveringly by devout holiness.

As spokesmen for God, sometimes their message did deal with the future and they were foretelling, but their message was always the message of God, forthtelling. Further, their messages were always delivered with a sense of authority that left little question about who they represented.

The Message of the Prophets. In addition to being counter-cultural and disturbing people, the prophets were also 'sensitive'. This is a term that Heschel uses to describe the variety of issues dealt with in the prophetic writings.

The prophets had a great sensitivity to God. They had encountered him themselves and knew his attributes well. They desired to communicate the 'person' of God to their hearers as well as the message that he had given them. They knew him as the electing, covenant-making God. They knew him as the God who makes history, using even the enemies of Israel to do his bidding (Jer 25:9; Hab 1:5-6; Isa 45:1). They recognized the universality of God's domain. They knew him as the God of justice. They knew him as a God of wrath. They knew him as the God of loving mercy.

The prophets had a great sensitivity to the depth of sin and unbelief. Heschel says: 'They speak and act as if the sky were about to collapse because Israel has become unfaithful to God.'[20] And again: 'the prophets were unfair to the people of Israel. Their sweeping allegations, overstatements, and generalization defied standards of accuracy. Some of their exaggerations reach the unbelievable.'[21]

The prophets had a great sensitivity to bad religion. They were concerned with 'weightier matters of the law'. Religiosity did not impress them; they looked for true religion of the heart.

The prophets had a great sensitivity to values that were misplaced. They had nothing kind to say about the materialism, hedonism, idolatry, power-grabbing, and various social injustices of their day. They spoke in no uncertain terms about these issues.

The prophets also had a great sensitivity to God's warnings of coming judgment and also to his promises of mercy. They emphasized the conditional nature of the gloomy predictions they made and pleaded for the people to return to God.

Finally, the prophets had a great sensitivity to their own unenviable position as God's spokesmen. They were not necessarily a happy lot, often hearing the snide remarks of their fellow countrymen and feeling the pangs of rebuke. They were persistent, though, as they remained faithful to their calls.

The Literary Style of the Prophets. There are numerous kinds of literary materials found in the prophetic books. The effective preacher will need to recognize and properly integrate them into the sermons to be preached. Some of the literary styles to be found there include the following:

1. Sermons/speeches/or synopses of the same: four such addresses make up the book of Haggai. Large parts of the major prophets, especially Isaiah and Jeremiah, also contain long speeches.

2. Reports of visions: These are found in texts like Isaiah 6, Ezekiel 37, and large parts of Zechariah. These are some of the best-remembered parts of the prophets, though not always completely understood.

3. Series of woes: These are scattered throughout the prophets in texts like Habakkuk 2:6, 9, 12, 15, 19 and Amos 1:3, 6, 9, 13;

2:1, 4, 6. Some-times the word 'woe' is used, as in Habakkuk. At other times different wording is used. In Amos, the formula is 'for three sins of -----, even for four.' Isaiah uses the words 'an oracle against ----' as a formula (13:1; 15:1; 17:1; 19:1; 21:1, 11, 13).

4. Figurative language: The book of Hosea has a great many similes and metaphors. Isaiah 5:1-7 is one of the few parables found in the Old Testament. (Another is found in 2 Samuel 12:1-7, also told by a prophet.) Allegory is found in Ezekiel 17:3-10.

5. Symbolic actions: In Ezekiel 4, we find that prophet building a model of Jerusalem and then reclining for 390 days on his left side and another 40 days on his right, signifying first the sins of Israel and then the sins of Judah. In Hosea, we find an unusual marriage that carries a symbolic message. Symbolic actions were sometimes quite drastic, as can be seen in these examples.

6. Object lessons: Jeremiah 13:1-11 discusses a dirty linen belt. Jeremiah 18:1-10 uses the potter's wheel to make his point. While these are relatively rare in the prophets, those found are rich in imagery and meaning.

7. Narrative: (Jonah; Isaiah 36–38) Many of the prophetic writings have narrative portions interwoven with speeches or short pronouncements. This is seen in Jonah, Isaiah 36 –38, the book of Jeremiah, and the book of Ezekiel.

8. Poetry: While it is not readily apparent in some of the older translations, such as the KJV, a look at newer translations like the NIV or the NASB will show that a considerable percentage of the material in the writing prophets is in the form of poetry. The preacher needs to handle this genre with care, understanding the various forms of Hebrew poetry previously discussed.

9. Dialogical argumentation: This is especially prevalent in Malachi (1:2, 1:6, 1:12-13; 2:14, 17; 3:6-8, 13) and is also found in Amos 3:3-6.

10. Predictions of the future: Sometimes these are short-term predictions, as in the case of Habakkuk 1:5-6. At other times, the prophet speaks of something quite distant in time, as in Malachi 4. It would seem that they themselves were not fully aware of the amount of time that would pass before the prediction was fulfilled.

11. Affirmations of faith: Even when uncertainty is present, the prophets have a strong conviction about the faithfulness of God. An example of this is Habakkuk 3. Lamentations, written by Jeremiah, is another affirmation of faith in the face of difficulty.

Preaching from the Prophets. Because the prophetic literature is so diverse, there are few exegetical or hermeneutical steps to be taken by the preacher that are unique to this kind of text. There are, of course, some important general guidelines or cautions to keep in mind, some of which might easily fall by the wayside. For example, a text should be chosen that is a complete thematic segment. If the same theme runs on for an extended time, a segment can be chosen that accurately represents the larger passage. Similarly, a text should be a complete literary unit. It is generally unwise to choose only portions of poetry, narratives, dialogue, or parables. These should not be cut off unless the length is prohibitive. I'm not saying that everything in an extended passage must be included in a sermon, but that the entire passage should inform the sermon and drive it intentionally toward the purpose of the extended passage.

We should remember that the prophetic texts were mostly oral at the time of their original communication. While we speak of the 'writing prophets', in reality almost all of their messages were spoken. a particular audience was present and that the message was geared toward its needs. We must inquire regarding the parallels between that audience and our own. Mickelsen rightly says: 'To lose sight of the original hearers and to focus our attention on what may tickle the fancy of the curious minded in the present day is to lose sight of the very reason for the message.'[22]

When we preach on the prophets, we need to pay special attention to historical and contextual matters. These texts reflect circumstances that took place a long time ago, Even when a text deals with predictive prophecy we must first clearly understand the situation to which it was addressed.

Finally, emphasize the theology of the text. Since the prophet was a spokesman for God, what Divine truth was being communicated? The theological issues as understood in that historical context must be dealt with before jumping to theological conclusions based on present day knowledge of theology. The principle of progressive revelation must not be forgotten.

Preaching from Apocalyptic Literature

An Overview of Apocalyptic. The apocalyptic literature in Scripture is sometimes discussed with the prophetic literature as though there is no distinction. Yet it has unique literary qualities that demand special attention. 'Apocalyptic' comes from the Greek word *apokalupsis* meaning 'a revelation' or 'a disclosing'. The usage of the word as an alternate title for the Book of Revelation is an example of its meaning. Parts of both the Old and New Testaments are usually regarded as apocalyptic. The second half of Daniel, Zechariah, and passages in Joel and Amos are included in this category, as is Matthew 24, Mark 13, 1 Thessalonians 4:13ff, and the Book of Revelation. The genre is found also in non-biblical books including *1 Enoch, 2 Enoch*, the *Book of Jubilees*, the *Sibylline Oracles*, the *Testaments of the Twelve Patriarchs*, the *Assumption of Moses*, the *Apocalypse of Moses, 2 Esdras*, and the Qumran scroll called *The War of the Sons of Light with the Sons of Darkness*. This type of literature is generally dated from about 200 B.C. to about 100 A.D., although Daniel is dated earlier by conservative scholars.

There are several distinctives that typify apocalyptic literature. A single piece of this kind of writing may not include each of the following traits, but will include a majority of them.[23]

1. It is eschatological, being concerned primarily with future end-time events.

2. The revelation is often received by a 'hero' figure who is a member of the 'in' group. In reality the writings are almost always pseudonymous, i.e. the real author is unknown but he has expressed his message through the medium of a well known person.

3. The revelation is intended only for a special group, God's remnant. Thus the writings are esoteric in nature.

4. There is usually a strong messianic flavor, i.e. a savior is coming to deliver the struggling saints.

5. There is a strong flavor of pessimism present. Spiritual and political matters are seen as deteriorating until the final conflict when

the remnant will be delivered.

6. There is a sharp difference between good and evil and between good people and evil people (dualism).

7. Much symbolism is used including animals, numbers, colors, and heavenly phenomena. This gives the writings a mysterious character to be understood only by the remnant.

8. There is an emphasis on the spirit world with angels and demons being involved in a cosmic conflict.

9. The writings speak of the Divine wrath and judgment which are coming upon those outside of the elect (the remnant). They culminate with a final judgment and the ultimate triumph of God and His people.

The two primary pieces of apocalyptic literature in Scripture are Daniel and Revelation. In fact, because of their similarities, these books are often studied together. We must remember that the Book of Daniel is more than apocalyptic, however. The first six chapters are really narrative and biographical. The apocalyptic material begins in the seventh chapter with Daniel's vision of the four creatures. Much of the final six chapters contains apocalyptic characteristics.

Most preachers regard the Book of Revelation as the most difficult book in Scripture to preach. It is admittedly a challenge to understand and interpret this part of the Bible, including not only the many details found there but its overall design as well. Regarding this design, there are four primary positions held by biblical scholars. The *preterists* hold that the book deals only with conditions at the time of writing. *Historicists* interpret the book as predicting the various eras of Church history up through the final events of the ages. The *idealist* interpretation sees the book as a 'drama' of the conflict between good and evil. Finally, the *futurist* viewpoint is that the section of the book beginning with 4:1 to the end is a prophecy of the events which will occur at the end of the Church age.[24]

Those who fear attempting to preach from Revelation should be reminded that some of the book is relatively easy to understand. Chapter 1 is a Christocentric introduction to the book which, while using some symbolic imagery, is fairly straightforward in its overall intention. The next two chapters are clearly a series of seven letters written to seven churches that existed at the time of John's writing. One does not need to apply these letters to successive eras of church history (a somewhat dubious interpretation) in order to profit from their plain meaning.

Many other parts of the book can be presented confidently if the preacher avoids the temptation of majoring in the minutia. There are many details of interpretation on which the most godly preachers have disagreed through the centuries. In his opening remarks in a sermon on Revelation 12:11, C. H. Spurgeon made the following statement, one sure to elicit nods of agreement from many preachers:

> It is not my main object at this time to expound the chapter before us. I scarcely consider myself qualified to explain any part of the Book of Revelation, and none of the expositions I have seen entice me to attempt the task, for they are mostly occupied with a refutation of all the interpretations which have gone before, and each one seems to be very successful indeed in proving that all the rest know nothing at all about the matter. The sum total of substantial instruction in nearly all the comments upon the Revelation amounts to this, that our heavenly Father has said in his word some mysterious things which few of his children can yet comprehend.[25]

It should be pointed out that this book is the most intricately structured book in Scripture. Its contents are woven together in a highly organized pattern which makes outlining relatively easy. While outlining doesn't assure proper interpretation, it is a good step to take toward understanding the larger and smaller themes in the book. Nevertheless, understanding each part of the book and being able to preach through the book is not a simple matter.

Guidelines for Preaching on Apocalyptic. The following comments, while somewhat general, should assist the preacher who desires to treat the apocalyptic literature of the Bible with the care necessary to ensure sound interpretation and teaching.

1. Gain an understanding of the book (or section) as a whole. Get a feel for the whole before you attempt to deal with the details of the writing. The former is much more important than the latter in this type of literature.

2. Preach on longer texts rather than shorter ones.

3. Look for preaching texts which summarize in plain language the surrounding context. (for example: Matt. 24:36,42,44; Mark 13:35-37; Rev. 1:19; 17:17.)

4. Preach theological themes primarily, rather than prophetic (predictive) themes. For example, the Book of Revelation has a great deal to say about Christology making mention of Christ some ninety times. The doctrine of God is likewise prominent in the book and other theological concerns are found there as well.

5. If planning a series on an apocalyptic book, trace a subject or theme through the entire book. This will help to unify the writing in the minds of the hearers. In the book of Revelation, for example, potential series might include: 'Images of the Messiah'; 'Seven Letters to Seven Churches'; 'Who's in Charge?'; 'The Ultimate Struggle Between Good and Evil'; and 'What's Going to Happen to God's People?'

6. Exercise great caution in interpreting figures of speech and symbols: (1) Let the text interpret itself first (Dan. 2:36-43; 7:17; Rev. 1:20; 17:9-16); (2) If the immediate context doesn't explain a symbol or figure, is it used elsewhere in Scripture by the same author? (3) Allow the clear parts of Scripture to serve as a basis for an understanding of the unclear parts; (4) Keep the original hearers or readers in mind. What would they have understood the text to be saying? Why would this symbol have been effective for them? (5) Do not force symbols or figures into a preconceived mold. Allow each context to determine its own meaning (Compare Mark 8:15 and 1 Corinthians 5:6 with Matthew 13:33. What about the 'fig tree' passage in Matthew 24:32-35?); (6) Remember that each symbol or figure doesn't need to be fully understood to get the gist of a passage. The flow of the whole text is more important than isolated parts, although these details can certainly help to amplify the meaning being communicated; (7) Be willing to say 'I don't know' when it comes to the meaning of a given figure, symbol, or even text (Dan. 12:8ff).

While preaching on apocalyptic texts may be viewed as daunting, it can be done if caution is taken to avoid speculation and novelty.

The Teachings of Jesus

The earthly ministry of Jesus was characterized by both word and deed. Both should be preached regularly for they each teach us who he is and what he came to accomplish. His deeds teach us indirectly. An incident such as his remaining behind in Jerusalem at the age of twelve tells us something about his sense of identity and calling even at that young age (Luke 2:41ff). Likewise, his baptism by John is a public announcement of 'the Lamb of God who takes away the sins of the world'. The miracles of Jesus tell us about his compassion for the needy as well as his access to Divine power. They are also a powerful apologetic regarding his messianic identity. This is clearly seen in the purpose and structure of John's Gospel where selected 'sign miracles' are used to bring people to saving faith (John 20:30-31). And the cross, even apart from the 'seven last sayings', speaks volumes about the Savior's person and purpose. A great deal about Jesus can be known by studying and preaching these indirect lessons presented in his deeds.

In addition to the indirect teachings of Jesus' deeds, there are many teachings that are more directly communicated by his words. These cover a broad range of subjects and are found in various formats.

The Content of Jesus' Teachings. In terms of subject matter, a multitude might be named including happiness, sadness, humility, righteousness, purity, peace, persecution, heaven and hell, witness, the Jewish law, murder and hatred, sexual impurity, marriage and divorce, keeping one's word, revenge, loving one's enemies, benevolence, prayer, fasting, materialism, anxiety, judging, the 'golden rule', false teachers, and wise and foolish choices. And this is just the Sermon on the Mount! Elsewhere, Jesus teaches about discipleship, money, the Holy Spirit, spiritual destitution, evangelism and missions, coming judgment, man and religious law, Satan, the nature of God's kingdom, relative values, faith, hypocrisy, his own identity, true greatness, forgiveness, grace, fulfilled prophecy, the new birth, various Divine attributes, true nourishment, depravity, authority, civil government, life after death, pride, religious oppression, Jesus' coming death and resurrection, the end of the age, the Second

Coming, the Lord's Supper, the great commission, and Christ's continual presence. Around sixty subjects are listed here with no attempt being made to name them all. We stand amazed at the comprehensiveness of Jesus' teachings.

While his teachings are indeed quite broad, there are several subjects taught by Jesus that appear to be at the heart of his earthly ministry in terms of the relative amount of time spent on them. The Kingdom of God is an area, for example, which he addressed on many occasions. He spoke of the Kingdom both in present and future terms and related it to the individual as well as to the corporate entity of God's people and **reign**. Spiritual regeneration itself is taught in terms of God's Kingdom. Eschatological matters are also related to this subject.

A second core area of Jesus' teachings is that of ethics, especially on the personal level. He spent a great deal of time talking about how people ought to live in terms of their behavior. Many of those subjects listed above fall into this category.

Third, Jesus taught about the promised Messiah and his own identity as that person. Sometimes he was rather obtuse about this, but on other occasions he allowed the truth that he was the Christ to be comprehended by his listeners.

Fourth, Jesus presented the ministry of the Holy Spirit in his teachings. This is seen primarily in John's Gospel, but is also found in the Synoptic Gospels in texts such as Matthew 10:19-20 and 12:28 and Mark 12:36 and 13:11. The Holy Spirit was to indwell his followers and empower them for ministry.

Finally, Jesus' teachings included his 'marching orders' to his followers. These are seen most clearly in the multiple texts known as great commission passages, but the necessity of ongoing gospel witness is seen elsewhere as well. In the Sermon on the Mount, for example, Jesus speaks of his followers as being the light of the world, people who should bring glory to God by letting their lights shine brightly. In the same text, believers are also called the salt of the earth. Their influence should be a preservative one.

The Forms of Jesus' Teachings. Jesus' teachings were diverse not only in terms of subject matter, but also in terms of their literary nature. Several characteristics are readily apparent when his teachings are studied from this perspective.

First, it is clearly seen that Jesus was a master of metaphor. Sometimes these were one-liners – whitewashed tombs, sheep without a shepherd, sheep among wolves, faith like a small seed, shrewd as snakes and innocent as doves, the bread of life – in the style of similes or metaphors. Sometimes, they were more extended as in the case of parables or even allegories. In short, figures of speech of comparison abound in Jesus' teachings.

He also used hyperbole. Sometimes these statements are rather humorous as we visualize the literal statement. We imagine a person with a piece of lumber sticking out of his own eye as he attempts to examine a speck of dust in someone else's. Such a picture brings a smile to our face, but we can't escape the poignant message it communicates. Or we see a camel struggling to fit into the eye of a needle and understand the difficulty of a person who clings to his riches trying to get into heaven.

We also see the use of paradox by Jesus. Speaking of discipleship, Jesus said, 'Whoever wants to save his life must lose it, but whoever loses his life for me will find it' (Matt 16:25). A few chapters later, when he spoke of greatness, he said, 'Whoever wants to become great among you must be your servant' (Matt 20:26). This kind of statement immediately grabs our attention and allows its significance to sink into our souls.

In addition to diverse figures of speech, Jesus used argumentation effectively. He had the ability to rebut accusations and tricky questions to the point that his accusers were astonished. A series of these refutations is found in Matthew 21:23-27 (Jesus' authority); Matthew 22:15-22 (paying taxes); Matthew 22:23-33 (marriage and the resurrection); Matthew 22:34-40 (the greatest commandment); and Matthew 22:41-46 (the parentage of the Messiah). These are only five examples; there are others as well.

Some of the teachings of Jesus are found in long sections. Two lengthy examples are the Sermon on the Mount, as found in Matthew 5–7, and the Upper Room Discourse found in John 13–17 (chapter 17 is actually a prayer, but this is usually included as part of this discourse. Some are of the opinion that the former text is actually a series of shorter sayings as is seen in the parallel passages in Mark and Luke. They argue that Matthew edited this material to make it appear as a single setting, while in Mark and Luke this material is found in several different settings. Such a conclusion seems to ignore the possibility that Jesus doubtless said the same things on more than one occasion. D. A. Carson, in fact, says in this regard: 'The pithier the saying, the more likely it was to be repeated word-perfect.'[26]

There are other relatively long speeches of Jesus such as the 'I am' discussions in John's Gospel and the eschatological speeches in the Synoptics. These are usually clearly defined literary units that can readily be utilized for sermon purposes.

Noteworthy among Jesus' teachings are the numerous parables. As mentioned above, these fit into the broad category of figures of speech of comparison. Some are quite brief and are basically extended similes. Others are longer and more detailed with a few actually being interpreted by Jesus in an allegorical fashion. The majority of parables are stories that are rather realistic – the elements in the story are culturally familiar to the listeners and easily understood. This does not mean that the point of the story is easily grasped, however. In fact, Mark's Gospel includes these statements:

> The secret of the kingdom of God has been given to you. But to those on the outside everything is said in parables so that, 'they may be ever seeing but never perceiving, and ever hearing but never understanding; otherwise they might turn and be forgiven!' (4:11-12).

> With many similar parables Jesus spoke the word to them, as much as they could understand. He did not say anything to them without using a parable. But when he was alone with his own disciples, he explained everything (4:33-34).

The clear implication of these statements is that parables are a bit on the mysterious side, their point being not as clear as first supposed. This is doubtless due to the fact that parables usually contain a surprise element, an unexpected twist in the story that is instrumental in conveying the point of the story.

One example of an unexpected twist is seen in the parable of the laborers in Matthew 20. The workers are hired and sent into the vineyard at various times of the day including some who began work at the eleventh hour, shortly before the end of the workday. When wages were given out, those who were hired last received the same pay as those who had worked all day! It is needless to say that this seems very unfair and the workers in the story grumbled accordingly. In the parable, Jesus gives the landowner's response and then his own final word:

> Take your pay and go. I want to give the man who was hired last the same as I gave you. Don't I have the right to do what I want with my own money? Or are you envious because I am generous? 'So the last will be first, and the first will be last' (Matt 20:14-16)

Jesus' listeners would have been surprised and dumfounded. This is so unexpected and seems to be so unreasonable. And in a sense it is for the parable is a teaching about grace, not a very 'reasonable' concept from the perspective of the world.

Another example of outlandish surprise is seen in the parable of the good Samaritan in Luke 10. It is a question by a Jewish expert in the law, 'And who is my neighbor?,' that prompts Jesus to tell the story of a man robbed, beaten, and ignored by a priest and Levite. To the surprise and probable chagrin of the Jewish lawyer, Jesus elevates a lowly, despicable Samaritan to the role of a true neighbor. The questioner apparently got the message, however, for he responded correctly to Jesus' inquiry by identifying the real neighbor as 'the one who had mercy on the needy victim'.

Preaching from the Teachings of Jesus. Because the teachings of Jesus are so diverse, a great variety of sermon approaches can be used.[27] Because of this literary diversity, care must be taken to match an appropriate approach with the text. What will work well with a discourse, for example, may not work well with a parable.

Preaching from this part of Scripture is a great opportunity to explore the tremendous wisdom and breadth of our Savior's teaching ministry. It is also an opportunity to model good hermeneutics, exegesis, and application in a public way. The benefit of this, of course, is that we not only preach this part of the Word, but we also assist our listeners to become more proficient at handling the Word for themselves.

Preaching from the Epistles

The Nature of Epistles. Twenty-one of the twenty-seven books in the New Testament are in the epistolary form. As far as form is concerned, these letters were not unusual in the ancient world. Epistles were widely used, both in and out of the church, to engage in personal conversation, to send information, and to present formal arguments regarding some issue under debate. Widely regarded as the greatest orator of the Roman Empire, Cicero (106–43 BC), was also a profuse letter writer, with some 835 still in existence. The philosopher Seneca (4 BC–AD 65), tutor and advisor to Nero and one of the most powerful men in first-century Rome, wrote 124 letters known as the *Epistulai Morales*. These deal with moralistic themes and problems from a philosophical perspective. In the early Christian era, many of the Church Fathers such as Polycarp, Clement of Rome, Origen, and Ignatius made use of epistles to encourage and instruct their flocks, and to deal with doctrinal and practical issues related to the life of the church.

It is evident that the epistolary form was quite common for an extended period of time both prior to and following the coming of Christ. It should not therefore surprise us that several of the epistles found in the New Testament – James, 1 and 2 Thessalonians, 1 and 2 Corinthians, Romans, and Galatians – are the earliest Christian writings known. (It's possible, if not probable, that the Gospel of Mark was also written during this period of A.D. 44–58.)

Some scholars dispute whether or not the New Testament letters should be called epistles in the literary sense of that classification. They argue that the biblical epistles are more personal and less formal than the secular epistles of the same period. This is obviously an overstatement as is seen in the variety of both the New Testament epistles and those from outside the canon. The letters of John are warm and personal and utilize a very common form of language. The letter to the Hebrews, on the other hand, is quite formal and is characterized by a style that is a sermonic, though it concludes in a way that is typical of an epistle. The letter to Philemon is quite personal and informal, yet, it is also a carefully crafted argument. In short, the New Testament letters differ in their styles and subject matters – even Paul's epistles vary in these regards – but this is typical of epistolary literature in general. A study of non-biblical epistles will confirm this is the case depending on the nature of the purposes and subjects of these letters.

The New Testament epistles, of course, are quite special in comparison to other epistles from the ancient world. While their writers never guessed their letters would be studied and utilized throughout the following centuries and millennia, this has been the case. Early on the church recognized the uniqueness of these letters in terms of truth and authority. They became part of the Christian canon and possibly the part preached from most often.

Suggestions for Preaching from the Epistles. Compared to some of the literature in Scripture, the epistles are relatively easy to handle homiletically. This is due to the discernible structures that characterize most of them. Main ideas or topics generally are clear and so are the supporting arguments. This flow of ideas can often be followed for the purpose of sermon outlining, though care should be taken to assure that a sermon is being outlined and not just a lecture or running commentary.

While outlining the content of the various epistles is relatively simple, the preacher will be more than adequately challenged to handle the broad diversity of doctrinal and ethical issues discussed in these letters. Some sermons will come together fairly quickly as they reflect the direct thrust of their respective texts. Others, however, will take a great deal of thought as the preacher attempts to move from a specific issue important to a given time, place, and persons and speak to a corresponding issue to today's hearer. This will be less difficult with doctrinal texts than with those that are ethical in nature.

For example, what Paul says in his letters about sin and its consequences, justification, sanctification, grace, the church, and similar theological subjects are as relevant today as when first addressed. This is not to say that care will not be needed in the use of terminology and in the selection of understandable illustrations and appropriate applications. But the theology of such texts remains unchanged. On the other hand, to preach from Philemon (an escaped slave becoming a Christian brother), 1 Corinthians 8 (food offered to idols), or even 1 Peter 4 (where persecution for being a Christian is discussed) may require the preacher to think in terms of equivalencies and principles rather than exact duplications in our present culture.

As with other kinds of literature in the Scripture, the preacher will need to select and utilize thematic segments for preaching texts. In the epistles, this means that paragraphs, minimally, will be selected as the basic text to develop sermonically. This doesn't mean that every phrase in the one or more paragraphs chosen must be covered in detail, but it does mean that the message of the entire thematic segment must be honored and conveyed in the sermon. It should be remembered also that when a broad subject is treated in a text that runs for several paragraphs, it is likely that the subject needs to be narrowed down in order to reduce the length of the text being used and to make the sermon more manageable from the preacher's perspective as well as from the listener's. The doctrinal discussions in Romans come to mind as examples of this. Some broad subjects such as sin, justification, and sanctification cover two or more chapters, far too much text to do justice to in most sermons. (The survey-type sermon would be an exception to this.) It is imperative, therefore, that the preacher divides these texts according to certain aspects of the subject. These will generally be discovered as the preacher studies the various paragraphs, for each paragraph should discuss some specific aspect of the broader subject.

The preacher will make decisions regarding the length of the preaching text on the basis of matters such as overall preaching schedule, specific purposes for specific sermons, the needs of the listeners, length of sermon, exegetical skill, and homiletical skill.

These decisions are somewhat arbitrary. For example, suppose one wishes to preach on the subject of Christian love and chooses 1 Corinthians 13 as the text. This might be done in a single sermon using the entire chapter. Or, it might be done as a series of three messages, each utilizing one of the three usual paragraphs (1-3, 4-7, 8-13). Other series arrangements might also be considered, but this seems to be the most natural way to divide the text for homiletical purposes.

The epistles, especially the shorter ones, are prime candidates for preaching series. Many of them divide into preaching segments that are manageable without being too numerous. An ordinary outline of an epistle will offer helpful insights into potential preaching texts. Such an outline will necessarily be divided according to subject matter and this will be suggestive for sermon pericopes. The concept of sermon series will be discussed in a subsequent chapter.

Because the epistles contain a great variety of literary material – biography, instruction, exhortation, Old Testament quotations, and poetry, to name a few – homiletical variety can be easily achieved with a little effort. There is no excuse, structurally speaking, to use the same homiletical method over and over. This is especially important when preaching a series through a book, but it is important for one's overall preaching plan in general. The epistles lend themselves to a great deal of structural variety.[28]

Finally, sermons from the epistles should include a brief mention of the fact that the Scripture being considered comes from an actual letter. I am always amazed when I hear a sermon based on a text from an epistle – especially a single sermon not part of a series – that never refers to the fact that the original message was in a letter sent to distinct recipients who needed to hear what was being written. The audience needs to understand that there was a time in which a letter writer wrote to people in a given place (usually), with a particular agenda to address. As with sermons from other biblical genre, pertinent background information helps listeners connect with the ancient text. They need to understand that what made the text relevant and important in the original setting is still applicable today. This part of preaching, it seems to me, is becoming increasingly important as culture becomes increasingly biblically illiterate. The preacher who ignores doing this robs the hearers of an opportunity to better understand the nature of the Bible.

Preach Both Familiar and Unfamiliar Texts

In this chapter we have thus far emphasized the issue of preaching from both the Old and New Testaments and we have also discussed the necessity of preaching from all of the various kinds of literary materials found in the Bible. Now I will mention briefly the importance of preaching both familiar and unfamiliar texts.

Preaching Familiar Texts

Sometimes texts will be familiar to the preacher but not as well-known to his hearers. The opposite may be true on occasion as well. Familiarity should not be the determinative factor in whether or not a given text is preached. Rather, we should be prayerfully asking for Divine guidance regarding the needs of our listeners and appropriate texts to address those needs. At times, such texts may be familiar to one party or the other. At other times, our prayerful inquiry and study may lead us to appropriate texts that are rarely known among our listeners and barely known to the preacher.

We may have a tendency to avoid some well-known texts simply because they are so familiar. We must not mistake this with being 'too familiar'. When can a text become so well-known that it needs to be ignored? I think, for example, of John 3:16. Without doubt this is one of the best known verses in Scripture. It has been many, many years, however, since I last preached or heard a sermon based primarily on this text. Yet as a child, I recall this verse being called 'the gospel in a nutshell'. Has something changed? Do folks, including Christian folks, no longer need to hear this truth? I'm not suggesting that John 3:16 needs to be mentioned every week or be the basis of a sermon every month. Still, it is an important text that should not be totally ignored. In fact, the text is familiar because it is so important!

Perhaps we preachers fear being labeled as too repetitive. We don't want to be accused of dabbling only in 'basic truths', so we go on the prowl for provocative texts that are sure to arouse interest and curiosity. While it is good to assist ourselves and our listeners to develop a growing knowledge of the entire Bible, and this is surely a by-product of using unfamiliar texts, this must be a secondary consideration. As mentioned above, some texts are well-known simply because they are texts that are crucial to our understanding of the Christian Faith. As preachers, we must never lose sight of the need to teach and remind our people of the foundational truths of the Faith as well as expand their knowledge of the deeper truths.

Converted people do not need to hear the basic gospel week after week. Such a preaching agenda can lull folks into stagnation. They may wrongly assume that this is all there is to Christianity and they miss out on the opportunity of being motivated to grow toward spiritual maturity. Having said this, I would also assert that it is important for believers to be reminded of the basic gospel as they hear occasional evangelistic messages. Such sermons serve as necessary reminders of our former condition apart from Christ and the change that has been made through his saving grace. Such preaching will help us to remain grateful and assist in keeping us from forsaking our 'first love', a fault Jesus found in the Ephesian church in Revelation 2. The Christian's heart can be warmed as one's own conversion experience is revisited. It is good to return to the foot of the cross and be reminded of where our walk with Christ began.

One of the challenges of preaching well-known texts is that of remaining fresh. We must guard against the temptation of laziness in our preparation with the result that we preach 'familiar sermons' when we use familiar texts. A sermon that is predictable is a sure invitation to the listener to tune out and use his or her time more profitably, perhaps planning a schedule for the next week, or daydreaming about the family vacation, or thinking through a school assignment, or even counting the beams in the ceiling. Not everyone who seems to be listening to our pulpit fare is. One of the reasons they stop listening is because sermons are predictable. They don't have to be, even when we preach on familiar passages.

I recall listening to a sermon three decades ago in which a Native

American evangelist spoke on John 3:16 by skillfully interfacing it with the part of Paul's prayer in Ephesians 3 in which he speaks of the love of God:

> I pray that out of his glorious riches he may strengthen you with power through his Spirit in your inner being, so that Christ may dwell in your hearts through faith. And I pray that you, being rooted and established in love, may have power, together with all the saints, *to grasp how wide and long and high and deep is the love of Christ*, and to know this love that surpasses knowledge – that you may be filled to the measure of all the fullness of God (Eph 3:16-19, italics mine).

He explained and clarified the concept of God's love in John 3:16 by utilizing Paul's expression concerning the width, length, height, and depth of divine love. This was a memorable sermon that held people's attention throughout while reminding them of some very basic gospel truths.

Sermons on familiar texts do not have to be predictable. If we're willing to spend a little extra time in preparation and think about some alternate approaches, we can preach these 'old' texts with a sense of newness that will help our listeners stay tuned. A text we are tempted to treat in a straightforward deductible fashion might be presented instead in an inductive mode. Some well-known biblical stories might be presented in a narrative style – perhaps even in the first person – to help assure the retention of attention. This can be done without compromising the meaning of the text in any way. And, in fact, a fresh approach may assist the listener to grasp truths that might otherwise be missed.

Preaching Unfamiliar Texts
In addition to preaching familiar texts, we must also break out of our comfort zones and preach texts that are unfamiliar. Most preachers seem naturally to gravitate toward a particular kind of text. Some, for example, may preach almost exclusively from the epistles while others prefer the wonderful stories of both the Old and New Testaments. This is probably attributable, at least to some

extent, to one's gifting and calling as a preacher. Those who love to teach doctrine, for example, may prefer epistolary texts while shepherds and encouragers may lean toward people-passages such as biographical and narrative texts. When we move from the kind of text we tend to prefer to another kind of text, there can be a sense of leaving our comfort zones.

When Paul gave his farewell thoughts to the Ephesian elders, he reminded them, 'For I have not hesitated to proclaim to you the whole will of God' (Acts 20:27). Preachers often speak of the necessity of declaring the 'whole counsel of God', and so we should. In order to do this, it must be understood, we will need to preach from all parts of Scripture, and for some preachers this will be a challenge. It will be a challenge because we will be leaving our comfort zones in terms of the kinds of texts we're accustomed to working with.

Seminarians are generally trained in the skills of hermeneutics and exegesis. They're taught the differences between the various literary types in Scripture and the processes to be followed and the cautions to take with each one. They may even be taught how to move from the exegetical study of a text to the homiletical steps and how these vary from literary type to type. What often happens, however, is that after a few years in ministry, the person has gravitated to a particular kind of text. While the processes and 'rules' for this type of text are well known and faithfully practiced, the processes and 'rules' for working with other kinds of texts may have been largely forgotten because of lack of use. When this is the case, the preacher needs to go back to the basics of how to study unfamiliar kinds of texts.

Ideally, preachers should preach from a variety of literary genre from the very beginning of their preaching ministries. Experience tells me, however, that this is seldom the case. Suffice it to say that the development of good study skills – hermeneutical, exegetical, and homiletical – will result in a much richer ministry as 'the whole counsel of God' is presented faithfully.

In addition to preaching the unfamiliar texts that are found in those parts of Scripture that we tend to ignore, there are also unfamiliar texts that go unpreached simply because they are difficult texts to handle. They may contain a variant reading that is awkward to explain when various translations are used by hearers. They may present a doctrinal issue that is difficult to resolve. For example, unless a congregation is totally Reformed or totally Arminian, a sermon on Hebrews 6:1-8 will leave some listeners perplexed and unhappy. Some texts may discuss an ethical matter that will open up a 'can of worms'. The Imprecatory Psalms come to mind as an example. And some texts are simply hard to understand. They may be complicated in terms of structure or unclear in terms of meaning. Regardless of what makes them difficult, they are.

There are a few basic principles to keep in mind when being confronted by such texts. First, study and think independently as you initially deal with the text. Do the best you can do in terms of understanding and interpreting the text yourself before seeking help elsewhere. Be certain that your study of the text's background is adequate to help you understand its original setting, situation, and purpose.

Second, after exhausting your own study skills, seek counsel from others. Both your present peers in ministry and prior generations may be available to share their opinions with you. Since you've already come to some conclusions on your own, you're not likely to be swayed unduly by unsound viewpoints. On the other hand, when your own conclusions are confirmed by others who are known for their faithfulness to sound study, this can encourage you to proceed. If your tentative findings are unverified by other trusted persons, you will need further study.

Third, remember that today's interpreter does not stand alone. There is a long history of scholarship produced throughout the church's history that should not be ignored. This is not to argue for some type of inherent authority in church tradition such as that advocated in Roman Catholicism. Nor is to blindly accept what some respected scholar of the past has said about a particular text. It is simply to say that in the case of difficult interpretational matters, it would be foolish to ignore the groundwork others have laid.

Fourth, do not expect to resolve every issue associated with difficult texts. Rather, concentrate on what you can conclude with confidence. If this is sufficient to utilize for preaching purposes, fine. If not, then save it for another occasion.

Fifth, be willing to say, 'I don't know what the precise meaning of this text is.' In such cases, put the text on the back burner until more helpful information and insights are forthcoming. This is not an admission of stupidity but a humble recognition that mortal man cannot understand all there is to know of God and his Word.

Sixth, do not use the pulpit as an extension of your study. Generally speaking, a sermon is not the appropriate place to discuss the processes you've gone through or the various options you faced in wrestling with this passage. Instead, emphasize what you've discovered in your study, the fruit of your labor. Devote the sermon to the proclamation of the truth you've found, not a discussion of other possibilities.

Finally, avoid uncertainty and subjectivism in the pulpit. Little phrases such as 'it seems to me', or 'in my opinion', do little to instill the listener's confidence in what you are saying. They are not there to listen to *your opinions*, but to hear a sure word from the Lord! If the difficulty of a given text prevents you from speaking the truth with a bold certainty, then speak from a different text.

Summation

This chapter has reminded us of the importance of preaching all of the Word of God. We must preach regularly from both Testaments for each is inspired Scripture and thus profitable. In this regard it is important to understand the progressive nature of biblical truth and to preach from the Old Testament in such a way that honors the completeness of God's revelation in Christ.

A balanced view of the biblical foundations for preaching also includes the recognition of many kinds of literary genre in Scripture. This necessitates an understanding of these genre and the development of appropriate skills to deal with each kind.

While it is tempting to preach only from the kinds of texts with which we are most comfortable, it is important to challenge ourselves to preach from other texts as well. This may result in dealing with texts that are difficult to understand and utilize for preaching purposes, or we may face texts that are not very familiar to us or our audience. Still, our calling as preachers of the Word implies that all of the Word needs to be taken seriously and communicated to those for whom we have responsibility.

A healthy philosophy of preaching will include the concept of a balanced perspective on the Scriptures we're called to proclaim. If we limit ourselves to one Testament or to one or two literary types, we and our people will be deprived of the fuller picture of God and his will that he intends for us to have.

Points to Ponder

1. Why do some preachers preach almost exclusively from one Testament or the other, generally the New Testament?

2. What are some possible misuses of the Old Testament in terms of sermon content?

3. How many different types of literature are common to both the Old and New Testaments? Are there literary types unique to one Testament or the other?

4. What is the relationship between hermeneutics and homiletics? Think of some specific examples of how good hermeneutical skills might save a sermon from homiletical error?

5. What constitutes a familiar text? Why should such texts be preached and if so, how often?

6. Are there some texts that should not be preached? Explain what you mean.

Step Four

Maintain a Balance in Preaching Purpose

The purpose of preaching is to inform, persuade, and call forth an appropriate response to the God whose message and instruction are being delivered. The response will consist of repentance, faith, obedience, love, effort, hope, fear, zeal, joy, praise, prayer, or some blend of these.... The purpose of preaching is not to stir people to action while bypassing their minds, so that they never see what reason God gives them for doing what the preacher requires of them (that is manipulation); nor is the purpose to stock people's minds with truth, no matter how vital and clear, which then lies fallow and does not become the seed-bed and source of changed lives (that is academicism). The purpose is, rather, to reproduce, under God, the state of affairs that Paul described when he wrote to the Romans, 'You wholeheartedly obeyed the form of teaching to which you were entrusted' (Rom. 6:17). The teaching is the testimony, command, and promise of God (J. I. Packer).[1]

There is an old story of a guest preacher moving across the rostrum of a church in which he had never before preached. As he approached the pulpit and began to spread out his Bible and sermon notes, he observed a small card taped in place on the desk top. It read: 'What in the world are you trying to do to these people?'

Good question! It's one that should be asked each time we prepare and preach a sermon. To fail to ask and answer that question is to validate the false assumption that preaching is without real merit and only a tradition to be maintained as a part of public church meetings. I assert, however, that preaching in general is quite purposeful and that individual sermons should each be focused in a purposeful direction.

In terms of the general purpose of preaching, we might well say that preaching is intended to proclaim and explain the Word of God so that the multifaceted truths of Scripture can be understood, embraced, and acted upon in appropriate ways. This assumes, of course, that the Scripture is the authoritative Word of God, that Scriptural truth is relevant to people today, that people are capable of receiving and processing information, that people will either embrace or reject what they've heard, and that a failure to give people the opportunity to respond either behaviorally or attitudinally to proclaimed Scriptural truth results in the short-circuiting of the preaching task. Preaching is intended to assist in the changing of lives.

What is true in a general sense of preaching as a whole is also true, though in more specific ways, of particular sermons. Effective sermons will have definite purposes for being preached. The preacher will have a clear idea of both the subject being preached and the purpose in preaching it. These two concepts are not the same and the preacher who formulates and articulates only the sermon subject will probably be dealing with vagaries as far as 'what he is trying to do to these people' is concerned.

Determining a sermon's subject remains only half-done when the preacher has discerned what the biblical writer was saying. We do not fully understand the subject until we have also determined its reason or cause. Consideration of a message's theme ultimately forces us to ask, 'Why are these concerns addressed? What caused this account, these facts, or the recording of these ideas? What was the intent of the author? For what purpose did the Holy Spirit include these words in Scripture?'

Until we have determined a passage's purpose, we should not think we are ready to preach its truths. Yet, as obvious as this advice is, it is frequently neglected. Preachers often think they are ready to preach when they see a subject in a passage, though they have not yet determined the text's purpose.[2]

Every biblical text has some underlying purpose for its inclusion in Scripture. As a whole, the Bible affirms that 'All Scripture is God-breathed and is useful for teaching, rebuking, correcting and training in righteousness, so that the man of God may be thoroughly equipped for every good work' (2 Tim 3:16-17). What is true of the whole is true of each part that constitutes the whole. Every passage in Scripture – yes, every preaching text! – is there for some specific purpose or purposes. Part of the preachers exegetical task is to determine what that purpose is and to subsequently shape the sermon in such a way that the purpose can be effectuated in the life of the listener.

Preachers need to take their cue from educators at this point. School teachers have long known the value of including learning objectives in lesson plans. For example, a fourth grade teacher giving instructions in mathematics might teach a lesson on fractions in which the stated learning objective is: 'Each student will learn how to reduce fractions using the multiplication and division factors already known.' In the area of fourth grade science, appropriate learning objectives might be: 'Students will discover how structures added to a beach can change the shape of that beach;' or, 'Students will learn how air temperature causes changes in air pressure and wind.'

These examples are obvious in terms of specificity and clarity. Nothing is left to chance. The teacher knows exactly what it is that needs to be accomplished in the respective lessons and the success or failure of each lesson can be readily measured.

While it must be acknowledged that preaching, unlike classroom instruction, involves a spiritual dynamic that will ultimately determine the success of a sermon in individual lives, we should not assume, therefore, that dealing with the issue of sermon purpose is unnecessary. The letters of Paul were written to address certain needs and accomplish certain purposes. The prophets of old likewise spoke to certain needs with specific intended results in mind. Indeed, this is true in principle of each part of Scripture including the teachings of Jesus. Again, one of the tasks of the preacher is to discover the intended purpose of a text and then to properly reflect on that purpose and restate it for today's listener.

I believe that every sermon should have a focused proposition statement (central idea, big idea, thesis statement) that clearly expresses what a given sermon is about thematically. Every sermon should also have a focused purpose statement. While the former will be stated and emphasized to the congregation, the latter probably will not. Sometimes the two statements will be somewhat similar. Regardless, the preacher must have no doubt as to what this particular sermon is meant to accomplish. The best way to assure clarity on this is to actually write out the statement and include it with the outline or manuscript so that your purpose in preaching this particular sermon is never far from your thinking and praying.

For example, a sermon on 'The New Birth' from John 3 might employ a propositional statement that says: 'It is necessary to experience a second birth in order to be part of God's kingdom.' The purpose statement for the sermon might be worded: 'This sermon is intended to inform each listener of the absolute need of spiritual conversion and to motivate them to respond affirmatively if they haven't done so previously.' In this instance, the two statements are clearly related and somewhat similar. On the other hand, a sermon that focuses on teaching about one or more of God's attributes may have as its purpose: 'To bring about a sense of worship and awe regarding the great God we serve.' In this instance the proposition might not allude to worship or awe but might be fairly didactic in its statement. A very helpful discussion, including examples, of the relationship between a text's central idea, the sermon's proposition, and the sermon's purpose statement is found in *Power in the Pulpit* by Vines and Shaddix.[3]

How many broad purposes might be possible in Christian preaching? The quotation from J. I. Packer at the beginning of this chapter mentions eleven (repentance, faith, obedience, love, effort, hope, fear, zeal, joy, praise, and prayer).

Lloyd Perry, in his *Manual for Biblical Preaching*, lists nine aims as examples of preaching purposes:

1. To heal the broken hearted
2. To make man conscious of God's presence
3. To develop social consciousness
4. To make man aware of his soul
5. To show man his spiritual need

6. To encourage the expression of Christian grace toward others
7. To promote communion with the Father, Son and Holy Spirit
8. To overthrow error
9. To explain biblical truths[4]

Baumann suggests 'four distinct purposes for contemporary preaching'.

1. Redemption
2. Teaching
3. Personal healing
4. Social healing[5]

The first of these, Baumann states, is aimed at unbelievers while the other three are pointed toward believers.

In an earlier work, I alluded to seven possible purposes of given sermons. Again this list is meant to be suggestive rather than comprehensive.

1. To inspire
2. To move toward deeper consecration
3. To evangelize
4. To motivate to action
5. To bring comfort
6. To instruct
7. To bring warning[6]

A word of caution: we must not settle on a term or phrase such as those above to represent our sermon objective. These give us a general category but it is necessary to get totally specific in our statement of what we want this specific sermon to bring about on this particular occasion.

For the purpose of this present volume, we will consider the necessity of maintaining a balance in preaching purpose under two general headings: preach evangelistically and edificationally; and, preach pastorally and prophetically. The first category addresses desired outcomes in view of the two broad categories of listeners, those who are 'in Christ' and those who are not. The second speaks of the tone of the sermon in relation to some desired outcomes. There is doubtless some overlap in these suggested distinctions, but the following discussion hopefully will help clarify our thinking.

Preach both evangelisically and edificationally

The great commission given by Jesus in Matthew 28:18-20, mentions two great emphases in the work of making disciples: evangelism ('baptizing them') and edification ('teaching them to obey everything I have commanded you'). It appears, therefore, that the basic purposes of preaching, in terms of desired outcomes, are bringing people to faith in Christ and building them up toward spiritual maturity.

It has been argued by some that in terms of New Testament word usage, only evangelism is actually *preaching*. This is based on the alleged New Testament usage of the word *kerugma* and its verb form *kerussō*, 'to proclaim or herald forth.' This view was popularized by the British scholar C. H. Dodd in his noteworthy volume, *Apostolic Preaching and Its Development.*[7] It was the position of Dodd that the New Testament presents a sharp contrast between preaching and teaching, that is, between *kerugma* and *didache*. The former, according to Dodd, always has to do with the proclamation of the gospel – the preaching of the saving work of Christ and an appeal to the hearer to respond appropriately. *Didache*, on the other hand, is the instruction of the early church regarding Christian doctrine and ethics.

A study of some pertinent texts in the New Testament, however, shows that Dodd's conclusions are not entirely accurate. While it is true that *kerussō* is often – even usually, in fact – used in conjunction with the preaching of the salvation message, this is not always the case. Sometimes the term is used to describe a message that is something other than the gospel of Christ. For example, while the message of John the Baptist can be considered as preliminary to the person and work of Christ, it is not the gospel *per se*. Yet Luke records that John 'went into all the country around the Jordan, *preaching* a baptism of repentance for the forgiveness of sins' (Luke 3:3, italics mine). In his address to Cornelius' household, Peter uses the same term to describe John's preaching, though he seems to differentiate between it and the gospel of Jesus.

> Then Peter began to speak: 'I now realize how true it is that God does not show favoritism but accepts men from every nation who fear him and do what is right. You know the message God sent to the people of Israel, telling the good news of peace through Jesus Christ, who is Lord of all. You know what has happened throughout Judea, beginning in Galilee after the baptism that John *preached* – how God anointed Jesus of Nazareth with the Holy Spirit and power, and how he went around doing good and healing all who were under the power of the devil, because God was with him. We are witnesses of everything he did in the country of the Jews and in Jerusalem. They killed him by hanging him on a tree, but God raised him from the dead on the third day and caused him to be seen' (Acts 10:34-40, italics mine).

The term is also used in reference to concepts that are distinctly Jewish rather than Christian. In his summation remarks at the Jerusalem council, when the relationship between law and gospel was being clarified, James says:

> It is my judgment, therefore, that we should not make it difficult for the Gentiles who are turning to God. Instead we should write to them, telling them to abstain from food polluted by idols, from sexual immorality, from the meat of strangled animals and from blood. For Moses *has been preached* in every city from the earliest times and is read in the synagogues on every Sabbath (Acts 15:19-21, italics mine).

Paul uses it to refer to the rite of circumcision: 'Brothers, if I am still *preaching* circumcision, why am I still being persecuted? In that case the offense of the cross has been abolished' (Gal 5:11, italics mine).

The use of *kerussō* in reference to concepts that are broader than the gospel is seen in Scripture as well. In Romans, Paul asks, 'You who preach against stealing, do you steal?' (Rom 2:21). In his second pastoral letter to Timothy, Paul instructs the young pastor:

> In the presence of God and of Christ Jesus, who will judge the living and the dead, and in view of his appearing and his kingdom, I give you this charge: *Preach* the Word; be prepared in season and out of season; correct, rebuke and encourage – with great patience and careful instruction. For the time will come when men will not put up with sound doctrine. Instead, to suit their own desires, they will gather around them a great number of teachers to say what their itching ears want to hear (2 Tim 4:1-3, italics mine).

In this latter passage, it is clear that the apostle is referring to far more than the saving works of Christ. He speaks of correction, rebuke, and instruction, terms found in the preceding paragraph where the useful purpose of all Scripture is discussed: 'All Scripture is God-breathed and is useful for teaching, rebuking, correcting and training in righteousness, so that the man of God may be thoroughly equipped for every good work' (2 Tim 3:16-17).

Finally, the word *kerussō* is found to be used interchangeably with the word *didaskō*. In Mark 1:39, for example, it says 'So he traveled throughout Galilee, preaching in their synagogues and driving out demons.' In Matthew, however, the term *didaskō* is also used: 'Jesus went throughout Galilee, teaching in their synagogues, preaching the good news of the kingdom, and healing every disease and sickness among the people' (Matt 4:23). The same kind of statement is found later in Matthew as well: 'Jesus went through all the towns and villages, teaching in their synagogues, preaching the good news of the kingdom and healing every disease and sickness' (Matt 9:35). It is doubtful that Jesus presented two different messages. Rather, he brought one message that could rightly be described as teaching *and* preaching. Two different words are utilized in good Hebraic style (synonymous parallelism) to compliment each other and present a fuller meaning.

The same sort of expression is used of Paul's ministry in Rome: 'Boldly and without hindrance he preached the kingdom of God and taught about the Lord Jesus Christ' (Acts 28:31). Again, there was only one message, the presentation of which could rightly be described as both preaching and teaching.

The point I am making is this: the use of the term 'preaching' should not be limited to evangelism alone. The term is much more comprehensive than this. *Kerusso* is an important New Testament word but it is not the only term used for either evangelism or preaching.[8] Having said this, I must immediately emphasize that a balanced pulpit ministry will include evangelistic preaching as well as edificational preaching.

Preach Evangelistically

What is evangelistic preaching? How can it be done well? What emphasis should it have in a pastor's preaching agenda? Let's deal with these questions one at a time.

Understanding Evangelistic Preaching

What is evangelistic preaching? Before defining and explaining evangelistic preaching, let me first state what it is not. This is necessary because the term is used frequently, but not always accurately. There are some who claim to be evangelistic in their preaching when an examination of their sermons would reveal otherwise.

I've just concluded reading a sermon in a book dealing with evangelistic preaching, a good book (it will remain unidentified) with many solid ideas regarding the nature and process of preaching evangelistically. The preacher whose sermon I read is widely known as an effective preacher and I would concur eagerly. This particular sermon is astute and hard hitting. It clearly reflects the intent of the chosen text and beautifully bridges the gap from the ancient text to the contemporary listener (or reader). It's a sermon I wish I had preached! It is not an evangelistic sermon, however, but one that calls people to live better, rightly understanding what it is that God expects of his people. There is no mention of the saving work of Christ or any appeal to respond to him in faith. At best, it might be considered 'pre-evangelistic', but even this is doubtful.

Evangelistic sermons are not simply sermons about our walk with God and our desire to live in a way that pleases him. While this is part of evangelism, every sermon deals with these kinds of truths.

Nor are concepts like incarnational preaching or confessional preaching the same as evangelistic preaching, though these types of preaching may well include elements helpful for evangelistic purposes. Evangelistic preaching is not preaching that simply tells the stories of persons apart from the Faith who have gotten their lives straightened out and are now living for Christ. Such stories may well play an important role in pulpit evangelism but do not in themselves necessarily present the *evangel*. Evangelistic preaching is not preaching that attempts to motivate people to affiliate with the local church. It is not preaching about the need to evangelize, of the necessity of church members to share their faith with those apart from Christ. Again, such preaching might have an evangelistic element involved, but this is not direct evangelism aimed at the present hearers.

What, then, is evangelistic preaching? It is preaching based on the unique nature of the *evangel*, the gospel. It has been traditional to ascribe the term 'evangelists' to the writers of the four Gospels. While the Gospels are biographical, in a sense, they are less than biography while being more. They are less because, unlike usual biographical writing, they give relatively little information about the person of Jesus. They skip over huge parts of his life and there is more unsaid than said. They are more than normal biography, however, because they present carefully chosen vignettes from the life of Christ in order to make a theological statement. That statement is the essence of the gospel. John's Gospel illustrates this clearly. This writer chooses a limited number of sign-miracles performed by Jesus as well as some selected discourses. He describes what he has done and why he did it: 'Jesus did many other miraculous signs in the presence of his disciples, which are not recorded in this book. But these are written that you may believe that Jesus is the Christ, the Son of God, and that by believing you may have life in his name' (John 20:30-31). John's overarching purpose was to explain the identity of Jesus, the purpose of his coming into the world, his atoning work on the cross and his subsequent resurrection, and then to call people to the Savior. This is the core of evangelism.

Evangelistic preaching is preaching in which Christ, the Son of God and Savior of the World, is presented as the solution to man's spiritual separation from God because of sin, and people are encouraged to place their trust in him for their own personal salvation. When people respond in faith to Christ, including confession and repentance, they are forgiven of their sin, regenerated by the Holy Spirit, adopted into God's family, and become a part of Christ's body, the church. This, of course, is only a summary of all that is involved in the presentation and appropriation of the gospel, but it is a starting point if one is to preach evangelistic sermons. Preaching that neglects the essentials and essence of the *evangel* cannot rightly be called evangelistic preaching.

Effective Evangelistic Preaching

How can evangelistic preaching be done well? This is a challenging question, especially for those who tend to emphasize a so-called teaching approach in the pulpit or for those who major in what Wayne McDill calls 'do-better preaching'.[9] Six suggestions follow which should be of help to the preacher who may not feel entirely proficient in the task of preaching evangelistic sermons.

Suggestion One. Be very intentional about your evangelistic preaching endeavors. Do not be content with attaching a few 'gospel remarks' to a sermon on tithing, for example, and congratulating yourself on having preached evangelistically. Is this really the case? When this sort of thing is done, it is doubtful that either the concept of tithing or an adequate explanation of the gospel has been presented. Sermons are fortunate to accomplish one aim, let alone two or more. Sermons that aim at multiple targets are quite likely to hit nothing!

Evangelism is a crucial part of the church's ministry and in most churches it is appropriate to do evangelism through the pulpit. The effective preacher will devote some of the preaching schedule exclusively to the presentation of the message of the gospel. This will help assure that evangelism, including pulpit evangelism, retains a high significance in the overall ministry of the church. It will also help assure that when pulpit evangelism is done, it is done in a thorough way that presents the gospel adequately.

Suggestion Two. Involve the congregation in the excitement of reaching people for Christ. Pulpit evangelism will fail unless unbelievers are present when such preaching is done. In larger churches this may not be a problem in that sheer numbers will result in the unsaved being in attendance on a weekly basis. The preacher can assume that some who need Christ will be present whenever the gospel of salvation is preached. When the evangelistic seed is sown and people respond and come to Christ, a climate of excitement and thanksgiving will prevail and folks will be encouraged to continue inviting folks who need to know Christ.

In small churches, however, there may be many services when unbelievers are not present. In such a situation, the pastor will need to plan special occasions when the gospel will be presented and then involve his people in the gathering of people to hear it. This, of course, takes advance planning and strategizing. A brief announcement from the pulpit or in the bulletin will not suffice. The pastor may need to see that his people are suitably trained to build relationships with unbelievers and engage in friendship evangelism. Church members may need to be motivated toward outreach and a brief series of messages prior to the special evangelistic occasion might be useful to emphasize the condition of the lost and the need and means to reach them. It may be helpful also to present a workshop or training sessions so that church members are equipped to actually lead a person to Christ or deal with other spiritual issues in the lives of seekers. All of these things and more might help to create the kind of evangelistic environment necessary to have a continuing effective outreach.

Suggestion Three. This relates to the matter of the foundation of evangelistic sermons. It is a plea to strive toward messages that are text-driven. Perhaps I'm reflecting unduly on the kind of evangelistic preaching I've been exposed to in my particular circles, but I'm concerned that most efforts heard have been biblically shallow.

There is often a poorly conceived approach taken that reminds me of hummingbirds. Preachers flit from verse to verse and book to book without alighting long enough to experience the sweet nectar of any one of them. Please note that I'm opposed neither to topical preaching nor to using a topical approach to present the gospel. I am strongly opposed, however, to the misuse of the topical method as is the case when the various texts used are not sufficiently dealt with to assure that the message is firmly rooted in Scripture.

In this regard, I would encourage the frequent use of the so-called expository method. This term is used with various understandings by different preachers and these variations will be discussed in Chapter 5. For our purpose here, I'm referring to exposition in the sense of basing the sermon on one text, possibly a paragraph or so in length, and then allowing that text to serve as the source of the sermon's main points and supporting material. This is not to say that other Scriptures are off limits. Another passage or two might be used to augment the argument being made or to illustrate what the primary text is saying. But the preacher will never stray from the focus of the main passage. This will assure that this sermon, like every biblical sermon, will be driven by a desire to help the listener comprehend and respond to 'thus says the Lord'.

Do not be confused regarding preaching method and message. Some might differentiate between expository preaching and evangelistic preaching, but these are not mutually exclusive terms. Exposition refers to how Scripture is handled in a particular sermon, while evangelism is one purpose of preaching. An expository sermon might very well be evangelistic in its intent.

Biblical preaching at its best is just as necessary for the effective evangelism of the lost as it is for the edification of believers. In a passage that reiterates the gospel and the need to proclaim it, Paul reminds us, 'So then faith comes by hearing, and hearing by the word of God' (Rom 10:17, NKJV). Likewise, James ascribes saving power to God's word: 'Therefore, get rid of all moral filth and the evil that is so prevalent and humbly accept the word planted in you, which can save you' (Jas 1:21-22).

It is interesting to note that in the Book of Acts, as the early apostles initiated evangelistic efforts, there are at least twenty-three instances in which the presentation of the gospel is said to be the preaching of 'the word of the Lord' or 'the word of God'. Effective Christian evangelism does not occur apart from the presentation of God's word.

As he reflects back on his evangelistic endeavors, Paul often recalls that it was the word of God – inseparable from the gospel – that was presented, resulting in people becoming believers. Three examples will suffice. To the Colossians Paul wrote:

> We always thank God, the Father of our Lord Jesus Christ, when we pray for you, because we have heard of your faith in Christ Jesus and of the love you have for all the saints – the faith and love that spring from the hope that is stored up for you in heaven and that you have already heard about in the word of truth, the gospel that has come to you. All over the world this gospel is bearing fruit and growing, just as it has been doing among you since the day you heard it and understood God's grace in all its truth (Col 1:3-6).

And to the Ephesians:

> And you also were included in Christ when you heard the word of truth, the gospel of your salvation. Having believed, you were marked in him with a seal, the promised Holy Spirit. . . (Eph 1:13)

And finally, Paul reminded the Thessalonians:

> ... we speak as men approved by God to be entrusted with the gospel. We are not trying to please men but God, who tests our hearts . . . And we also thank God continually because, when you received the word of God, which you heard from us, you accepted it not as the word of men, but as it actually is, the word of God, which is at work in you who believe. (1Thess 2:4, 13)

However and whenever evangelism is done, whether through personal witness or through preaching, the Bible must play the leading role in defining meanings, motivating toward conversion, and establishing converts in the Faith with a sense of assurance. When Scripture is ignored or minimized, it is probable that the gospel seed will fail to take root and produce the kind of harvest that is normative. Even in evangelism, preach the word!

Suggestion Four. Embrace theology enthusiastically in your sermon content. Evangelistic sermons should be theological sermons. Some might protest, 'We don't need to preach doctrine; we just need to preach the gospel.' This kind of statement is pure nonsense!

To preach the gospel means to preach Christ. But, which Christ? Some years ago there was a popular television game show called 'To Tell the Truth'. The show consisted of a moderator, a panel of celebrities, and a series of guest contestants. This latter group consisted of three people each claiming to be the same person. They each introduced themselves with the same phrase, something like, 'My name is Don Hamilton and I teach preaching in a theological seminary.' The moderator then explained that one of these people was the real Don Hamilton. The job of the panel was to ask probing questions of each contestant. The rules permitted two of these contestants to tell untruths, but the contestant who was the actual person had to answer each question truthfully. At the end of the questioning, the moderator had the panel cast and reveal their votes as to who they thought the real person was. Then the moderator would say, 'Will the real Don Hamilton please stand up?' One or two contestants would then pretend to begin standing and then the real person would stand. The object of the game was to fool the panel and collect money for each misplaced vote.

What does this have to do with preaching Christ theologically? Simply this: there are many 'christs' who are being introduced as the real Christ. There is the 'gentle Jesus meek and mild' christ. There is the 'great religious thinker' christ. There is the 'wonderful moral example' christ. There is the 'incredible teacher' christ. There is the 'religious prophet' christ. There is the 'lesser god' christ of the Jehovah's Witnesses. There is the 'metaphysical healer' christ of the Church of Christ, Scientist. There is the 'unfortunate martyr' christ. There is the 'delusional' christ, *vis a vis* Albert Schweitzer in *The Quest of the Historical Jesus*. And the list could go on. Theology is crucial to a seeker's understanding of Christ the Savior, who is the heart of the gospel!

Theology is also crucial in the presentation of various aspects of the gospel such as sin, confession, repentance, faith, forgiveness, regeneration, and eternal life. While church people may profess a good understanding of these terms – this is probably somewhat questionable in many churches – the general unchurched populace is, for the most part, biblically and theologically illiterate. The preacher should never assume that the seeker has an understanding of such concepts that will be sufficient to make an informed decision for Christ.

Does this mean that the potential convert must first become a theologian before becoming a Christian? Not at all. But it does mean that we do a disservice to people when we ask them to respond to the gospel without first informing them sufficiently of what the gospel is. This is like selling a product and having folks sign on the dotted line without knowing what they're buying. This is both unwise and unethical.

Sometimes evangelistic sermons are story-driven rather than text-driven. When this takes place the theological moorings of the gospel are undermined or at least trivialized. This is potentially detrimental to effective evangelism. At best, this kind of presentation might have a role in pre-evangelism. When sermons consist primarily of human interest stories strung together around the theme of changed lives, positive illustrations of the transforming power of the gospel are presented and people may be motivated to experience spiritual change themselves. What is generally lacking, however, is a sufficient explanation of the terms of the gospel from a biblical-theological perspective. Salvation is not based on emulating the experiences of other people but on appropriating the message of the gospel for ourselves. This appropriation includes a basic understanding of what the gospel is. Theology must be embraced by the preacher even in evangelistic preaching.

Suggestion Five. This suggestion relates to general sermon content. The preacher must keep in mind the concerns and needs of the unconverted person who will hear the message. While this will not always be the case, we should usually assume that this person is not a frequent church goer and that he or she has preconceptions of what being a Christian is all about. Some of these may be accurate, but many will be misunderstandings that need to be clarified when possible.

For example, there is the issue of an assumed lifestyle. When I was much younger, I learned a humorous caricature of what being a Christian was all about: 'We don't smoke; we don't chew; we don't go with girls that do!' In the past, I heard (on numerous occasions) well-meaning preachers rail – interestingly, this verb comes from the Latin *ragere*, 'to bray' – against smoking, drinking, gambling and other such behavior. It was strongly implied, if not stated, that either one *becomes* a Christian by giving up these habits, or that every true Christian *will* give up these habits.

The first assertion is legalism pure and simple, the teaching that one becomes a Christian by doing something. Salvation is no longer a free gift but rather a reward for being the right kind of person. This is works-righteousness and it is wrong! The list may have changed in our day, but the teaching has not. It is still present in some so-called evangelistic preaching. The careful gospel preacher will avoid any hint of this false teaching.

The second assertion confuses salvation and sanctification. While we desire to see people put off worldly pursuits and values (whatever they may be) and put on the things of Christ, this will happen as a result of *being and growing in Christ* (sanctification), not for receiving forgiveness (salvation). While conversion sometimes instantly releases a person from particular sins or a certain lifestyle, this is not usually the case. Thus, Paul writes to Colosse:

> Since, then, you have been raised with Christ, set your hearts on things above, where Christ is seated at the right hand of God. Set your minds on things above, not on earthly things. For you died, and your life is now hidden with Christ in God. When Christ, who is your life, appears, then you also will appear with him in glory. Put to death, therefore, whatever belongs to your earthly nature: sexual immorality, impurity, lust, evil desires and greed, which is idolatry.... You used to walk in these ways, in the life you once lived. But now you must rid yourselves of all such things as these: anger, rage, malice, slander, and filthy language from your lips. Do not lie to each other, since you have taken off your old self with its practices and have put on the new self, which is being renewed in knowledge in the image of its Creator (Col 3:1-10).

Our evangelistic preaching must carefully avoid confusion regarding the work of salvation which happens instantaneously by God's grace, and the work of sanctification by his ongoing grace.

Another misconception held by some is that Christians are doomed to dull, funless living. While it is true that some Christians look and act as if they have been baptized by immersion in pickle juice, the fact is that Christ came to give us *abundant* life. In the NIV, Jesus says, 'I have come that they may have life, and have it to the full' (John 10:10). This is why the gospel is *good news*! To be a Christian is to enjoy life to the maximum. Our message should therefore be a positive one presented with a positive demeanor.

At the same time, we must be careful to avoid the false promise of panacea. Becoming a Christian is not a cure-all for all illnesses, evils, or troubles. Christians still live in a fallen world. They are still passengers in hijacked airliners, occupants of blown-up buildings, sufferers with terminal diseases, victims of crime, and subject to fear, loneliness, and depression. Believers do not have perfect lives thrust upon them at the moment of conversion. What they have, however, are the spiritual resources to help them cope with their less-than-perfect world. The evangelist should not ignore this part of the truth of the gospel. This too is *good news*!

Finally, in regard to general content, the evangelistic preacher should avoid Christian jargon. This might vary from church talk like 'chancel,' 'offertory,' and 'dearly beloved' – a single lady in a small church said she blushed every time the preacher said this – to the use of terminology that might be foreign to the potential convert. Terms that are clear to the mature Christian may be entirely new to an unchurched person. Words like 'regeneration,' 'confession,' 'justification,' and 'atonement' should be used sparingly and with ample definition, explanation, and illustration to assure that the message is connecting with the hearer.

Suggestion Six. Effective evangelistic sermons should conclude with specific, clearly stated appeals for decision. This may or may not mean a 'walk the aisle' type of invitation. Whether this kind of invitation is given should depend on the particular setting including a clear-cut plan for dealing with those who, by God's grace, respond.

But whether or not this traditional type of altar call is given, an appeal of some sort must be given to assist the person in the valley of decision to decide for Christ.

Invitations can vary in the way people are asked to indicate their desire to make a decision for Christ. A prayer to receive Christ can be led line-by-line with responders praying along silently. Or, such a prayer can be led with everyone in attendance praying aloud as long as an explanation is given regarding the propriety and meaning of everyone, Christians included, praying this prayer. People who pray this prayer with the intention of receiving Christ may then be invited to meet with the pastor or appropriate counselors for further instruction. Or, those who respond in faith to the gospel may be invited to indicate this decision on their attendance card. This necessitates the practice of having each person present fill out a card and then having all the cards collected at the end of the service. Such cards can also be used to indicate other needs or prayer requests in addition to indicating attendance, so they have multiple purposes.

An invitation may also be given in which the pastor asks seekers to meet in an adjacent room immediately following the service and that trained counselors of both genders will be happy to meet briefly with them there. Such a room can be prepared with seating arranged in pairs and appropriate counseling materials in place.

The key to an effective invitation is to give sincere seekers the opportunity to embrace the gospel without manipulation or coercion, treating all persons with respect while at the same time urging them to decide for Christ and experience salvation. To preach the gospel without giving the opportunity to respond is to short-circuit the process.

The appeal to make a decision for Christ does not usurp the role of the Holy Spirit in convicting, extending grace, or bringing about the new birth. No one comes to the Savior unless the Spirit draws him or her. This is true, but it is also true that when Christ called someone in the Gospels, he always did so publicly. He stated, 'Whoever acknowledges me before men, I will also acknowledge him before my Father in heaven' (Matt 10:32).

It is not a good idea, in my judgment, to offer 'mixed' invitations. It is customary in some circles to give a threefold or even fourfold invitation at the conclusion of every sermon. People are invited to become a Christian, be baptized, rededicate their life, or join the church all in the same 'walk the aisle' (generally) type of invitation. While these are all worthy decisions to invite people to make, it is my fear and even conviction that this is not a good idea. When the gospel has been preached and evangelism has taken place, the emphasis in whatever kind of invitation is given must focus on that, at least initially. If, after a suitable time, the preacher opens the invitation to include other appropriate responses, fine.

Finally, avoid a lack of clarity when asking people to respond to an evangelistic invitation. To simply say 'whatever decision you need to make for Christ, now is the time to do it,' may be confusing to those contemplating the meaning and urgency of the gospel. A greater effectiveness can be gained when the person extending the invitation is specific and focused.[10]

The Place of Evangelistic Preaching in the Local Church
Having discussed briefly what is meant by evangelistic preaching and having looked at some suggestions on how to do it well, we turn our attention to the emphasis pulpit evangelism should be given in relation to the pastor's overall preaching schedule. This is not a simple matter for each church is somewhat unique in the way evangelism is done. It is assumed that the normal church will be an evangelistic church – one that reaches out to the lost both near and far. If this is not true in a particular church, then the issue is not the frequency of evangelistic preaching but rather the essential nature and task of the church.

A church must do evangelism! Whether or not it is done primarily through the pulpit is another matter. In a sense, Sangster overstates the case when he says, 'Unquestionably, the great end of Christian preaching is to win men and women to a whole-souled committal to Christ and to their spiritual upbuilding in him. Where the evangelical appeal is rarely or never sounded, an awful incompleteness hangs over the whole work.'[11] I appreciate the sentiment but would prefer substituting the word 'ministry' for 'preaching' because preaching is only one way to fulfill the evangelistic mandate given by Jesus. There are other important methods as well. I agree with the statement of George Sweazey in his excellent book, *Preaching the Good News*:

> The best occasion for evangelism is not a church service, it is a private conversation, but each can help the other. A sermon can tell more about Christian truth and life than can be readily told in private talk. A sermon can make a more extended appeal for faith. Talk about what Christ can do for life has its best setting in the surroundings of the daily life, but a worshipping congregation also offers some powerful advantages. Cold hearts are warmed by the glow that is kindled in a praying, singing fellowship; there the reality of Christian love and the presence of the Holy Spirit may be strongly felt. Faith, which in solitude may have seemed eccentric and unconvincing in such a company, may seem natural and right and greatly to be desired.[12]

Evangelism done in the 'gathered church' should not be thought to be distinct from that which is done in the 'scattered church'. That which is done in the auditorium and classroom is complimentary to what is done in the community, and *vice versa*. The local church must cultivate an evangelistic mentality on all fronts so that its constituents are constantly concerned with winning the unsaved to Christ and building them up in the Faith.

Let's return to the question of a desired frequency for evangelistic preaching. Is there some kind of formula to follow? I think not. Instead, the pastor must look at the overall effectiveness of the church's evangelistic outreach and ask, 'How can pulpit evangelism augment what is already taking place?' If outreach is successfully being carried out beyond the walls of the church, then evangelistic preaching inside may not need to be too frequent. If, on the other hand, the harvest outside is meager, then at least two things will probably need to occur: (1) the church membership will need to be helped and motivated to 'do the work of ministry' (Eph 4:12) in the area of evangelism; and (2) the pulpit probably will need to be utilized at frequent intervals to assist the laity as they are growing in their ability to do personal evangelism.

In either scenario above, the frequency of focused evangelistic preaching will vary from place to place depending on specific circumstances. The leadership of the church needs to collectively seek God's wisdom about this. He is more concerned about the lost than are we and we need to come to know his heart in this matter.

Not only is frequency an issue, so is setting. Should pulpit evangelism be done during Sunday morning services, Sunday evening services, or perhaps during other times set aside for outreach meetings?

There was a time when many churches utilized Sunday evening services for evangelistic outreach. This is rarely the case today. Many churches, including growing churches, no longer have Sunday evening services but devote that time to training, benevolence, and outreach ministries. And the fact remains that in churches that have such a service, attendance is almost always less – usually considerably less – than attendance at a morning service. Furthermore, the likelihood of unbelievers attending Sunday evening services in comparison to the likelihood of their attendance at morning services is generally very small. There may be some exceptions to this such as a concert or children's program, but this is usually the case. Therefore, as far as regular Sunday services are concerned, Sunday morning is by far the best time to preach evangelistically.

In certain sub-cultures in America, special week-night services are still held for evangelism purposes. Sometimes called 'revivals', the frequency of such meetings seems to be diminishing rapidly as Americans continue to work longer work-weeks on average. As recently as two or three decades ago, many churches held one-week revivals or evangelism crusades once or twice a year. Gradually, these were reduced to four- or five-day meetings and in many places have been discontinued altogether. Some see this as a failure on the part of the church to maintain evangelistic vigor. I do not. How the church does evangelism will vary from generation to generation. The method is not the issue. Doing it is.

Special days in the church calendar provide very natural settings to preach evangelistically because unbelievers may well be present.

I think especially of Christmas and Easter. These are Christian holy days, yet they are also observed by numerous unbelievers. People who have little relationship with a church and no personal grasp of the significance of these days will often attend church services at these times of the year because it is a socially acceptable thing to do. This is a wonderful opportunity for the congregation and pastor to welcome them warmly (no snide remarks about C-E Christians, please) and share with them the real meaning of these very special days. Actually, they expect to hear about this and are exceptionally open to the presentation of the gospel at these times. If it is done in a winsome, non-threatening way, bridges are built for further opportunities for gospel presentations.

A different kind of special occasion might be a baptismal service to which unsaved family members and friends are invited. Many in our culture view such an event as an important 'life passage' whether or not they embrace the meaning of baptism. Such a setting gives the opportunity to speak of the meaning of baptism in an evangelistic way as those participating give testimonies of the spiritual work it signifies.

The church calendar will doubtless offer other opportunities to make an effort to reach out to the unconverted with evangelism or pre-evangelism efforts. These may be concerts, children's programs, men's or women's programs, or even public forums on current issues. In regard to the latter, for example, a church might sponsor a public forum on the teachings of Islam. An expert in the field could be invited to make a presentation and material could be included comparing and contrasting Islam and biblical Christianity. The creative church, driven by a passion to see people brought to Christ, can take advantage of many such opportunities for evangelistic outreach. Preaching will play an important role in many of them.

Finally, it should be recognized that the ordinary activities and preaching ministry of the church will sometimes produce converts when least expected. I recall the conversion of a young father and Ph.D. candidate in the first church I served as pastor. His wife had become a Christian through a small group Bible study for ladies. He remained skeptical but began attending services with his wife and small son. After several months of observing what the church was all about, including attending a Communion service, he gave his life to Christ. This was not in response to an evangelistic sermon, though he heard the gospel on many occasions. It seems his conversion was motivated primarily by simply seeing the church be the church.

Ken Hemphill tells the story of another such a 'surprise' conversion.

> One Sunday morning I preached a message on commitment to service. I extended the invitation and the first person down the aisle was my next door neighbor. His wife had been led to Christ some months earlier by one of our visitation teams. He had listened to the gospel that evening but did not respond. He did, however, begin attending church with his family. After he made his public commitment that day he remarked to me about why he came on that particular Sunday. He told me that he had heard the gospel on several occasions and knew how to be saved, but he had never seen the real point of salvation until I preached on total commitment.[13]

These kinds of experiences take place countless times in the lives of vibrant churches in which the living Christ is exalted. The church today must conscientiously reflect the early church in this regard: 'Day after day, in the temple courts and from house to house, they never stopped teaching and proclaiming the good news that Jesus is the Christ' (Acts 5:42).

The pulpit is not the only place for evangelism to take place, nor is it the chief place. But it is a proper place. As we seek to see preaching in terms of biblical balance, we must certainly include the role of preaching evangelistically as mandatory rather than optional.

Preach Edificationally

The Apostle Paul engaged in an emotional encounter when he met with the Ephesian church leaders for the last time. He had earlier invested three years of his life – more time than at any other church plant – bringing these people and others to Christ, helping them toward Christian maturity, and establishing a strong local church.

Now he was headed to Jerusalem, facing uncertain peril. The danger ahead, however, was not as disconcerting as his farewell to this group of men whom he loved dearly. He reminds them of his faithful ministry among them in which he labored 'night and day with tears' (Acts 20:31). He gives them warning about the potential spiritual battles ahead, and then he offers encouragement and instruction as to how to remain both vigilant and victorious: "Now I commit you to God and to the word of his grace, which can build you up and give you an inheritance among all those who are sanctified' (32).

Paul understood that it is the Word of God that enables people to serve Christ effectively. It is the 'word of his grace' that builds us up. Paul's ministry of the Word at Ephesus had been both evangelistic and edificational (see Acts 19). This is the same model that we must pursue in our pulpit ministries today, but this is sometimes easier said than done. The challenge is to preach to the needs of the converted and to reach out to the unconverted at the same time.

Edificational preaching, like evangelistic preaching, must be Christ-centered. 'We proclaim him, admonishing and teaching everyone with all wisdom, so that we may present everyone perfect in Christ' (Col 1:28). The objective, however, is different. In evangelism, we introduce people to the Savior and, through God's grace, we see them come to know God's forgiveness and to experience spiritual regeneration, the new birth. This is the beginning of the Christian life. It is an absolute necessity for everyone who would be a part of God's family. It is not the end of the story, though, but only the beginning.

The Need of Edification

I attended high school with a fellow named Nick. He was a great guy and everyone liked him. In fact, he was elected president of the freshman class and continued to have a positive influence on the school's student body throughout our four years of high school. But Nick was genetically different from others. He was what we called a 'midget' in those days. More properly, he was a dwarf. This was not by his choosing. He had no control over it nor did his parents, once he was conceived. His genetic condition resulted in what a dictionary might call 'a pathological condition of arrested physical growth.' Nick appeared to be 'normal' in every way except in terms of physical stature.

I have often thought of Nick as I've observed what happens to many Christians following their conversions. They appear to be 'normal' in many ways. They do certain Christian things such as attend and support their churches. Yet they remain shallow in their Christian experience. They fail to comprehend and live by the wonderful teaching of Scripture. They are like children who never pass much beyond childhood. They seem to be affected by 'a condition of arrested spiritual growth'. They remain 'spiritual dwarfs' throughout their lives and, as a result, their Christian experiences are minimally rewarding to them personally and minimally effective in influencing others toward the things of Christ.

A handful of years after his emotional departure from the Ephesian elders, Paul finds himself in prison, probably in Rome. He writes a letter to believers in the area of the Lycus Valley in the province of Asia. What we know today as the Ephesian epistle was possibly a circular letter to several churches in this region – the specific address 'in Ephesus' is missing from some important manuscripts. Nevertheless, one of these would have been the church in Ephesus, the largest and leading city in the entire area. This letter is perhaps the loftiest, most comprehensive of Paul's letters. He writes in exalted tones of God's sovereign role in bringing humanity together through the person of Jesus Christ. At the same time, the letter is so very practical as he writes of Christian living in the midst of the spiritual battles in which believers are engaged.

One of the subjects Paul discusses is spiritual maturity. He speaks of it as the goal of every believer in this lifetime. The process begins in the responsible ministry of church leaders and continues to be pursued through the ministry of all of the members of the Body to one another. Speaking of the risen and exalted Christ, Paul says:

> It was he who gave some to be apostles, some to be prophets, some to be evangelists, and some to be pastors and teachers, to prepare God's people for works of service, so that the body of

Christ may be built up until we all reach unity in the faith and in the knowledge of the Son of God and become mature, attaining to the whole measure of the fullness of Christ. Then we will no longer be infants, tossed back and forth by the waves, and blown here and there by every wind of teaching and by the cunning and craftiness of men in their deceitful scheming. Instead, speaking the truth in love, we will in all things grow up into him who is the Head, that is, Christ. From him the whole body, joined and held together by every supporting ligament, grows and builds itself up in love, as each part does its work (Eph 4:11-16).

The Means of Edification

It should first be noted that the common task of the church leaders discussed in this text is that of the proclamation of the Word of God. The New Testament prophets and apostles conveyed the Word. Sometimes this message was temporary, for the moment. At other times their messages became part of the New Testament Scriptures. Evangelists were those who were gifted primarily in the declaration of the gospel to the unconverted. Sometimes the apostles did evangelistic work, but there were others who apparently were known for their special calling to this task. Then there were the 'pastors and teachers', most likely, in view of the language structure of this text, one group of persons. Like these other persons gifted for leadership in the church, pastor-teachers too were charged with the responsibility of communicating the Word.

The Short-range Purpose of Edification

Note that collectively, the responsibility of these leaders was to 'prepare God's people for works of service' (4:12). There are two important concepts in this part of the verse. The first suggests what it is that should be happening in the lives of Christians as they are taught the Word. The NIV says, 'to prepare God's people.' The King James Version translates it, 'for the perfecting of the saints.' Some translations use the term *equip*: 'for the equipping of the saints' (NASB). The term in question is the Greek word *katartismon*. This very visual term is the basis of our English word, artisan. It refers to the process of shaping something for a purpose, to complete something thoroughly, to repair or adjust. Its various renderings in the KJV include frame (1), mend (2), make perfect (2), perfect (2), prepare (1), and restore (1). In Hebrews 11:3, it refers to the *framing* of the world. In Matthew 4:21, it is used of *mending* nets. In Hebrews 10:5, it refers to the *preparing* of Christ's incarnate body. In Galatians 6:1, the term is used of *restoring* a brother who has sinned. Church leaders are to do the work of artisans as they 'shape up' believers. They are 'preparing' them for an important role in the church and in the world.

What is this role? Believers are to be 'shaped up to do ministry'. The NIV says, 'for works of service.' The KJV says, 'for the work of the ministry.' The NASB uses the phrase, 'for the work of service.' The older American Standard Version says, 'unto the work of ministering.' The meaning should be obvious. While the traditional church has neatly distinguished between the clergy and the laity, between ministers and lay-people, this verse says that it is the body of believers as a whole who should be doing ministry! The word used is *diakonia*. This word, along with its cognates, is used more often than any other in the New Testament to refer to Christian ministry, literally dozens of times. To assign it only to a specific group of 'deacons' in a church's organizational structure is to overlook clear biblical teaching. All believers are to be doing ministry and they are equipped to do it through the perpetual influence of the Word of God that teaches and motivates.

The Long-range Purpose of Edification

The purpose of this process begins to be explained in the last part of Ephesians 4:12 and continues through verse 13: '...so that the body of Christ may be built up until we all reach unity in the faith and in the knowledge of the Son of God and become mature, attaining to the whole measure of the fullness of Christ.' Paul says that the Body of Christ must be 'built up'. This is edification. In fact, the KJV says, 'for the edifying of the body of Christ.'

One of the images of the Church used in the New Testament is that of a building, or even a temple. Peter, for example, uses this picture: 'As you come to him, the living Stone – rejected by men but chosen by God and precious to him – you also, like living stones, are being built into a spiritual house to be a holy priesthood, offering spiritual sacrifices acceptable to God through Jesus Christ' (1 Pet 2:4-5).

In the Ephesian verse, Paul seems to be mixing his metaphors somewhat as he uses two images, body and building. The Greek term is *oikodomeō*, which is used of building a building either literally or figuratively. To 'edify' is to construct an edifice. While this term may remind us of a dusty old world cathedral, this is the wrong picture. The Church of Jesus Christ is a spiritual temple being built to his honor and glory. It is to be dynamic, not dust-filled. It is a work-in-progress, and the preaching of the Word has an important role in this construction process.

Some Descriptions of Effective Edification

As the Word of God is allowed to do its work in building up God's people, the result might be summarized as stable maturity. Paul uses some vivid descriptions to drive this point home. Negatively, he says maturity leaves infanthood behind. New born Christians are 'babes in Christ', but they should not stay that way (4:14a). He then describes doctrinal uncertainty as a sailing craft in a stormy sea 'tossed back and forth by the waves, and blown here and there by every wind of teaching and by the cunning and craftiness of men in their deceitful scheming' (4:14b). Positively, he speaks of the maturing church as 'growing up into Christ' (4:15). Reverting to his image of the body of Christ, Paul says that all the parts of the body will be properly related, 'joined and held together by every supporting ligament' (4:16a). Twice he speaks of the *agapē* love that will be present as we are characterized by 'speaking the truth in love' (4:15a) and 'growing and building itself up in love' (4:16b).

These descriptions are just part of the result of a maturing process that takes place when the church does what the church ought to be doing. Only when this is established is Paul free to give the detailed instructions that follow as far as living the Christian life is concerned.

A vital and foundational part of this process is the edificational preaching of the Bible. As emphasized repeatedly, it is the Word that brings spiritual fruit both in terms of evangelism and in terms of edification. Thus, Peter can encourage his readers: 'Therefore, rid yourselves of all malice and all deceit, hypocrisy, envy, and slander of every kind. Like newborn babies, crave pure spiritual milk, so that by it you may grow up in your salvation, now that you have tasted that the Lord is good' (1 Pet 2:1-3). He speaks, of course, of the milk of the Word because it has all of the nutritional ingredients necessary to build healthy, growing Christian lives.

Like evangelistic preaching, edificational preaching must be a regular part of the pastor's preaching agenda. In my judgment, it should be the primary part in terms of ministry to the gathered church. The church gathered is not primarily a soul-saving station, but a station of saved souls. The church is the *ekklesia*, the 'called-out assembly' of those who have been baptized by the Holy Spirit into the body of Christ (1 Cor 12:13). Believers do not need to be evangelized over and over again, though hearing the gospel repeated occasionally can contribute to the edification process. The crucial need of the believer, once the rudiments of the gospel are clearly understood, is to be taught the doctrines and disciplines of the Christian life in such a way that spiritual growth continuously takes place.

Preach Both Pastorally and Prophetically

We have seen two broad categories of sermons related to their desired outcomes. Some sermons seek to evangelize, to bring people to a saving knowledge of Jesus Christ. Other sermons are intended to be edificational, to help people move beyond their initial Christian experience and to become mature believers in matters of knowledge, attitudes, and behavior.

Now we move to a second set of categories under the general heading of sermon purpose: pastoral preaching and prophetic preaching. This couplet relates to the matter of what I call sermon tone and as well as to the matter of sermon content. To be certain, the term 'tone' appears to be a bit vague, yet I believe that some sermons have a pastoral tone while others have a prophetic tone.

Pastoral preaching is warm and embracing, while prophetic preaching is solemn and confrontational. These diverse 'tones' are closely related to the kind of content being presented. Some preacher long ago described his task as 'comforting the afflicted and afflicting the comfortable'. To a large extent, this describes the difference between pastoral and prophetic preaching. Pastoral preaching seeks to contribute to the well-being of the listeners by teaching, guiding, comforting, and encouraging. Prophetic preaching seeks to contribute to the well-being of the listeners by challenging, rebuking, and warning. While these are not mutually exclusive categories, they differ in terms of emphasis.

Preach Pastorally
Pastoral preaching is not about the position of the person who preaches nor is it about the place where a sermon is preached. Rather, it is about the manner and substance of the sermon's presentation. While most preaching takes place in a pastoral context – the preacher being a pastor in a local church – pastoral preaching can occur when this is not the case. It can take place in a college chapel service, in a youth meeting, or by a graveside. It takes place when the preacher exercises the role of a pastor in ministering to needy people.

The concept of 'pastor' is based on the figurative language of Scripture in which people are likened to sheep and those who care for them are called shepherds. A pastor is a shepherd who feeds and cares for the people of God. In terms of church leadership, it should be noted that the terms pastor (*poimen*), elder (*presbuteros*), and bishop/overseer (*episkopos*) are used interchangeably by both Paul and Peter. In Acts 20, the church leaders at Ephesus are called elders, but Paul also speaks of them as overseers and pastors: 'From Miletus, Paul sent to Ephesus for the elders of the church.... Keep watch over yourselves and all the flock of which the Holy Spirit has made you overseers. Be shepherds of the church of God, which he bought with his own blood' (Acts 20:17, 28). In his first letter, we find Peter giving instructions to church leaders: 'To the elders among you, I appeal as a fellow elder, a witness of Christ's sufferings and one who also will share in the glory to be revealed: Be shepherds of God's flock that is under your care, serving as overseers – not because you must, but because you are willing, as God wants you to be; not greedy for money, but eager to serve; not lording it over those entrusted to you, but being examples to the flock' (1 Pet 5:1-3). It is interesting that in the evolution of various church polity structures through the centuries, the term that remains most common for the leader of a local church is pastor. The metaphor of sheep and shepherd seems to be understood universally.

Pastoral preaching is that kind of pulpit ministry in which the pastoral heart recognizes and embraces the needs of the flock, striving to help meet them by God's grace. The pastoral heart cares about the welfare of God's people. It desires to both tend and feed the sheep. Like the shepherd described by Jesus in Luke 15, this person searches out the one sheep who is in trouble, brings deliverance, and rejoices that 'the lost has been found'. Pastoral preaching reflects the loving heart of God, full of compassion and empathy. As we explore this idea further, let's note some special emphases often present in pastoral preaching.

Preaching as Counseling

It was Harry Emerson Fosdick, the noted champion of theological liberalism during the heyday of the modernist-fundamentalist debate, and arguably the best known American preacher of the first half of the twentieth century, who popularized a method of preaching that is variously called 'life-situation preaching', or 'counseling preaching.' In his autobiography, a book that is helpful reading for any pastor regardless of theological persuasion, he says in regard to the development of his preaching method: 'Little by little, however, the vision grew clearer. People come to church on Sunday with every kind of personal difficulty and problem flesh is heir to. A sermon was meant to meet these needs; it should be personal counseling on a group scale.'[14] This statement by Fosdick has been often quoted, being both praised and ridiculed. Perhaps it is an overstatement. Perhaps some sermons should not be thought of as 'personal counseling on a group scale'. In fact, unless one greatly enlarges the meaning of 'personal counseling', the statement is excessive.

Having said this, however, the reader should be aware of the very next statement made by Fosdick, a statement that has obvious merit.

> If one had clairvoyance, one would know the sins and shames, the anxieties and doubts, the griefs and disillusionments that filled the pews, and could by God's grace bring the saving truths of the gospel to bear on them as creatively as though he were speaking to a single person. That was the place to start – with the real problems of the people. That was a sermon's specialty, which made it a sermon, not an essay or a lecture.[15]

While we might be tempted to 'deconstruct' Fosdick's statement as far as the meanings of his terms are concerned, let's avoid this and simply take the statement at face value. It is true that as our listeners attend our services, they bring their 'baggage'. Paul alludes to this in Galatians 6 where he says:

> Brothers, if someone is caught in a sin, you who are spiritual should restore him gently. But watch yourself, or you also may be tempted. Carry each other's burdens, and in this way you will fulfill the law of Christ. If anyone thinks he is something when he is nothing, he deceives himself. Each one should test his own actions. Then he can take pride in himself, without comparing himself to somebody else, for each one should carry his own load (Gal 6:1-5).

At first glance, verses 2 and 5 seem contradictory. A study of the words shows otherwise. The word translated 'burdens' in verse 2 is *baros*, meaning 'weight, a load, or burden.' The term in verse 5 is *phortion*, derived from a word meaning 'an invoice (as part of freight)', and used figuratively of 'a task or service'. In verse 2, Paul is saying that the duty of the church is to help the person who is carrying a burden that is too heavy to bear by oneself. In verse 5, on the other hand, Paul points out the importance of personal responsibility in 'shouldering one's own pack'.

What does this have to do with preaching? Simply this: while believers are to assume personal responsibility in dealing with routine issues, there are sometimes heavier burdens to bear that require the assistance of the Body of Christ. Sometimes this help comes through personal, one-on-one interaction, but at other times it can come through pastoral preaching. The wise preacher knows that many of his hearers are struggling with various life issues. While every sermon may not be 'group therapy', the overall scheme of preaching should include a healthy dose of godly, biblical counseling. Sweazey argues:

> A minister performs the same function in his private counseling and in the pulpit. Each depends on the other. . . .
>
> Every church service should be a healing service. Worship can be medicine. Participation in a fellowship of singing, praying believers, the symbols, the suggestions of health and happiness, can lift people out of their unhealthy states. This meets directly such problems as loneliness, anxiety, a lost sense of God, a colorless daily routine. . . .
>
> A church service is intended to be preventive medicine. It can keep people built up so that healing is not necessary. . . .
>
> It is a minister's incomparable good fortune to have very definite ways by which his sermons can help people with their personal problems.[16]

While I am not entirely comfortable with some of these statements – there seems to be a minimizing of worship as being God-focused – it is true that the overall effect of the gathered church can be therapeutic for those who are hurting. Preaching that helpfully addresses the everyday problems people face reflects the loving heart of God as exemplified in the Great Shepherd who lovingly tends the flock. It is one way in which the pastor can 'fulfill the law of Christ' as commanded by Paul (Gal 6:2).

Preaching as Exhortation

Some years ago, a seminary student and I were engaged in an informal conversation. I inquired about his future plans for ministry, specifically the kind of ministry he thought he would be doing. Among other responses to my question, he said he felt he had the 'gift of exhortation'. As I probed further, I soon discovered he meant that he felt gifted by God to correct people when they get out of line, 'to set people straight' (my words). This is a false understanding of the term that I fear is shared by too many well-meaning Christians, including ministers. I sometimes hover on the brink of cringing when I hear the word used with a questionable bias.

With one exception, the words 'exhort' and 'exhortation,' as found in the KJV, are always based on the Greek word *parakaleō* and its cognates. It literally means "to call a person to the side." It can mean 'to beseech, to entreat, to encourage someone toward a certain course of action or conduct.' In addition to this usage, *parakaleō* is often translated 'comfort' in the KJV (25 times including the cognates). It is translated as 'consolation' some 14 times. Finally, it should be pointed out that this Greek word is closely related to the special name given to the Holy Spirit by the Apostle John, *paraklētos*, the 'comforter, advocate, one called along side to help.'

This look at how these terms are used in the KJV of the New Testament indicates that the term is more 'pastoral' in its tone than 'prophetic'. While the concept of exhortation may include some amount of correction, this is not foundational to the meaning of the term. One dictionary of the English language defines exhort as 'to urge by strong argument, advice, or appeal; to make urgent appeal'.[17] We see, then, that the basic ideas of exhortation is 'to encourage people toward positive action; to comfort and console them.' We see this modeled in the ministry of Paul in Thessalonica: 'For you know that we dealt with each of you as a father deals with his own children, encouraging, comforting and urging you to live lives worthy of God, who calls you into his kingdom and glory' (1 Thess 2:11-12).

Obviously, this concept is related somewhat to the idea of preaching as counseling. But whereas the former category tends to describe sermons which identify certain specific problems for the reason of offering answers and perspective, preaching as exhortation is more about an overall attitude that is communicated. It is the attitude that says, in effect, I know you are struggling but I want to encourage you and urge you to do what God wants you to do.

A very natural place for exhortation to surface in any sermon is in the area of application. We do not preach simply to dispense information. We preach to inform, explain, and apply. The heart of a sermon's content might be said to consist of:

Information: The preacher speaks of a subject needing explored and presents his pertinent knowledge, including biblical knowledge, about this subject.

Explanation: The preacher takes care to make certain that situations, words, and concepts are understood by the hearers. This might include material ranging from definitions to illustrations.

Exhortation: The preacher urges the listeners to respond appropriately to what has been presented.

This exhortation may appear throughout the sermon body and it may (should) also be found in the sermon's conclusion. Such applications should be made with an attitude of urgency, but also with understanding and love.

Preaching as Compassion

I find myself writing this six months to the day after the September 11, 2001 terrorist attack on America took place. I still recoil when I think about the grisly scenes later viewed by people around the world. Our nation was in profound shock. I personally knew no one whose life was lost that day and yet felt that I knew each one. In the days that followed, the certain Word of God was addressed time and time again as we grappled with the profound uncertainty of those terrible events. Pastors preached with compassion to a grieving nation. Their purpose, for the most part, was not to attempt to answer questions concerning the 'why', but to bring hope and assurance that God is still in control even when mankind is unbelievably inhumane.

Some sermons have as their primary purpose the task of bringing encouragement and comfort to those who are mourning. A funeral is one such occasion, but there are others as well. Sometimes events occur in the experiences of our listeners when grieving takes place, whether or not the death of a loved one has occurred. The occasion might be a serious conflict at the office, a confrontation with a wayward child, the loss of a job, or dealing with divorce. At such times, a pastoral sermon, one in which the compassionate heart of the preacher accurately reflects the compassionate heart of God, can be a gift from God to a wounded heart. John Stott comments:

> Every Christian pastor today has the same feelings of tender love towards those who have been committed to his care. As he speaks to them every Sunday, he knows something of the burdens they are bearing. One has soon to face major surgery, another has recently been told he has an incurable illness, yet another has just been bereaved. Then there is the couple whose marriage is falling apart, that man whose wife has been unfaithful.... As he looks at their faces, there seems to be tragedy behind every brave facade.... It is true that some need to be disturbed from their complacency, but others need above all else the comfort of God's love.[18]

It should be remembered that grief is not a momentary reality. Some grief lasts a lifetime. I was asked to fill the pulpit in my home church a few years ago and decided to preach a message based on the entire book of Habakkuk, a message entitled 'When We Wonder Why.' It echoed the dialog between the prophet and God, a dialog in which Habakkuk first inquires about the need for punishment for sinful Judah:

> The oracle that Habakkuk the prophet received. 'How long, O LORD, must I call for help, but you do not listen? Or cry out to you, "Violence!" but you do not save? Why do you make me look at injustice? Why do you tolerate wrong? Destruction and violence are before me; there is strife, and conflict abounds. Therefore the law is paralyzed, and justice never prevails. The wicked hem in the righteous, so that justice is perverted' (Hab 1:1-4).

God responds that he will in fact punish his people and will do so by sending the Babylonians to do the deed.

> Look at the nations and watch – and be utterly amazed. For I am going to do something in your days that you would not believe,

even if you were told. I am raising up the Babylonians, that ruthless and impetuous people, who sweep across the whole earth to seize dwelling places not their own. They are a feared and dreaded people; they are a law to themselves and promote their own honor. Their horses are swifter than leopards, fiercer than wolves at dusk. Their cavalry gallops headlong; their horsemen come from afar. They fly like a vulture swooping to devour; they all come bent on violence. Their hordes advance like a desert wind and gather prisoners like sand. They deride kings and scoff at rulers. They laugh at all fortified cities; they build earthen ramps and capture them. Then they sweep past like the wind and go on – guilty men, whose own strength is their god (Hab 1:5-11).

Habakkuk is indeed utterly amazed. How can God use such a vile people to accomplish his purposes? He offers his protest to God:

O Rock, you have ordained them to punish. Your eyes are too pure to look on evil; you cannot tolerate wrong. Why then do you tolerate the treacherous? Why are you silent while the wicked swallow up those more righteous than themselves? (Hab 1:12b-13)

The prophet withdraws to ponder what kind of response God might have to his protest. And then God gives his bottom line:

Then the LORD replied: 'Write down the revelation and make it plain on tablets so that a herald may run with it. For the revelation awaits an appointed time; it speaks of the end and will not prove false. Though it linger, wait for it; it will certainly come and will not delay. See, he is puffed up; his desires are not upright – but the righteous will live by his faith' (Hab 2:2-4).

The answer to all of Habakkuk's inquiries was to trust God for he is trustworthy. He knows the end from the beginning and those who are truly his will live by their faith. This lesson is learned by the prophet for he responds affirmatively in chapter 3:

LORD, I have heard of your fame; I stand in awe of your deeds, O LORD. Renew them in our day, in our time make them known; in wrath remember mercy.... I heard and my heart pounded, my lips quivered at the sound; decay crept into my bones, and my legs trembled. Yet I will wait patiently for the day of calamity to come on the nation invading us. Though the fig tree does not bud and there are no grapes on the vines, though the olive crop fails and the fields produce no food, though there are no sheep in the pen and no cattle in the stalls, yet I will rejoice in the LORD, I will be joyful in God my Savior. The Sovereign LORD is my strength; he makes my feet like the feet of a deer, he enables me to go on the heights (Hab 3:2, 16-19).

In my sermon I spoke of how events in life often seem unfair. Why do people, even God's people, sometimes experience difficult and even devastating situations? Why do we have to deal from time to time with tragedy? Why does God allow such things to take place? What can we do when we wonder why?

On the Sunday I preached this sermon, my wife and I had unexpected company for the weekend. Cousins on my wife's side of the family visited our home from out of state. They met me after the service with tears in their eyes, thanking me for a message that ministered to their grief. They had lost a son in Viet Nam almost three decades earlier and the grief was still there, dulled by the years, but real nevertheless.

Pastoral preaching can bring needed comfort to those who are hurting. This comfort can be communicated both in the message we present and also in the empathetic attitude we bring to the situation. This, of course, cannot be feigned. William Willimon asks:

A sermon might be the only contact many people in the congregation will have with the pastor. What impressions will the people receive from their preacher? Will the preacher be experienced as someone who is sufficiently open and empathetic to the discussion of tough, personal issues? Or is the preacher the sort of person who always has an easy answer to every problem on the tip of the tongue?[19]

Surely, we should emulate the master teacher, the Lord Jesus Christ in this matter of compassionate, pastoral preaching.

Jesus went through all the towns and villages, teaching in their synagogues, preaching the good news of the kingdom and healing every disease and sickness. When he saw the crowds, he had compassion on them, because they were harassed and helpless, like sheep without a shepherd (Matt 9:35-36).

Preaching as Nurturing

Pastoral preaching should also be preaching that nurtures. The responsibilities of the shepherd include supplying the sheep with food and caring for their basic needs. Interestingly, the final reiteration of the Great Commission in John's Gospel is couched in this kind of language:

When they had finished eating, Jesus said to Simon Peter, 'Simon son of John, do you truly love me more than these?' 'Yes, Lord,' he said, 'you know that I love you.' Jesus said, 'Feed my lambs.' Again Jesus said, 'Simon son of John, do you truly love me?' He answered, 'Yes, Lord, you know that I love you.' Jesus said, 'Take care of my sheep.' The third time he said to him, 'Simon son of John, do you love me?' Peter was hurt because Jesus asked him the third time, 'Do you love me?' He said, 'Lord, you know all things; you know that I love you.' Jesus said, 'Feed my sheep' (John 21:15-17)

'Feed my lambs.' 'Take care of my sheep.' 'Feed my sheep.' The NIV rendering reflects the four different words used by the apostle. To 'feed' (*boskō*) is 'to pasture, to graze, to provide fodder.' To 'take care of' (*poimainō*) is 'to tend as a shepherd.' 'Lamb' (*arnion*) refers to a baby sheep. 'Sheep' (*probaton*) refers to a grown sheep. The pastor who truly loves Christ will provide nurture for Christ's flock.

This responsibility can also be thought of as the parenting role. When Paul wrote to the Thessalonian Christians, he reminds them of his care for them:

. . . but we were gentle among you, like a mother caring for her little children. We loved you so much that we were delighted to share with you not only the gospel of God but our lives as well,

> because you had become so dear to us. Surely you remember, brothers, our toil and hardship; we worked night and day in order not to be a burden to anyone while we preached the gospel of God to you. You are witnesses, and so is God, of how holy, righteous and blameless we were among you who believed. For you know that we dealt with each of you as a father deals with his own children, encouraging, comforting and urging you to live lives worthy of God, who calls you into his kingdom and glory (1 Thess 2:7-12).

Another figure of nurturing used frequently in Scripture is that of agriculture. We're told about planting, watering, and pruning. We learn in 1 Corinthians 3:6-9 that the church is God's field (*georgion*) and the planters and waterers are workers in that field.

As a widow in her mid-nineties, my mother lived alone and had a special activity to keep her occupied, her garden. She planted and watered, but she did much more. She cultivated and loosened the soil so that her plants were not trapped in concrete-like dried mud. She fertilized so that the plants had plenty of nutrients. She 'hilled' the potatoes so that the dirt was thick and the 'spuds' were not exposed to the sun's harmful rays. She pulled weeds so that they did not steal the moisture needed for health and growth. She pinched off the 'suckers', those branches on tomato plants that will never bear fruit. She attempted to protect her plants from raiding birds and bunnies. She sprayed and dusted to help protect her garden from insects and disease. She *nurtured* her garden so that the harvest would be as plentiful as possible.

Pastoral preaching is preaching that nurtures the souls of those entrusted to our care. The preacher must feed, water, protect, and cultivate those who are growing in the 'field of the Lord'. When we do our part, God gives the increase and the harvest will bring joy to him.

Preach Prophetically

Now having looked at the importance of pastoral preaching, we turn our attention to the matter of preaching prophetically. In one sense, all preaching is prophetic. Prophecy has to do with the *forthtelling* of the Word. This is the primary meaning of the Old

Testament word *naba*, to prophesy. This verb is used more than 100 times in the Old Testament and its noun form is found more than 300 times. Generally, we think of a prophet as one who foretells, one who predicts what will happen in the future. But this is not the primary idea. A true prophet was a messenger of God. This message may or may not have included predictions of the future. In fact, the majority of the prophetic writings and speeches in Scripture are not about the future but relate to situations at hand at the time the prophet spoke.

The Greek word *prophetes* is the same in meaning as the Hebrew *nabi*. It too refers to someone who speaks forth a message. In the Septuagint, it is used to translate both *nabi* and *roeh* ('seer'), and in the New Testament it is used variously to refer to Old Testament prophets, John the Baptist, Jesus, the future prophets of the Book of Revelation, and to the prophets in the early church. The function of this latter group, like their Old Testament counterparts, was to 'forthtell' the Word of God. They were God's mouthpieces.

If, in terms of the biblical usage of these words, a true prophet is one who speaks forth the message God has for his people, why should we discuss the concept of prophetic preaching? Is this not a redundancy? Are 'preaching' and prophecy' not synonymous terms? In an etymological sense, yes. But, as noted earlier, the concepts of pastoral preaching and prophetic preaching are about *the tone of a sermon*. They are being used in this discussion not as explanations of what preaching *is* primarily, but of what preaching *does*. They relate to sermon purpose.

The term prophetic preaching is used today to refer to the kind of preaching that emulates that which was done by the Old Testament prophets. While this concept is helpful and will therefore be discussed, it should immediately be clarified that the term is used arbitrarily of a particular kind of sermon that, while reflecting the passions and concerns of much Old Testament prophecy, fails to reflect the entire genre. Those who use the term are at least a little guilty of generalization. Old Testament prophecy covers a tremendous range of topics and emotions. At best, therefore, any discussion of prophetic preaching will probably fall short of adequately reflecting the entire gamut of themes and moods of biblical prophecy.

A good place to begin is to look at the Old Testament prophets themselves. What kinds of persons were they? Are there some common traits, concerns, and emphases that will guide us as we consider this matter of preaching prophetically? I believe so.

Urgency and Boldness

While the prophets of old came from various stations in life, they were almost always characterized by an acute sense of urgency – Jonah alone seems to be an exception to this. They were compelled to say what God wants them to say. Amos was a farmer who also cared for livestock. He was keenly aware of his lack of qualification but also tuned in to his mandate from God. When confronted by a religious hireling of King Jeroboam II, Amaziah, this occurs:

> Then Amaziah said to Amos, 'Get out, you seer! Go back to the land of Judah. Earn your bread there and do your prophesying there. Don't prophesy anymore at Bethel, because this is the king's sanctuary and the temple of the kingdom.' Amos answered Amaziah, 'I was neither a prophet nor a prophet's son, but I was a shepherd, and I also took care of sycamore-fig trees. But the LORD took me from tending the flock and said to me, "Go, prophesy to my people Israel." Now then, hear the word of the LORD. You say, "Do not prophesy against Israel, and stop preaching against the house of Isaac." Therefore this is what the LORD says: "Your wife will become a prostitute in the city, and your sons and daughters will fall by the sword. Your land will be measured and divided up, and you yourself will die in a pagan country. And Israel will certainly go into exile, away from their native land"' (Amos 7:12-17).

Or consider Jeremiah, a man ensnared in self-pity as he was continuously ridiculed and persecuted by his audience, yet who had little choice but to declare God's truth.

> 'O LORD, you deceived me, and I was deceived; you overpowered me and prevailed. I am ridiculed all day long; everyone mocks me. Whenever I speak, I cry out proclaiming violence and destruction. So the word of the LORD has brought me insult and reproach all

day long. But if I say, "I will not mention him or speak any more in his name," his word is in my heart like a fire, a fire shut up in my bones. I am weary of holding it in; indeed, I cannot' (Jer 20:7-9).

What would have motivated Isaiah to remain faithful to his task in spite of widespread unbelief among those to whom he preached? He was, in fact, forewarned that his ministry was doomed to fail, yet he boldly persisted.

Then I heard the voice of the Lord saying, 'Whom shall I send? And who will go for us?' And I said, 'Here am I. Send me!' He said, 'Go and tell this people: "Be ever hearing, but never understanding; be ever seeing, but never perceiving." Make the heart of this people calloused; make their ears dull and close their eyes. Otherwise they might see with their eyes, hear with their ears, understand with their hearts, and turn and be healed.' Then I said, 'For how long, O Lord?' And he answered: 'Until the cities lie ruined and without inhabitant, until the houses are left deserted and the fields ruined and ravaged, until the LORD has sent everyone far away and the land is utterly forsaken' (Isa 6:8-12).

Only a profound sense of God-induced urgency could enable mere mortals like Amos, Jeremiah, and Isaiah to 'keep on keeping on'. This same kind of bold urgency will characterize prophetic preaching today, that urgent boldness which Montoya calls 'sanctified madness'.[20]

Writing in *The Christian Ministry*, first published in 1830, Charles Bridges comments on this matter of bold preaching, warning those who are lacking:

This Ministerial Boldness is fenced... by warning and encouragement. Yet many probably know, and even feel, more truth, than they have the courage to preach. Want we then a further motive? Think of the despised Saviour in the judgment hall, 'before Pontius Pilate, witnessing a good confession' (1 Tim 6:13) – an example of fidelity enough to make a coward bold!

The deficiency of this spirit lowers us in the estimation of our people, as time-servers, whose moral and religious integrity are alike suspected. Many who love the 'smooth things' we should 'prophesy', would despise us in our hearts for this accommodation to their sinful indulgences; whilst Christian boldness awes the haters of our message, and secures the confidence of the true flock of Christ, and the approbation of our conscience in the sight of God.[21]

To be a prophetic preacher, then, is to be utterly motivated by a sense of Divine urgency with the result of the attainment of a holy boldness. This should not be thought to be the exclusive domain of just a few preachers uniquely gifted to be modern day prophets. Rather, this is the legacy of every preacher truly called by God. In this sense, every preacher should be a prophetic preacher.

Individual and Corporate Morality

A second concern seemingly held in common by the Old Testament prophets is that of the need to return to God's standards of righteousness, both individually and corporately. They address personal and national sin in no uncertain terms.

Nathan, a prophet in David's time, is such an example. Following the king's affair with Bathsheba and the disposal of her husband Uriah, Nathan marched into the court and told a story seemingly unrelated to David, a story about a man who steals and butchers the only sheep of a poor man when he had plenty of his own. David was furious, decreeing that this person ought to be put to death. Nathan then, unabashedly, turned his finger straight into David's face and declared, 'You are that man.'

Prophetic preaching includes a straightforward denunciation of sin as sin. It doesn't sidestep around the issue of morality. This is true not only of 'their' sins, but 'ours' as well. Most any preacher can puff out his chest and preach 'boldly' about the sins of others, those on the outside. There will probably be a few 'amens' voiced, whether audibly or silently. But what about the sins of those within sound of our voices? Surely, the typical congregation is not composed of sinless saints! What about the sins of covetousness, lying, cheating, sloth, avarice, lust, lack of self-control, bitterness, prejudice, corporate stealing, spousal abuse (yes, even in churches), unethical business dealings, materialism, hedonism – and the list could go on and on. And these are all sins of commission. What about the sins of omission: sins like neglecting the poor, failing to speak the truth in love, and faithlessness.

I'm not suggesting that every sermon should be a moral witch hunt; I am suggesting that God takes sin seriously and so must the preacher. The prophets did not sweep sin under the rug of vague euphemisms like moral lapses, weaknesses of the flesh, mistakes, ignorance, or errors in judgment. Neither am I suggesting that our preaching on sin should be only confrontational, without an attitude of humility, grief, and love on the part of the preacher. But I fear that much preaching today is more geared to platitudinous generality than to a prophetic recognition of sin's awfulness.

Prophetic preaching must address not only the matter of personal sin, but corporate sin as well. The subject of such preaching might be the church's failure to do that which is right while priding itself on being a good church. There are ample examples in the Old Testament of a people who correctly practiced all of the external forms of their religion and yet completely missed doing that which was expected by God.

> With what shall I come before the LORD and bow down before the exalted God? Shall I come before him with burnt offerings, with calves a year old? Will the LORD be pleased with thousands of rams, with ten thousand rivers of oil? Shall I offer my firstborn for my transgression, the fruit of my body for the sin of my soul? He has showed you, O man, what is good. And what does the LORD require of you? To act justly and to love mercy and to walk humbly with your God (Mic 6:6-8).

While the tone of this is somewhat individualistic, Micah's message was intended for the nations of Judah and Israel. They were quite content in keeping external religious observances without considering what God really desires. Similarly, Amos strongly denounces the northern kingdom of Israel:

'I hate, I despise your religious feasts; I cannot stand your assemblies. Even though you bring me burnt offerings and grain offerings, I will not accept them. Though you bring choice fellowship offerings, I will have no regard for them. Away with the noise of your songs! I will not listen to the music of your harps. But let justice roll on like a river, righteousness like a never-failing stream! Did you bring me sacrifices and offerings forty years in the desert, O house of Israel? You have lifted up the shrine of your king, the pedestal of your idols, the star of your god – which you made for yourselves. Therefore I will send you into exile beyond Damascus,' says the LORD, whose name is God Almighty (Amos 5:21-27).

These warnings to religious people are precipitated by their sinful behavior. The prophets are not bashful about naming names and pointing fingers, even in terms of God's covenant people.

The prophets also warn about national sin. Because of the nature of the relationship between God and the Jewish people in the Old Testament, it is impossible to completely distinguish where 'church' sins stop and national sins begin. There are instances, however, in which the prophets speak of national sins to those who are not part of the covenant. One such example is found in Obadiah where Edom is addressed:

The pride of your heart has deceived you, you who live in the clefts of the rocks and make your home on the heights, you who say to yourself, 'Who can bring me down to the ground?' Though you soar like the eagle and make your nest among the stars, from there I will bring you down, declares the LORD (Obad 1:3-4).

In this citation, Edom is being confronted for her pride in her safeness. This accusation is confounded by Edom's failure to assist Judah in their time of need.

On the day you stood aloof while strangers carried off his wealth and foreigners entered his gates and cast lots for Jerusalem, you were like one of them. You should not look down on your brother in the day of his misfortune, nor rejoice over the people of Judah in the day of their destruction, nor boast so much in the day of their trouble. You should not march through the gates of my people in the day of their disaster, nor look down on them in their calamity in the day of their disaster, nor seize their wealth in the day of their disaster. You should not wait at the crossroads to cut down their fugitives, nor hand over their survivors in the day of their trouble. The day of the LORD is near for all nations. As you have done, it will be done to you; your deeds will return upon your own head (Obad 1:11-15).

Other prophets who address the issue of national sins include Jonah and Nahum, both of whom speak the Word of the Lord to Nineveh.

There are parts of the book of Hosea, addressed to the northern kingdom, that strongly condemns sin on a national level.

Hear the word of the LORD, you Israelites, because the LORD has a charge to bring against you who live in the land: 'There is no faithfulness, no love, no acknowledgment of God in the land. There is only cursing, lying and murder, stealing and adultery; they break all bounds, and bloodshed follows bloodshed. Because of this the land mourns, and all who live in it waste away; the beasts of the field and the birds of the air and the fish of the sea are dying' (Hos 4:1-3)

The prophets take sin seriously whether it is on the personal, corporately religious, or national levels. Abraham Heschel, a well-known Jewish scholar in Old Testament studies, says regarding the prophets' concern for sin, 'They speak and act as if the sky were about to collapse because Israel has been unfaithful to God.'[22] To preach prophetically is to echo this concern. The Bible says, 'If we claim to be without sin, we deceive ourselves and the truth is not in us' (I John 1:8). The preacher who neglects preaching on sin is guilty of participating in the self-deception of his congregation as well as his own self-deception.

Social Justice

There is a fear held by some in evangelical circles that to preach social justice is to preach a 'social gospel'. This is based on the memory of what took place during the early years of the twentieth century, when many liberal theologians and pastors forsook the message of personal repentance and conversion, attempting instead to Christianize society. As this was taking place, conservatives were increasingly obsessed with the defense of orthodoxy theology and in turn, unfortunately, increasingly neglected social ministries and matters of social justice. There was a general concern voiced that 'true Christians' should avoid the appearance of the evil of the 'social gospel'.

It is important to remember, however, that effective social ministry has often, if not always, been seen as part of the obligation of the church. The New Testament church shared material wealth to those outside the church as well as to those within: 'Therefore, as we have opportunity, let us do good to all people, especially to those who belong to the family of believers' (Gal 6:10). The late James Montgomery Boice makes a persuasive argument that it is the sharing of money that is the main topic here.[23] Even if Paul meant something other than money – perhaps good works in general, for example – the principle remains. The early church was encouraged to serve the needs of society at large.

The New Testament epistles presented socially constructive principles that have positively influenced culture when they have been rightly applied. Equal standing before God, regardless of race, gender, economic worth, or social status, was established. The epistles also taught proper relationships between employer and employee, respect and help for the poor, and the danger of the abuse of power. Women were elevated from servitude to a position of respect.

Under Roman Catholicism, monasticism has often included groups that emphasized social ministries. The Jesuits, for instance, while noted for their missionary activities, have long been involved in education endeavors and social work among the needy. Others in the monastic tradition have begun hospitals and orphanages, and have worked among the poorest of the poor, Mother Teresa being one such example.

During the Reformation period, some church leaders were deeply involved in societal matters. Sweazey comments:

Actually, what some of the Reformers slighted in their teaching they more than made up for in their conduct. As the pastor of the church, John Calvin was almost the dictator of the morality of business and government in Geneva. Queen Mary bitterly protested the strong part John Knox took in the affairs of the realm.[24]

I think also of notable persons from later church history like John Wesley, William Booth, and Dwight Moody. These individuals, known primarily for their public evangelistic ministries were also extremely involved in social ministries. Wesley and his Methodist movement did much to alleviate inhumane prison conditions in England and was also involved in literacy programs, medical assistance, education, and the distribution of money, clothes, and food to the poor. Booth, the founder of the Salvation Army, was similarly dedicated to giving assistance to the 'down and out' of society, a tradition that still guides this organization today. Moody, whose fame usually extends only to his evangelistic meetings and to the founding of the Chicago Bible Institute, later Moody Bible Institute, had a far larger influence. In a late nineteenth century article in MacClure's Magazine, Henry Drummond wrote:

> There is no large town in Great Britain, and I find that there are few in America, where this man has not gone, where he has not lived, for days, weeks, or months, and where he has not left behind him personal inspirations which live to this day; inspirations that from the moment of their birth have not ceased to evidence themselves in furthering domestic happiness and peace; in charities and philanthropies; in social, religious, and even municipal and national service.[25]

I dwell on this matter to make an important point. The church today must not turn its back on the needs and issues of society. To do so is to forsake our Christian heritage. We must both speak out and act in matters of social justice and societal needs.

That Christians have always served society should not surprise us. The roots of social justice and serving the needs of the poor extend back to the warnings of the prophets.

> You trample on the poor and force him to give you grain. Therefore, though you have built stone mansions, you will not live in them; though you have planted lush vineyards, you will not drink their wine. For I know how many are your offenses and how great your sins. You oppress the righteous and take bribes and you deprive the poor of justice in the courts. Therefore the prudent man keeps quiet in such times, for the times are evil. Seek good, not evil, that you may live. Then the LORD God Almighty will be with you, just as you say he is. Hate evil, love good; maintain justice in the courts. Perhaps the LORD God Almighty will have mercy on the remnant of Joseph (Amos 5:11-15).

Jesus reiterated this theme:

> Then the King will say to those on his right, 'Come, you who are blessed by my Father; take your inheritance, the kingdom prepared for you since the creation of the world. For I was hungry and you gave me something to eat, I was thirsty and you gave me something to drink, I was a stranger and you invited me in, I needed clothes and you clothed me, I was sick and you looked after me, I was in prison and you came to visit me.' Then the righteous will answer him, 'Lord, when did we see you hungry and feed you, or thirsty and give you something to drink? When did we see you a stranger and invite you in, or needing clothes and clothe you? When did we see you sick or in prison and go to visit you?' The King will reply, 'I tell you the truth, whatever you did for one of the least of these brothers of mine, you did for me' (Matt 25:34-40).

Prophetic preaching includes the addressing of social justice issues. To treat these themes as unimportant is to be less than Christian in our ministry.

Judgment and Blessing
Prophetic preaching also includes the declaration of coming judgment and blessing. In recent years, my experience has been to see the latter greatly emphasized and the former almost ignored. The idea of judgment has fallen on hard times as moral relativism and political correctness have made their inroads into our culture. We often hear that we should not judge the actions of others, and sometimes this

opinion is given with an attached biblical quotation. And as judgment is now forbidden to us, it seems to be thought unworthy of God as well. After all, God is 'a God of love'. The wrong assumption, of course, is that love and justice are somehow mutually exclusive ideas. But make no mistake, judgment is coming and preachers need to talk about it! Macpherson makes a summative statement in this regard:

> This is a note that needs sounding in the pulpit today. Jesus is to be our judge. Our lives matter morally. They are to have an ultimate ethical evaluation. At last they are to be subjected to the awful magistracy of the Most High. Bad behavior is not to be blamed upon heredity or 'glands' or environment: it is to be charged upon the recalcitrant human will. We are responsible creatures, and that means not only that we are responsible *for* something but also that we are responsible *to* Someone, and that Someone is Jesus Christ. Strike that deep chord in your preaching and the hearts of your hearers will be filled with a fresh sense of the solemnity and dignity of human life.[26]

To preach prophetically is to include the truth regarding coming judgment in our extended preaching ministry. This theme must never become a hobby horse, but it must be included if we are to faithfully proclaim all of God's truth.

The subject of judgment creeps into Scripture in unlikely places. Lectionary preachers find it among advent readings. Texts that offer wonderful promises also include dire warnings.

> 'See, I will send my messenger, who will prepare the way before me. Then suddenly the Lord you are seeking will come to his temple; the messenger of the covenant, whom you desire, will come,' says the LORD Almighty. But who can endure the day of his coming? Who can stand when he appears? For he will be like a refiner's fire or a launderer's soap. He will sit as a refiner and purifier of silver; he will purify the Levites and refine them like gold and silver. Then the LORD will have men who will bring offerings in righteousness and the offerings of Judah and Jerusalem will be acceptable to the LORD, as in days gone by, as in former years. 'So I will come near to you for judgment. I will be quick to testify

against sorcerers, adulterers and perjurers, against those who defraud laborers of their wages, who oppress the widows and the fatherless, and deprive aliens of justice, but do not fear me,' says the LORD Almighty (Mal 3:1-5).

Other advent texts also include the note of judgment.

We must preach this theme prayerfully and with a sense of humility and brokenness. It should bring us no joy to remind people that many will suffer the displeasure of God because they do not measure up to his standards.

Even as we declare the truth about judgment, however, we must also speak about future blessing. The hard, but necessary, sayings of the pulpit must never be allowed to overshadow the wonderful truths of grace and mercy. Future blessing awaits those who are 'joint heirs with Christ.' In his teaching of the Old Testament prophets in the seminary classroom, Walter Kaiser often referred to the 'rosy tinted promises' tucked into their messages about coming judgment. For example, the prophet Hosea severely rebukes Israel for their spiritual adultery, yet promises forgiveness and future blessing if repentance is forthcoming.

'Return, O Israel, to the LORD your God. Your sins have been your downfall! Take words with you and return to the LORD. Say to him: "Forgive all our sins and receive us graciously, that we may offer the fruit of our lips. Assyria cannot save us; we will not mount war-horses. We will never again say 'Our gods' to what our own hands have made, for in you the fatherless find compassion."

'I will heal their waywardness and love them freely, for my anger has turned away from them' (Hos 14:1-4).

God has always delighted in forgiveness and reclamation. Throughout the Old Testament prophets, similar promises of forgiveness and future blessing can be found.

As we scour the New Testament writings, we discover that the promise of blessing is there also. Our salvation and its accompanying blessings are secured through the finished work of Jesus Christ on the cross: 'Therefore, there is now no condemnation for those who are in Christ Jesus, because through Christ Jesus the law of the

Spirit of life set me free from the law of sin and death' (Rom 8:1-2).

Prophetic preaching, while often somewhat harsh in its subject matter and tone, must also be tempered with hope and forgiveness. To preach prophetically is to warn and chastise, but it is also to plead with the wayward to repent and turn to God.

Summation

This chapter has approached our overall concern of developing balance in our preaching philosophy by exploring the issue of purpose. I have painted with broad strokes and therefore we've looked at purpose in terms of four distinct kinds of sermons: evangelistic preaching, edificational preaching, pastoral preaching, and prophetic preaching. Some may regard these categories as arbitrary and this may well be the case. The number and nomenclature of categories is not crucial in itself, but we must recognize that sermons are addressed to different kinds of people with varying needs. In terms of an effective long-term preaching ministry, the biblical preacher will desire to faithfully address all of the important subjects and moods of Scripture. This chapter has attempted, therefore, to remind the preacher of these related issues.

Points to Ponder

1. How does our theology of the church impact the way we plan our preaching agenda?

2. What are the arguments, pro and con, for including an evangelistic element in every message we preach in the local church?

3. In a local church congregation, are there any dangers to the believers who hear only a steady diet of edificational preaching?

4. Is it likely that strong pastoral preaching will increase counseling opportunities for the preacher? If so, what provisions will need to be made to accommodate those seeking help?

5. Is it possible to preach pastorally from the prophets, or prophetically from the epistles? Why is this the case?

Step Five

Maintain a Balance in Sermon Variety

> A preacher needs a wide variety of sermon styles. Never let the congregation guess what you are going to do. If they know as soon as you get into the topic how you will treat it, there is no novelty and no excitement to keep them listening. Those who anticipate the preacher's methods are inclined to be bored (George E. Sweazey).[1]

Familiarity can be a comfort. Change can be threatening, even ominous, but sameness seems to assure us that all is well with the world. This is true in most walks of life and it is true of people's attitude toward church. The majority of church attendees prefer that wholesale changes in the order of worship, the style of music being used, and the decor of the worship center not take place on a weekly basis! While there may be some truth to the old adage that says 'variety is the spice of life', most of us prefer that this not extend to our corporate worship. We tend to find comfort in sameness and prefer that change be gradual.

What is true of attitudes toward the corporate worship experience is probably true for preaching as well. Those who listen to sermons may find a kind of comfort in the familiarity of particular kinds of sermons. It may be reassuring to have a sense of knowing where the preacher is headed once the sermon has been launched. At the same time, it must be said that a familiar type of preaching practiced continuously results in a high degree of risk in terms of boredom and lack of attention. Such preaching invites the listener to listen 'in spurts'.

Maintaining consistent attention span on the part of every listener is a worthy goal for the preacher. Realistically, however, we must understand this is an ideal goal that will never be achieved. Studies through the years have regularly shown that absolute attention span is quite limited. It is estimated that the average listener takes a mental 'side trip' every ten or twelve seconds, and that a 'major excursion' is taken every few minutes! Thankfully, most of the side trips and excursions end with the wanderer rejoining the sermon and the listener is able to fill in the missed gaps without having done irreparable harm to the process of grasping the gist of the message. It can be disconcerting nevertheless to the preacher to realize that at any moment during a sermon, twenty percent of the audience may be temporarily (at least!) 'tuned out'.

It is important, then, to prepare and deliver a sermon in a way that assists the listener to maintain good attention. Short of utilizing theatrics and other dubious means, there are relatively few legitimate ways of doing this. One way of helping do this is to strive for relevance, making certain that the topic presented is understood by the listener as being of personal importance. (This matter of relevance will be discussed in a later chapter.) Another useful means of aiding attention span is the utilization of attention-attracting techniques such as body language and vocal variation. This, of course, can be overdone and actually distract from the sermon's message, but delivery can also be a legitimate tool for enhancing attention span. Still another approach is the use of content materials purposely chosen to attract attention such as stories, figures of speech, examples, provocative statements, and humor. Finally, one other means of grabbing and holding attention is to arouse curiosity.

There are at least two primary ways that curiosity can be evoked in a sermon as far as the content is concerned. One way is to utilize various rhetorical devices specially chosen for that purpose. For example, an illustration may be used without its purpose or ending being clear until it has been concluded. Or, a provocative quotation might be inserted while keeping the audience in suspense as to who said it. Dialogue, in which the speaker portrays two sides of an argument, may be used to explain an issue in a message. Questions might be raised which remain unanswered for a period of time. Basically, curiosity is aroused in a sermon when predictability is absent. If the content in each part of a sermon is predictable – known or surmised in advance – the listener will not be motivated to remain engaged. Some element of suspense must be present.

Just as predictability can be minimized within the various parts of a message, it can also be minimized by varying the overall sermon designs we utilize. The preacher needs to deviate frequently from the normal expectations of listeners. We can do this by adding the element of homiletical surprise. Larsen rightly remarks that 'One of the curses of the contemporary pulpit is its total predictability. This is lethal.'[2] Yes, predictability is lethal whether it relates to topic, purpose, presentation style, internal content, or homiletical design. Elliott observes:

> Many of our church members ... live in a world of compact disc players that shuffle ten discs, remote controls that herd five hundred channels and Wal-Marts with the square footage of a small county. Church members have grown accustomed to and even *demand* variety. My wife admits she no longer can listen to just one compact disc. At the grocery store, I expect to find wines from Chile, Australia, and South Africa.[3]

The agenda of this chapter is to discuss the matter of overall sermon design. Homiletical variation will be addressed by discussing sermon propositions, basic structural guidelines, comprehensive expositional preaching, deductive and inductive preaching, and creativity. As Sweazey remarked, 'Never do anything always.'[4]

Preach Propositionally for Maximum Thematic Clarity

When an earlier book, *Homiletical Handbook*, was being considered for publication, one of the reviewers – a person unknown to me – took issue to the section in which I insisted that every sermon ought to have a propositional statement.[5] The reviewer felt this claim was exaggerated and that some sermons do not require propositions. The editor with whom I was working asked me to consider this input but gave me the freedom to do with it as I liked. I chose to keep my original statement and actually augmented it a bit. I'm glad I did for I'm more convinced than ever regarding the absolute cruciality of a carefully conceived and stated propositional statement as the guiding force of a sermon, both in the formation of the sermon and in its delivery, both for the sake of the preacher and for the sake of the audience.

The Importance of Sermon Propositions

I use the term 'sermon proposition' as a synonym for thesis statement, central idea, big idea, theme statement, and other similar concepts. Please understand that the term 'proposition' is not the issue. I could not care less what this statement is called as long as there is one. It is the term I personally use consistently in order to avoid confusion on the part of my readers and students. Further, it must be said that this concept is not original with me. Many outstanding homileticians of the past and present – for example, John Broadus, John Henry Jowett, Harwood Pattison, Charles Koller, Lloyd Perry, Haddon Robinson, and Bryan Chappell – endorse this idea.

Clear sermon propositions are crucial, in my judgment, to clear sermons. We've all had the experience of listening to sermons that seems to meander here, there, and everywhere. This is often, though not always, the result of an unclear propositional statement. No single homiletical component is more helpful in keeping a sermon focused that this statement. Some may argue that it is the subject or theme that provides focus for a sermon. (Some, like myself, differentiate between the subject and theme while others do not.) While the subject or theme is helpful in this regard, neither is sufficient. Let me explain.

I find it helpful to distinguish between the subject and theme in the following way. I see the subject as the single, broad concept presented in a Scripture text and subsequently in a sermon suitably based on that text. Generally, the subject can be stated in a single word (eg. love, prayer, faith, doubt, anxiety, salvation) or perhaps two words (eg. Holy Spirit, second coming, and the new birth). These subjects are, in my opinion, *much* too broad to use as the main idea of a sermon. A sermon based on 'love' would have insufficient parameters to keep it sharply focused. Such a message might go any one of many directions, especially if it is developed as a topical sermon.

As far as the theme is concerned, I see it as a narrowing down of the subject, reducing it to a more manageable size. Each subject may have quite a few possible themes but the right theme should reflect that aspect of the subject which the text emphasizes. There are, for example, many texts that present the broad subject of prayer. But one may discuss 'how to pray'; another may present 'praying with faith'; while yet another may present 'faithfulness in prayer'. Quite a few other themes relating to prayer might fit given texts. Generally, the theme can be stated as a phrase in which the single-word subject is present.

In most kinds of sermons, the proposition will be a complete sentence that includes the theme phrase. Thus, the single-word subject is found in the theme and the theme-phrase is found in the proposition. This simple process alone helps to keep the developing sermon on target. Suppose that you are preparing to preach on Philippians 2:1-4. You might choose the word 'unity' as the broad subject of the text. You then inquire as to what it is about unity that this text is emphasizing. You might settle on 'achieving unity in the church'. This phrase then becomes the basis of the sermon's proposition which might be stated: 'We can achieve unity in the church.' This particular sermon would be a 'how to do it' kind of message and would proceed to explain how to behave in according to the instructions in the text and thus achieve unity in the church. Each main point would be one of these instructions.

Another example is seen in an approach to Matthew 6:5-8. The subject of this text is clearly 'prayer'. The theme might be stated as 'when prayer fails' with the proposition stated in the form of a question: 'Why is it that prayer sometimes fails?' The sermon's main points would consist of a series of 'reasons' for the failure of prayer such as: prayer fails when it is done to impress others (vv. 5-6); prayer fails when it consists of empty words (vv. 7-8); prayer fails when it is not specific (v. 8b); and prayer fails when it is not offered at all (v. 5a, implied). (Usually, I prefer that propositions be stated as declarative sentences in keeping with the idea of 'that which is being proposed'. In homiletics, however, the primary purpose of this statement is to be the integrative center of the sermon.

Functionally, therefore, an interrogative may occasionally be used.)

Before discussing how propositions might be treated to enhance balance in sermon structure, let me mention one additional thought regarding subjects and themes. Since these are both present in the statement of the proposition, which should be clearly articulated for the audience, it is both unnecessary and ill-advised to state the subject and theme as separate entities. This would be too repetitive and extremely mechanical. The broad subject can be alluded to early in the sermon introduction without saying 'My subject today is _____.' The thematic direction of the subject should be made clear as the introduction progresses as well. Then, when the proposition is clearly stated, often just prior to the sermon body, the listener will be informed sufficiently of the subject and theme since they are included as part of the proposition.

It is helpful to remember that a good, carefully thought out propositional statement can be a great asset to both the preacher and the hearer. As mentioned earlier, it will assist the preacher to keep the sermon focused and on track. Like a navigational device, the proposition sets the direction for the message and helps assure that it will not deviate off course. As the preacher does his preparation, the proposition should remain in the forefront of his thinking. As each part of the sermon is considered, the question should be asked, 'How will this relate to the sermon proposition?' If it doesn't – and this includes main points, supporting materials, illustrations, and applications – this part should be eliminated. Only material which contributes to the establishment of the proposition should be included. Otherwise, the preacher gets off track and begins 'chasing rabbits'.

The proposition can be an important help for the listener also *if* the preacher uses it well. It should not be thought of only as a homiletical device, something meant for the study. In essence, the propositional statement communicates what the sermon is about. It has been called 'the sermon in a sentence'. This being the case, the audience needs to be informed at the appropriate time of the precise proposition. Without a clear proposition being understood, the listener will understand only the approximate idea of the message, generally the broad subject. Using the examples mentioned previously, the listener might understand that the preacher 'spoke on something about unity', or the preacher 'talked about prayer'. Ideally, when asked about the sermon just heard, the listener should be able to respond, 'The preacher talked about how we can achieve unity,' or 'The sermon was about why prayer sometimes fails.'

If the listener hears and understands the proposition as the main idea of the sermon, every other part of the sermon can be related to it. The hearer will grasp the notion that the main points are not arbitrary statements without an inherent relationship, but rather statements which support the main idea of the sermon, the proposition. Listening to a sermon should not be the undertaking of a mystery to be solved, but a coherent presentation of a central idea with all other ideas related to it in a clear way. The proposition clues the audience in so they can listen intelligently.

Varying Our Propositions

A great variety of kinds of propositions and propositional functions can be utilized to help achieve homiletical variety and balance. This necessitates, of course, an understanding of more than one approach to homiletical structuring. Unfortunately, some preachers have been taught only one method of homiletics – it may be a very good method – and the result is that sermons often become predictable. If, on the other hand, we're able to utililize various homiletical methods, it will be much easier to vary our propositions.

Kinds of Propositions

Different kinds of propositions can be used with various types of sermon structures. Following is a table of some sample propositions based on some common sermon methods.[6] You will note that the broad subject of each one is 'worship', but that the themes expressed in the different propositions vary. You will note also that at least three different kinds of propositions can be used with the Keyword method and that the same kind of proposition is used with both the Syllogistic and Inductive methods. These examples are meant to be suggestive rather than exhaustive.

Table 1: Propositions and Sermon Methods		
Proposition Type	*Example*	*Sermon Method*
Obligation	Each of us should worship God daily	Keyword
Ability	Each of us can experience meaningful worship.	Keyword
Value	It is better to worship God than to exalt man.	Keyword
Analysis	A study of the concept of worship in Psalm 24 will help us correct any basic misunderstanding we have about this important privilege.	Analytical
Impression	'Worship the Lord in the beauty of holiness' (1 Chron. 16:29)	Textual
Interrogation	What is God's perspective on proper worship?	Problem Solving
Clarification	A study of the nature of the Old Testament priesthood will clarify the concept of worship (1 Peter 2:5).	Comparative
Conclusion	Therefore, worship must be our highest priority.	Syllogistic, Inductive
Plot resolution	We can be involved in doing so many good Christian things that we forget the importance of worship.	Narrative

This table demonstrates that different kinds of sermon structures require different kinds of propositional statements. Using a variety of structures, therefore, will lead to the positive result of varied propositions. This is a small but important help to avoiding predictability.

Functions of Propositions

Not only can propositions vary in terms of the way they are stated, they can also vary in regard to their stated or implied function. This is seen in the first column of Table 1. Some propositions are statements of obligation, ability, or value. Some state that a sermon will study some biblical concept with an anticipated result. One method of textual preaching is to allow a short, pithy text to serve as the proposition by being repeated quite a few times – perhaps twelve or fifteen times – in a sermon. This is what is meant by a proposition of impression. A problem-solving sermon explores and provides answers for some significant issue. This proposition asks about God's answer or perspective. A proposition of clarification is useful when a sermon deals with a figure of speech. The spiritual meaning of the figure is ascertained as it is studied. When sermons are structured on the basis of formal reasoning, whether deductive or inductive, the 'argument' produces a conclusion statement. This serves as the proposition.

Finally, narrative sermons need a propositional statement so that the hearer understands the purpose of the story. As I've listened to students experiment with narrative sermons, I'm usually struck by the fact that the central point of the story can be easily lost. There needs to be a clear statement that summarizes the single truth this story proposes. While this is generally offered at the end of the narrative as a 'bottom line' kind of statement, it can be stated or at least suggested earlier in the story as well. One way of doing this is to frame it as a rhetorical question early in the sermon and then state it as a declaration toward the end. Since the sermon itself is presented as a narrative, it is preferable to present the proposition as a natural part of the story rather than something thrust into the story from outside.

The kinds and functions of propositions just discussed are simply examples of the numerous possibilities that exist. There are other kinds of sermon methodologies that have been and can be developed. The point to be gained from this discussion is that a listener-friendly and preacher-friendly variety of approaches can be achieved even in the way propositions are framed.

Clarity

It must be added that sermon propositions need to be carefully crafted to be as clear as possible. The listener should be able to recognize this statement as being the heart of the sermon and should also be able to grasp what it means. A proposition should be a simple sentence, grammatically speaking, devoid of multiple clauses, phrases and words that are not crucial to its meaning, and conjunctions. It should be edited to assure brevity and forthrightness.

It must be remembered that the listener is 'in the dark' as far as prior knowledge of the sermon is concerned. While it is assumed that the preacher has spent many hours studying the text and working on the message, the listener has probably spent no time at all. What is hopefully a well-traveled landscape for the preacher is new territory to those in the audience. Further, unlike the reader of a book, the listener is at the mercy of the speaker. A reader can always go back and re-read an unclear idea, but a listener generally doesn't have that option. Therefore, the preacher must take every possible measure to make this proposition as clear as possible.

Clarity is important both in the way the proposition is formulated as well as in the way it is presented. When the preacher arrives at the point in delivery when the proposition is stated, care must be taken to vocally highlight it. It needs to be recognized as different in kind than other statements in the sermon. When it is spoken, the listener needs to have an 'aha! moment' with an understanding that this is what the sermon is about. Preachers can assist the listener by pausing before and after the statement of the proposition, by repeating it immediately the first time it is mentioned, by reminding the hearers of it during the course of the sermon (depending on the nature of the sermon), and by utilizing it as a part of the final transition into the conclusion. If the proposition is not grasped by the listener, the task of understanding the sermon as a whole will be more difficult. A good effort by the preacher to make the proposition clear will be appreciated by the hearer.

Utilize Good Structure Without Being Mechanical

While this book's primary intention is not to emphasize homiletics but rather a larger, more philosophical perspective on preaching, how we arrange sermons structurally is, in fact, an important aspect of our preaching philosophy. It relates directly to the means by which we hope to 'connect' with our hearers. Some homileticians have argued that structure is a relatively minor issue. This is reflected in the lack of emphasis given to the subject in some books on preaching. While extremely fine thought is given to many aspects of preaching, detailed explanation about how to move from a text to a sermon and how to organize the ideas of the sermon into a smooth flowing structure is sometimes minimally discussed in only one chapter or so. While the amount of discussion on the subject in the present volume will necessarily be limited, the important role of structure in the communication process still needs to be considered.

The Basic Purpose of Sermon Structure

We need to remember that sermon structure is a tool, a means to an end. It is not the end itself. A beautifully structured sermon can fail miserably while a message that is poorly conceived organizationally may succeed in helping people respond to its purpose. Preaching is a dynamic enterprise that cannot be reduced to simple formulas. Furthermore, we must affirm that preaching is a spiritual encounter, one in which the Holy Spirit of God moves upon the hearts of hearers after first, hopefully, ministering to the preacher.

Nevertheless, preaching is also about communication. It is about shared information, experiences, and values. It is about a Spirit-controlled person encountering the revealed Word of God and then passing along that Word to others. In the communication process, clarity is always preferable to ambiguity.

There are, of course, some who might chafe at this view of communication. Because of their understanding of some theory of language or because they're convinced of the rightness of postmodern thinking, they conclude that propositional truth cannot be communicated or understood. They would argue that the job of the preacher is to create a mood, a setting in which listeners can 'feel' that which becomes 'truth' for them, or has 'meaning' for them. I find it interesting, however, that these folks market their ideas via books and articles which, for the most part, consist of statements of opinion, i.e. 'propositional truth.' Furthermore, speaking very practically, we all live out our daily experiences on the assumption that words have meaning and that we can understand 'conversations' on numerous levels. Few embrace the ultimate end of postmodern thinking which is a nihilism that rejects all values and asserts that nothing is knowable or can be communicated.[7] Actually, to embrace philosophical nihilism seems to be contradictory to one's supposed position. If nothing is knowable or capable of communication, how can the supposed nihilist know this or talk about it?

I reiterate, then, that in the communication process, clarity is always preferable to ambiguity and that clear structure is one means of assisting clarity. This is true for preachers, for good structure will assist their clarity of thought, as well as that of the listener. When hearers are able to grasp the relationships between the many ideas in a sermon, they are well on their way to understanding the *message* in the sermon. A clear structure can help them do this.

The Essentials of Good Structure

It is not as difficult to arrange sermons with an adequate degree of structural integrity as some preachers seem to think. The starting point is the sermon proposition. As discussed in the previous section, this is a carefully planned sentence that states what this particular message is about. It is, in effect, the mission statement of the sermon. Everything in the sermon should somehow relate to it.

To support the proposition, the homilitician will devise two or more main points. These are sometimes called 'heads' or 'Romans' or 'moves'. They form the structural backbone of the sermon body.

The nature of the points will vary depending on the type of sermon being preached. In a sermon that seeks to prove the proposition through persuasion, these points may be thought of as 'proofs'. In a sermon that seeks to teach the listener how to do something, the main points will function as procedures to follow. In an inductively arranged sermon, these points will be 'particulars' which collectively lead to the general truth that will be announced toward the end of the message. In a narrative sermon, these points will be less obvious and not even formally announced, but they will guide the preacher and hearer through the stages of the narrative's development so a sense of progress is maintained. Regardless of the overall sermon design, the main points have the basic function of supporting the proposition.

In turn, each main point will be established by sub-points which I simply call supporting material. This will consist of the major part of the sermon's content and will be explanatory, illustrational, and applicational. Just as each main point must relate to and help support the proposition, so all of the supporting materials must relate directly to their respective main points. This sometimes requires self-discipline that is painful. It can be tempting to slip in exegetical gems or wonderful illustrations that don't relate directly to the thrust of a main point. One of the difficult parts of writing sermons is the decisions to be made regarding what *not* to include!

Regardless of the overall homiletical design of a sermon, this kind of structural integrity should characterize the sermon body. If it does, the preacher is well on the way to present a message that is clearly focused. It should be remembered that a sermon should have a single goal or purpose. This is not to say that collateral benefit will not be realized apart from this intended purpose. It undoubtedly will thanks to the Holy Spirit's ministry in meeting needs at different levels. The preacher, however, must keep in mind that a sermon that aims to do many things will probably do very little and be helpful to few.

Beyond the sermon body, the introduction and conclusion must be given careful thought. It is important, in my opinion, to prepare these *after* the body of the sermon has been completed. It's difficult to introduce a total stranger properly, but easier to introduce someone we know well. This is the way it is with a sermon. A general idea about the subject of a message is inadequate information for formulating an effective introduction. Similarly, we cannot summarize what a sermon has been about or call for a proper response until we know exactly what it is that we will have said. Thus, the conclusion of a sermon will ordinarily be considered as the last step in the sermons preparation.

A sermon introduction has four basic purposes. It must disclose the sermon's broad subject; it must arouse the listener's interest by promoting the importance (relevance) of the subject; it should indicate directly or indirectly, depending on the sermon style, how this message will be developed; and, it should enhance the good will of the audience toward the speaker. An introduction should be brief and should avoid material that is irrelevant to the sermon. Keep in mind that it is usually during the first two or three minutes of a sermon that hearers will decide whether or not it is worthwhile to listen. The introduction should be crafted carefully, therefore, to help those in attendance become an actual *audience*.

Unfortunately, conclusions are often ill-prepared or simply presented in an 'off the cuff' manner. In a very real sense, this part of the sermon is the most important part for it is here that people will act or fail to act on what they have heard. The conclusion should generally be quite brief, simply reminding people of the main thrust of the sermon and inviting them to respond in a way that is appropriate for this particular message. This final application should not detour from the sermon's propositional intention. For example, a sermon dealing with financial stewardship should not conclude with an evangelistic appeal. To do so is to create a twofold problem. First, hearers are given permission not to respond to the sermon's purpose – they're left 'off the hook'. Second, persons being asked to respond to Christ for salvation probably are being asked to 'sign a blank check – to respond without adequate knowledge of what it means to become a Christian. If a subject is worth preaching it's worth asking people to respond to appropriately.

The Misuse of Structure

My wife and I recently had two living room chairs upholstered. We were apprehensive about doing this because we chose a fabric with stripes for chairs with curved backs. The owner of the fabric shop told us this was probably not a good idea. On the other hand, the upholsterer assured us that the fabric would work well. When he delivered the chairs following the completion of the job, he knocked on the door and I asked how they turned out. He replied with only a faint trace of a grin, 'They're a work of art.' It was evident that he took a great deal of pride in his workmanship, but he was right. The chairs were really beautiful. Suppose, however, that the fabric had been properly installed and the stitching carefully done, but he had not replaced the cushions, cushions with broken springs. The chairs might have looked like a work of art, but their functionality would have been almost worthless.

It can be that way with our preaching. Good structure should enhance the effectiveness of sermons, not simply be a work of art. Our goal should not be to have people think, 'What a well-crafted sermon!', but rather, 'What a powerful message!' It may be, for example, that a person is skilled in the art of alliteration. This is sometimes a helpful mnemonic device. If not practiced with restraint, however, alliteration can overpower what is being said by becoming the center of attention. Further, if a person is not skilled in this art, a lot of time can be wasted in attempting to come up with a beautifully alliterated outline, time that might better be used in the preparation of other parts of the sermon.

Good sermon structure is an important means to an end, but we must be clear as to what constitutes this end. It is the clear communication of a message. This purpose is worth the time investment if treated with balance. It is a misuse of structure to regard it as having a purpose other than the enhancement of communication.

Structure can be misused also by presenting it in a mechanical fashion. While the listener needs to be made aware of the proposition and understand the relationship of the rest of the sermon's ideas to it, this should not be done in a rigid, formal way. The introduction should not begin with the preacher saying: 'My subject today is "prayer" and my theme is "effectiveness in prayer". Further, my proposition is that "we can indeed have a prayer life that's effective".' Nor should the sermon body be presented by saying, 'My first main point is that effective prayer is a result of a properly placed faith.' And then later, 'My second main point is that effective prayer is a result of knowing God intimately.' Later still, we should not say, 'Now in conclusion...' This kind of presentation creates an unnecessary formality that is impersonal and artificial.

The various components in a sermon can be articulated in less formal ways that flow naturally along with what is being said otherwise. The introduction might begin like this:

It's been said that communication is the key to any good relationship. This is true and I believe too that prayer is our communication link to God. Yet, we struggle with prayer, don't we? And few of us claim to have an outstanding prayer life. The good news is that we can indeed have a prayer life that's effective.

In five short sentences, this introduction approaches the general subject area (prayer), the sermon theme (effective prayer), and the proposition (we can indeed have a prayer life that's effective). This example is not a complete introduction but shows that basic structural components can be presented conversationally rather than mechanically. Other important structural components can likewise be presented in a normal, relational, conversational way. Our usage of structure need not deteriorate into a reflection of a high school public speaking course.

Why does good structuring relate to the matter of sermon variety? It relates because variety is the result of rearranging the normal structural components. For example, a deductively arranged sermon will state the proposition prior to the sermon body while an inductively arranged sermon will delay the propositional statement until the body has been concluded. As seen earlier, propositions themselves can take different shapes and serve different functions. Because of this, main points will necessarily vary in their statement and function. Still, it must be emphasized that regardless of the arrangement and style of the structural components, structural integrity must be valued and maintained.

UNDERSTAND TRADITIONAL CATEGORIES

When I use the label 'traditional categories,' what do I mean? I am not using the term in any biased sense; rather, Im simply recognizing that there have been some methods utilized through the centuries that have had merit and continue to be effective. Fant wrote of preaching's double stubbornness. He said it is stubbornly there and it is stubbornly the same.[8] In what sense is this latter opinion generally true?

Henry Grady Davis and others have pointed out that Christian preaching falls within the general framework of classic rhetoric. Davis argues:

> This is not a plea for an intensive formal study of rhetoric. Just the same, it is chastening to remember the proud history rhetoric has had, from Aristotle to Brooks and Warren, as the art of communication in language. Many of Christianity's great preachers were rhetoricians before they were preachers, among them Ambrose, Augustine, and Chrysostom.[9]

This link to the widespread understanding of rhetoric by many preachers in the early church is doubtless the reason preaching has maintained many of the same traits and methods down through the years. It has a history that continues to be an influence with the result of being stubbornly the same in some ways.

Three Traditional Categories

A study of the literature on preaching from the mid-nineteenth century until about 1980, will disclose that three primary kinds of sermons are discussed: topical, textual, and expository. Some of these books devote individual chapters to each of these approaches.[10] These three categories are actually much older, however, dating back to at least the thirteenth century where a book attributed to Thomas Aquinas, probably erroneously, *A Treatise on the Art of Preaching* (*Tractatus de Arte Praedicandi*), speaks of these approaches.[11]

I've never found these categories overly helpful because they seem to overlap. Does not every sermon have a topic? Should not every sermon have a text? Should not every sermon expose the meaning of the text? I find myself nodding in agreement with Davis:

The terms, topical, textual, and expository, are used loosely and not at all uniformly in homiletical literature, and are of limited usefulness. Having a topic does not necessarily make a sermon topical. A good textual or expository sermon also has a topic expressed or unexpressed, a unitary idea, an inclusive subject with one or more predicates.[12]

Topical Sermons

Though Davis is correct is asserting that these terms are not used uniformly, it can be said that, in general, a topical sermon is one in which supporting material for the topic (often extracted from some text, though not always in a hermeneutically sound way) is found in places other than the main text. Main points, for example, may be 'proof-texts' from various parts of Scripture and ideas may also be imported from outside the Bible.

The topic is preached not on the basis of a focus-text, but from the tenor of Scripture as a whole. Some even assert that specific biblical support isn't required as long as the topic is addressed from the perspective of 'the gospel. One proponent of this idea states his opinion in a rather extreme way:

... the Bible is not the only guide for the Christian life. Furthermore, the Bible is silent on some subjects and can be scarcely used to address others. Occasionally the Bible is not the best guide and, in some few instances, the Bible is actually an unreliable guide.[13]

Thankfully, many topical preachers do not stand in such judgment over the Scriptures, but rather allow the Scriptures to stand in judgment over them. I'm hard pressed to think of a topic needing to be preached to a Christian congregation that is not addressed in Scripture, at least in terms of biblical principles. Nor do I believe the Bible, when properly understood, to be an unreliable guide.

Textual Sermons

As usually presented in the literature as well as in the pulpit, textual sermons are those which focus on a specific text, a verse or two at most, and which find both the subject and the main ideas in that text. The main points are generally based on explicit statements in the text or on implications inferred from the text. Materials from other parts of Scripture may be used also along with material from outside the Bible. Baumann offers a positive assessment of this type of message:

> One of the values of this type of preaching is that it is biblical and therefore restrains the preacher from perpetrating an exclusive diet of personal ideas upon his congregation. It also affords the opportunity for study in depth; that is, an intensive scrutiny of a single biblical concept found in a verse or two of Scripture.[14]

Expository Sermons

What is expository preaching? The answer to this depends on whom you ask because explanations and definitions of this method are quite varied.

I recall attending the Congress on Biblical Exposition in Anaheim, California in 1986. Many well known 'expository preachers' spoke in the plenary sessions. On the second night of the conference, following three other plenary messages spread over that two-day period, John Stott spoke. He electrified the audience by beginning with a statement something like the following: 'We are at the Congress on Biblical Exposition. We have heard several sermons but have not yet heard one that was expositional.' Folks in the audience looked at one another nervously but were then treated to an outstanding expository sermon.

Many differentiate this approach from a textual sermon solely on the length of the text. If one preaches on a text longer than one or two verses, it is an expository sermon. The homiletical structure or the handling of the text does not seem to matter. This is the viewpoint of Andrew Blackwood, the venerable former professor of preaching at Princeton Theological Seminary.

In the present book preaching means the interpretation of life today, in light that comes from God today, largely through the Bible. Expository preaching means that the light for any sermon comes mainly from a Bible passage longer than two or three consecutive verses. This kind of message differs from a textual sermon chiefly in the length of the Bible passage.[15]

Baumann makes a similar statement: 'Expository sermons are based on a biblical passage longer than two verses.'[16]

Some understand expository preaching only as a verse-by-verse running commentary, not necessarily unified by a thematic direction or designed with main points and sub-points.[17] While this approach may have some value in terms of the teaching of biblical information, it usually fails to present a focused purpose and anticipated response.

Another concept of expository preaching is that of doing a series of sermons based on a particular book of the Bible. Donald Barnhouse's four volumes on Romans are often singled out as a collection of expository messages. I've seen books of sermons with titles like *Expositions on Revelation* or *Expository Sermons on Matthew*. An examination of the sermons within these volumes shows that some of them may be expositional but others better fit into the topical or textual categories. A series of sermons connected only because they're based on the same book of Scripture doesn't necessarily assure that individual sermons are expository.

Some expositors insist that all of the parts of the sermon be based on all of the sentences, clauses, phrases, and words in the text. Every idea in a text, they say, should correlate to some part of the sermon. Thus, the subject, theme, and proposition must come from the text along with every main point idea, but so must every sub-point and other sermon detail. This seems to be a rather laborious approach that might easily become tedious and even overwhelming to the listener.

Other expositors agree that the subject, theme, proposition, and main points should come from the text, but that sub-points, illustrations, and other sermon materials might come from elsewhere in Scripture or even from outside of Scripture. Further, they do not believe it is necessary for the sermon to comment on every detail in the passage. The sermon should instead clearly present the thematic thrust of the passage utilizing the text's various statements to clarify and enhance it. This is not to say that textual details should be ignored in one's study, but that the sermon should have an objective that has been carefully thought through – one that echoes the intended purpose of the text – and that the sermon use those parts of the passage which benefit this objective. This is an overview of the kind of exposition with which I am most comfortable.

In a book unfortunately long out of print, *Power in Expository Preaching*, Faris Whitesell gives a lengthy introduction to this subject and then concludes that this kind of preaching involves several factors:

1. It is based on a passage in the Bible, either short or long.
2. It seeks to learn the primary, basic meaning of that passage.
3. It relates that meaning to the context of the passage.
4. It digs down for the timeless, universal truths stemming out of the passage.
5. It organizes these truths tightly around one central theme.
6. It uses the rhetorical elements of explanation, argument, illustration, and application to bring the truth of the passage home to the hearer.
7. It seeks to persuade the listener to obey the truth of the passage discussed.[18]

This is an excellent summary of the character of expository preaching, but it leads to the distinction between these three traditional methods beginning to blur somewhat.

The Limitation of the Traditional Categories

Having looked at the three traditional categories of sermons – topical, textual, and expository – I return to my earlier statement: I've never found these categories overly helpful. Yes, I've used them to distinguish one form from another, but a larger issue is always present. Did the sermon, regardless of category, faithfully proclaim the Scripture by allowing the text to make its *own* statement? If a sermon does this, then I am comfortable calling it expository in the larger and proper sense of the word. If it didn't, then I question whether it is biblical or Christian preaching. The task of the Christian preacher is to be an ambassador of the King. This means telling forth *his* message, not the preacher's own views about something. James Stewart speaks eloquently to this point in his classic work, *Heralds of God*, as the first of three pleas:

> The first is a plea for expository preaching. This is one of the greatest needs of the hour. There are rich rewards of human gratitude waiting for the man who can make the Bible come alive. Congregations are sick of dissertations on problems, and essays on aspects of the religious situation: such sermons are indeed no true preaching at all. Men are not wanting to be told our poor views and arguments and ideals. They are emphatically wanting to be told what God has said, and is saying, in His Word.[19]

More than half a century after these words were penned, Stewart is still correct. Sermons that deal with the themes of 'pop psychology' or the fads of the day may tickle the listeners' ears for a moment, but without a deep rootedness in Scripture they will result in little in the way of real and eternal benefit.

It should be kept in mind that Stewart was not necessarily speaking of texts that are three or more verses in length, though his sentiments would be true of longer texts as well as shorter ones. Rather, he was referring to the way texts are handled. Longer texts can be handled poorly without really allowing the passage's own statement to be clear. On the other hand, a short text might be preached with astute expository ability.

The formal definition of expository preaching given by the Olfords further demonstrates the point I'm attempting to make:

> Expository preaching is the Spirit-empowered explanation and proclamation of the text of God's Word with due regard to the historical, contextual, grammatical, and doctrinal significance of the given passage, with the specific object of invoking a Christ-transforming response.[20]

This brief yet comprehensive definition says nothing about the length of the passage. Again, its emphasis is on the way the passage is presented. Elsewhere, the Olfords make this statement about preaching:

> ... a sermon is the proclamation of the Word of God only if the text of the Word is accurately expounded and preached. So, in the strictest sense of the term, *authentic* preaching is expository preaching.[21]

John Stott echoes this sentiment. He writes of the traditional categories and purposes as 'simpler classifications'. He continues:

> There are topical sermons and textual sermons, they say. Some are evangelistic or apologetic or prophetic, others doctrinal or devotional or ethical or hortatory, while somewhere down the line 'exegetical' or 'expository' sermons are included. I cannot myself acquiesce in this relegation (sometimes even grudging) of expository preaching to one alternative among many. It is my contention that all true Christian preaching is expository preaching.... The expositor prizes open what appears to be closed, makes plain what is obscure, unravels what is knotted and unfolds what is tightly packed. The opposite of exposition is 'imposition', which is to impose on the text what is not there. But the 'text' in question could be a verse, or a sentence, or even a single word. It could equally be a paragraph, or a chapter, or a whole book. The size of the text is immaterial, so long as it is biblical. What matters is what we do with it.... In expository preaching, the biblical text is neither a conventional introduction to a sermon on a largely different theme, nor a convenient peg on which to hang a ragbag of miscellaneous thoughts, but a master which dictates and controls what is said.[22]

These and others bear witness that Christian preaching must be expositional. The issue is not length of text or homiletical arrangement; rather it is the reiterating and applying of that which God has already spoken. Vines and Shaddix comment:

Expository sermons may or may not stand in contrast to other traditional sermon forms. Because exposition is a *process*, it should never be put in juxtaposition to other sermonic models. All preaching should be expositional in nature. The preacher should utilize only sermon forms that issue forth from good hermeneutics, thorough exegesis, and credible homiletics.[23]

Rather than pondering the artificial differences between the three traditional categories of topical, textual, and expository sermons, the preacher should instead determine to make every sermon, regardless of homiletical arrangement, a clear statement of what God has said. This is exposition rightly understood.

Use Exposition Creatively

As with sermon structure, creativity is not an end in itself. It is a means to the end of grabbing and maintaining the attention of our potential listeners. Preachers do not need to work hard at entertaining because that is not our calling. We don't need to labor long hours to discover a text never before preached or a truth never before told. Creativity is not a matter of pursuing our own cleverness in order to 'wow' those who hear us. These endeavors are all preacher-centered rather than God-centered. Whatever we do that is creative must be done as a reflection of God's own creativity and must ultimately focus attention on him. As Elizabeth Achtemeier wrote:

> We preachers need to labor over our words, so that they may mirror at least a hint of such a God of glory, though we know that heaven and and the highest heaven cannot contain him, much less our awkward phrases.... We preachers are called to be nothing less than the mediators of the speaking and doing of God.[24]

We need to work hard at presenting our sermons in ways that attract and maintain a hearing for it is our creative God whom we represent.

Be Willing to Experiment

As a young person, I was never fond of 'classical' music. Then I heard a composition by Joseph Haydn (1732-1809), prolific Austrian composer, older friend of Mozart, and instructor of Beethoven. The piece is his Symphony No. 94, in G, fondly referred to by his London audiences for whom it was written as the 'Surprise Symphony'. It is so-called because at various intervals the listener is lulled into solitude by eight bars of soft music followed by eight bars of even softer music. Then, unexpectedly, a sudden explosion of the full orchestra resounds and the listener moves from complacency to excitement. Yet, it has been said of this composition:

> ... all of Haydn's work is full of just such surprises, such swift changes of mood, and that the surprise in Symphony No. 94 is a small one compared with the breath-taking new departures that Haydn kept making, over and over again, from the music that had gone before him.[25]

Haydn was a creative genius and his music enthralled me as it had previous generations. I began listening to the works of other composers and became a devoted fan of all the styles – baroque, classical, romantic, neo-classical, and contemporary – of so-called classical music. This happened because one noted composer refused to be in a rut.

Many preachers are in a rut! They plod along using the same homiletical method week after week, year after year. This is usually the method learned in seminary but might be one developed afterward. It may be a very good method. It may be useful with more than one kind of biblical text. It may allow a text to make its own statement. It may be easy to organize and easy to follow. But regardless of the method's virtues, it can still keep the preacher in a rut. This can easily contribute to frustration both on the part of the preacher and the listener. The 'same old, same old' can quickly become *old*!

Preachers locked into one method may suffer from homiletical boredom. The excitement of seeing a message framed in a fresh way is seldom realized as it was earlier in one's ministry. It is a positive thing to experience the satisfaction of a well-formed sermon come into being from a plan that has been carefully thought through.

Listeners can also suffer from homiletical boredom, though they wouldn't call it that. They simply know that a lot of sermons sound the same, even though subjects and texts may vary, and there is little in them to hold one's attention.

It can be uncomfortable for the preacher to experiment with sermon structure. After all, this new arrangement has to be preached and maybe it will bomb! We know all too well that creative presentations will not necessarily be welcomed by every hearer, yet this is a risk that must be taken if we're to get out of our homiletical rut.

As suggested previously, creativity for its own sake is not the point. We must therefore be aware of our true motivations. Are we experimenting with a new structure to be clever or to appear to be creative geniuses? If so, we're drawing attention to ourselves and this is the very antithesis of preaching. The whole point of pulpit creativity is to give the gospel a new hearing, to reenlist listeners who have tuned us out, at least temporarily, because they're bored with what seems to be a lot of repetitious preaching whether in subject, style, or both.

Use Deductive Approaches in a Variety of Ways

As discussed among homileticians, the term *deduction* is used in two ways. It is used to speak of the kind of argument being made and it is also used to speak of the arrangement of the sermon homiletically. These uses of deduction often come together in a single sermon but at other times a sermon may be arranged inductively with an deductive argument, or arranged deductively with an inductive argument.

Deductive Argumentation

A sermon can be presented as a deductive argument by using formal syllogistic reasoning. This kind of sermon presents a major premise, a minor premise, and a conclusion that is logically deduced. While the sermon arrangement is inductive in form, the reasoning process employed is pure deduction. Sangster gives a simple example of this approach:

> All men need a Saviour.
> You are a man,
> Therefore, you need a Saviour.[26]

The preacher might consider this to be a three-point sermon, or possibly a two-point sermon with the conclusion of the syllogism serving as the foundation of the sermon's conclusion. This probably doesn't matter to the hearer. The important thing from the listener's perspective is to make certain that the flow of the argument is clearly presented. Otherwise, the purpose of the message has been lost.

When a syllogistic approach is used, the preacher must take special care to assure that each of the premises represents a statement of truth that can be established, and that each of the premises properly relates to the other. In a categorical type of syllogism such as that above, the major premise sets forth a universally true statement while the minor premise then introduces a particular part of that universal. In this case the universal has to do with 'all men' and the particular selects one part, 'you are a man.' Because the two premises are true, the conclusion must necessarily be true.

Another type of syllogism is hypothetical in nature. The major premise raises the possibility of something being true and then sets out to prove it is. It looks like this:

> If you are a human being, you need a Savior.
> You are indeed a human being.
> Therefore, you need a Savior.

Another example of a hypothetical syllogism could be stated:

> If all people are by nature spiritually dead, they need to find spiritual life.
> All people are actually spiritually dead by nature.
> Therefore, all people need to find spiritual life.

This syllogism raises the possibility of spiritually dead people needing life, shows that we're all spiritually dead, and establishes that we therefore need spiritual life.

A third type of syllogism is called a disjunctive syllogism. This kind of argument presents two possibilities and then eliminates one as being undesirable or untrue.

> We can either pray or give up hope.
> We should not give up hope.
> Therefore, we should pray.

Or, again:

> Christ is either God incarnate or a mere human being.
> Christ is not a mere human being.
> Therefore, Christ is really God incarnate.

With a disjunctive syllogism, care must be taken to assure there are only two valid possibilities. Otherwise, the either/or choice of the major premise is a false choice.

It is not my purpose to suggest that syllogistically arranged sermons be standard pulpit fare or that the preacher present such sermons with technical language intact. There will be occasions, however, when this type of sermon may be useful to present an old truth in a fresh way. Sangster's statement shows wise balance regarding the use of deductive reasoning:

> A preacher need not be familiar with the technical terms of logic and may seldom (if ever) use them in the pulpit, but the discipline of logic will do him incalculable good. Exercise in the clear definition of terms, studies in classification, the development of a keen scent for fallacies, marking the limits of legitimate inference – all these are of unspeakable help to a preacher. If the opportunity to study formal logic passes him by, let him at least scrutinize, in the light of God, the chain of reasoning in every sermon that argues a case. Let it be, to the limit of his ability, *honest* arguing.[27]

Deductive Sermon Arrangements

In terms of sermon arrangement, it can be safely said that the vast majority of sermons preached today are arranged deductively. The subject to be considered is introduced, some kind of thesis statement about the subject is given, and then main points are set forth to establish or demonstrate the validity of this thesis. The generic outline would be something like the following:

Introduction (broad subject, theme, text, textual background)
Proposition (thesis statement)
Main Point I
    Sub-points: explanation, illustrations, application
Main Point II
    Sub-points: explanation, illustrations, application
Main Point III
    Sub-points: explanation, illustrations, application
Conclusion: summation, final application

This type of approach is sometimes caricatured as: 'Tell them what you're going to say, say it, and tell them what you've said.'

Depending on the nature of the proposition (thesis statement), the main points might seek to persuade the listener of the importance of certain values or actions, or they might attempt to persuade toward actually modifying one's behavior or to encourage the listener to take certain steps toward better living. Main points might also be primarily explanatory or even illustrational. Usually, the sermon develops in a somewhat argumentative way, perhaps not as finely tuned as a legal brief, but an argument nevertheless.

Deductive sermons have been a tried and true general approach for centuries. Yet, although they have a deductive approach in common, it should not be thought that all deductive sermons are the same. Various types can be presented in terms of the kind of text used, the sermon purpose, the type of proposition utilized, and the number and style of main points.

Neither this book in general nor this chapter in particular is intended to be a treatise on precise homiletical structuring. There are other volumes that will be much more useful to the reader in this regard.[28] Through the years, I have found three particular methods of deductive preaching to be especially useful in terms of being applicable to a great many texts and in their ability to be varied from sermon to sermon.

The Keyword Method

This basic approach was clarified in the mid-twentieth century by Charles Koller and subsequently popularized by some of his students who themselves became teachers of preaching. The method was doubtless used long before Koller, however, though perhaps not in a highly polished form. It is often utilized by preachers today who in spite of a lack of training in the precise method, instinctively approach a text and its structure with a keyword outline in mind.

The body of a keyword sermon has main points that fall into some category described by a keyword device. This device is a single plural noun that describes the nature of each of the main points. For example, the main points of a given message might each be an instruction to follow. Thus, the heart of the sermon might say that 'We can experience the daily presence of God (this is the proposition) by following the instructions given in our text.' This becomes a clue to the listener as to how the message will proceed point by point.

The main points of a keyword sermon are based on parallel concepts in the preaching passage. These are often discovered by means of a 'mechanical layout' of the passage. This is not a grammatical diagram, but rather a schematic arrangement of the text in terms of the relationships of the various ideas it contains. It shows how primary clauses, secondary clauses, phrases, and connectives all relate. Such a layout will show one or more sets of parallel ideas. There may be, for example, two or more *imperatives* to obey; two or more *warnings* to heed; two or more *steps* to take; two or more *blessings* to be gained. It is my opinion that taking the time to produce such a layout as part of one's exegetical study will help assure that the preacher really does understand what the text is all about.

The usual 'lazy' way to do a keyword sermon is to announce a somewhat general theme (without stating a specific propositional statement) and then transition into the sermon body by saying something like: 'There are *three things* in this passage that we ought to notice about God's love,' or whatever the broad theme happens to be. I suppose there are worse homiletical sins committed but we can do better than peddle vagaries. Preciseness of language in a clear propositional statement, in a carefully chosen keyword device, and in crisply stated main points that are actually parallel conceptually will do wonders in terms of our hearers knowing precisely what we are talking about. Following is a brief outline of a keyword sermon. Another example is found in chapter 3.

The God Who Demands Priority (Haggai 1:1-15)

Subject: Priorities

Theme: The priority God expects

Proposition: We must give God the priority He demands. (Implies 'where?')

Transitional Sentence (with keyword device): God demands priority in all the *areas* of our lives as is seen in Haggai 1.

I. God's priority must overshadow our use of time (vv. 2-4).

II. God's priority must overshadow our quest for a living (vv. 5-6).

III. God's priority must overshadow our desire for personal wealth (v. 9).

IV. God's priority must overshadow every concern of our heart (vv. 5, 7). ('Give careful thought to your ways')

Once a basic outline of this nature has been formulated, the preacher can proceed to add sub-points (including explanation, illustration, and application) to the main points, and then do an introduction, and conclusion. This type of sermon allows for a cogent presentation in terms of argumentation, and it accurately reflects the thrust and content of the preaching text. It is a basic approach to expositional preaching that I've used for many years. I highly recommend it.

The Analytical Method

This approach is based on the idea of taking a whole and breaking it down into its parts for closer scrutiny. This is what happens when we analyze virtually anything.

I've found this method to be useful with narrative and biographical sermons, as well as with sermons that are doctrinal or ethical in nature. Whereas a keyword approach is often useful with texts that are relatively brief – a paragraph or so in length – an analytical structure tends to work best when there are two or more paragraphs under consideration as long as they each deal with the same topic.

Based on the text at hand, a subject will be chosen and this subject is then broken down into its parts. This is done by noting how the text presents the parts of the whole and this is often reflected in the paragraphing. A good paragraph has thematic unity. When two or more paragraphs discuss the same broader subject, each one generally speaks to some aspect of the whole.

This is seen clearly, for instance, in 1 Corinthians 13 where the broad subject is love. The first paragraph (1-3) speaks of the comparative value of love, the second paragraph (4-7) gives us descriptions of how love behaves, and the third paragraph (8-13) tells us that love lasts forever. Or again, Philippians 2:1-4 gives a plea for humility, verses 5-8 present the great example of humility, and verses 9-11 describe the result of Christs humility. Following is a simple example of an analytical sermon outline.

God's Kind of Marriage (Ephesians 5:22-33)

Proposition: A study of marriage in Ephesians 5:22-33 will show us the rightful responsibility of husbands and wives.

I. The wife's role in marriage is seen in verses 22-24.

II. The husband's roles in marriage are seen in verses 25-33.

Sometimes the parts of the whole are found within a single paragraph. According to the NIV, Ephesians 6:10-18 is one paragraph. Yet, there are natural sub-themes within this passage that would allow for an analytical treatment such as this.

Doing Battle with the Enemy (Ephesians 6:10-18)

Proposition: A study of the concept of spiritual warfare in Ephesians 6:10-18 will help us live victoriously in Christ.

I. The reality of spiritual warfare is seen in verses 10-12.

II. The weapons for spiritual warfare are seen in verses 13-17.

III. The underlying resource for spiritual warfare is seen in verse 18.

These simple outlines are nicely unified around a clear subject and each sermon body breaks down its subject into graspable parts. Another example of an analytical outline is found in chapter 3.

Textual Sermons

My concept of textual sermons is somewhat different from the traditional use of the term, though I hasten to add that traditional textual sermons are often well done and faithful reflections of the thrust of their texts. My style of textual preaching takes a brief verse, or even part of a verse, and utilizes that verse as the sermon proposition itself. While some propositions *analyze* (as in the case of an analytical sermon) and others *obligate* or *demonstrate ability* or *value*, (as with the keyword approach), I use this textual proposition to *impress*. (A chart with various kinds of propositions can be found earlier in this chapter.) When preaching a textual sermon, it is my goal to leave the hearer with the text/proposition reverberating in his or her mind long after the sermon has ended. To this end, I repeat the proposition numerous times while I proceed through each part of the sermon.

I owe the insight for doing this to E. V. Hill, the late, long-time pastor of the Mount Zion Missionary Baptist Church in Los Angeles, and one of the outstanding preachers in the country. Speaking in chapel on the campus of Columbia International University in the 1980's, Dr. Hill spoke of the needs of the children of Israel during their bondage in Egypt. God called Moses but he was slow in getting the message even though confronted with the burning bush. Moses asks, 'God, I know my people are in trouble. What's the answer?' God responds, 'Moses, you are the answer!' This statement, 'you are the answer,' was repeated throughout the remainder of the message more than a dozen times, perhaps closer to two dozen. As the needs of our world were presented, 'you are the answer' rolled forth from the preacher with convicting power. I doubt that any person walked away from chapel that day without clearly understanding what they had heard and what bearing it had on their lives. Hill's proposition was strongly impressed and imbedded into the consciousness of each one.

The text/proposition selected must be fairly brief so it can be repeated many times throughout the sermon without sounding awkwardly redundant. A one-liner such as 1 Peter 5:7, for example, works quite nicely: 'Cast all your anxiety on him because he cares for you.' A single verse like this can stand on its own merit and provide wonderful encouragement if it can be properly impressed.

The sermon body might be developed in several different ways. It might present a series of *illustrations* of persons in Scripture who experienced the truth of the statement.

Proposition: Cast all your anxiety on him because he cares for you.

I. This is illustrated in the experience of the chronically ill woman in Mark 5.

II. This is illustrated in the experience of Paul and Silas in Acts 16:25-34.

III. This is illustrated in the experience of the church in Acts 12:1-17.

The main points might break down the text into appropriate parts. This is sometimes called the *telescopic method*.

Proposition: Cast all your anxiety on him because he cares for you.

I. *Cast all your anxiety* . . .

II. Cast all your anxiety *on him* . . .

III. Cast all your anxiety on him *because he cares for you*.

Another way to design the sermon body is to identify and discuss *implications* of the text. This approach requires two cautions. First, the main points must indeed be implied by the text and context without eisogesis being done. Second, these points must be implications of the text, not something already stated explicitly in the text.

Proposition: Cast all your anxiety on him because he cares for you.
 I. This implies that anxieties come our way sooner or later.
 II. This implies that we are incapable of handling anxieties by ourselves.
 III. This implies that another can handle our needs sufficiently.

Another example of a textual-implicational sermon is found in chapter three.

Finally, textual propositions can sometimes be developed by using the so-called *ladder method*. This is accomplished when the last part of a main point becomes the first part of the next main point.

Proposition: Cast all your anxiety on him because he cares for you.
 I. Dealing with anxiety is a serious matter.
 II. Serious matters require the right kind of help.
 III. The right kind of help involves someone who empathetically cares.

There are many ways to construct deductively arranged sermons. These three approaches have been found to be useful by many. They can be used with many kinds of texts and provide needed homiletical variety.

Use a Variety of Inductive Approaches

The past three decades have seen a rising interest in a 'new' approach to sermons called inductive preaching. The method was discussed in earlier works, but it was Fred Craddock's *As One without Authority*, published in 1971, that was the chief catalyst for the method's rise in popularity. Not everyone has warmly embraced inductive preaching. Some see it as less than biblical preaching because it appears, at first glance at least, to lack the firm ring of authoritative proclamation. It is feared by some to be antithetical to expositional preaching and deficient in terms of proper application.

It must be said, however, that the worth of inductive preaching has been affirmed by many who take biblical authority seriously. Among those who have written favorably on the subject since the time of Craddock are J. Daniel Baumann, *An Introduction to Contemporary Preaching* (1972, 79-81); Haddon Robinson, *Biblical Preaching* (1980, 125-127); Ralph and Gregg Lewis, *Inductive Preaching* (1983); Harold Freeman, *Variety in Biblical Preaching* (1987, 171-174); John Brokhoff, *As One With Authority* (1989, 158-164); Ralph and Gregg Lewis, *Learning to Preach Like Jesus* (1989), and the present writer, *Homiletical Handbook* (1992, 97-103).

Definition and Explanation

The term 'inductive preaching' needs to be carefully defined for it can be used in at least three ways related to preaching. First, the term is used to describe elements in sermon such as story telling, analogies and other figures of speech, examples, questions, drama, and dialogical statements. Second, the term is used also in reference to a specific kind of formal reasoning, an argumentation from particular instances that leads to a general truth. Third, among homileticians, the term is used to speak of the structural plan of a sermon, one in which the proposition is not announced formally until the concluding stages of the sermon.

It is possible that either or both of the first two usages may be present in a sermon without the sermon being an inductively structured sermon. Some inductive elements such as illustrations, analogies, or rhetorical questions may be present in a deductively arranged sermon. It may be that some sub-points under a main point will use inductive argumentation. Still, the entire sermon is not structured inductively. Thus, it can be argued regarding the preachers and preaching in *Twenty Centuries of Great Preaching* that

... All ninety-six of the notable speakers included in this thirteen-volume work used some inductive ingredients and showed signs of inductive process. The common thread through their greatness was not some secret aspect of exposition or oratory. It was induction.[29]

It may be that this opinion is overstated, yet it illustrates that inductive elements alone do not constitute inductive preaching that is thoroughly inductive. Indeed the preachers represented in *Twenty Centuries of Great Preaching* overwhelmingly utilize deductive approaches to structure.

When the term inductive is used in the sense of overall sermon design or structure, this type of sermon would be one in which a broad theme is set early, issues and questions are raised, but the precise proposition is not revealed until the transition into the sermon's conclusion. The basic flow of its outline might look something like this:

Introduction: (Question, illustration, Rhetorical questions, teasers, statistics, examples, etc.)
Theme (usually in the form of a question)
Main Point I
    Sub-points, examples, partial affirmation
Main Point II
    Sub-points, examples, partial affirmation
Main Point III
    Sub-points, examples, partial affirmation
Proposition (total affirmation of the sermon's main idea)
(Read the text)
Closing appeals and applications

It should be noted that inductive reasoning is not fully indispensable to inductive structure. A syllogistic sermon employs deductive reasoning – an argument that moves from the general to the specific – yet is arranged inductively with the proposition, which is the logical conclusion of the major and minor premises, announced at the end of the sermon.[30]

For our discussion here, the idea of inductive preaching will include all three of the above meanings: sermon elements which are inherently inductive, some form of inductive reasoning that presents the sermon's agenda convincingly, and an overall homiletical arrangement in which the proposition of the sermon is not fully announced until the end of the sermon body where it will be clearly stated and emphasized so that each listener will understand that this is the major truth being declared in this message.

Issues Related to Inductive Preaching

Because the concept of inductive exposition may be new to some, it may be helpful to discuss several issues related to preaching in general and inductive preaching in particular. These include audience involvement, authority, effectiveness, and difficulty.

Audience Involvement

In regard to audience involvement, it is an obvious truism that preaching is irrelevant if there is no audience. The most carefully prepared and articulately delivered sermon is pointless if no one hears it. We may rightly assume that some are listening. Some members of our audiences have a heart for God and sufficient self-discipline to cause them to listen to almost any kind of sermon, interesting or otherwise. But do as many listen – really listen – as we think? And, do they listen well?

A classic example of poor listening took place on the evening of October 30, 1938 when huge numbers of American radio listeners were persuaded by actor Orson Welles that their country was being invaded by creatures from Mars. These extra-terrestrials were described as creatures who spit flames, looked like snakes, and stood as tall as large bears. In spite of the fact that it was Halloween and that several clear announcements were made regarding the nature of the program, there was widespread panic among many 'listeners'. The broadcast began with the following introduction: 'The Columbia Broadcasting System and its affiliated stations present Orson Welles and the Mercury Theater of the Air in *The War of the Worlds*, by H. G. Wells.' At the half-way point of the program, two announcements were made that informed the listeners that what they were hearing was a dramatization of a work of fiction. At the end of the program, the same announcement was given. Yet, it has been estimated that over one million people did not hear those announcements and thought the unimaginable was happening.[31]

A study was done in the mid-twentieth century regarding attention active listening. It took place among school children of various ages and involved a number of teachers suddenly interrupting themselves by announcing 'time out'. They then asked two questions: 1) 'What were you thinking about?' 2) What was I talking about? Among first graders, 90 percent were listening to their teachers. Over 80 percent of second graders were listening. In the junior high grades, less that 44 percent were listening and among high school students, the average dropped to 28 percent.[32] It would appear that listening doesn't improve with age.

It has been estimated that the typical adult listener has an absolute attention span on only 12-14 seconds! This means that while the preacher is waxing eloquent, folks in the audience are going on side trips every few seconds. Furthermore, studies have shown they go on a major excursion every 8-10 minutes! In view of this, keeping listeners involved with what is being said is indeed a major challenge.

Another issue related to audience involvement is that it appears that people listen and process information differently. In recent years much has been written about left-brain and right-brain people. While the final word on this has yet to be written and we ought to jump on this bandwagon cautiously, it appears that the left hemisphere of the brain is analytical and verbal while the right hemisphere is instinctive and visual. The left side tends to break ideas apart in order to understand them in-depth. It processes abstractions. The right side sees things comprehensively and concretely. It is theorized that while everyone uses both sides of the brain, most people tend to use one side more than the other. Some are 'left-brain thinkers' and some are 'right-brain thinkers'. Left-brain thinkers tend to think deductively and analytically, while right-brain thinkers tend to think inductively and visually.

If the theory advocated in the previous paragraph is even partly true, it would make good sense to utilize both deduction and induction in our preaching since our audiences will include both left-brain and right-brain people. If we preach deductively arranged sermons exclusively, we will miss the opportunity to minister effectively to a sizeable portion of those present.

Cultural learning style is a third issue regarding audience involvement. There may have been a time when westerners treasured words and thought by means of linear reasoning. This is not a dominant trait of our culture today. David Larson rightly describes our culture as having a preference for the nonverbal.

> Words, propositions, and carefully reasoned arguments are less appealing than images, and most preachers tend to be image-poor communicators whose specialty is propositional revelation and who preach best from the didactic sections of Scripture. Ours is an age attuned to feeling, while many of us preach in a context still reacting against excess in feeling.[33]

Craddock gives the following rationale for preaching that is inductive.

> The inductive process is fundamental to the American way of life. There are now at least two generations who have been educated in this way from kindergarten through college. Experience figures prominently in the process, not just at the point of *receiving* lessons and truths to be implemented, but in the process of *arriving* at those truths.[34]

And again Craddock states:

> The plain fact of the matter is that we are seeking to communicate with people whose experiences are concrete. Everyone lives inductively, not deductively. No farmer deals with the problem of calfhood, only with the calf. The woman in the kitchen is not occupied with the culinary arts in general but with a particular roast or cake. The wood craftsman is hardly able to discuss intelligently the topic of 'chairness,' but he is a master with a chair. We will speak of the sun rising and setting long after everyone

knows better. The minister says 'all men are mortal' and meets drowsy agreement; he announces that 'Mr. Brown's son is dying' and the church becomes the church.[35]

The preacher must meet the listeners where they are before attempting to lead them to a better place. Surely Jesus did this as is seen in his encounters with the Samaritan woman, hungry multitudes, and Mary and Martha at the tomb of Lazarus.

A fourth concern regarding the involvement of the audience is that of ownership. How can the preacher best help the listeners appropriate the truth for themselves? The key involves more than simply listening. It involves discovery and participation. Chapell refers to Jay Adams who argues that 'it is only when a truth touches us experientially or when we sense the impact it could have upon us that we can comprehend it fully.'[36] Likewise, those who are experts in the field of adult learning affirm that students learn best when discovering and appropriating new ideas for themselves. In this way, inductive preaching helps to promote a strong sense of ownership in the listeners.

... Jesus-style inductive preaching moves toward and comes to the same conclusion deduction begins with. The inductive process allows the people to become involved, to explore and own the concepts in the course of the sermon. An inductive sermon becomes something more than decreed dogma. The congregation can claim it as conviction. It becomes personal. And real.[37]

Authority
To this point, I have emphasized the issue of the involvement of the audience with preaching, especially in regard to inductive preaching. A second issue, that of authority, must also be discussed. What is the relationship between inductive preaching and authority?

It is likely that for many the least palatable part of Craddock's book, *As One without Authority*, is the title. It may leave the reader with the impression that inductive preaching *per se* has no authority. But is this necessarily the case? Is it possible that this concern confuses the concepts of authority and authoritarianism?

If a sermon that is inductive declares the truth of the text that is under consideration – that is, it allows the passage to make its own statement – then the sermon has inherent authority of the proper kind. It does not depend on the perceived authority of the speaker or any demeanor on his part, but the sermon's authority comes instead from the authority of Scripture itself. Timothy Warren speaks to this concern:

> If people are listening for messages that carry elements of authority to guide their lives, where will they find such authority? What in the preaching event is authoritative? Is it the preacher himself? No. It is the Scripture that confers authority.[38]

Warren continues by citing the Sidney Greidanus statement below, a statement which I've enlarged slightly:

> Since the prophets proclaimed *God's* word, their preaching was authoritative. This relationship suggests that the authority of the prophets did not reside, ultimately, in their person, their calling, or their office; rather, their authority was founded in the word of God they proclaimed.
>
> For with the prophets we noticed that their authority did not reside, ultimately, in their calling or office but in the words they spoke, whether they were from the Lord. So it is with preachers today: they have a word from the Lord, but only if they speak the *Lord's* word. The only norm we have today for judging whether preachers speak the word of the Lord is the Bible.[39]

As Warren and Greidanus affirm, real authority in preaching depends on its biblical content, not the personality or forcefulness of the preacher nor, I might add, the structural style of the sermon.

Effectiveness

A third issue needing to be mentioned is that of effectiveness. Evangelicals have a time-tested tradition of deductive expository preaching. We can agree that lives have been changed as God's Spirit has blessed and continues to bless this method of faithful proclamation. Can we expect the same of inductive exposition?

Actually, the issue is not that of deduction or induction. Rather, the issue is that of exposition. If the truth of the Word of God is clearly presented, listeners will be taught, rebuked, corrected, and trained in righteousness as purported in 2 Tim. 3:16. Homiletical methodology is not the point; the clear and accurate presentation of the Word to listeners is.

We need look no further than Jesus to see that inductive messages are effective. An examination of the Sermon on the Mount, for instance, will show that proposition-type ideas are sometimes stated at the end of sections. An example of this is seen in the account regarding worry in Matthew 6:25-34. The 'bottom line' of the text is verse 33, 'But seek first his kingdom and his righteousness, and all these things will be given to you as well.'

Perhaps Jesus' most prolific use of induction is seen in his parables. About a third of all Jesus teachings are parabolic in nature and many of these are directed toward unbelievers. These parables are generally narrative in style as well as inductively arranged. The result is that the unsuspecting listener finds himself inside the story processing its meaning.[40]

Taken as a whole, the Gospel of John is inductively arranged. The thesis of the book is not disclosed until next to the last chapter:

> Jesus did many other miraculous signs in the presence of his disciples, which are not recorded in this book. But these are written that you may believe that Jesus is the Christ, the Son of God, and that by believing you may have life in his name (John 20:30-31).

Even Paul, though often arguing and presenting his materials deductively, sometimes resorts to an inductive approach. This is seen in his sermon on Mar's Hill (Acts 17:16-34) and in the messages related to his conversion which he uses in his personal legal defense (Acts 21, 24, 26). His argument in Galatians has a very strong inductive flavor as does his approach in Philemon.

Why are we so hesitant to agree that inductive sermons can be as effective as deductive ones? The New Testament evidence doesn't support this hesitancy. In fact, we can induce from the above examples that inductive preaching can be effective.

Difficulty

Finally, the matter of difficulty needs to be addressed. The issues of audience involvement, authority, and effectiveness all relate to the worth of inductive preaching. The matter of difficulty, on the other hand, relates to proficiency. This is a practical issue which is quite important.

In a paper titled 'Reclaiming the Deductive Sermon' presented to the Evangelical Homiletics Society, Kenneth Bickel accurately describes the differences between inductive and deductive sermons and, in fact, presents a very good case for inductive preaching. He stops short of completely endorsing the method because of one important issue – difficulty. He says, '. . . that which sounds sensible in theory is not always valid in practice. The reality is that inductive sermons are very hard to preach well.'[41] Bickel then explains in detail some of his concerns:

> Sustaining unity, order, and progress in an inductive sermon takes a skillful communicator. Preachers must be able to help listeners sense a unity to the message without the central theme of the sermon being disclosed until late in the presentation. In addition, they must be capable of using transitional statements very effectively so that listeners can sense an order to the sequence of ideas that are delivered. They must also know how to communicate to listeners an awareness that: a. More needs to be said, b. All that is being said is leading to a climax and closure, and c. The stream of consciousness that is coming forth from the preacher has meaning and relevance for the central thrust of the sermon (as well as for their lives).[42]

These concerns are legitimate. I concur that preparing and presenting inductive sermons is more difficult than following a deductive methodology, especially since most preachers have been trained to prepare deductive sermons. Still, I believe that a preacher or student with average ability can preach well inductively.

Preparing Inductive Expositions

While preparing inductive sermons is admittedly more difficult than preparing those that are deductive – primarily because we've been taught to preach deductively and have had deductive sermons modeled for us almost exclusively – inductive sermons are both do-able and enjoyable for both the preacher and the listener. Following are three suggestions as to how one might begin to develop inductive sermons while remaining expository.

Use a Semi-inductive Approach

While 'inductive purists' might chafe a bit at this suggestion, I believe this approach will help ease preachers into using an inductive approach in two ways: 1) it will enable them to apply the process of inductive thinking to sermons that also have a more familiar deductive quality; and 2) it will provide practice in delivering sermons without stating their propositions too early for inductive purposes. At least two particular approaches lend themselves to this.

The Problem-solving Method. There are many ways to do a problem-solving sermon. In my *Homiletical Handbook*, for example, I present an approach with three main points:

   I. We need to solve the problem of .
   II. There are some solutions to that have been suggested (these may be non-biblical or otherwise not fully adequate)
   Proposition: What is God's solution to the problem of ?
   III. God's solution to the problem of is seen in (text).

The proposition, stated as a question, is asked as part of the transition into the third point. (Some may question whether a proposition can be a question. Ordinarily, I question the practice because a question doesnt *propose* anything. In this case, however, I believe it is valid to do this because the function of a sermon proposition is to focus attention on precisely what the message is about. An interrogative type proposition accomplishes this.) Since the proposition precedes the last main point, I refer to this as a semi-inductive method.[43]

Harold Freeman has a more detailed seven-move approach to a problem-solving sermon that also retains an inductive flow.[44]

1. You are 'here'. (statement of the problem)
2. How did you get here? (the problem's origin)
3. What's it like to be here? (complexities of the problem)
4. Has anyone else ever been here? (contemporary and other examples)
5. What if you don't get out of here? (consequences)
6. How *could* you get out of here? (alternate solutions)
7. What's the *best* way out of here? (a biblical solution)

The Syllogistic Approach. As mentioned earlier, while this method is based on deductive reasoning, the argument itself is communicated inductively. This is because the conclusion of the syllogism is not announced until the sermon is nearing its end.

Mark 2:1-12

I. Forgiveness of sin comes from God only. (7)

II. Jesus claimed to forgive sin. (10-12)

III. Therefore, Jesus claimed to be God. (Proposition)

The sermon's proposition, point III in this example, is the same as the syllogism's conclusion.[45]

Recycle Deductive Sermons

A second way to experiment with inductive preaching is to try to rearrange previously used deductive sermons into an inductive format. This will permit the comfort of familiarity while nudging the preacher toward the edge of his comfort zone homiletically speaking. Many years ago, I preached a sermon on Acts 2 according to the following simple deductive structure:

'God's Kind of Church'

(Read text: Acts 2:42-47)

Introduction: The most unique church in history was this church in Acts 2. (Other information about the early church and today's church)

Context: (The setting of this text in Acts)

Proposition: Our church can move toward being God's kind of church. How? By pursuing the *characteristics* of the church in Acts 2:42.

I. We must be a church of sound doctrine (42a).

II. We must be a church of meaningful fellowship (42b).

III. We must be a church of true confession (42c).

IV. We must be a church of devout prayer (42d).

Conclusion: These are the characteristics of God's kind of church that we must pursue today.

More recently, I recycled the sermon using a more inductive approach.

Introduction: There are many differences in churches today (examples). Let me tell you about the most impressive church I've ever encountered.

Theme: As I reflect on my encounter with this church, there seems to be several *emphases* that stood out.

I. An emphasis on sound teaching was evident.

II. An emphasis on community living was evident.

III. An emphasis on observing certain rituals was evident.

IV. An emphasis on corporate prayer was evident.

Transition: There were other practices carried on in this church, but these seemed to be the most important.

Proposition: This church gives us the right model to follow as we seek to build our local churches.

Closing: If you want to investigate this church further, its address is Acts 2:41-47. (The text was read.)

Application

It was fascinating to watch the audience – seminarians and professors – as this sermon unfolded. Some began to catch on at about the third point. Others began to smile and nod knowingly a little later. Most importantly, the audience was 'with me' throughout the message.

Experiment with Full Inductive Approaches
There are doubtless many structures that legitimately could be called fully inductive. Following are four approaches that have been used with success.

The Building-block or Chain Method. This method finds its main points in a single paragraph or two of Scripture, or perhaps in the larger context of a chapter or two. These might be examples that support the main truth of the text or they could be statements that prove the sermon's proposition. These points will each provide partial answers to the thematic question raised in the introduction. Together, they affirm the proposition statement.

1 Corinthians 13:1-3

Thematic question: How does Christian love compare to other virtues?
   I. Love outshines spiritual giftedness (1-3a)
   II. Love is better than martyrdom (3b)
   III. Love results in behaviors that are supra-human (4-7)
   IV. Love will last forever (8-13)
Proposition: Christian love is the virtue that surpasses all others.

The Rebuttal Method. The main points in this approach are a series of questions which will be answered *negatively* in their respective sub-points. These collective responses inductively 'prove' the truth of the proposition statement.

1 Corinthians 15:12-28

Thematic question: How can Christians cope with the reality of death?

I. Is Christ still in the grave? (12-19, 20)

II. Is Christ the only one to be raised from the dead? (21-22)

III. Will death continue to destroy life indefinitely? (26)

IV. Is someone other than God in charge of human affairs? (24-25)

Proposition: Christians can cope with death because it is subject to our all-loving, all-powerful God.

Another example of a sermon outline using the rebuttal method is based on a well-known passage in the book of Romans, a text that has brought comfort to many.[46]

Romans 8:26-39

Thematic question: Does God really care about the difficult circumstances of our lives?

I. Do we face difficulties that are unknown to God? (26-27)

II. Do we face these difficulties apart from God's grace to us? (29-30)

III. Does God withhold that which is for our good? (31-32)

IV. Do we live outside the scope of His purposes for us? (28)

V. Can any circumstance overpower God's love? (35-39)

Proposition: God really does cares about all of the difficult circumstances in our lives.

The Affirmation Approach. This is somewhat the opposite of the previous method, though the structure will appear to be quite similar. The difference is that the main points present a series of questions which evoke *positive* responses. Inductively, arguing from particular truths to a general truth, these lead to the 'proof' and statement of the proposition.

Hebrews 11:1-12

Thematic question: Why is faith as important as everyone seems to think?

I. Does faith enable us to worship God properly? (Abel, 4)

II. Does faith enable us to walk in fellowship with God? (Enoch, 5)

III. Does faith enable us to obey God in the face of uncertainty? (Noah, 7)

IV. Does faith enable us to believe God for the impossible? (Sarah, 11-12)

V. Does faith enable us to gain God's eternal promises? (Abraham, 8-10)

Proposition: Faith is the necessary means by which we can please God. (6)

The following is a second example of this type of approach.[47]

1 Corinthians 6:9-20

Thematic Question: Does God have a personal interest in our sexual behavior?

I. Does God have a claim on our total selves, including our bodies? (19-20)

II. Does the Holy Spirit reside within us? (19a)

III. Does sexual immorality harm the Spirit's dwelling place? (18)

Proposition: The way we behave sexually is extremely important to God.

With both the rebuttal and the affirmation approaches, it is important that only one method be followed in a particular sermon. It would be very confusing to the listeners to have some main points that evoke negative responses and some that call forth positive responses.

The Narrative/Inductive Approach. This fourth type of inductive sermon tells a biblical story, or series of stories, and then concludes with a clearly stated propositional truth. Each movement (main point section) tells a story and then concludes with a clear statement that labels that movement. These labels collectively will lead to the statement of the proposition at the end of the sermon. Following is a brief summary of the main movements of a sermon recently published in a collection of communion sermons. The sermon consists of five movements, each presented in a narrative style and each dealing with a particular perspective on Jesus being the Lamb of God.[48]

BEHOLD THE LAMB! (John 1:29)

It is a time long ago and a place far away. Barely daybreak: 4 leave home for unknown mountain destination. (Story of Abraham preparing to offer Isaac.)

BEHOLD, THE SUBSTITUTE LAMB!

Time passes and things change. God is faithful to His covenant. New nation; numerical strength; political weakness; slavery! (Story of Moses and the exodus)

BEHOLD, THE PASSOVER LAMB!

Time continues to pass: Canaan is claimed. Temple is built. Not coincidently, this temple is built on Mount Moriah. (Account of OT sacrificial system)

BEHOLD, THE SACRIFICIAL LAMB!

Another scene unfolds before us: a future unknown time. (Rev. 4 & 5) Apart from the Father, one other is the focal point (28 times). He is worshiped; He's often in center of the throne. (Account of the Lion and the Lamb)

BEHOLD, THE TRIUMPHANT LAMB!

One last setting: It's the beginning of Jesus' earthly ministry. He has been baptized; suffered 40 days of fasting; tempted. (Story of John introducing Jesus)

"BEHOLD, THE LAMB . . . WHO TAKES AWAY THE SIN OF THE WORLD.

Conclusion: This title and this communion table remind us of the accomplishments of the Lamb. Do you see Him? Do you see the Lamb? John invites you: "Look, the Lamb of God who takes away the sins of the world." From Genesis to Revelation, you're urged to see Him. There He is! . . .in the shadow of a cross, wearing a crown!

Proposition: JESUS, THE LAMB OF GOD, IS WORTHY OF OUR COMPLETE WORSHIP AND DEVOTION.

Interestingly, the editors of the book in which this sermon was published apparently did not fully understand the intent of induction. Rather, the main point statements ('Behold, the Substitute Lamb!' etc.) were each stated prior to their respective sections rather than at the end of the sections. Whether in print or in speech this has the effect of undermining the inductive thinking process.

More recently, I preached an Advent sermon using the same basic approach. In this instance, I presented three movements, each of which was a specific case study, and then had a fourth movement that was a summation of several cases.

THE COST OF CHRISTMAS

Introduction: Have you done it yet? Have you done that part of Christmas which is most unpleasant? Not decorating, or shopping, or wrapping, etc. Have you figured out how much the whole thing is going to cost! Christmas is always costly. It's always been that way.

Thematic question: Am I suggesting that Christmas is always costly for everyone?

Case Study #1: He was an everyday sore of fellow; a blue-collar worker who crafted things by hand. He worked with wood. (Other details about Joseph) His young lady was only a teenager. (Other details about Mary) Then the news came about her pregnancy. (Discussion of the aftermath and the issues involved)
CHRISTMAS WAS COSTLY FOR JESUS' EARTHLY PARENTS.

Case Study #2: The giving of this special gift had long been considered. He thought about it for what seemed an eternity. It would be a gift with an unimaginable price tag. (Discussion of God's perspective without disclosing prematurely that it is God who is the subject)
CHRISTMAS WAS COSTLY FOR GOD THE FATHER.

Case Study #3: What would it be like to give up everything for nothing? To be a ruler and become a servant? To give up unquestioned authority, unbelievable power, and unsurpassed status? (Discussion from Jesus' perspective without disclosing his identity prematurely)

    CHRISTMAS WAS COSTLY TO JESUS.

Case Study #4: The birth of Jesus affected everyone. The innkeeper; the shepherds; the wisemen; King Herod; Jesus' contemporaries; Pontius Pilate. All of these had to pay the price of a decision.

    CHRISTMAS WAS COSTLY TO THIS WHOLE ASSORTMENT OF PEOPLE.

Proposition: THE BOTTOM LINE IS THAT CHRISTMAS IS COSTLY FOR EVERYONE FOR ALL MUST PAY THE PRICE OF A DECISION ABOUT CHRIST.

Just as induction works best when the precise proposition is not announced until the concluding part of the sermon, so in the case of this style of narrative/induction it is important that the statement of each respective main point is withheld until that point is being completed. By doing this, the preacher is more likely to keep the listener 'tuned in' throughout the message.

It is important to note that each of the examples presented above falls into the general category of expository preaching. Exposition can be done inductively.

I do not believe for a moment that inductive preaching is the only method to use. Most of my preaching is still deductive. I continue to find that deductive sermon arrangements still communicate well with traditional audiences, especially those composed primarily of folks who are in substantial agreement with what is being said. I find myself using inductive methods more often than in the past, however, especially when the audience is perceived as being somewhat doubtful or even hostile to what will be said. Induction has a way of disarming wary listeners and bringing them along slowly. Perhaps this is one of the reasons Jesus often spoke inductively. Finally, induction exposition provides some much needed variety for listeners who tend to get bored with hearing the same sermon approaches time after time after time. A touch of surprise may well be a helpful tonic for tired listeners.

Summation

This chapter has discussed sermon structure in terms of balance in homiletical variety. First, the importance of sermon focus was addressed with propositional preaching being advocated as the means by which every sermon can begin, proceed, and conclude without deviating from its specific purpose. Speaking about a general theme is not sufficient to keep a sermon on course. Themes tend to be broad and difficult to control in terms of sermon structure. A carefully composed proposition that clarifies some specific aspect of a theme can be invaluable in helping a sermon remain focused on a precise objective.

Lest homiletical structure be thought of as the end-all of preaching, we need to remember that sermon structure is a tool, a *means* to an end. All oral communication has structure of some type, but not all structural plans are equally helpful. Poor outlining can contribute to confusion on the part of the listeners and might cause some to drop out. Poor outlining might also fail to contribute to the establishment of the proposition and the ultimate purpose of the message. Poor outlining is often an indication that the preacher is not entirely clear on how the various ideas in the sermon actually fit together. If the preacher is confused about this, the audience will be even more uncertain.

It is equally dangerous to have an outline that is so meticulously crafted that it actually distracts from that which is being said. Attention is drawn to the rhyme, rhythm, or alliteration of the main points and sub-points instead of to the truths being proclaimed. Any of these devices may be helpful, but care must be taken not to allow them to usurp the sermon's content.

Exposition, properly understood, must be the norm of the Christian pulpit. The single unique contribution that the church can make in the lives of people is to let them know what God has to say about the issues of life. To be an expository preacher is to act as a conduit for that which God has already spoken. It is to present the Scripture in such a way that it makes its own statement. Whether the texts used are single or multiple, short or lengthy, a sermon worthy of utterance in a Christian setting must be Word-based and focused.

To preach with needed variety means to think creatively about the audience and the best way to communicate a particular text to them. In some instances this may require a more traditional deductive approach, while in others an inductive treatment may be most effective. Texts vary, audiences and their needs vary, subjects vary, and preaching purposes vary. One sermon size does not fit all. The wise preacher will carefully consider appropriate alternate homiletical approaches so that each sermon can be optimally effective from a human perspective.

Points to Ponder

1. Is the time invested in thoughtful sermon structures worthwhile? How might good structure be a help to the preacher? How might it be a help to the listener? Is it possible that good structure might it be a liability to a particular sermon?

2. What is the proper relationship between the preaching text(s) and a clear, concise sermon proposition?

3. In what ways are the traditional sermon categories of topical, textual, and expository helpful? What are the shortcomings of these terms?

4. Think of a deductively arranged sermon you've preached. Did this arrangement help the sermon's effectiveness? How might this sermon be arranged in a more inductive style? Would this revised structure be a help or a hindrance?

5. For those of us who are not especially creative in terms of homiletics, where might we go to find help in being more imaginative in the way we prepare sermons?

Step Six

Maintain a Balance in Sermon Content

> Horses are not to be judged by their bells or their trappings,
> but by limb and bone and blood; and sermons, when criticised
> by judicious hearers, are largely measured by the amount of
> gospel truth and force of gospel spirit which they contain.
> Brethren, weigh your sermons. Do not retail them by the yard,
> but deal them out by the pound. Set no store by the quantity
> of words which you utter, but strive to be esteemed for the
> quality of your matter (Charles H. Spurgeon).*

The heart of every sermon is its content. What is the preacher saying?
What ideas are being expressed? Where did they come from and
what is meant by them? What bearing do they have on those who
listen?

It is true that some sermons are heard not because of content but
because of style. Some preachers are entertaining to watch whether
or not they have much to say. Pulpit antics, an enthralling voice, and
a charismatic personality can sometimes make preaching a spectator
sport instead of authentic proclamation of the Word aimed at
receptive hearts. When this occurs, folks can be heard saying things
like 'He was good today', or 'the preacher was hot', instead of
remarking on how the sermon impacted their lives by what God has
said. This kind of preacher-centered activity dishonors God and his
revelation to us. It maximizes the preacher, minimizes God, and robs
God of the glory that belongs to him.

Having something important and interesting to say sermon after
sermon after sermon would be a daunting task if we were left only
to our own ingenuity. Thankfully, this is not the case. We have the
Word of God as a complete reservoir of that which God intends for
us to know. Indeed, it is an inexhaustible treasure trove of that which

needs to be preached. If we preach only our own ideas and insights, we will soon have little left to say. If, on the other hand, we discipline ourselves to be diligent exegetes of the Scripture, we will never run out of substantive content.

In the previous chapter, attention was given to the homiletical aspects of preaching. These are the main structural designs or outlining methods that are used to give sermons a sense of unity, coherence, and movement. While the main structural components – broad subject, narrower theme, precise proposition, and main point statements – are crucial in limiting a given sermon to a desired subject and purpose, they are not the conveyors of the bulk of a sermon's content. Rather, most of a sermon's content is communicated through the introduction, sub-points, illustrations, applications, and conclusion. It is the job of the structural components to help keep these conveyors of content on track in terms of the overall flow of the sermon.

We will now turn our attention to the content of our preaching, first as it relates to some specific parts of the sermon that convey most of our content. Then, we will look at the issue of content in some broader contexts that are somewhat more philosophical in nature.

Vary the Content Components

I've proposed that preaching with balance requires variety in terms of overall sermon structure. Such variety will help keep both the listeners and the preacher enthusiastic about the preaching event. But variety need not be confined to the overall structural issues discussed previously. It can also impact the various parts of sermons including the sub-pointing material, illustrations, applications, the introduction, and the conclusion. Briefly, let us look at some suggestions as to how this might be done.

Vary the Supporting Material that Explains and Persuades
The bulk of the content in the body of the message consists of four kinds of material: explanation, argumentation, illustration, and

application. This supporting material, often called sub-points, is the 'meat on the bones', the weighty part of the sermon. It establishes and applies that which has been (or will be, in the case of an inductive sermon) advanced in the proposition and main points.

Ordinarily, the supporting materials will follow the statement of their respective main points. In some forms of inductive structuring, however, the supporting material might precede the actual statement of the main point. This is the case in the final two inductive structure examples given in the previous chapter. In either case, it should be obvious that sub-points must support or 'prove' their respective main points, just as each main point must establish the factualness of the proposition. This might be thought of as a homiletical chain of command.

The Priority of the Text
Supporting material can be created and arranged in numerous ways. First, in terms of importance, the preaching text(s) must be allowed to speak. This is true of the main points for each main point should have specific textual support. Otherwise, the preacher may be guilty of emphasizing his own ideas at the neglect of the text. Similarly, it is also true of the sub-points in most kinds of sermon structures.[1]

When sub-pointing, therefore, we must first consider how to reflect the passage with which we're dealing so that our listeners can have a profitable encounter with the Scripture. Our ideas count for very little, but the Bible we preach has the information required to touch lives.

In our preliminary study prior to doing specific homiletical steps, we should have thoroughly studied both the context and the content of the text. The latter should have included detailed exegetical study that gives us a deep understanding of this part of God's Word. This study should have informed us of the proper direction to go homiletically in terms of basic purpose and design. Now it should be utilized to give us detailed textual information that undergirds the more general textual reflections seen in the proposition and main points.

Depending on the length and literary nature of the preaching passage(s), there might be a great deal of exegetical gold to be mined and distributed or there might be relatively little. The latter should not be assumed, however, until a thorough study has been carried out. Two or three verses in an epistle, for example, may contain a vast treasure trove of potential sermon material whereas a much longer passage of narrative may contain relatively little in terms of exegetical detail. Regardless, the biblical preacher should begin with the text as far as sub-pointing material is concerned. This requires diligent effort, but it is the only way to preach with integrity.

Theological Reflection
A second natural category to consider when sub-pointing would be Christian theology. The Bible is a book about God and our relationship to him. Everything in Scripture speaks to this and this is the basic essence of theology. Our preaching, therefore, should necessarily reflect this. There seems to be a popular misconception entertained by some that preachers must choose between relevant preaching and doctrinal preaching. Nothing could be further from the truth. This is a false dichotomy which is based, if one reasons through the issues involved, on the assumption that Scripture itself is irrelevant because it doesn't address the issues of life. Donald Macleod takes strong exception to this assumption.

> Equally, theological preaching is the primary means of pastoral care. The flock is to be fed – indeed, pastors must never forget that it is possible to kill them not only with heresy, but with starvation. Only the truth can sanctify them (John 17:17).... Doctrine cannot be set against experience... This is why, time and again, when the biblical writers were faced with problems in the realm of experience and practice, they appealed to Christian doctrine.[2]

Doctrine and relevance dare not be placed in opposition. The latter is determined by the former.

Supporting material in sermons must therefore be considered theologically. This doesn't mean that preachers should be theology books wired for sound. It doesn't mean that scholarly language should permeate every (or any) sermon we preach. It doesn't mean that our sermons should be theological treatises devoid of practicality. But it does mean that our listeners need to be aware of the doctrinal truths of Scripture and that life's experiences should be informed by these. Again, Macleod wisely observes:

> Theologically, nothing is to be held back. What God has revealed was not intended for academics and theological colleges, but for the people of God. If a thing is not biblical, it must have no place in our preaching. If it is biblical, we have no right not to teach it. We must wrestle with the great themes, even if they throw us. We cannot plead height or depth or complexity.[3]

Admittedly, it is hard work to discover the theological issues at work in a text and then to communicate them in clear, understandable language that relates to life. But this is the job of the preacher. We are the 'scholars in residence' in our churches, knowledgeable in both the content of the Bible and its theology.

Secondary Texts

Once supporting material has been gathered from the preaching text, both exegetically and theologically, the preacher may consider other similar passages that will have something to say about the main point being made. I urge caution, however, not to do this too quickly. Most preaching passages have a sufficient number of concepts in them to supply a sermon. To turn to other texts prematurely is an indication that we haven't really studied and contemplated the passage at hand. I find it interesting to compare my earlier sermons with those I've preached in recent years. My older sermons almost always had numerous texts cited from passages other than the main text. Sometimes, these citations numbered ten or twelve or even more. More recent sermons sometime have no extra-textual citations at all, and others may have only one or two. Why is there such a difference? In my earlier days as a preacher I spent less time studying the text at hand deeply. I found it easier to use a concordance, topical Bible, or chain reference device to find 'proof texts' than to do serious exegetical study in the main preaching passage.

In view of the wonderful Bible software widely available today, I wonder if contemporary preachers are even more tempted to do this than I used to be. If so, I fear that sermons will be increasingly 'dumbed down' and superficial. Christian preaching should be text-driven preaching, not a kind of canonical smorgasbord where preachers toss out a collection of texts from all over the canon with little regard for exegetical or contextual considerations. This can be further exacerbated by the multiplicity of translations available in the English-speaking world. If our preferred translation renders a verse in a little different way than we desire, we can always check out dozens of other translations until one is found that matches our own agenda.

Do these opinions sound overly cynical to you? Perhaps they are. But I'm concerned that the seeming popularity of topical preaching in many evangelical circles, coupled with the practice of arbitrary proof texting that sometimes strips the Word of any semblance of authority, is helping to produce a new generation of biblical illiterates in the church itself.

The Parts of the Whole

It is safe to say that every concept can be broken down into smaller ideas. Therefore, every main point in every sermon is a concept capable of being reduced to smaller parts. This is true of doctrinal concepts, ethical ideas, narrative events, and biographical information.

For example, if the main point concept is related to time, then smaller ideas like past, present, and future come to mind. If the main point relates to a person, then we may well think in terms of background, character, personality, weaknesses, strengths, failures, likes, dislikes, and contributions. If the larger idea is related to an event, we might consider ideas like setting, time, cause, and effects.

Try to think of any concept that is incapable of being broken down into smaller natural parts. I'm not sure that it can be done. We can therefore formulate supporting material based on this process.[4]

Formal Reasoning

As mentioned in the previous chapter in relation to overall homiletical structuring, there are two kinds of formal reasoning processes and both of these can be utilized in preaching. As discussed, deduction and induction are invaluable ways of establishing proofs.

The former, deduction, is an argument from the general to the specific. It is known as syllogistic reasoning and employs a major premise and a minor premise which, when stated properly, lead to a conclusion. Some main point statements can be established by means of a deductive set of sub-points. Following are two examples, one positive and one negative, of how a main point might be developed with the use of deductive reasoning in the supporting material.

Main Point: How we live demonstrates our claim of knowing Christ (Rom 8:9ff).

All professing Christians should seek to be led by the Spirit.

You are a professing Christian.

Therefore, you should seek to be led by the Spirit.

Main Point: How we live demonstrates our claim of knowing Christ (Rom 8:9ff).

Being led by the Spirit is a characteristic of the normal Christian life.

You are not living a life that is Spirit-led.

Therefore, you cannot be characterized as a normal Christian.

These sample sub-points are explanatory and persuasive in nature. They might serve as the heart of supporting material under a given main point but they would also need to be augmented by illustration and application.

In addition to using deduction, the preacher can also use induction as the basis of the sub-points under a given main point. This type of reasoning argues from the specific to the general. It often takes a set of examples and draws a probable conclusion.

Now the word *probable* may be of concern to purists, but probability reasoning is acceptable in many walks of life. The scientific method is based largely on induction. New prescription drugs, for example, are researched and tested on the basis of field trials. These trials may show that 94% of the subjects receiving this drug responded favorably as seen in a particular illness cured or minimized. In comparison, only twelve percent of those receiving placebos were helped. There were three side effects observed (nausea, dizziness, and rash) but these were serious in less than five percent of the patients tested and seemed to dissipate over a period of time. If the population tested was large enough numerically, if sufficient time was allowed to observe long-range results, and if other proper testing procedures were followed, then the pharmaceutical company would probably apply to the FDA for government approval to market this medication. And this is done on the basis of *probability*. When my doctor gives me a prescription for this medication, there is no absolute assurance that it will help me, though there is a likelihood that it will and, hopefully, with no side effects.

If inductive reasoning is used carefully, it can be a proper and powerful means of informing and persuading. A main point can be stated and then a series of sub-points can be presented which collectively establish the (probable) certainty of that main point. We might be speaking on the concept found in 1 Corinthians 1:27, for instance, and support a main point idea with induction.

Main Point: God often uses weak people to accomplish his purposes.

God used barren Sarah to mother a nation.

God used a slave boy named Joseph to save his people.

God used a stammering, fearful Moses to confront Pharaoh.

God used a shepherd boy named David to slay Goliath.

God used a reluctant farmer, Amos, to speak his truth to Israel.

God used an unknown teenager to bring Jesus into the world.

God used impetuous Peter to lead the early church.

God used a sickly Paul to spearhead first-century missionary efforts.

God used an elderly, exiled John to bring visions of eternal victory.

Conclusion: God can use us in spite of our weaknesses.

In addition to these examples from Scripture, we could add examples from church history, people such as melancholy Luther, sickly Calvin, and uneducated Moody. When the hearer is reminded of these people, it becomes easier to understand that God can use all of us in spite of our seeming limitations. Thus, the main point is established.

The Basic Interrogatives

Another method of devising effective sub-points was probably learned in elementary school. We can reflect on the idea in a particular main point by asking questions like: What? Who? Where? When? Why? How? So what? This approach is so simple that it is sometimes overlooked by the erudite preacher, but it can be extremely useful if not overused. These questions can be used in the preparation of the sub-points without announcing them in the pulpit. To do so might be a bit mechanical.

Summary

These approaches to developing supporting material – exegeting the text, doing theological reflection, using parallel texts, breaking a concept into its parts, using formal reasoning, and asking basic interrogatives – are all helpful processes to consider when fleshing out the body of the sermon. The first two approaches should be considered normative and usual. The other methods can be used as appropriate and with variation.

Utilize Varied Illustrations

Sermon sub-points which explain and persuade tend to be abstract, and those who preach have the sometimes difficult task of taking these abstractions and converting them to concrete truths, truths that are seen and felt, truths that are sensory. This is done by utilizing language that is carefully chosen to be visual. It is also done through the use of what is commonly called illustrations. To illustrate means 'to cast light upon something' as suggested by the Latin root, *lustrare*, 'to illuminate.' The idea is to make something clear, in this case some concept in a sermon that is otherwise abstract.

The Worth of Illustrations

Some preachers, especially some who have a particular commitment to strong expositional preaching, question the need of including illustrative materials in sermons. Their rationale is that it is the Bible that needs to be presented, not stories and anecdotes. While this concern has a certain amount of validity, it fails to take into account several issues. First, illustrations are not always stories and anecdotes. Second, even stories, when properly used, can enhance biblical truth without necessarily detracting from it. Third, if Christian preachers can learn anything from the teachings of Jesus, it is that stories and other kinds of visual language can be incredibly helpful in communicating spiritual truth. If illustrations are used to clarify various parts of the sermon and not allowed to be the center of attention, then they can make a positive contribution to the explanation, argumentation, and application that should be the foci of our messages.

The Purposes of Illustrations

Illustrations have numerous purposes, some of which enhance the message and some of which assist the listener. In addition to the primary functions discussed above, illustrations also reinforce ideas by means of indirect repetition, they provide inductive argumentation, they help attention span by varying a sermon's conceptual intensity, they regain the attention of wandering minds, they impress important ideas by making them memorable, they establish connections with various persons in the audience, and they help provide intellectual and emotional balance in the sermon's content. They do much more than simply provide filler material!

Types of Illustrations

As mentioned earlier, illustrations should not be thought of as only stories or anecdotes. They come in all sizes, shapes, and substances. One illustration might be as brief as a simile or metaphor while another might be a narrative that lasts several minutes. In between these two extremes we find other kinds of illustrative materials such as analogies, parables, allegories, current events, personal experiences, statistics, quotations from famous persons, quotations from recognized authorities, poetry, hymns and other Christian music, non-Christian music, testimonies, object lessons, visual aids, film clips, myths and legends, fables, and news reports. This list is only suggestive and not one exhaustive. There are other kinds of illustrations as well.

Not all types of illustrations are equally effective. Some will infiltrate the heart and mind of the listener more readily than others. Keith Willhite wisely suggests the following hierarchy in relation to receptivity on the part of the audience. The kinds of illustrations at the top of the list have a higher receptivity than those toward the bottom.

From the experience of both the speaker and the listener (sic)
From listener's experience
From speaker's experience
From the experience of people we know
A true story about an unknown person's experience
'Somebody told me about . . .'
'I heard a story . . .'
'Suppose . . .'[5]

In general, I agree with this order though I would tend to place imagination ('Suppose . . .') a rung or two up the ladder. This is, after all, a method that Jesus used frequently.

Sources of Illustrations
Where does one find suitable illustrations? Actually, resources are as abundant as our imaginations will allow. There are, of course, collections of illustrations available both in print and digitally. Some preachers simply find and use these materials verbatim. This may be quite satisfactory with historical, literary, and factual materials, but I would urge caution with stories that appear to be anecdotal. There is simply no way to verify their truthfulness. Also, they sometime seem to be old and worn instead of fresh and vibrant. On the other hand, these kinds of stories can be quite useful in jogging the preacher's mind to recall similar events personally known.

Beyond published collections of illustrative materials, there are many resources available. Conversations (don't betray confidences or embarrass people), people watching, television, movies, radio, recreational reading, scholarly reading, nature, current events, the visual arts, music of various kinds, history, personal experiences, and creative use of the imagination are all examples of sources for illustrative materials. The sermons of others can also be helpful, but credit should be given when appropriate. Perhaps the most excellent source is the Bible itself. It abounds in interesting stories and sayings and this resource has the added merit of informing the listeners of biblical content even when it is being presented only as an illustration.

Basically, one must develop three skills in order to have access to good illustrations: first, be a keen observer of what is seen, heard, and experienced; second, note when and how these observations serve as analogies of spiritual truth; third, develop some kind of storage and retrieval system. In this last regard I've known some preachers who have developed extensive collections of illustrations. These are stored in files or data bases according to primary and secondary topics so they can be more easily located when needed. Other preachers collect materials – exegetical, homiletical, general content ideas, and illustrations – for messages only within the purview of the weeks or months sketched out as part of a fairly detailed preaching plan. This plan might cover six, nine, or even twelve months. They often have a file folder for each sermon anticipated and place various materials in each folder until the time comes for detailed preparation. I have used this approach many times over the years and have found it to be helpful.

Sermon Variety and Illustrations

No parts of sermons have more potential for using a variety of content in sermons than introductions and illustrations. In fact, most of what is true for one is also true for the other. Both can utilize many kinds of materials from many different places. The task of the preacher is to avoid ruts! It is a helpful exercise to periodically review one's recent sermons to see whether or not habits are developing in terms of homiletical designs as well as in terms of content within sermons, content such as introductions and illustrations. Some preachers would find that they use a lot of material that tends to be male-oriented, such as illustrations from sports. We must consider connecting with everyone in our audiences: men, women, teenagers, children, the elderly, white-collar workers, blue-collar workers, those who are academically inclined and those who are not. A good variety of illustrations will help us do this.

Presenting Illustrations in Sermons

Sermons are most enjoyed when the flow of the structure is seamless, yet the necessary transitions are sufficiently clear to guide the listener through the successive parts. It is much too mechanical, as well as unnecessary, to begin by saying 'Now for my sermon introduction today...,' and then a little later, 'My proposition today is...,' and still a little later, 'Now my first main point is...,' and then toward the end, 'Now in conclusion....' While few preachers (hopefully) would tend to do this sort of thing, many will formally introduce illustrations in just that way: 'Let me illustrate this for you,' or 'I thought of this story that might illustrate what I've just said.' It seems to me that to do this on a regular basis is to slip into the trap of woodenness. It is to bring homiletical process to the pulpit instead of just speaking conversationally with the audience. As with other sermon parts, we should think ahead of these transitions into illustrations so that they are presented as integral parts of the sermon, not something tacked on because of our lack of ability in verbalizing abstract concepts. Moving into an illustration and back out of it should be seamless and smooth.

Another matter to be considered is this: illustrations should be told, not read. It is far more preferable to paraphrase a story in one's own words rather than read it out of a book. To read any part of a sermon is to lessen the amount of eye contact and rapport building that needs to take place. A well-told story, on the other hand, will strengthen these.

It is imperative that illustrations be presented with accuracy. If this is not done, credibility is damaged. As a young preacher, I once used Billy Sunday as an example of someone who had been changed by God's grace. Because of a picture I had seen of him in a pugilistic pose, I ignorantly referred to him as a rough living professional boxer. My father, who seldom attended church in those days, corrected me afterward but I had doubtless lost some credibility in his eyes as well as the eyes of others who knew that Sunday had been a professional baseball player. I should have done my homework!

Should the preacher document his illustrations? At times, this might be cumbersome. On other occasions, however, it may well be a good idea to refer to one's source in a general way at least. To say 'a recent editorial in the Washington Post pointed out that...' is to assure your listeners that you know what you're talking about and that you're using a primary source. This is a way to gain their trust.

Balance Your Use of Application

The Importance of Application

Good preaching cannot be had without good application. It is application, clearly and pointedly made, that distinguishes a good sermon from a good lecture. Without answering the implied 'so what?' question on every listener's mind, the preacher has simply presented some information and this can scarcely be called a sermon. As Spurgeon aptly said, 'Where the application begins, there the sermon begins.'

Others have expressed similar opinions. Charles Koller stated, 'An exposition becomes a sermon, and the teacher becomes a preacher, at the point where application is made to the hearer, looking toward some form of response in terms of belief or commitment.'[6] Bryan Chapell believes it is the application which justifies a sermon. He says there is no reason for listeners to absorb exegetical insights, historical facts, and biographical detail without understanding the reason why. 'Through application the preacher implicitly encourages the parishioner to listen to the message's explanations because they establish the reasonableness and necessity of particular responses.'[7] Haddon Robinson similarly suggests that 'dull preaching usually lacks creative application'.[8] In keeping with his unique ability to catch attention while making a profound point, Howard Hendricks says that each time we observe and interpret but fail to apply, we perform an abortion on the Scriptures in terms of their purpose.[9]

Too often, the preacher treats application like an add-on, rather than the ultimate object or purpose of the sermon. We tack it on or leave it to chance. We might even spiritualize and say that we're planning to allow the Holy Spirit to lead us to make appropriate applications as needed. Interesting, is it not, that we limit the working of the Spirit to that short period of time during which a sermon is being presented rather than acknowledge his ability to lead us during the hours of preparation as well. Is this not a denial of his omniscient and omnipresent character? Is this not a form of blasphemy?

Application is at the very heart of preaching. It is, in fact, why we preach. We do not simply wish to impart information or feelings. We desire to see lives transformed in terms of values, motivation, and behavior. This is what application is intended to address.

The Foundation of Application

Where do applications come from? The necessary starting place is the text itself. The passage on which our sermon is based has not only a subject and thematic thrust, it also has some purpose. This may be stated explicitly or it may be implied. If the text is preachable, it is applicable.

As a student of the text, I must first allow the passage to be applied to myself. What does it demand or expect of me? What should my personal response to it be in terms of *being* and *doing*? We should not engage in preparing a sermon for others until we have first prepared it for ourselves. Then, and only then, we may inquire as to what the truth of the text demands of our hearers.

Words of caution and boldness are in order at this point. We must not expect more of ourselves and our listeners than that which is demanded by the Scripture. To do so is to become burdensome and dictatorial, ignoring the freedom that is ours in Christ. But, neither should we demand less than that which is demanded by the Word of God. To do so is to encourage casualness and nominalism, a 'country club mentality' of the church and Christianity that runs contrary to the costliness of discipleship. The Bible itself must be the source and guide for the application of our sermons and we dare not add to it nor subtract from it as we apply its truths to ourselves and others.

It is important that overall sermon purpose and appropriate application be thought through before a great deal of sermon structuring and writing has been done. The text should always be the prime factor in the shaping of our sermons, and part of this foundation is the applicational thrust of the text. Chapell wisely states, 'Application must precede final decisions about structure, wording, and even the tone of the message or else the preacher will be designing a highway without knowing its destination.' [10]

Some Characteristics of Good Applications.

As we consider how best to include appropriate application in our preaching, several characteristics come to mind.

The first is that application is always relational. As we just discussed, application will always be related to the text. What is this text stating or implying that we be or do? Application is also related to the audience. Therefore, the preacher will need to know, as much as possible, where listeners are spiritually so that application is timely, relevant, challenging, and do-able. Finally, application is also related to the central thrust or purpose of the sermon. It is helpful, as discussed elsewhere, to think in terms of a sermon objective. Write a statement that describes what you hope to accomplish through this particular sermon. This statement may include both a general purpose as well as a specific kind of response you want some or all of the hearers to make. For example, you might write a sermon objective that says: 'I want this sermon to produce increased faith in God, specifically to enable each hearer to be able to trust God despite delayed answers to prayer.' The entire sermon development process will be the servant to this overall sermon objective and the preacher will not deviate by tacking on other applications not dealt with in the message.

A second characteristic of good application is that it will summon to a decisive action or response. It will be noted for specificity. Good applications go beyond generalities and abstractions. They deal with family relationships, life in society, attitudes, life priorities, habits, business practices, spiritual disciplines, and moral choices. And they get down to cases! Instead of saying something safe like, 'Let us try to be better husbands,' try to be as specific as you can be. The following example comes to mind.

'Husbands, Christ loved his bride, the church, sacrificially. He has told us to love our brides in the same way. Does your attitude and behavior toward her reflect a sacrificial mindset? Are you willing to set aside your own agenda in order to sacrificially express your love for her? Think and pray about some specific way you can show Christlikeness toward your wife this week. Not something easy, not something costless, but something that is truly a sacrificial, loving thing to do.'

A third characteristic of effective application is that it leads to spiritual challenge, not listener frustration. Frustrating applications generally take three shapes. The first is that of trite or predictable applications. More Bible reading, witnessing, and better church attendance are all worthy desires for our people, but our applications must go beyond these basic expectations. They ought to address real issues faced by real people. They ought to address life's questions. A second type of frustrating application is that which is legalistic. Applications ought to carry biblical authority, but not the would-be authority of some preacher's whims. A third type of frustrating application occurs when we force applications on people without giving them the resources or 'know how' to carry them out. I recall the testimony of Dr. D. James Kennedy and his experience with evangelism that resulted in the church 'growing' from approximately 45 to 17 persons. Week after week he kept urging his small flock to share the Gospel but it wasn't until he began to teach them *how* to do it that conversions began to occur and the emergence of one of America's great churches, Corel Ridge Presbyterian Church in Ft. Lauderdale, began to take place.

A final characteristic of good application has to do with placement. When should application be made? There are two schools of thought on this. The first seems to be somewhat American and is the practice of placing application in the conclusion. This is exemplified, perhaps to excess, in the revival preaching of Charles G. Finney. Mr. Finney preached rather long sermons, often well over an hour in length, and these were usually divided into two major sections. The first was the formal sermon consisting of the usual homiletical parts. Following his conclusion, Finney would typically begin the second section of his presentation which was called the 'remarks.' This consisted of his applications, sometimes totaling fifteen or twenty in number and designed to be so comprehensive that virtually everyone in the audience was addressed by one or more. These were not 'one liners' but were full paragraphs or more of closely reasoned appeal. This part of the sermon often lasted thirty minutes or longer.

The second way of placing applications is to insert them throughout the sermon. This is, in my opinion, the preferable method in most cases. It is done by thinking of sub-points as being of three kinds: explanation, illustration, and application. Under each main point, then, there will be supporting material that is explanatory, supporting material that is visual and exemplary, and supporting material that appeals to the listener to respond either behaviorally or attitudinally. This approach will help keep listeners engaged throughout the message as the kinds of content will be shifting throughout the sermon including the body of the sermon. Listener fatigue is less likely to take place when content changes frequently and an attentive listener is more likely to respond to application than one who is tuned out.

Directness and Indirectness.

Whether or not our applications are perceived as direct or indirect will depend on the kind of language we use. Good application may be direct. An expression like "You need to. . ." is very direct. In some circumstances this kind of language might be to harsh. The attitude of the preacher will often determine how well this kind of very direct statement will be received. If it is spoken with genuine compassion, and not judgmentally, it may be accepted by the listeners as being in their best interest. An expression like "We need to. . ." is still direct, but not as harsh. 'You can do this' or 'we can do this' is direct in a promissory way. Sometimes we can ask direct questions:

'What will your response to this be?' 'What will you do with God's stated will in this matter?'

Good application may be also be indirect. An illustration often carries an applicatory thrust. John Knox's famous statement, 'Give me Scotland or I die,' communicates by way of example the kind of compassion we ought to have for those apart from the Faith. Questions can be another form of indirect application. We might ask rhetorically, 'How do you suppose people should respond to this?' Or, 'I wonder what this means for us?'" "Do you suppose this means that we should ...?' On occasion, we might make use of a multiple choice technique: 'Here are the choices before us: (make them clear one by one). Now, which choice is the appropriate one? Will you make it?' Another type of indirect application, a form of illustration, is narration or testimony. We can tell the story of someone who did the right thing. Still another other method is to use a 'visualization of success'. Using our imagination, we can tell what 'success' will look like when a certain course of action is followed.

Vary the Way Responses Are Conducted

Preachers, like most other living things, tend to become creatures of habit. We become comfortable with the way we do things and don't easily change. This kind of predictability is not helpful in regard to sermon applications, especially those that come at the end of sermons. Singing a familiar invitation hymn may be a proper thing to do following an evangelistic sermon. It is an improper thing to do if the sermon objective is something different. Likewise, having people respond by 'walking the aisle' may be the correct thing to do sometimes, but there are other legitimate forms of response as well.

First, remember that the final appeal or invitation should be specific in asking people to respond to the burden of this particular sermon rather than to every duty under the sun such as salvation, rededication, increased witnessing, church membership, baptism, and additional prayer. For example:

A sermon on prayer should 'invite' people to pray more effectively.

A sermon on spiritual gifts should urge folks to discover and use them.

A sermon on encouraging others should motivate people to practice encouragement.

A sermon on the greatness of God should move folks toward corporate and private worship.

These kinds of appeals can then be handled in creative and appropriate ways as is seen in the following short list:

Invite people forward for private prayer.

Invite people forward for spiritual counsel.

Lead a corporate 'responsive' prayer of affirmation

Use a response card from the bulletin or back of the pew and invite people to drop it in the offering or leave it in a receptacle at the door.

Invite folks to come forward to place their cards at the front.

Ask listeners to fill out a 'to do' card to stick on the bathroom mirror.

Ask people to engage is silent personal reflection and prayer in their seats.

Invite listeners to write a response on a card or sheet to keep in one's Bible.

Sing a congregational hymn of affirmation.

There are doubtless other approaches to use as well. Fresh methods are more likely to catch peoples' attention and encourage them to work through their response to the message.

The Preacher's Attitudes When Making Applications

It is a privilege to preach the Word of God and it is a privilege to see people respond to what God desires for them. We must always remember that we are mere spokesmen – ambassadors – and that it is God's Spirit who works in hearts to bring about change. Our job is to present the truth and not get in the way of what God wants to accomplish.

There are several attitudes that ought to be naturally present to the one who preaches the word and asks people to respond. First, be expectant. Assume that the majority of your listeners want to do the right thing and that others will be moved by the Holy Spirit. Second, be confident. Don't feel a need to apologize for that which

God expects. These are not your expectations, but his. Third, be humble. Don't present yourself as 'having attained', but 'attaining'. Fourth, be respectful. Don't talk down to people or underestimate their intelligence, understanding, or motivation. Fifth, be realistic. Avoid grandiose applications that are beyond doing, such as a plea to 'never to sin again'. Sixth, be understanding. Many aspects of life are complicated and should not be treated simplistically. And seventh, be a person of integrity. This does more to convince and motivate people than any other single factor on the human level. If you are trustworthy, then people will be more likely to respond positively to your preaching.

Vary Your Introductions

When the preaching text has been thoroughly studied, an appropriate homiletical plan has been designed, and interesting and helpful supporting material has been added to the outline, then the preacher is ready to spend serious time on the introduction. It may be that ideas related to this part of the sermon have been considered, but it is premature to settle on a precise introduction until the heart of the sermon – the proposition, main points, and sub-points – has been completed. An introduction can then be planned that is tailor-made for this specific message. Introductions should never be generic. The listener will assume that a generic introduction leads to a generic sermon.

The General Purposes of Introductions

Introductions have several basic purposes in common. When these are cared for, the sermon is considerably more likely to gain a hearing than if these purposes are ignored.

One purpose of an introduction is to gain attention. The first thirty to sixty seconds of a sermon are crucial in this regard. Contrary to what we preachers might assume, many in attendance do not have a sense of duty in terms of listening to a sermon. Many will use the opening statements as a guide to determine whether or not to actively invest their energies in what will be said. A 'ho-hum' beginning will doubtless persuade many not to bother.

A second purpose of an introduction is to present the subject that is to be dealt with in the message. At first, any allusion to the subject may be fairly broad but as the introduction progresses there should be a move from broadness to specificity. The subject will become real specific when the sermon's proposition is disclosed toward the end of the introduction, assuming the presentation is structured deductively. If the structure is inductive, then the thematic question will need to be raised. It is usually productive to pay special attention to the opening sentence or two (the approach sentence) so that the broad subject – or a parallel concept – is immediately disclosed. For example, a sermon on the subject of prayer might begin by speaking of the importance of good communication in any relationship. Some sample relationships might be quickly mentioned (marriage, parenting, work) and then it might be stated that good communication is a key ingredient in our relationship with God and that this communication is what prayer is all about. While prayer per se is not mentioned in the approach sentence, a more neutral term, communication, is.

Third, in conjunction with the disclosing of the subject, the speaker must show the relevance of this concept to those who listen. It has been my experience that church attenders do not come in droves to listen to messages on subjects that have no bearing on their lives. Preachers might get excited about many finer points of biblical history or doctrinal intrigue, but listeners want to hear what God has to say about issues that impact their lives. Listeners who judge the content of a sermon to be irrelevant will probably tune out or listen only sporadically. A good introduction should include motivating reasons as to why people should bother to stay engaged with what the preacher is talking about.

A fourth common purpose of introductions is to introduce the preaching passage. Preachers who take expository preaching seriously will take time to explain why the passage serving as the basis of a sermon deserves to be looked at and what it is about. I generally divide my introductions into three parts: the first gains attention, introduces the subject, and shows its relevance; the second introduces the text and shows its relationship to the subject; and the third (to be discussed next) states the proposition or thematic question and offers some hint as to how the sermon will proceed. This second part should not be long, nor should it be technical. Three or four sentences explaining what the book is about and how this text fits into the larger context should be sufficient to pave the way for the announcement of the proposition. Following is an example of what this might look like.

> Being the church in the world is one of the themes Paul writes about in Philippians. Keep in mind that what we know as the Book of Philippians is a letter – a thank you note actually – written by the apostle to what was one of his favorite churches. It was the first church he established in Europe and it was a church that stood by him in good times and bad. So he sends this letter and includes in it not only his words of gratitude, but some encouragement concerning how to live as Christians both in the gathered church and in the scattered church. We see this here in Philippians 2:12-16.

This kind of brief introduction to the preaching passage helps remove the sense of mystery that many church attenders have toward the Bible. It helps explain that the Bible is a knowable book when properly approached.

The final purpose of introductions is to disclose the sermon plan. The introduction should utilize clear transitional statements to inform the audience as to how the sermon will be developed. In a deductively arranged sermon, this can simply include a clear statement and restatement of the proposition and, as needed, a transitional sentence. The following kind of transitional paragraph might follow the paragraph above.

> We need to be the church in the world. It is not enough to be the church when we come together for worship or other activities. We must be the church in the world. But to do this, we'll need to be characterized by at least three distinctives. We find these distinctives in verses 12-16 of Philippians 2. The first distinctive is found in verses 12 and 13...

At this point a successful transition has been made from the introduction into the sermon body. The first main point can be stated (and repeated for the sake of clarity) and then the supporting material (sub-points) can be discussed. When this kind of transition is made, the listeners have a sense of where the sermon is going and there is a greater likelihood that they will stay tuned in. If the listener is confused here, a decision may be made to think about other things.

The Content of Introductions

Even though introductions have these general purposes in common, their content should vary widely. Every sermon needs and deserves a unique 'custom built' entry way into its special interior. Generic beginnings won't suffice!

There is almost no end to the variety of materials that can conceivably be used in introductions. Stories, rhetorical questions, startling statements, questions that seem to lead to a dilemma, current events, quotations, figures of speech, personal experiences, observations from life, brief poems or parts of poems, the words from hymns or praise songs, jokes, references to cartoons, hand-held objects, agree-disagree statements, happenings in the life of the church, excerpts from conversations, and lines from books or movies are all examples of the assortment of content the preacher can use from time to time. Granted, it takes some time to discover and put together just the right material for a given sermon, but isn't it worth the effort to discover that hearers are actually listening with anticipation rather than thinking, 'Here we go again.'

Weaknesses to Avoid

In addition to the weakness of sameness, just discussed, there are several other things that ought to be avoided when introducing sermons. One is excessive length. The purpose of the introduction is to *introduce*, not to usurp the sermon itself. An overly long introduction can become tedious and even discouraging to the listener. Suppose that in a given setting, the length of a sermon is assumed to be around thirty minutes. A guest speaker has an introduction that lasts fifteen minutes and then indicates there are four main ideas that will be presented. Listeners will become real nervous! Perhaps this doesn't seem very spiritual on their part, but this is the way it is for most listeners. Furthermore, the only way to honor the thirty minute expectation is to have abbreviated main points of three or four minutes. The result will probably be like an accomplished diver wading in the shallow end of the pool – disappointing.

A rule of thumb I've used through the years is that the length of an introduction should not exceed about ten to fifteen percent of the allotted preaching time. This, of course, means that discipline will need to be exercised regarding what *not* to say as well as deciding what needs to be said. As far as introductions are concerned, briefer is almost always better.

Another weakness to avoid is the inclusion of remarks irrelevant to the sermon. It is usually best for the pastor of a church to give announcements and acknowledgments at a different time in the service rather than as a preface to the sermon. A guest preacher should also avoid lengthy remarks that are outside the scope of the sermon. This is sometimes difficult to do, but it may be that greetings or words of appreciation can be offered either earlier in the service. Apart from remarks of these types, sermons should not begin with material other than what will lead to and enhance the establishment of the sermon theme. Telling a few jokes to warm up the audience, for example, undermines the seriousness of the preaching task and relegates the preacher to the role of a stand-up comedian.

A third weakness to avoid is an apologetic demeanor. This may happen when the speaker feels a sense of inadequacy because of lack of preparation time, fatigue, or illness. We sometimes think that an apology or other words of explanation will soften the attitude of the listeners toward us, but this is not the case. Instead, it tends to put them on guard against an inferior product.

Perhaps you've been present when a soloist stands up to sing and says apologetically, 'I've been fighting a cold this week and my voice is rather scratchy. So don't listen to my voice, just listen to the words of the song.' Now what is it that we listen to? The voice! Apologies are almost always counter productive. If we're ill or feel that we're less than fully prepared, this is between us and the Lord. It's best to keep it to oneself.

A final weakness to avoid is indecisiveness. A sermon should begin with a ring of certainty. Both the message and the messenger should be so well prepared that the opening remarks leave no doubt that the preacher is prepared and ready to proceed with exactly what needs to be said. Hem-hawing and vocal pauses communicate that the speaker isn't prepared to speak with a high degree of confidence and at least some in the audience will assume this is an invitation to stop listening.

Plan Effective Conclusions

It is quite likely that no single part of preaching is as consistently weak as conclusions. Homileticians as diverse as Ilion Jones, J. Daniel Baumann, and David Larsen believe this is the case. Yet, we neglect them to the detriment of the overall effect of our sermons. The conclusion represents a final chance to bring together the important ideas of the sermon and then confront the listener with the opportunity to make an appropriate response.

Every sermon deserves a conclusion that is unique. We should not think in terms of generic conclusions where only the subject and main points vary from sermon to sermon – a sort of recipe approach that takes little effort. Unfortunately, these generic conclusions also produce little in the way of attentiveness or response.

The Functions of Conclusions

What is it that conclusions ought to accomplish? There are some functions that most sermon conclusions have in common.

First, there is the function of bringing the sermon to closure.[11] Some sermons seem to just stop. Without warning the preacher ceases to speak, turns around and walks away. Or, perhaps in what seems like the middle of an idea, the preacher asks the listeners to bow their heads in prayer. Stopping is not the same as bringing a sermon to closure. Closure means that the message is coming to conceptual and emotional fulfillment. The listener is left with a sense that a unified and completed idea has been presented. There is neither a feeling that loose ends remain or that too much has been said, some of which has been overly repetitious.

Second, there is the function of bringing the thematic thrust of the sermon into a very clear focus. Previously, the preacher will have announced the sermon's big idea, the proposition. The main points will also have been presented. Now in the conclusion the speaker makes certain that these foundational ideas come together in sharp focus in the mind of each listener. When the sermon is finally over, there should be no fuzziness of thinking as people recall what this message was actually about.

Third, the conclusion also has the function of setting forth an appeal to the listeners to respond appropriately. Scriptural truth has been presented and this always calls for a response. Exposition is never an end in itself. Sometimes this response will be attitudinal. A sermon on the goodness of God may lead to the appropriate response of worship with the congregation entering into a time of corporate worship. A sermon on the sin of pride may ask people to do some introspective digging to discover areas of their lives in which pride may be present. Sometimes the proper response to a sermon will be behavioral. A sermon on financial stewardship may urge people to rethink their personal and family budgets to reflect God's perspective on material things. A sermon on forgiving others may invite listeners to seek out someone they need to forgive and bring healing to broken relationships. The sermon objective should be pursued in this final appeal. People should be challenged toward change.

The Elements of a Conclusion

While sermon conclusions will vary widely in terms of specific material, there are some elements which will be had in common. These will serve as a sort of skeletal framework for the specific materials used.

First, there should be a carefully composed transitional sentence connecting the sermon body to the conclusion. I call this the final transition. The easiest and clearest way to do this is to take the sermon's propositional statement and preface it with a transitional phrase such as 'Therefore, having seen (proposition)...' or 'Now we have examined how (proposition)....' This bridge statement serves double duty. It serves notice to the listeners that the sermon is entering a new phase, the conclusion phase, and it also reminds them of the sermon's main idea as summarized in the proposition. When this final transitional sentence is preceded by a suitable pause or change of body position, its clarity will be further enhanced. There will be no need to use trite, overused phrases like 'Now in conclusion...' or 'Finally....' A well-stated sentence of this type will accomplish a great deal in helping the listeners bring the sermon to closure in their own thinking.

Second, some sermons will probably benefit from a very brief recapitulation of the main points. This must not be a re-preaching of the sermon! Rather, a simple restatement of the points should be sufficient. This assists the listener to fit the primary concepts in the sermon together into a unified whole. It can also assist those who may have missed a key idea earlier. Brevity in this regard is essential. The final transitional sentence and the re-statement of the main points should not take more than half a minute, probably less.

Third, the conclusion should include a specific appeal for response, as discussed above. This should not be left to the whim of the moment but should be part of the total preparation process. Ask your listeners to respond in specific ways. To simply say, 'Let's meditate on these truths' does little to move people toward spiritual transformation.

Fourth, there should be a persuasive or motivational element in the conclusion. We must do more than appeal to the cerebral when we ask people to respond. Preaching must also touch the emotions and the will. There must be an emotional response and a volitional response, as well as an intellectual response. Jesus said that we're to love God with our whole 'heart, soul, mind, and strength'. We are whole beings and we must respond and urge others to respond with our total selves. While sermons and their conclusions should not sink to emotionalism, they should not hesitate to address the audience's emotional needs. They must also speak to the capacity of people to choose, exercising volition. While manipulation must be avoided, persuasion is at the heart of Christian preaching.

Fifth, a carefully worded closing sentence should be planned. Let the sermon end with a clinching statement rather than an off-the-cuff remark that accomplishes nothing. This is the last thing people will hear in this sermon. It ought to be significant.

Finally, various rhetorical elements and materials can be used to enhance the above. A human interest story might be used to make a final analogy. Questions might be raised to cause the listener to interact with what has been said. The preacher might return to a problem or unanswered issue presented in the introduction. Similarly, an opening illustration or statement might be reintroduced bringing the sermon full circle. A quotation might be used, though caution should be exercised in keeping it short and making certain that it says exactly what needs to be said. This is true whether the quotation is of prose or poetry. The latter should be used only with extreme caution because today's audiences have little use for literary niceties. A stanza of a hymn or worship song might be appropriate on occasion.

General Guidelines for Conclusions

The following suggestions will help assure that conclusions are effective.

Allow sufficient time for the preparation of the conclusion. This step often receives a minimum of attention, yet it is extremely important. Andrew Blackwood, in fact, spoke of the conclusion as being 'the most important part of a sermon, except for the text.'[12]

Second, keep the conclusion brief. Listeners will be tiring and an ending that is too long will prompt some to stop listening. A rule of thumb that I've tried to follow is to limit the conclusion to about five to eight percent of the total preaching time. This is sufficient to say what really needs said without dragging it out unnecessarily.

Third, do not introduce new ideas. Stick to reinforcing what has been said already. Any new concept will be out of place and irrelevant to this particular sermon.

Fourth, avoid humor. While humor might be used effectively elsewhere, it should never be used in the conclusion. To do so is to undermine the importance of what is being said and the response that is being expected.

Finally, when wrapping up the sermon, avoid anything that is apologetic. Perhaps the sermon has not gone as well as you had hoped. Don't apologize for it. Leave that verdict with God. Perhaps you've preached too long. Don't apologize for this. The deed has already been done and your apology will not change anything. Leave this with the listener to deal with. It is important that sermons end on a positive, expectant note. An apology will destroy this.

Be Historical Yet Contemporary

To preach balanced sermons in terms of content means to recognize and deal with two spheres of reality. One is the historical setting of the Bible and the other is the present day situation in which we and our audiences live. John Stott referred to this as being 'between two worlds'.[13] Sidney Greidanus titled one of his books *The Modern Preacher and the Ancient Text*, a title that aptly reminds us of these two spheres with which we must deal.[14]

Many preachers, and I count myself among their number, enjoy stepping into the world of the Bible. We feel at home there. We've studied the times, the nations, and the cultures of Scripture. Perhaps we've studied the biblical languages. We've learned exegetical and hermeneutical skills. It's not a stretch to say that we feel fairly comfortable with the prospect of digging into less familiar parts of Scripture, perhaps it even excites us to do so. Our listeners, on the other hand, are far less knowledgeable about biblical matters and far less motivated to do deep study. They don't care particularly about the details of investigation in the text that tend to boost our scholarly adrenalin. They only want to know the bottom line and they usually want to know it only if it has relevance to their lives. Keith Willhite[15] vividly describes this dichotomy.

> As a student of Scripture, trained in exegesis and theology, I can 'get lost' in the study of the Ancient Near East's worship of Baal, the composition of the tribes of Israel, or the debates about James' theology. As a preacher, give me good biblical-historical-theological evidence, and I'll buy the sermon's big idea or homiletical proposition.
>
> In doing so, I'm thinking as a preacher because I'm living in a

preacher's world. The people to whom I speak on Saturday night and Sunday morning live in a world of bioethics, violence, car payments, sitcoms, and dot-coms. Trying to explain to them Elijah's conflict on Mount Carmel (1 Kings 18) by giving an abbreviated history lesson on Baal worship is like trying to sell flood insurance in the desert.

That's because I'm talking in the preacher's world.[16]

Multiply this one historical example by a couple of thousand and it becomes apparent that the preacher faces a tremendous challenge in trying to bridge the gulf between the world of Scripture and the world in which we live.

Honor the Historical Roots of Scripture

As we contemplate the daunting chasm that exists between the world of the Bible and our contemporary world, we must first reflect on the fact that this has not taken God by surprise. He has chosen to reveal Himself in history fully understanding that it is not a fixed, static commodity. The affairs of the human race have been in a state of flux from the very beginning. Places, values, practices, belief systems, and a myriad of other human attachments have changed numerous times. God has been fully aware that this would occur.

We seem to think that the gulf that presently exists between our time and Bible times is unique, but this is not so. There was a cultural gulf that existed between the ancients of the early chapters of Genesis and the patriarchs. There was a gulf that existed between the patriarchs and the generation of Moses. There was a gulf that existed between the Jews of the Exodus and those who settled in Canaan. There was a gulf that existed between the monarchy and the Babylonian exile. There was a gulf that existed between the exile and the resettlement of Judah. There was a gulf that existed between the writings of the Old Testament and New Testament times.

When Isaiah prophesied the coming of the Messiah, the two kingdoms of Judah and Israel were the homes of God's covenant people. When Messiah came, neither kingdom existed and hadn't for centuries. Christians of the first century had to examine the Old Testament writings, affirmed by Jesus as authoritative, and strive to understand and apply them in view of the times in which they were living. Baal worship may have been as foreign to them as it is to us. The armies of Shalmanesar of Assyria and Nebuchadnezzar of Babylon were old memories compared to the armies of Caesar. Furthermore, these Believers had to wrestle with issues like the Jewish Law and whether or not to worship in the temple. Still further, the pastoral world of the past was giving way to a world that was becoming cosmopolitan, as is seen in the tri-lingual sign posted on the cross of Jesus. These spiritual ancestors of ours had to live in two spheres also, the sphere of their Scriptures and the sphere of their ever-changing culture. This sounds familiar.

It may be granted that some of the cultural changes being experienced by first-century Christians were not as drastic as ours. Still, the changes in the area of religion were significant. We are not unique in having to build bridges between the past and the present.

Having observed all of this, we must still deal with the task of the preacher regarding the ancient world of the Bible. There is a cultural gap between us and the early Christians. There is an even larger gap between us and the various periods included in the Old Testament. We cannot simply ignore the differences, nor can we assume that the realities of biblical times are readily known and understood by contemporary congregations.

Most Christians don't need to know every detail of biblical history and culture in order to mature in their faith and function as God intends. This is not to say that such knowledge is fruitless nor would I discourage people from learning as much as possible. It is simply to recognize that most people have an array of responsibilities that prevents 'full time' study of the Bible. It is also my opinion that preachers, with the possible exception of those who are bi-vocational, are blessed with enough time to devote sufficient attention to the scholarly examination of the Scriptures. This is both a privilege and an obligation. Even in the midst of unrealistic (and often unbiblical) job descriptions, preachers must give priority to the Bible!

The Life Situation
One of the tasks of the expository preacher is to discover the situation

that was in place at the time of the biblical account. This is known by some scholars as the *Sitz im Leben*, a German term. While it is not always possible to discover the precise life situation being experienced in the text, the preacher should be diligent to get as close to it as possible. This will help assure that the preacher will be able to bring to sermon preparation as much knowledge as possible about the setting of the preaching text.

There are some obvious steps that need to be taken when approaching a text. The speaker or writer needs to be identified. Biographical information on this person should be researched as necessary. Where does this passage fit in terms of his or her life span and other contributions in the biblical record? The original recipients of the text should also be identified. Who were they? When and where did they live? What were their cultural situations in life? How does their chronology fit into the rest of biblical revelation? Geographical places and issues should be looked at and a determination made regarding the relevance of these to the sermon.

Apart from the text itself, and its larger context, it is helpful to look at information that is available apart from the Bible. Secular history and the science of archeology can often shed light on a people or time that may not be detailed in Scripture. The writings of Josephus, for example, offer insights into Jewish history that is quite informative. Tacitus, a Roman historian, is profitable reading in terms of developing an understanding of the culture in which the early church existed. A familiarity with archeology will sometimes help explain the meaning of biblical texts and the culture involved. Genesis 23, for example, contains the story of the death and burial of Sarah, the wife of Abraham. An interesting part of the story is the dialogue between Abraham and Ephron the Hittite. Ephron attempts to give a parcel of land with a cave for burial to Abraham, but he refuses to receive it as a gift. Finally, Ephron agrees to sell the land for four hundred shekels of silver while still protesting that he would prefer giving the land to Abraham without cost. We might wonder why Abraham didn't accept the land as a gift. Archeological discoveries in southeastern Turkey (in the area of ancient Hattusa, the center of Hittite culture) include at least 25,000 cuneiform tablets, some of which contain Hittite law codes. Among these codes was information explaining Abraham's insistence on paying for the land. To have received it as a gift would have resulted in a permanent indebtedness to Ephron in terms of required military service, if required. Abraham wisely chose not to become involved in this cultural situation.

I am not suggesting that we should devote huge amounts of time to this kind of study. I am saying, rather, that some time spent will greatly enrich our understanding of that world which often seems far removed from our consciousness. As we become increasingly familiar with that world, we will be better equipped to understand the relationship between that world and our own. This will help inform our sermon preparation and enrich our preaching. It will also help assure that we preach the Bible's message.

Harold Bryson, in an excellent book dealing with the methodology of preaching through books of the Bible, uses the analogy of sitting under the big top at the circus and compares this to visiting the circus's side shows. He then likens this to proper and improper preaching.

> Every text in the Bible book comes under the big top of historical background. Interpreting a text without regard to its historical background turns the text (and sermon) into a sideshow. Studying biblical background helps the preacher show the overall cover for each text in the Bible book. Studying these life situations is hard work, but the careful expositor knows that it is worth the effort because it pays off in authentic biblical sermons.[17]

The Faith Situation

In addition to the importance of understanding the life situation of a biblical text, some have also emphasized the importance of understanding the faith situation, the *Sitz im Glauben*.[18] Mickelsen differentiates between the life situation and the faith situation in terms of 'the horizontal: man and his environment; the vertical: man and his relationship with God.'[19] Both of these perspectives must be understood to comprehend and communicate the biblical account adequately.

The biblical writers and speakers were themselves people of faith. They were concerned primarily with God's revelation to people and their response to him. While they were not systematic theologians, they were concerned with matters of theology and how their audiences understood and responded to these issues. They were themselves God-focused individuals who deeply desired their hearers or readers to be the same.

As preachers, then, we have the responsibility of getting to know the spiritual conditions of the various people involved in the biblical accounts. This will help us better understand precise contexts and it will assist us as we apply the Scripture properly to ourselves and our audiences.

As we deal with Old Testament texts we might ask, for example: where were these people in terms of their relationship with the Abrahamic covenant? What was their stance in regard to the Mosaic Law? Were they practicing idolatry and if so, what kind? What type of deviation from Orthodox Judaism did this represent? What did they understand or misunderstand about God? What change(s) needed to be made in order to please God? What were their relationships with others like in terms of religious values? Were they people of faith or people of a mere religious tradition? Did their profession of faith match their behavior? What was their understanding of the messianic promises available to them?

As we preach on New Testament passages we also need to study the faith situation of those original hearers or readers. What was their understanding of Jesus the Christ and his relationship to God the Father? Were believers or unbelievers being addressed? What steps toward saving faith or a deeper faith were needed? What areas of Christian doctrine were misunderstood? What areas of Christian behavior were misunderstood? What corrective measures were being prescribed by the speaker or writer?

These are representative of the kinds of questions the preacher should ask in order to gain a feel for the faith situation found in each text. We can then make comparisons to ourselves and our own audience. This will help insure that our preaching is both truly biblical and truly relevant.

Accumulating Historical Knowledge
It may seem that coming to a good comprehension of the life and faith situations of every text we preach on is a task too formidable to tackle. While it is true that in-depth study of this nature takes time, it is time well spent. Furthermore, this time is part of the total preparation time that should be budgeted as a priority in the preacher's schedule. It must also be said that some sermons will not require a great deal of time in this regard.

This kind of knowledge is cumulative. As we continue to engage in serious study of biblical texts, we are enlarging our knowledge of historical and spiritual contexts. We don't have to start from scratch with each sermon. Our first sermon from a particular book of the Bible may require a couple of hours or more of studious digging into atlases, histories, encyclopedias, and commentaries. When we return to preach from that book again, we don't need to repeat all of the same processes. We are gaining a cumulative knowledge of Bible contexts.

This is one of the great advantages of preaching expositionally through a Bible book. We can prepare and preach stronger sermons by building on what we've discovered previously. Some of our study time will be reduced because we're not starting all over again with each message. At the same time, our listeners are being taught more fully about the Scripture than if we jump from book to book each week or if we preach only topical sermons.

Communicate the Historical Roots Relevantly
There are, as stated earlier, two spheres with which the preacher must be competently familiar. One is the sphere of Scripture; the other is the sphere of the contemporary situation. In the previous section, we looked at the former. Now let us look at the latter. To do so is to be reminded of the need of relevant preaching.

The Reality of the Bible's Relevance
Almost half a century ago, Ian Macpherson rightly decried the misuse of the concept of relevancy in regard to Christian things.

> That word 'relevance' is the epidemic word in religious circles nowadays. It is on every lip. People talk about the 'relevance' of the Bible, the 'relevance' of the Church, the 'relevance' of Christianity. James Denney and F. R. Barry started it, and now everybody has become infected. Prominent among the things thus put to the proof is preaching. Is preaching relevant?[20]

Macpherson did not appreciate the implication that the Bible, the Church, Christianity, and preaching had to be defended from claims of irrelevancy. He also did not appreciate that some ministers, including the two he named, believed that these things must be *made* relevant. He contended that all of these things, including the concept of preaching, were relevant in and of themselves.

Biblical preaching is relevant because Scripture is 'living and active' (Heb. 4:12) and it meets real needs in people's lives. Vosteen poses the key question: 'Does God's Word really change lives? That is the question that must be realistically faced by every minister of the Word. Unless we can say a resounding yes, the church of Christ is in deep trouble.'[21]

It is my assumption that we who affirm the authority of Scripture in its teaching and our practice believe that the Bible is indeed relevant. This is true even when we struggle to effectively communicate that relevancy.

Preaching Relevantly

While it is true that Scripture is most certainly relevant, it is also true that relevant truth can be communicated in such a way as to make it seem irrelevant. Not all sermons based on Scripture are highly relevant to listeners, though they ought to be. When they're not, it's usually either because the preacher doesn't really know the audience and its concerns, or the preacher has failed to connect the life situation and faith situation of the text to the audience. Each of these has to do with achieving and maintaining relevance.

In regard to this latter concern, that of failing to connect the text and the audience, there are two possible errors to avoid. One is to begin with the felt situation of the audience and never move beyond this to the authoritative teaching of the text. The preacher must never bow the sermonic knee to the god of relevance at the expense of eternal truth. As David Henderson rightly observes:

> There is a fine line here. It is important to begin where our audiences are. It is a fundamental communication principle: begin where people are, not where you wish they were. Our words should intersect with the issues and concerns of their daily lives. Only then is it possible for our hearers to get a sense of the functional relevance of the Bible.... But this is a key. While we need to start with the pressing issues of our hearers, we cannot stay there. We must move on from a person's experience to God's view of the issue... [22]

The other error is to begin with the text and never move to the audience. Biblical preaching must move beyond the Bible. As Larsen notes, 'The purpose of preaching reaches beyond the accurate exposition of the biblical text. The sermon which starts in the Bible and stays in the Bible is not biblical.' [23] Clyde Fant makes a similar statement: 'Our sermons cannot reflect profound knowledge of the first century and abysmal ignorance of the twentieth century. No one can be true to the biblical text and ignore the congregation. The biblical word is never a word in abstraction. It is always a specific word to a specific situation.' [24] Homiletician Ian Pitt-Watson wrote that 'preaching which is rooted in the text of Scripture alone can still be unbiblical, unreal, and irrelevant unless it is also rooted in the text of life. [25]

Other effective preachers from a wide variety of backgrounds have understood the importance of preaching biblical truth relevantly. Spurgeon, in his own inimitable way, taught his young students:

> I suggest again that in order to secure attention all through a discourse we must *make the people feel that they have an interest in what we are saying to them*. This is, in fact, a most essential point, because nobody sleeps while he expects to hear something to his advantage. I have heard of some very strange things, but I never did hear of a person going to sleep while a will was being read in which he expected a legacy, neither have I

heard of a prisoner going to sleep while the judge was summing up, and his life was hanging in jeopardy. Self-interest quickens attention. Preach upon practical themes, pressing, present, personal matters, and you will secure an earnest hearing.[26] (Emphasis his)

A contemporary of Spurgeon, the Episcopalian bishop Phillips Brooks, stated in his Yale Lectures that 'truth and timeliness together make the full preacher.'[27] In the early part of the twentieth century, theologian Karl Barth spoke of preaching as having the Bible in one hand and the newspaper in the other.

All of these expressions remind us of the importance of preaching relevantly. Listeners must identify with a sermon's concerns if it is to be effective. It is necessary that people in the audience feel this message has relevance to them. If not, they will likely stop listening actively.

Understanding the Audience
Some preachers speak of 'exegeting' the audience or doing audience analysis. Calvin Miller, referring to Vohs and Mohrman,[28] discusses three kinds of audience analysis: demography, motive, and range-of-receptivity.[29] Keith Willhite, in an excellent chapter titled 'Look from the Pew's Perspective', devotes several pages to some tools for audience analysis. He includes general analysis that is sociological and cultural in nature, local analysis that is community-based, and particular analysis which relates to a specific congregation. In regard to particular analysis, he deals with theological analysis, psychological analysis, demographic analysis, and purpose-oriented analysis. He then suggests some suitable ways of adapting to audience expectations. Finally, he presents some practical sample grids that can be developed.[30] There is some overlap between Miller and Willhite but both are very helpful treatments of the importance of understanding one's audience and some practical ways of doing so.

At the very least, an effective preacher will have a general understanding of the make-up of his hearers. The preacher will be aware that a significant number of marriages are dealing with some conflict, that some families are being tried and tested by problematic teenagers, that a goodly number of those who attend are in the throes of grief, and that many are suffering from emotional problems of various kinds. The preacher will understand that some within hearing distance are battling habits that are health and life threatening, that a substantial number are under extreme stress at work, and that many who are younger face stress of various kinds at school. Preachers should be aware that many who want to live faithful lives struggle with temptation, besetting sins, or even moral failure with its subsequent guilt. Others face fears and anxieties. Relatively few of our listeners, if any, 'have it all together.' Still, we have been called to be messengers of grace to these needy people, people with whom we can readily identify because of our own struggles.

Lest this generalization appear to be too pessimistic, let us recall that early word from the public ministry of Jesus, a word given in his own synagogue in Nazareth as his public preaching ministry was launched. The text was read from Isaiah 61:1-2:

> The Spirit of the Lord is on me, because he has anointed me to preach good news to the poor. He has sent me to proclaim freedom for the prisoners and recovery of sight for the blind, to release the oppressed, to proclaim the year of the Lord's favor (Luke 4:18-19).

Jesus echoed the prophet in identifying the poor, the imprisoned, the blind, and the oppressed as those to whom he came to minister. As he continued speaking to those in the synagogue, Jesus also identified those outside the fold – a Gentile widow and a Gentile leper – as being recipients of God's grace. Our Lord recognized hurting people and came to serve them. So must the relevant preacher.

Thankfully, not all of our listeners are in pain. Some are experiencing joyful circumstances and our preaching must be relevant to them also. We are to hurt with those who hurt and rejoice with those who rejoice. We must warn and we must encourage. We must teach and we must apply. Basically, we must touch their lives in a multitude of needful ways, being led by the Holy Spirit to present the right truths at the right time in the right way so that these truths can be understood and embraced by our people in their various life experiences.

Be Both Broad and Deep

Another area of content in which balance must be brought to our preaching is that of depth. We face a kind of dilemma each time we prepare a message, each time we plan a series, and each time we do long-range planning regarding our preaching. This dilemma relates to how in-depth a given sermon, or a series, or our total preaching ministry will be. Should we preach in great detail, or should we preach the broader themes of the Bible? The answer, I believe is 'yes'. But how can a suitable balance be achieved?

Broad Preaching

Many observers of America speak of our present day cultural situation as being post-Christian or even pre-Christian. This is seen in a number of ways including the rise of secularism and the introduction and growth of many religious movements outside of the country's Judeo-Christian roots including Islam, Buddhism, Hinduism, and New Age thinking. In spite of the rise of the megachurch boom, attendance in Christian churches is falling at a serious rate, perhaps for the first time since the latter part of the 17th century. While many people have their names on church roles, attendance is often sporadic. Furthermore, serious engagement in Christian practices seems to be waning and an understanding of biblical teachings and values may be at an all-time low. Even in many evangelical churches there appears to be a high degree of biblical illiteracy as well as an absence of Christian thinking and practice.

Tolerance, of course, is the magic word these days. Our pluralistic culture is seen as a good thing and everyone's opinion about religion and morality is considered of equal value. Truth is either thought to be elusive (unknowable) or relative (non-existent). This is what is consistently communicated in the vast majority of media presentations including radio, television, and the print media. The exception to this inclusivism is often biblical Christianity. At best, evangelical Christians are begrudgingly tolerated by the media elite. At worst, we are regarded as dangerous 'fundamentalists' akin to those responsible for the Twin Trade Towers attack. It is not a stretch to say that

Americans live in a post-Christian culture.

In such an environment, the broad themes of Scripture need to be presented constantly to our regular listeners and to others as we have opportunity. We preachers must be persuaded that Truth is a reality. In a culture that cynically echoes Pontius Pilate ('What is truth?'), we must instead reflect the certainty of Christ who daringly asserted that he is the Truth and that he came to make the Truth known (John 14:6, John 18:37-38).

If the Bible is indeed the authoritative Word of God, then all of its theological and ethical teachings must be presented over the long haul of our ministries. We will first need to be fully knowledgeable of and thoroughly committed to these truths ourselves. Then, we will need to determine how best to present them to our people.

I think of the Apostle Paul in this regard. He spent three years in Ephesus, a pagan city in which there was much opposition to the Christian message. Later, when he met with the Ephesian elders, he reminded them: 'you know that I have not hesitated to preach anything that would be helpful to you' (Acts 20:20); and again, 'I have not hesitated to proclaim to you the whole will of God' (Acts 20:27). The word translated 'will' in the NIV is *boulē*, which can also mean advice, purpose, or counsel. Paul had a preaching ministry in Ephesus that was exhaustive in terms of its breadth.

Preaching in the local church should also be broad. Our listeners are bombarded by a steady stream of ideas and opinions. Some of these are acceptable from a Christian perspective and some are not. 'Equipping the saints' (Eph. 4:12) must include a pulpit ministry that presents the full teachings of Scripture. This will help enable Christians to engage the culture in an informed way that honors Christ.

Still the question remains as to the best way to accomplish broad preaching. Long-range pulpit planning, it seems to me, is the best way to achieve this. When we plan our sermons a week or two in advance, we tend to choose from a limited number of subjects, those with which we feel most comfortable and those which appear to be most immediately relevant. Many other important topics will wait for a later time which somehow never seems to come. Long-range planning helps bring the bigger picture to our attention. It gives us the opportunity to consider a variety of subjects to cover in the next six, nine, or twelve month period. It also prompts us to re-examine what we've preached on during the past extended period of time. This kind of planning has the potential to help us achieve a tremendous amount of balance in our preaching ministries. It will help us achieve a proper balance in sermon purposes, doctrines discussed, and behavior promoted. This will result in helping us "preach the whole will of God." Practically, it means that subjects will be greatly varied and that texts will come from all of the major parts of Scripture.

Another way to achieve broadness in our pulpit fare is to plan occasional series which are purposely broad. While I've never done it, it seems that a series of eight or ten messages on the Apostles Creed would be a great way to present some broad doctrinal truths. In churches that often recite this creed, such a series of sermons would make its recitation much more meaningful. It would also be a way of presenting some basic tenets of Christian theology without coming across like a systematic theologian. In churches that are 'non-creedal', a series of this type would be an opportunity to remind our congregation of the larger Body of Christ and some of her roots. Most churches have a 'statement of faith' of some sort. A series on this statement is also worthy of consideration. A doctrinal series of this kind would need to include a heavy emphasis on the practical ramifications of each truth presented. The preacher would need to work hard at communicating 'eternal truths that impact daily living'.

In addition to an occasional doctrinal series, a balanced preacher might wish to address the moral teachings of Scripture in an occasional brief series. One such approach would be to address the myriad of moral systems in our culture (relativism, pragmatism, utilitarianism, Christian legalism, anti-nomianism, etc.) and to address each of these from a biblical perspective. Paul's first letter to the Corinthians is a great foundation for such a series.

We should be less concerned with the *how* than the *what*. How we present the broad teachings of Scripture is not as important as doing it. Many, if not most, of our listeners face a culture hostile to our Faith and they do so with a meager amount of biblical knowledge.

How can they function as healthy Christians in this situation without adequate grounding in God's truth? It is the responsibility of the church, including those who preach, to prepare them to successfully engage the world beyond the church's walls. Our preaching must be broad if our people are to be adequately equipped to bear witness to the truth.

Deep Preaching

While our preaching must necessarily be broad, we also need to preach with specificity and great depth as we address many of the themes in Scripture. Our people need more than a steady diet of 'Bible lite,' the standard fare in many pulpits today. This is where the choice between breadth and depth becomes difficult. How do we choose wisely between that which can be presented with broadly painted strokes and that which ought to be presented with careful detail work? Both are important.

The difference might be seen in the following example. I have a former colleague who preached a series of twelve sermons on the Minor Prophets. Each of these books is important and has relevance to the contemporary person. Hosea, for example, speaks of unfathomable love that is scarcely understandable in today's self-centered culture. Obadiah addresses the issues of pride and disloyalty. Zephaniah emphasizes coming judgment and promised blessing. Malachi asks pointed questions of those who are self-righteous. The others are also thematically of value yet few people in our churches have heard preaching from these twelve books. So, my friend painted with broad strokes by preaching twelve sermons, one per book.

I've also preached on the Minor Prophets, at least some of them. I've done four sermons on Jonah, several on Hosea, a few on Amos, a couple on Malachi, and one covering the whole of Habakkuk. I've also preached the obligatory Christmas sermon on Micah 5:2. My sermons based on Jonah were much more detailed than the single sermon preached by my friend as were my messages on Hosea and Amos. Yet, both approaches were needed and helpful.

Another example of the contrast of breadth and depth is the way one might preach on the person of Jesus. A doctrinal series on a statement of faith, as discussed in the previous section, would have a sermon or two on Christology. A few highlights could be covered briefly, such as his eternality, his deity, and his humanity. I've preached this type of sermon on occasion. I've also preached an eight-part series on the person of Jesus based on the sign-miracles in John's Gospel. This enabled me to be much more in-depth than the single sermon. Again, both approaches met a legitimate need at the time.

A word of caution needs to be mentioned. Preaching deeply does not mean that our sermons should become mere lectures, filled with biblical and theological facts. We preach not simply to impart information but to persuade our listeners to act on what they've heard. They need to experience transformation as the Holy Spirit of God implants the Word into their inner beings. Our motivation should not be primarily to produce systematic theologians and biblical scholars, but mature followers of Jesus Christ.

Balancing Breadth and Depth

There are times when the need of the congregation is to be broadened. The people may have heard certain subjects covered in a deep way, but are relatively uninformed about other biblical truths. This may be because previous pastors have failed to preach broadly, or it may be because the current pastor similarly is locked into favorite subjects. Most preachers, if we're honest, have our pet subjects and texts. We believe that sermons based on these are crucial, we're comfortable addressing these areas, and we may find ourselves facing intimidating challenges if we begin to address subjects and parts of Scripture with which we are less than familiar. So we continue doing what we've always done. And our people continue to languish where they are in terms of learning, growth, and hunger for the Word.

Sometimes, the opposite is true. There are some who tend to be surface-level preachers. They speak on a wide variety of topics and passages, but seldom speak at an in-depth level. They are either unconvinced of the importance of deep, challenging, thought-provoking preaching or they see themselves as incapable of doing it. The result is that the church is 'a mile wide and an inch deep.' People continue to be fed on the milk of infancy, while the Bible says that 'solid food is for the mature' (Heb. 5:14). Peter was told by Jesus to feed the flock (John 21). Paul writes that the church's gifted leaders, including pastor-teachers, are to contribute to the maturation of believers. They are

> to prepare God's people for works of service, so that the body of Christ may be built up until we all reach unity in the faith and in the knowledge of the Son of God and become mature, attaining to the whole measure of the fullness of Christ. Then we will no longer be infants, tossed back and forth by the waves, and blown here and there by every wind of teaching and by the cunning and craftiness of men in their deceitful scheming. Instead, speaking the truth in love, we will in all things grow up into him who is the Head, that is, Christ (Eph. 4:12-15).

Balancing breadth and depth is not always easy. It involves making good judgments about which subjects are worthy of an in-depth treatment. Spurgeon gave good advice to his students: 'Do not make minor doctrines main points. Do not paint the details of the background of the gospel picture with the same heavy brush as the great objects in the foreground of it.' [31]

Be Rooted in Sound Scholarship but Readily Understandable

To utilize sound scholarship in our sermon preparation is not the same as delivering sermons that sound scholarly. The pulpit's purpose is not to present argument and counter-argument, nor is it to explain the nuances of the process of exegesis. It is to present in understandable terms what God has said.

The Substance of Sound Scholarship
Effective preaching cannot be separated from biblical scholarship. The preacher must be a student of the Word and always pressing to know it better. While all preachers do not have the same depth of training or even intellectual capacity at their disposal, each should

have the same drive to understand as fully as possible the teachings of Scripture. Neither laziness nor lack of interest should ever characterize us.

The Product of Biblical Scholarship.

As we diligently study the pages of the Bible, there are three large categories of materials we will encounter: theology, history, and ethics. These categories are not mutually exclusive. When we study biblical history, for example, we may well encounter theological and/or ethical teachings. We may study a text that is primarily ethical in nature only to discover its theological basis. A theological passage may disclose its historical roots. Still, I find it helpful to think in terms of these broad categories.

Sermons which are text-driven, therefore, will usually fall into one of these categories. Given sermons will tend to be theology-based, history-based, or ethics-based. As with the texts themselves, however, our messages will sometimes reflect a necessary blend of two or three of these categories. Nevertheless, I find it helpful to treat a text according to its primary emphasis.

Some of our preaching will therefore reflect a doctrinal emphasis. We must not shy away from this. I concur with Timothy George's emphatic statement that 'the recovery of doctrinal preaching is essential to the renewal of the church'.[32] Such a statement will not find universal agreement. Some would argue that doctrine is not nearly as important as those issues encountered by our listeners day in and day out in homes, schools, and the marketplace. They would emphasize subjects like the importance of knowing how to cope with daily stresses, how to have healthy relationships, and how to handle the ethical choices regularly faced. What does theology have to do with these?

I believe that theology has *everything* to do with these. Without a clear understanding of who God is, what he is like, what he has done for us in Christ, and what he continues to do in us through the Holy Spirit, the above issues cannot be addressed adequately. We can only attempt to do what the secular authorities do. Do we have nothing more to say than the philosopher, social scientist, professor, or psychologist? I believe we do, and it must be grounded in theology. This is not to suggest that a dry recitation of systematic theology will suffice. Theology is never an end in itself. Rather, it must always be the starting point. Doctrinal preaching is therefore necessary to ground our listeners in basic Christian truth. All other ideas will need be filtered through this.

Some of our preaching will be historical in its emphasis. That is, it will deal with an incident or biographical account from the Bible's huge amount of narrative material. This doesn't mean that these sermons will be history lessons with all the names and dates neatly arranged. A sermon of this type is probably doomed before the first word is uttered. Few people are interested in relatively recent history, such as the founding of America or the Revolutionary War. Should we expect them to be excited about something that happened two or three thousand years ago? To assume that they are is to be extremely naive.

The preacher's task is to communicate that such history is important and even exciting because it tells us about God's dealings with people in the past and, by extension, with us today. From biblical history we can learn a great deal about ourselves for we see ourselves mirrored in the lives of those we study. We see what God expected of them and what he expects of us. Sermons based on these accounts can encourage and warn, comfort and condemn, inform and inspire.

Some of our preaching will be ethical in its emphasis. It will reflect the Bible's teachings regarding right behavior and wise choices. Such passages are found in the sayings of Jesus, the most obvious being the Sermon on the Mount in Matthew 5-7. But they are not limited to the Gospels. Ethical teaching is also found throughout the Old Testament and in the New Testament epistles as well.

Biblical ethics are revolutionary to say the least. These teachings come to completion in the remarkable teachings of Jesus. Raymond Bailey captures this well:

> The theology of Jesus demands a radical ethic. Those who have been forgiven of their sins and have yielded to the rule of God in their lives are called to live God's standard of life. 'You therefore,

must be perfect, as your heavenly Father is perfect' (Matt. 5:48), Jesus said on the mountain.[33]

Bailey then gives practical results of this radical ethic:

Perhaps if all preachers were as clear about what it means to 'follow' Jesus, churches would not operate on the premise that only half of the membership will be active. Do you think we have been clear about counting the cost (Luke 14:25-33) when 20 percent of the congregation bears 80 percent of the cost of ministry? What does it mean when a hundred people are cajoled to the altar during a revival but a year later eighty of them can't be found? . . . At no time did Jesus mince words about what it meant to be a kingdom person.[34]

Diligence in biblical scholarship will produce an understanding of the kind of text on which we plan to preach. It will also enable us to balance our presentations of these kinds of texts.

Scholarship Beyond Biblical Studies
First and foremost, the preacher should practice sound biblical scholarship. The Scripture must be front and center, the focal point of our preaching ministry. But we should be knowledgeable regarding other areas of life as well.

There was a time when the clergy were the best educated people around. In fact, the word 'parson' comes from the Latin *persona*. This title indicated that this individual was the leading person around. This is no longer the case and has not been in quite awhile. Many in our churches are equally or better educated than we. Collectively, they are conversant in a great many areas of knowledge. While preachers can't hope to know everything, we shouldn't be content to wallow in our ignorance either. We should be life-long learners not only in biblical matters, but in various disciplines that impact the human race. Our preaching will be greatly strengthened if we continue to discipline ourselves to read widely and discuss a variety of issues with others.

I'm reminded of Charles Spurgeon. While lacking a formal

education, he nevertheless was a remarkably learned person. His personal library numbered some twelve thousand volumes and included books not only in the biblical and theological disciplines, but a wide collection in the sciences and arts. One need only read a few of his sermons to discover that he illustrated profusely from a tremendous breadth of human knowledge and that his figures of speech reflect the same.

Being well educated has many advantages and no disadvantages, except perhaps the temptation to flaunt it. Being broadly knowledgeable helps us think critically, it enables us to relate to others in our sphere of influence, it reminds us of many examples and analogies of the varied concepts on which we preach, and it keeps us informed of the kind of world in which we live even to the extent of current events.

Casual Reading

In addition to continuing education in the forms of serious reading, professional dialogue, and attendance at conferences and workshops, I believe that casual reading is worthwhile for the preacher. While some may see this kind of reading as mere recreation, this is not so. The reading of novels, short stories, newspapers, and magazines can be profitable if done wisely in terms of selection and time usage. This kind of reading often helps to keep us informed of our current culture and trends toward the future. Paul quotes from secular literature in his sermon to the Greek philosophers in Acts 17.

There is also something to be learned stylistically from those who write professionally. Craddock remarks:

> Reading good literature enlarges one's capacities as a creative human being and has a cumulative effect on one's vocabulary, use of the language, and powers of imagination. Not by conscious imitation but through the subtle influence of these great storytellers and poets, a preacher becomes more adept at arranging the materials of the sermon so that by restraint and thematic control, interest, clarity, and persuasiveness will be served.[35]

The Use of Sound Scholarship

While preaching informed by scholarship is desirable, we must use our research with great care. Scholarship is a tool, not the end result of our endeavors. It should be used, but not paraded in such a way as to call attention to itself. Sermons that sound ostentatious usually turn people off. When attention is drawn to our scholarship, it is drawn to us rather than what we are proclaiming.

There are three immediate dangers that come to mind that ought to be avoided in this regard. The first is the pitfall of intellectualism. Writing from the perspective of the 'Reformed Faith,' Geoffrey Thomas addresses this matter in a pointed way.

> One of the great perils that face preachers of the Reformed Faith is the problem of a hyper-intellectualism, that is, the constant danger of lapsing into a purely cerebral form of proclamation, which falls exclusively upon the intellect. Men become obsessed with doctrine and end up as brain-oriented preachers. There is consequently a fearful impoverishment in their hearers emotionally, devotionally, and practically. Such pastors are men of books and not men of people; they know the doctrines, but they know nothing of the emotional side of religion.[36]

God has made us to be whole persons. Our minds must be nourished, but so must our emotions be satisfied and our volitions be challenged. Preaching that is only intellectual quickly becomes stagnant like a water hole without an outlet.

The second danger of the misuse of scholarship is that our sermons might deteriorate into something other than sermons. James Stewart, both an able scholar and a fine preacher, wrote:

> Remember, first, that what you are hoping to produce is a sermon – not an essay, not a lecture, not a college exegesis, but a sermon. That is to say, when you sit down to write in your study, you must visualize a gathered congregation. This will give your work those qualities of directness, liveliness, verve, and immediacy which are so essential. . . . It will eliminate irrelevances. It will constrain you to clarify your own ideas. . . . It will embolden you to use personal

forms of address. It will banish the dull stilted tediousness of the
sermon-essay. It will keep the dominant notes of urgency and reality,
of appeal for a verdict, sounding unmistakably.[37]

This seems to be a particular danger to those who are gifted
teachers. They love the Word and they love helping others
understand it better. Giving detailed background information on the
text, explaining the nuances of exegetical findings, and discussing
the fine points of theology all bring a sense of excitement to the
teacher. Unfortunately, these processes can become a steady barrage
of facts – good facts to be sure – but a barrage of facts that fails to
move beyond information. This is not preaching. It is a duplication
of the lecture hall.

The third danger is that of sending a wrong message to our
listeners, communicating that only scholars are capable of studying
the Bible. The pulpit is a place where teaching takes place not only
directly as we present the truths of Scripture, but indirectly as well.
For example, we can present a poor model of biblical interpretation
and then find ourselves wondering why our people don't handle the
Word of God properly. Or, we can preach with a negative and
judgmental spirit and wonder why we have a congregation of
negative, fault-finding people. Another message we may
unintentionally send is that serious Bible study needs to be left in the
hands of the scholars. We might decry the practice of some in church
history who withheld the Scriptures from lay people lest they
misinterpret it and fall into heresy, yet we may inadvertently
encourage the same thing to happen.

When we emphasize the use of the original languages, for instance,
we may send the message that without a knowledge of Greek and
Hebrew the Bible can't be properly understood. Charles R. Brown,
former dean at Yale Divinity School and the presenter of the Beecher
Lectures at Yale in 1906, wrote: 'The expository sermon is a product
of exegesis, but not an exhibition of it. It is altogether wise to dig
beforehand with your Greek spade and your Hebrew shovel but
not to be digging while you are preaching.'[38] We should use our
language tools to the extent of our ability, but it is both unnecessary

and unwise to present our findings using the technical language of the study process. The pulpit should communicate the truth of our findings, not the process.

To say something like, 'The main verb in this verse is in the aorist tense and this means punctiliar action,' is to leave our listeners shaking their heads in bewilderment. Instead, we could simply say, 'and this is something that happens in a moment of time.' We could say, 'There are several different words translated "power" in the New Testament, words like *dunamis, exousia, ischus, dunaton* and *arche*, but the word used here is *kratos*.' But it is far better to get to the point simply and quickly by saying, 'The kind of power spoken of here is "strength in action".' Again, it is the bottom line that is important in a sermon, not the exegetical process.

The Importance of Being Understood

Preachers have the challenging task of being scholars who know how to effectively speak in a clear and interesting way. Listeners must understand what is being said. Truths that are abstract must be made concrete. The unfamiliar must be made familiar. The familiar must be said with a sense of freshness.

A very common criticism of preaching is that it contains Christian jargon that is not easily understood by the unchurched person, the casual attender, or even the committed follower of Christ. Henderson says we make the mistake

> . . . of being so confident of the relevance of the Bible that we fail to translate what it says into language that is meaningful to Average Joe and Average Josephine. And there it goes – *zing* – right over the person's head.
>
> God's Word speaks with relevance to all humans, crossing every cultural line. But not until it has been translated into words and concepts that speak with particular meaning to each particular culture. You will not overhear many conversations at McDonald's in which words like repentance, tithe, sanctified, or fellowship figure prominently. We redeem bottles, save dying trees, give testimony in the courtroom, have stewards on cruises, and give justification for showing up late for meetings, but what do those words mean when we use them in church?[39]

I must confess that the criticism of using biblical terminology in our preaching is a bit difficult for me to swallow. In fact, this criticism seems to imply that listeners aren't intelligent enough to comprehend biblical concepts. David Martyn Lloyd-Jones, in commenting on the perceived difficulty of understanding the language of the King James Version, remarked:

The simple answer to all this is that people have always found this language to be strange. The answer to the argument that people in this post-Christian age do not understand terms like Justification, Sanctification and Glorification is simply to ask another question. When did people understand them? When did the unbeliever understand this language? The answer is: Never! These terms are peculiar and special to the Gospel. It is our business as preachers to show that our gospel is essentially different and that we are not talking about ordinary matters. We must emphasize the fact that we are talking about something unique and special. We must lead people to expect this; and so we are to assert it. Our business is to teach people the meaning of these terms.[40]

Many walks of life have a unique vocabulary. My father was a railroader. As a young child, I recall him saying things like 'I plan to deadhead,' 'I've been bumped,' 'I'll mark off,' or 'I'm late because we had a hotbox.' I didn't initially know what these expressions meant, but I made it a point to find out. If I was in a gathering of railroaders, such as their annual picnic, I expected to hear them use some strange words. This didn't cause me to think of railroaders as being irrelevant. I simply understood that I was not very well informed regarding this particular vocation. The same can be said for many vocations.

The difference between this analogy and Christian preaching is that my dad was not attempting to convert me to his way of life. I was simply outside his vocational circle and was expected to stay there. Our preaching, on the other hand, is expected to clearly communicate the truth of the gospel in a way that is conducive to a 'vocational change'. We desire to see those who apart from Christ come to him. We wish to see those who are 'nominal believers' commit their lives fully to him. The clear understanding of truth is necessary for these changes to occur and unclear jargon can be a hindrance if suitable explanations aren't given. On the other hand, those who profess to be committed Christians have little excuse to remain ignorant about the meaning of significant biblical terms and concepts. I have little patience for those who choose to wallow in a self-imposed ignorance of significant Christian truths.

The task of the preacher, then, is to perform a sermonic wedding of sound scholarship and effective communication. This is an important part of balancing our sermon content. We must never shrink from speaking forth the truths of Scripture in a significantly informed way, and we must do this in a way that is significantly understandable to our listeners.

Summation

This chapter has dealt with the wide variety of materials the preacher should employ as sermons are being prepared. Sermon components such as the supporting material (sub-points), illustrations, applications, the introduction, and the conclusion were all discussed. These are crucial to the success of any sermon for they carry the bulk of the sermon's content and clarify the sermon's purpose. They are also crucial because they are a major factor in determining the interest level of the hearers. An effective preacher will continue to hone skills in these areas.

Then, the issue of the 'old and the new' was explored. The preacher's source of authority is the Bible, the newest parts of which are almost two millennia old. While we must necessarily deal with ancient history and teaching, these truths must be communicated with effectiveness to people who live in the twenty-first century. We must be able to successfully bridge the gap between these two spheres with relevant sermons.

The person who desires to be a faithful preacher of the Word will strive to achieve a proper balance in sermon purposes, doctrines discussed, and behavior promoted. This will result in what is sometimes called "preaching the whole counsel of God." Practically, it means that subjects will be greatly varied and that texts will come from all of the major parts of Scripture. It means that our preaching should be both broad and deep. Some sermons will examine large concepts and will necessarily be broad. Others will deal with smaller details of doctrine or behavior and will tend to be deeper in terms of detailed examination and explanation.

Finally, the tension between scholarship and understandability was explored. While we need to work hard at supporting our sermons by means of biblical and cultural research, and while we need to be constantly growing as persons on both the spiritual and intellectual levels, we also need to keep scholarship in its rightful place. It is a means to the end, not the end itself. The end of sermon-making must be people-making. Our task is to communicate God's truths in ways so clear that people can't miss them and in ways so winsome that people will embrace them and be utterly changed.

Points to ponder

1. What specific part of sermon preparation seems to be most problematic to you? What steps might you take to improve your skills in this area?

2. Do you find yourself in a 'rut' in terms of the kinds of materials you use in creating supporting material (sub-points, illustrations, applications)? What ideas have you gained from this chapter that might help you be more diversified?

3. Do your sermon introductions compel people to want to listen? Do you vary them and make them 'case specific?'

4. Do your sermon conclusions briefly remind your listeners of the message's primary thrust and then clearly invite and motivate them to respond in a specific appropriate way?

5. What struggles do you have in balancing the historical with

the contemporary? Do you tend to emphasize one and neglect the other? What can you do to correct any imbalance in this regard?

6. Are you continuing to grow as a scholar as well as spiritually? Does your preaching reflect diligent study and the cumulative effect of your personal growth as a person?

Step Seven

Maintain a Balance in Sermon Delivery

And delivery does not consist merely, or even chiefly, in vocalization and gesticulation, but it implies that one is possessed with the subject, that he is completely in sympathy with it and fully alive to its importance; that he is not repeating remembered words, but bringing forth the living offspring of his mind (John A. Broadus).[1]

Our work as a preacher is not finished when the homiletical outline has been completed or the sermon manuscript has been written. The most important part is still to take place. The message must be delivered to an audience. It might well be argued, in fact, that there is no sermon until this has occurred. We may well be in possession of sermon materials, but the actual sermon is that which is spoken. The very word, sermon, is from the Latin *sermo*, meaning 'a spoken discourse'. Thus, Brown, Clinard, and Northcutt state:

> The delivery of the sermon is the most dynamic moment of the preaching experience. In that moment all sermon preparation is brought to fruition or frustration. If the sermon is delivered effectively, the minister, in grateful joy, forgets the long hours of toil in preparation. But if he fails, all his labor in the study haunts him as a heavy and useless burden. The gospel is a proclaimed gospel. Thus, a sermon is never a sermon until it is delivered. A minister is never a preacher until he communicates his message to others.[2]

Sermon delivery is no small task, even for the accomplished public speaker. For the typical, less-than-accomplished speaker, it can be downright intimidating! There is so much to consider including the audience with its varied opinions regarding effective preaching. Some listeners prefer a composed delivery style, forthright but not too loud or energetic. Others don't think preaching has really taken place unless the preacher has shouted himself hoarse vocally and worn himself out physically. The fact is that no style of delivery will please everyone and the preacher who desires to 'be all things to all men' will die trying.

It is my purpose in this chapter to offer some practical, sensible advice about the delivery of sermons that will be helpful to those who are learning to preach as well as to those experienced preachers who may feel a sense of frustration or struggle in this area of ministry. The chapter will not offer detailed anatomical descriptions of our vocal mechanisms. The reader is directed to other helpful books on this subject.[3] Instead, I will endeavor to emphasize some practical considerations regarding preparation for delivery and some important aspects of the delivery process itself. This should serve as a primer for inexperienced preachers and a reminder for those who preach often.

Be Aware of a Basic Tension Inherent in Preaching

Delivering a sermon is no small matter. With the Lord's help we may have worked long and hard. We may have done an extraordinary job of studying our passage. We may have created a sensible homiletical structure that reflects the text and is understandable to the listener. We may have come up with important thought-provoking content for the various parts of the sermon. We may have found just the right illustrations to make everything clear. And we may have developed perfect points of application. All of this may come to nothing if these materials are not presented to our hearers in a way that clearly communicates God's truth in the power of the Holy Spirit.

I recognize that a superior sermon presented with outstanding delivery skills may fall flat. I also recognize that a relatively weak sermon presented with mediocre ability may be the means God uses to change lives. This is the sort of thing Paul wrote about to the Corinthians:

When I came to you, brothers, I did not come with eloquence or superior wisdom as I proclaimed to you the testimony about God. For I resolved to know nothing while I was with you except Jesus Christ and him crucified. I came to you in weakness and fear, and with much trembling. My message and my preaching were not with wise and persuasive words, but with a demonstration of the Spirit's power, so that your faith might not rest on men's wisdom, but on God's power (1 Cor 2:1-5).

He wrote something similar to the Thessalonian church:

For we know, brothers loved by God, that he has chosen you, because our gospel came to you not simply with words, but also with power, with the Holy Spirit and with deep conviction. You know how we lived among you for your sake (1 Thess 1:4-5).

For the appeal we make does not spring from error or impure motives, nor are we trying to trick you. On the contrary, we speak as men approved by God to be entrusted with the gospel. We are not trying to please men but God, who tests our hearts. You know we never used flattery, nor did we put on a mask to cover up greed – God is our witness. We were not looking for praise from men, not from you or anyone else (1 Thess 2:3-6).

The preaching of the Word of God involves a spiritual dynamic that most of us struggle to fully understand. We know that it is the Holy Spirit who ultimately convinces people of the reality of sin, the means of righteousness, and coming judgment (John 16:8). We know that the Holy Spirit leads people into truth and teaches them (John 14:26; 16:13-15). At the same time we're aware that God has chosen to present this truth through people. Paul speaks of this in his second letter to the church at Corinth:

For we do not preach ourselves but Jesus Christ as Lord, and ourselves as your servants for Jesus' sake. For God, who said, 'Let light shine out of darkness,' made his light shine in our hearts to give us the light of the knowledge of the glory of God in the face of Christ. But we have this treasure in jars of clay to show that this all-surpassing power is from God and not from us (2 Cor 4:5-7).

And he explains this concept further in the next chapter:

> All this is from God, who reconciled us to himself through Christ
> and gave us the ministry of reconciliation: that God was reconciling
> the world to himself in Christ, not counting men's sins against them.
> And he has committed to us the message of reconciliation. We are
> therefore Christ's ambassadors, as though God were making his
> appeal through us. We implore you on Christ's behalf: Be reconciled
> to God (2 Cor 5:18-20).

There is a tension that exists. On the one hand, human beings are
given the responsibility of ministering the Word. On the other, the
Holy Spirit accompanies this ministry and assures that it will be fruitful.

As preachers, we are stewards (overseers) of the gospel. We
are required to carry out this responsibility faithfully: 'Let a man so
account of us, as of the ministers of Christ, and stewards of the
mysteries of God. Moreover it is required in stewards that a man be
found faithful' (1 Cor 4:1-2, KJV). Thus, we must prepare and
preach as though success depended on us, all the while aware that
it doesn't! Ultimately, it depends on God and we can be fully assured
that the Holy Spirit will faithfully execute his ministries of conviction
and teaching.

Practically, this means that the preacher must be a person both
of prayer and preparation, of devotion and diligence, of reliance
and resolve. The responsibility is a grave one. The omnipotent God
has chosen to use weak people as his mouthpieces, the means by
which his truth is made known. Surely, there could have been another
way, a way more God-like, a way that would be more sure, a way
that would bypass human frailties. But he chose this approach!

Perhaps this is an ongoing reflection of the incarnation of Christ.
God chose to meet us on our own turf as a helpless baby. Jesus did
not come accompanied by all the splendors of heaven. The
incarnational statement was one of simplicity, humility, and suffering.
While his deity was not left behind, Christ willingly laid aside his
divine prerogatives. He became a man and told us about God in a
human way. Now, through the presumed foolishness of preaching,
God has again chosen to speak in a human way.

Find Your Optimal Delivery Method and Work to Perfect It

There is no set way to prepare sermon materials and deliver them. We preachers need to do a bit of experimenting in order to find the method that enables us to be most effective in the pulpit. Following is a discussion of the primary methods that have been used down through the years by various preachers.

Extemporaneous Preaching

This approach is sometimes thought of as impromptu speaking without any advance preparation or speaking 'off the cuff.' Generally, however, this type of preaching is not devoid of preparation, but rather employs a sort of informal preparation. Henry Ward Beecher (1813–1887), for instance, thought extensively about two or three sermon ideas each week and did some reading and studying on these ideas. But he didn't normally decide on his theme and prepare a working outline until the time between breakfast and the morning service. A few ideas were hastily jotted down on paper but these were not usually consulted during the preaching event. Evening sermons were sketched after afternoon tea. Phillips Brooks, a contemporary of Beecher and a highly respected preacher himself, described him as 'the greatest preacher Protestantism has produced'.

Charles Spurgeon is also known to have been an extemporaneous preacher, though his hundreds of printed sermons appear to be carefully outlined. He said that he never composed a sentence in advance.[4] It must be remembered that from almost the beginning of his preaching ministry, the sermons of Spurgeon were stenographically transcribed and put into print, doubtless being edited in the process. Nevertheless, to have preached his sermons without the use of pulpit manuscript, outline, or notes was a tremendous accomplishment.

Today, we might speak of this kind of preaching as 'winging it'. Many do it from time to time, but very few do it well. Few of us have the genius possessed by people like Spurgeon. Jones wisely says in this regard:

This way of preaching is effective for a few men who, like Beecher and Spurgeon, have unusual abilities for speaking often and for putting their thoughts together quickly, but who nevertheless are all the time working hard at the tasks of reading, gathering ideas and putting them into proper form, and improving their methods of expressing themselves clearly and forcefully. But it is a dangerous method for the average preacher. As described above, it sounds like hasty and careless preparation. In the hands of less capable men, this sort of sermon preparation is careless.[5]

If attempted, it must be remembered that this kind of delivery is not devoid of preparation. This method will work only if the preacher's mind and heart have been thoroughly saturated with the sermon content that needs to be spoken, is able to place these ideas into a sensible order while actually speaking, and is capable of recalling and communicating clearly the essence of what has been studied. This is no small task if it is to be done well.

Reading the Sermon from a Manuscript

The practice of reading sermons apparently began in the sixteenth century during the reign of Henry VIII as a sort of reaction against the free preaching of the independent clergy of that day. The method fell out of favor in England within a century. A letter from Charles II, written in 1674, shows that he strongly condemned this practice. In 1720, the General Assembly of the Church of Scotland declared that the reading of sermons was 'displeasing to God's people and caused no small obstruction to spiritual consolation'.[6] Still, the practice has persisted in many parts of the church, especially in those congregations that are liturgical in worship style. Among well-known preachers of the past who have preached by reading a manuscript are Richard Baxter, Jonathon Edwards, Henry Liddon, R.W. Dale, Horace Bushnell, John Henry Jowett, and George Buttrick. More recently, I've observed Robertson McQuilkin, former president of Columbia International University, preaching from a complete manuscript, sometimes reading it almost word for word, yet in a very conversational tone.

We should not assume arbitrarily that reading from a manuscript spells doom for the sermon. One of the most famous sermons in history, 'Sinners in the Hands of an Angry God,' was given as Jonathon Edwards read the sermon (not very well, I understand) from a manuscript. The sermon succeeded in spite of its apparently poor delivery because preaching is ultimately a spiritual activity that is not necessarily short-circuited by our own ineptitude. While being thankful that this is the case, we should not plan to deliver sermons poorly. God expects our best efforts.

There are some possible advantages of reading a sermon from a manuscript. In comparison to other delivery methods, it probably requires less time and energy in both the preparation process and the delivery itself. It relieves the fear of forgetting, which is a major concern with other types of delivery. This, in turn, reduces the sense of nervousness felt by practically every public speaker. It is also very precise in style.

There are disadvantages as well. While reading a manuscript may help relieve nervousness, it should be remembered that some nervousness is good. It helps energize our preaching and, if properly channeled, can enhance body language. This method can also produce a dependence on manuscripts that may not serve well in settings other than the pulpit. Another serious disadvantage is that reading minimizes eye contact. Each time the preacher looks at the manuscript the audience is being temporarily cut-off. Good eye contact is crucial to establishing and building rapport with listeners and reading doesn't assist this process. Also to be considered is the generally accepted opinion that congregations overwhelmingly prefer that sermons not be read. The typical listener wants to be spoken to, not read to, and there is a definite difference. In assessing student sermons during more than two decades of classroom teaching, I've observed that when students resort to reading, the audience tends to become detached. Listeners become observers rather than participants. Finally, it must be mentioned that many churches have become less formal as society has become more casual. A read sermon seems to be out of place in an informal setting.

Reading a manuscript effectively is not an easy thing to do. Andrew Blackwood said that, 'Except in the hands of a minister with rare pulpit gifts, the use of a manuscript constitutes a handicap.' [7] Almost all who comment on this method agree: those who use a manuscript should not try to conceal the fact. Most in the audience will be aware that the sermon is being read and will not appreciate any attempt at deception.

One further word about manuscripts: whether the preacher plans to read from a complete manuscript or not, it is a worthwhile discipline to write out sermons completely, at least on some occasions. This is particularly helpful for younger preachers and those who may struggle in linking ideas together in oral form. This discipline will greatly assist growth in wordsmithing, phraseology, and the development of a clear style. It must be remembered, however, that a sermon manuscript is meant to be *heard*, not read. Therefore, it must be written in an oral style that will indeed be conversational in nature and pleasing to the ear. This may not be as easy as it sounds because most of us are used to writing for the eye.[8]

Memorizing the Sermon Verbatim

Another approach to sermon delivery is to memorize the sermon and recite it. This is done by first writing out a complete manuscript and then committing it to memory. This was done in seventeenth century France by a group of Roman Catholic priests who became famous for delivering their sermons *memoriter*.[9] I'm not aware of anyone today who actually does this on a regular basis except, perhaps, some itinerant speakers who use the same message numerous times. I've noticed some novices who, when required to speak without notes, end up trying to memorize large parts of the sermon. Interestingly, the tone of voice and the demeanor of the preacher almost always tips off the listener that this is the case.

There are two possible advantages with this approach. First, because a full manuscript is first prepared, there would be a precise style with exact wording chosen carefully by the preacher, just as with a sermon that is read from a manuscript. Second, good eye-contact can be maintained with this method, though I suspect that the preacher's own attention would tend to be on 'what comes next' rather than actually connecting with the audience.

Several disadvantages come to mind. To begin with, most people do not have great memories and this ability is not stressed in today's educational processes. As a student in the mid-twentieth century, I was often required to memorize fairly lengthy poems. I still recall verses from Coleridge's 'The Rhyme of the Ancient Mariner' and other poems. This skill is seldom emphasized today. Even the memorization of 'math facts' is often looked down upon by modern educators as being too mechanical and outmoded! Mediocre memories require a great amount of time and this method is thus rendered highly inefficient. Further, the congregation will tend to be ill-at-ease when they perceive this is taking place. They can't help but wonder what will happen if (when?) the preacher forgets his lines. Then too, the preacher is not free to be himself for his chief concern is not just to get the message over, but to remember the next sentence, and the next, and the next. It may also be argued that this method of delivery is a type of performance. The preacher is not conversing, but reciting. Finally, and this is most obvious, if the mind gets untracked, the sermon is doomed. This fact alone seems to disqualify this delivery method.

Preaching without Notes
With this approach, sermons are carefully prepared either in full outline form or by writing a complete manuscript. This preparation includes formulating a clear structure, thoroughly preparing the sermon content, and wording the message in a proper oral style. The preacher then internalizes the message thoroughly so that it can be delivered without notes and these are not taken into the pulpit. The message is *not* memorized word for word, however, but thought for thought. This approach is sometimes called 'free preaching'. Preparation is done in such a way that each idea in the sermon leads naturally into the next one. James S. Stewart shares a wise word about the importance of sensible preparation.

> . . . it is worth emphasizing that freedom of delivery in the pulpit depends upon carefulness of construction in the study. It is surprising how often this point has been missed in the debate between read and spoken sermons.

He then mentions some conditions of effective note-free preaching:

> The conditions are clarity of logical structure; well-defined divisions
> and sub-divisions; exclusion of irrelevancies; short paragraphs with
> a single clear-cut thought in each, not long unbroken stretches,
> where a dozen ideas jostle; balance and progress and development;
> with one or two strong and vivid illustrations marking out the track.
> The point is that freedom of delivery will tend to vary in direct
> proportion to accuracy of construction. If you can fashion a sermon
> which stands out clearly in all its parts before your own mind, the
> tyranny of the manuscript is broken.[10]

A considerable number of preachers have used this approach.
Many of the sixteenth century reformers, including Calvin, spoke
without notes. So did George Whitefield in the eighteenth century
and Alexander Maclaren and John A. Broadus in the nineteenth.
The twentieth century saw great preachers like G. Campbell Morgan,
the predecessor and co-worker of David Martyn Lloyd-Jones at
London's Westminster Chapel, Clarence McCartney, best known
as pastor of Pittsburgh's First Presbyterian Church, and Charles
Koller, former president of Northern Baptist Seminary, all preach
without notes. Some recent homileticians have also advocated this
approach including Koller[11] and Wayne McDill.[12]

There are certain advantages of preaching without notes. First, if
the preacher is well-prepared and confident, this method has the
great potential of giving a sense of freedom that will energize the
delivery. Second, it provides a natural condition for listening. This is
the way most verbal communication takes place. Third, this approach
greatly enhances eye-contact and other non-verbals. Fourth, this
approach appeals to the majority of church attenders. If given a
choice, this method of sermon delivery would be preferable
compared to the others. Finally, note-free preaching requires a
thorough job of preparation and this helps assure that both the
preacher and the sermon itself will be potentially at their best.

Disadvantages should be considered also. First, this approach
requires a longer-than-usual time for preparation. Either a complete
manuscript or detailed outline will need to be prepared and then

read and digested repeatedly until it is thoroughly internalized. Second, some degree of lack of preciseness may slip into delivery. Grammatical errors and other misstatements will sometimes occur. Sometimes statements are made that are not entirely accurate either because of a slip of the tongue or a misstatement of a fact. Third, it is also possible on occasion that the sermon's line of thought may be lost. At such times, the preacher will need to backtrack a bit to get his mind in gear. Fourth, when preaching without notes the speaker may forget to include something that had been planned such as an illustration or even part of a line of argument. Finally, to preach without notes may be the most exhausting kind of preaching delivery-wise. It is hard work mentally, emotionally, and physically.

Preaching from Notes

The use of notes in the pulpit ranges from utilizing a few brief notes at crucial places in the sermon to the use of an extensive outline that includes quotations and even various biblical materials. Preaching from notes of some sort is probably the most popular method used today. Baumann says 8 out of 10 preachers do this.[13] I suspect the percentage is even higher now than when Baumann made this statement more than thirty years ago.

There are some definite advantages to this kind of delivery process. In comparison to note-free preaching, preparation time is considerably lessened because the sermon doesn't have to be internalized quite as thoroughly. There is a helpful security in having notes present and this may well give the preacher a little extra confidence as the daunting task of delivering a sermon is faced. Notes also help the preacher give quotations, statistics, illustrations, and technical information accurately, a deficiency in note-free preaching unless these kinds of materials are allowed to be an exception to the method. Also, in spite of the fact that notes are present, there is still a fair amount of eye-contact possible and non-verbals are not totally thwarted. Finally, this approach provides a comfortable listening environment for the audience. Listeners still have a sense that conversation is taking place but without the worry of the preacher forgetting the sermon material.

As with all possible delivery methods, there are some disadvantages to be forewarned about. First, if overused, notes can be as distracting as a manuscript. The secret, of course, is to either use a minimal amount of notes or to discipline oneself to avoid using them except when absolutely necessary. Second, notes will tend to tie the speaker to the podium. This problem can be alleviated by physically reducing the size of the outline or other materials and attaching them to the Bible, perhaps opposite the preaching text. This will, however, tend to limit the use of the hands for gesturing. A third disadvantage of this delivery method is that it can become a lazy method if the preacher does not sufficiently internalize the message. We might easily assume that the sermon's preparation is complete once the notes have been prepared. This is, of course, not the case for the message must still be sufficiently internalized. Without sufficient internalization, delivery effectiveness is greatly reduced.

Act and Speak Naturally

Now that we have examined the options related to preparing our sermon materials for delivery, we will move on to discuss the delivery itself. For some preachers, especially younger ones, this can be an intimidating task. Some experience what might be called stage fright. Others are concerned about the proper approach to delivery in terms of formality and informality. These are issues to consider as we begin thinking about the actual act of sermon delivery.

The Fear Factor

Many people are not overly comfortable with public speaking and some are just downright fearful. This reality makes a natural delivery difficult. One of the most frightening experiences of my younger days was a high school speech course that was required. In retrospect, it was quite helpful. At the time, it was terribly fear-provoking. If someone would have told me then that in a few years I would be preaching regularly to a congregation, I would have ridiculed the notion.

Stage fright, as this type of fear or nervousness is often called, manifests itself in various ways. It might consist of physical feelings of weak knees, butterflies in the stomach, dry mouth, and shaky hands. It might manifest itself in verbal uncertainty, stumbling over words, a 'bleached' facial appearance, and excessive vocal pauses such as 'er' or 'uh'. Eye contact may be severely limited and varied facial expression non-existent. It is not a pleasant experience.

Various polls down through the years have repeatedly shown that public speaking ranks at or near the top in terms of people's fears. In fact, Litfin reports:

> In *The Sunday Times* (London) of October 7, 1973, there appeared an article on 'Things That People Fear Most.' Can you guess what topped the list? The fear of public speaking! The fear of death ranked only sixth![14]

Given a choice, I suspect that most people would opt for the former, but speaking to a public gathering can indeed be frightening.

The highly opinionated Spurgeon spoke of this kind of fear as an evil.[15] Perhaps it is if we are simply afraid of man's opinion of our message. But there are other causes of fear such as a feeling of inadequacy or a concern of forgetting what we want to say. Rather than labeling fear as an evil, I prefer to think of it as an obstacle with which we must deal. I've been preaching for some four decades but rarely stand up to preach without a fairly significant sense of nervousness. There may be some who thrive on being in front of a crowd: I'm not one of them.

This has been the experience of many in the public arena. Cicero, perhaps the most famous Roman orator said:

> Assuredly, just as I generally perceive it to happen to yourselves, so I very often prove it in my own experience, that I turn pale at the outset of every speech, and quake in every limb and in all my soul.[16]

In each of two independent studies, it was found that among experienced, successful speakers, 77% still experienced stage fright.[17] While these studies were done several decades ago, it is doubtful that the results would be much different today. Speaking to a group of people can be a very uncomfortable thing to do.

It helps to recognize that feelings of nervousness are natural and can be utilized by channeling them in productive ways. Brown, Clinard, and Northcutt state:

> It is an error to believe that all fear should be removed from the speaker. The minister who comes to the pulpit without nervous tension is unlikely to preach well. Tension is necessary to effective public speech. It makes for readiness, for zest in delivery. But if poise is to exist, fear must be controlled.[18]

Litfin agrees:

> Within limits your stage fright is actually a positive (though uncomfortable) thing. It is your body's way of preparing you to speak. The adrenalin begins to flow; the heart rate steps up; your breathing quickens a bit. All of these are positive symptoms.[19]

These symptoms can be recognized and utilized to enhance our delivery. They provide a boost in our energy level and this can result in a freer delivery in terms of our voice and our body language. There is no easy recipe for accomplishing this, however, except to be aware of these factors while gaining speaking experience at every available opportunity. The practical steps that are most immediately productive in helping to minimize fear are good preparation, thorough internalization of your material, and a total reliance upon the faithfulness of God to his Word. Undue nervousness can also be alleviated in part by learning to relax tense muscles prior to preaching, by joining in the singing and other worship activities, to speak prior to the sermon (perhaps reading Scripture, praying, or greeting those present), and to purposely smile and use the body in gesturing while preaching.

The Importance of Natural Delivery

Every preacher has an important decision to make about sermon delivery. Basically, there are two approaches to the task: to *perform* the sermon's delivery or to *present* the sermon in a natural manner. Some readers might discount the first option as non-existent. No one does this, it might be argued. Think again. I've seen many preachers who either emulate the sermon delivery of others or who rehearse their sermons with such preciseness of speech and mannerism that delivery is actually a performance. Pitt-Watson reminds us to be ourselves:

> We are not professional actors playing the part of a preacher – perhaps even consciously impersonating our own favorite role model. The actor can be many characters, saint or sinner, genius or fool, hero or villain. We can only be ourselves.[20]

Have you ever seen anyone try to preach in the style of Billy Graham, Charles Stanley, D. James Kennedy, Ben Haden, or Robert H. Schuller? I have. While each of these persons may have worthwhile delivery skills to model (though all are markedly different), those who try to imitate their styles do so at the risk of appearing artificial. The styles of these well known preachers are their own, and so should ours be.

Or think in terms of groupings of churches. Isn't it interesting that a television preachers affiliation or circle of influence can often be recognized by the way he presents his message? But do all Baptists have the same personality and temperament? Do all Methodists or Pentecostals? Of course not. Then why do so many seem to present their messages in similar ways both in terms of voice and mannerism?

In regard to preaching a sermon that has been precisely rehearsed – including varying tones and pitches of voice, studied hand gestures, body movements, and well-placed pauses – the preacher again runs the risk of merely performing. In a previous age, public speaking was sometimes taught in such a way and some ministers adopted this method as their own. Known as the elocutionary movement, it began in the eighteenth century and lasted more than one hundred years.[21] Interestingly, most of the founders of this movement were actors, but its influence quickly spread to the pulpit. The line of thinking that was central to this approach was that correct pronunciation, including, tone of voice, and correct body movement were crucial to the ideas being communicated. Public speaking was taught with this in mind and, as mentioned, many ministers appropriated the method for themselves.

The result of either of these approaches is that preaching degenerates into a performance, something to be heard, seen, and experienced, but not really listened to. The preacher may succeed in communicating *himself* or *herself*. People may leave the preaching event with a real sense of excitement because 'the preacher was hot today.' But they may also leave without being overly aware of what was actually being said in terms of sermon content because that was not effectively communicated. Speaking is not the same as communicating.

Our overall demeanor when preaching needs to be a proper balance between formality and informality. It will be noted by some, of course, that this balance may be affected by the specific setting in which the sermon is delivered. A liturgical or formal worship setting would seem to require a presentation style that fits in appropriately. A setting such as a youth rally or an informal 'seeker service' would seem to require a less formal approach to delivery. While I tend to agree with these assumptions, I quickly add that preachers must be themselves regardless of the type of setting. Yes, we must make adjustments in our presentations conducive to the occasion. But we must never pretend to be something that we're not. As Chapell wisely observes, 'Congregations ask no more and expect no less of a preacher than truth expressed in a manner consistent with the personality of the preacher and reflective of the import of the message.'[22]

The Focus of Natural Delivery

This brings us, then, to a brief summary of what is meant by natural delivery. In short, to speak naturally means to speak conversationally, not in the manner of a public orator.

There was a time when oratory was highly respected. As far back as the ancient Greeks there were those who made their living by traveling from city to city giving speeches. They were highly respected persons, the stars of their day. Amphitheaters were built, at least in part, for this 'spectator sport.' Speeches were presented in a dramatic oratorical fashion that was impressive. This type of presentation was doubtless in the mind of the Apostle Paul as he explained his manner of speaking to the Corinthians and Thessalonians, contrasting it to the expectations of the day.

Preaching as oratory was especially practiced during the nineteenth century, often called the golden age of preaching. In the United States, Henry Ward Beecher of Brooklyn's Plymouth (Congregational) Church is an example of a pulpit orator. Andrew Blackwood, in fact, spoke of him as 'the foremost pulpit orator in our history.'[23] In England, Joseph Parker of London's City Temple was characterized by an oratorical style. He is described as having had 'an impressive appearance, regal personality, commanding voice, impeccable diction, and histrionic manner,'[24] this latter term used to describe his flair for the dramatic. Pulpit oratory was apparently fairly common as Spurgeon often railed against it in his *Lectures to My Students*.

The remnants of this style of speaking still persist in some places. It is seen, for instance, when a minister engaged in normal, personal conversation enters the pulpit and switches on his 'preacher's voice.' It is seen when body language not normally utilized in ordinary conversation finds its way into sermon delivery. These are subtle indications that something artificial is taking place. The preacher is probably aware of this, though this kind of behavior easily becomes habitual. The listeners are most certainly aware of it if they know the speaker on a personal level. The pretense is generally not appreciated.

The focus of effective sermon delivery is to be natural, to be conversational. To his young ministerial students, Spurgeon said:

> Gentlemen, I return to my rule – use your own natural voices. Do not be monkeys, but men; not parrots, but men of originality in all things. . . . Your own modes of speech will be most in harmony with your methods of thought and your own personality. . . . I would repeat this rule till I wearied you if I thought you would forget it; be natural, be natural, be natural evermore.[25]

Let me be clear. Preaching conversationally doesn't refer to casual chit-chat. This kind of delivery is sometimes caricatured as being too laid back, as though the preacher was perched in a recliner barefooted. As we shall see shortly, this is *not* what I'm referring to. Rather, I'm saying that preachers have a *real* message to proclaim and they can't do this effectively unless they are *real* themselves. If they're perceived as being phony, even in matters of voice and gesture, their credibility will be harmed and their message hindered.

Speak Authoritatively, but Maintain a Conversational Tone

How do we speak both authoritatively and conversationally? At first glance this seems to be inherently contradictory. I don't believe it is.

The Preacher's Authority

Historically, preachers have often been viewed as authority figures. Many have been well educated, particularly in terms of theology. Some have been strong public personalities who have had a following in their churches and beyond. Their ideas have been widely respected and when they spoke, people listened. Even pastors serving in small towns or pastors of small congregations have traditionally been given a fair amount of respect as people who ought to be listened to.

This is increasingly less true today. Ministers are thought to carry far less authority than previously. They are simply one voice in a milieu of many. Thus, when a well-known preacher is interviewed on a television talk show regarding a particular divisive issue, viewers who already agree are further convinced and those who disagree are often further alienated from the position being advocated. Being a minister is seldom more advantageous than being a lawyer or a medical doctor. If there ever was an assumption that a preacher has something special to say on a controversial issue, this is no longer the case. This is certainly the way it is with non-churched people, and, I fear, a growing sentiment within the wider church.

Can preachers speak authoritatively? Does the preacher have any authority on which to stand? In a word, yes! But it is not an authority brought about by one's personal qualifications or even by ordination. It is a conferred authority. The Olfords describe this well:

> A person 'under authority' has a derived authority from the one he is under. The minister is under the authority of his Lord. The authority of the preacher should be matched by humility and simplicity (reality). It is then that authority will be expressed without carnality or willful manipulation. True authority in preaching cannot be forced or faked. . . . You cannot work up authority to gain respect or response. Real authority in preaching ultimately is derived from the Lord . . . [26]

To speak with authority is first to recognize the true source of that authority.

Further, authoritative preaching requires transformation and personal ownership on the part of the preacher. We cannot speak authoritatively about anything until we have understood and absorbed it for ourselves. I enjoy playing golf, or perhaps I should say that golf enjoys playing me! I am only a duffer, however, and have no right to speak with authority on the finer points of the game. Jack Nicklaus, on the other hand, has the right to speak about them and he commands people's attention in the process. He didn't invent the game, nor has he perfected his playing of it. Still, he understands golf with an extraordinary degree of thoroughness on both the hypothetical and experiential levels. He has the right to be regarded as an authority figure on the game.

As a preacher, then, my only right to speak authoritatively rests on my relationship to the Lord and my ownership of the message entrusted to me. Again, the Olfords instruct us:

> Authority has to do with being mastered by the Word and by the Spirit.... It is a product of the preacher's calling, gifting, relationship with the Lord, knowledge of the Word, readiness to preach, fullness and anointing of the Spirit, and presence under authority at that moment.[27]

Authority is not something that we have a right to nor is it something that can be achieved by our own efforts. It is conferred authority that gives us the right to boldly speak forth God's truth with confidence that comes from beyond ourselves. We are God's ambassadors. Our only authority is to accurately deliver his message, the authentic message of Scripture. Allow the words of Jim Shaddix to remind you of this:

> The body of truth that is revealed in the Bible, given for the purpose of godliness (see 2 Pet. 1:2-4) and righteousness (see 2 Tim. 3:16), can be called *God's stuff*. It is the stuff of the Bible – its very essence. On the other hand, there is much helpful advice in life that is comprised of information or principles gleaned from simple observation and research. That is *good stuff*. Let us be very clear – the shepherd has not been charged with the task of speaking on all matters of *good stuff*. . . .
>
> The shepherd's authority is to stand and speak 'Thus saith the Lord' is not in *good stuff*, but *God's stuff*. While biblical truth surely informs certain principles that might be categorized as *good stuff*, its primary intent is more specific and far-reaching. The faithful shepherd will rightly interpret, exegete, and proclaim the truth of Scripture so as to allow it to accomplish its purpose in people's lives. But when the shepherd prostitutes *God's stuff* for *good stuff*, anarchy occurs. And the biggest tragedy is not what people are *getting* but what they are *not getting*. While they certainly are getting some helpful information, they are being robbed of the truth that is necessary for realizing God's end and subsequently bringing glory to Him.[28]

We can see, therefore, that preachers speak authoritatively *only* when their sermons speak what God has spoken. For example, he does not intend for us to be authority figures in matters of civil government except when his Word speaks on that subject. It does that on occasion and we can preach such texts authoritatively. But when we move away from the revealed Word to the findings of current political scientists, somehow equating their opinions with the revealed truth of Scripture, we have no authority on which to stand. At that point we cease to be preachers and join the ranks of other public speakers.

The Preacher's Conversational Tone

Our tone in delivery ought to be conversational, but it should be different from the kind of quiet, slow-paced conversation between two persons enjoying a meal together in an upscale restaurant. Instead, the kind of conversational tone used in preaching should be similar to a family member telling the others that she has been named the recipient of some prestigious award; or that he has been promoted to executive vice-president; or that a long lost wealthy uncle, recently deceased, included someone in the family in his will. It ought to mirror the conversation of two close friends who meet again after a separation of many years. Yes, our speaking should be conversational, but it should be expanded or enlarged conversation.

The subject matter given by preachers is far too important to treat with either pretense or with a casual tone of voice. We ought to speak with a sense of conviction about important, eternal truths. We should not give the impression of hesitancy or uncertainty, but instead engage in straightforward conversational speech that is passionate and bold. Spurgeon said in this regard:

> The world also will suffer as well as the church if we are not fervent. We cannot expect a gospel devoid of earnestness to have any mighty effect upon the unconverted around us. One of the excuses most soporific to the conscience of an ungodly generation is that of half-heartedness of the preacher. If the sinner finds the preacher nodding while he talks of judgment to come he concludes that the judgment is a thing which the preacher is dreaming about, and he resolves to regard it all as mere fiction.[29]

Are we enthusiastic about the privilege of preaching the truths of God? If not, we should certainly reexamine our calling, gifting, and present walk with the Lord. If we are, then we should reflect that enthusiasm with a sense of excitement for both our message and audience. Spurgeon rightly said that 'A dull minister creates a dull audience'.[30] Our conversation should be animated.

Are we passionate about the truth we proclaim? The way we speak, even though it is conversational, must reflect passion. Jerry Vines calls this 'heart preaching'. He says:

When the preacher's heart is on fire, his speech comes as lava from a volcanic flow. We desperately need this element in modern preaching. Preaching, to be genuinely effective, must be eloquence on fire. The preacher must preach from his heart as well as from his head. He must combine proper exposition with heartfelt exhortation.[31]

Fuller said, 'Surely that preaching which comes from the soul most works on the soul.'[32] The first co-superintendent of American Methodism appointed by John Wesley (along with Francis Asbury), Thomas Coke, wrote:

> . . . a holy minister, a man of prayer, with only moderate talents, will be more successful, will leave his congregation more affected and influenced by his discourse, than many others whose talents are vastly superior, but who have not by prayer drawn down that unction, that tender taste of piety, which alone knows how to speak to the heart. A minister speaks very differently the truths he loves, and which he is accustomed to meditate upon, and taste all his days, at the feet of Jesus Christ! The heart has a language which nothing can imitate.[33]

To preach with our hearts means, of course, to preach with emotion. To say this may raise fears or a sense of uncomfortableness with many. Some of us have seen emotional excesses and we want to avoid that. Others may serve in a tradition that seems to frown on emotionalism. Others of us may simply prefer to guard our own emotions lest we show personal weakness. But make no mistake about it, true preaching can't be isolated from the emotional element. The gospel itself is intrinsically intertwined with emotion. 'God so *loved* the world . . .' '*Love* the Lord your God with all your *heart* and with all your soul and with all your mind and with all your strength.' '*Love* your neighbor as yourself.' Or consider the resurrection account given in Matthew:

> After the Sabbath, at dawn on the first day of the week, Mary Magdalene and the other Mary went to look at the tomb.... The angel said to the women, '*Do not be afraid*, for I know that you

are looking for Jesus, who was crucified. He is not here; he has risen, just as he said. Come and see the place where he lay. Then go quickly and tell his disciples: "He has risen from the dead and is going ahead of you into Galilee. There you will see him." Now I have told you.' So the women hurried away from the tomb, *afraid* yet *filled with joy*, and ran to tell his disciples. Suddenly Jesus met them. 'Greetings,' he said. They came to him, *clasped his feet and worshiped him*. Then Jesus said to them, *'Do not be afraid*. Go and tell my brothers to go to Galilee; there they will see me' (Matt 28:1, 5-10).

The italicized words in these texts are all words of emotion and this small sample demonstrates the link between the gospel we preach and the emotional elements involved.

This should not surprise us for we have been created not only as intellectual and volitional beings, but as emotional ones as well. Writing several decades ago from a seminary setting wary of the emotional element in preaching, Ronald Sleeth observed: 'The tragedy is that the preacher who keeps all emotion out of his preaching is not communicating on a deep and important level in the interaction between human beings.' [34] Many centuries ago, the early church father Jerome made a corollary statement: 'When teaching in church seek to call forth not plaudits but groans. Let the tears of your hearers be your glory.' [35]

The element of emotion – heart preaching – is an important part of the persuasion process. We preach to persuade both intellectually and behaviorally. We want our listeners to make right choices, to exercise their volitional capacities in appropriate ways. People make right choices, however, only when both the mind and the emotions have been stirred. If persuasion takes place in the mind alone, behavioral change does not occur. If people are moved emotionally without any sensible information being given, then the action that take place may be wrong. Both the mind and the heart must be rightly persuaded. Vines speaks powerfully to this:

The preacher who learns to preach from his heart will move men to action. Our purpose is not merely to present a Bible message for the purpose of information or display. We preach in order to bring men to decision. Our purpose is to change behavior for the better, to bring men to obedience to God, and to lead them to accept the challenge of a Christ-centered life. Heart preaching will help us accomplish those goals. When Cicero spoke to the people it was said, 'How well Cicero speaks.' But when Demosthenes spoke the people said: 'Let us march against Carthage.' [36]

Again, our tone of speech in sermon delivery should be conversational, but it should not be casual conversation. It must be characterized by enthusiasm, boldness, straightforwardness, and passion. When this is the case the preacher will be believable, at least in terms of delivery.

Develop Strong Communication Skills

Sermon delivery has to do with communication. It is never an end in itself but a means to a more important end. It is possible to become so wrapped up in the finer points of public speaking technique that effective communication is hampered. The wise words of Clyde Fant are worth pondering: 'Delivery is not an art form; it is a communication channel. Being a good speaker is not particularly important; being a good communicator is. Of course, good communicators are good speakers – but the opposite is not always true.' [37] This means that we should study the area of public speaking insofar as it will assist us to become better communicators.

Effective communication has long been a concern of preachers and those who would instruct them. In the eighteenth century, Richard Baxter penned his classic work *The Reformed Pastor*, a book dealing not with reformed theology but with reviving ministers spiritually. Much of this worthwhile volume deals with the ministry of preaching. In one place, he says:

In preaching, there is a communion of souls, and a communication of somewhat from ours to theirs. As we and they have understandings and wills and affections, so must the bent of our endeavors be to communicate the fullest light of evidence from our understandings to theirs, and to warm their hearts, by kindling in them holy affections as by a communication from our own.[38]

Baxter cuts to the essential idea of communication, passing along realities from one person to another. The Latin root *communicare* has to do with having things in common. While more recent usage elevates the idea that communication is about expressing one's ideas effectively, it is helpful to be reminded of the core meaning of the term and what it is that requires effectiveness.

Some years ago I was one of several regular speakers on a radio program called 'Pressing On.' The other speakers and I were all faculty members at what was then known as Columbia Bible College and Seminary, now Columbia International University. After one of my weekly series I received a letter from a somewhat irate listener taking me to task for using the word 'share'. I had said something such as, 'Today I would like to share with you...,' and then I stated the theme or proposition of my short talk. The letter writer complained strongly that 'share' is weak and not biblical and that I should use a stronger word like 'preach'.

The fact of the matter is that communication is about sharing! As preachers, we have been affected, presumably, by the message we plan to present. We have studied to understand it as thoroughly as possible and we have embraced its truths personally. Now we have the opportunity to pass along that which has come to be ours. This is the essence of communication as far as the ministry of preaching is concerned.

As we consider effective oral communication in a preaching setting, there are three primary areas that require our attention. The first has to do with verbals, the second with vocals, and the third with nonverbals.

Verbals

The verbal aspect of communication relates to the choice and use of words. Some, in their efforts to emphasize the importance of the nonverbal aspects of speaking, tend to minimize the importance of verbals, or at least exaggerate the importance of nonverbals. This is unwise, in my judgment. Wayne McDill, for example, repeating the opinion of Raymond Ross's *Speech Communication*, says, 'When you are preaching face to face with your hearers, they are receiving 65 percent of your message by means other than words.... Amazing as it is, only 35 percent of speech communication may be verbal.'[39] Such a statement implies that a sermon without any verbal message would still be somewhat effective – perhaps 65% effective, in fact. Such an idea, though popular, is ludicrous. While nonverbals are certainly important helps or hindrances to communication, a sermon without verbals is doomed to be a 100% failure. As we consider verbals, I want to emphasize the importance of word choices.

As we formulate our sermon plan and then begin to think in terms of the content itself, we must make choices about the words we choose to speak the message. Words are tools. They are 'the primary means of conveying information in public speaking'.[40] They help us in our efforts to communicate clearly if we choose them well. On the other hand, they can de-rail our efforts if we make poor choices.

Words are more than sounds accompanied by a wisp of air. They are symbols, representing ideas. They can explain or question. They draw analogies. They disclose or invite. They can inspire or they can discourage. They can convey truth or lies. They link us with the ideas of others and are a vital component in human relationships.

Words are also uncommonly strong. Once spoken, they cannot be withdrawn. They have staying power. James says words appear to be small and insignificant, but they're like a bit in a horse's mouth which, though small, steers the steed to its destination; they're like the rudder of a ship used by the captain to guide it to port even through gales; they're like a small spark that ignites a great forest fire (Jas 3:3-6). We're told in Proverbs 25:11 that 'A word aptly spoken is like apples of gold in settings of silver' but we're also warned that 'The tongue has the power of life and death' (Prov 18:21).

If we are to be effective preachers, we must understand the role of words. We must remember with regularity that words link their listeners to a myriad of thoughts and concepts as well as to a vast array of emotions. We will therefore choose our words carefully. This is called being a 'wordsmith'.

As mentioned earlier, words are tools. They are the primary means of much that we do as preachers, both in the pulpit and out. A skilled carpenter learns to use saws, planes, hammers, and drills as extensions of himself. This enables him to create a quality product of wood. An auto mechanic grows in his ability to use diagnostic equipment, socket sets, and torque wrenches and becomes increasingly skilled at his trade. In comparison to these craftsmen, many preachers limp their way through sermon preparation never bothering to hone their wordsmithing skills. Calvin Miller throws down the gauntlet on this matter:

> One would think that evangelicals who are forever talking about the Word of God should ask themselves, 'Does *my* word complement *the* Word?' Assuming that preaching is a calling, preachers must choose their words to give reverence to the Caller. Poetry succeeds because it is an economical way to communicate. William Stafford was once asked when it was that he decided to become a poet. He responded: 'Everyone is born a poet – a person discovering the way words sound and work, caring and delighting in words. I just kept on doing what everyone starts out doing. The real question is why did other people stop?' Most pastors, too, at the outset of their calling, consider wordsmithing important. The question is, why did they stop?[41]

What a great question! To be true to our calling, we need to grow in our ability to use the tools of our trade – words.

Not everyone is quick to leap onto this bandwagon. Some tell us that words are antiques, relics of a pre-technical period. Pictures are in: words are out. I first encountered this opinion as a seminarian. While devouring a sandwich during a lunch break, I picked up the latest issue of *Time* magazine and turned to the religion section. I was horrified to discover that the demise of the traditional sermon was imminent because an entrepreneurial minister in Toronto was experimenting with multi-media sermons. Instead of a reliance on his own words, he was using some of the latest technology, things like film clips, slide shows, art works, and sound bites. (Remember, this was in the mid-sixties. Overhead projectors were still in the planning stages!) These were all 'spliced' together into a Sunday morning presentation, a new approach that would surely spell doom to the traditional pulpit offerings heard around the world each week!

Thirty five years have passed and traditional verbal preaching is still the norm. In spite of the availability of fantastic technological tools hardly imagined a generation ago, sermons are still predominantly verbal. Oh, some preachers make use of Power Point and similar computer tools (these are still primarily verbal) and even an occasional video clip. But words are still the most useful tools on the preacher's workbench.

While words are often criticized as being weak and pictures are promoted as being strong, it is important to grasp the visual power of words. As a youngster, I was one of the deprived few whose home didn't have a television set for a fairly long while. It was my lot in life to be content with a radio. I recall listening to radio adventures like 'Mr. And Mrs. North,' 'Clyde Beatty,' 'Mark Trail,' and especially, 'The Lone Ranger.' The only pictures I had were those conjured up in my own mind, conjured by a good choice of words and my own active imagination. I thrilled to hear the musical strains of Rossini's William Tell Overture as the masked hero rode into my mind. I could easily picture his beautiful horse, Silver, his faithful Indian companion, Tonto, and even Tonto's horse, Scout. I could see the terrains being traveled, the ranches being visited, the towns that were saved, and the villainous outlaws being pursued and brought to justice. I could almost smell the smoke of campfires and feel the trail dust blowing across my face. Powerful words had this effect on a young boy.

A few years later, the long-awaited television arrived in our living room. I recall eagerly turning the on-off knob and selecting the channel (we had three to choose from) for the television version of my favorite radio program. I was practically numb with anticipated joy. What a huge disappointment! It wasn't nearly as much fun as the radio show. Everything was spelled out and little was left to the imagination. I found myself watching black and white two dimensional images while previously I had been *listening* in three dimensional living color!

My purpose here is not to minimize the importance of visuals. I have no problem with video clips or Power Point presentations except when they are used as substitutes for good word choices. But remember that words themselves can be visual. If selected carefully, they can be *seen* as well as heard. They do not have to be abstract, but can be quite concrete.

Suppose you hear a report that a close friend of yours was stopped on a street corner by someone with a weapon. What can you visualize about this? It is difficult to see much because the words are vague and general. What does 'stopped' mean? What kind of 'street corner' was it? Where? What kind of person was this 'someone' who did the stopping. What 'weapon' was involved? These are just some of the questions that might be posed in your thinking, questions that hinder clarity and visuality. It might be that your friend was stopped by a policeman who was asking directions to the nearest donut shop!

Suppose instead that the report said that this friend was stopped for a red light in a poorly lighted part of town when a large fellow with a mask ran to the car window, waved a gun, and demanded money. More of a picture is beginning to emerge. We're beginning to *see* what took place in the incident. We still can't clearly visualize everything because some abstraction remains. For instance, what type of gun was waved? Was it a handgun, a shotgun, or a bazooka? Oh, it was a sawed-off shotgun. By simply choosing the most descriptive word available, the speaker can help the listener move toward concreteness in meaning. The words can be seen.

It is sometimes thought that adjectives and adverbs are the most crucial parts of descriptive language. This is not the case. They can be useful, certainly, and should be chosen with care. But strong language is carried to its destination by strong verbs and nouns, words that catch attention and yet accurately describe the concept being spoken of.

Think for a moment of the difference in similar verbs. A word like *walk* may be sufficient, but *meander* or *saunter* may be better.

Seize is stronger than *obtain*, and *junked* says more than *discarded*. A good thesaurus is a wonderful help for strengthening our word power. They are especially beneficial with verbs.

When it comes to nouns, be as precise as you can without being overwhelming. *Grave* may be the recognized name for a burial plot, but *hole in the ground* is more vivid and stimulating, though it may be inappropriate depending on the audience context. *Fly rod* is better than *fishing equipment*, and *747* is much more descriptive than *plane*.

Increasing our vocabulary skills without being ostentatious takes some focused effort. Our goal is not to use fancy words so that we impress our listeners with our learning, but to use words that best describe what we're talking about while being fully comprehendible. It is good to know that this is a cumulative skill, one that continues to build and improve as we pay special attention to word choices. With a little practice and experience, using the right word at the right time will become increasingly natural.

Vocals

In books dealing with public speaking or preaching, a discussion of vocals is sometimes consigned to the category of nonverbals. It can certainly fit there. In a sense, public speaking consists of words (verbals) and everything else (nonverbals). It is my present intention, however, to highlight some aspects of speaking which have to do with sounds that are not verbal. After this brief discussion, we will examine the nonverbals in delivery that are not sound related.

Tone

One of the most common vocal issues is that of tone. I'm not referring to sound quality, for that is an issue much too large to address here. Rather, I'm thinking of the emotional tone to be communicated by the speaker. I said earlier that our speaking should be conversational. But not all conversation has the same tone of voice. Think of the child being scolded by an unhappy parent. Think of the new widow being counseled by her pastor. Think of the student being guided through a tough math problem by his teacher. Think of the recipient of a 911 call who is being told of a severe medical emergency. Each of these persons presumably hear entirely different tones of voice. The child hears a voice that is stern and perhaps impatient; the widow hears a voice that is empathetic and consoling; the student hears a voice that is business-like, yet assuring; the 911 operator hears a voice that is panicky, urgent, and perhaps a bit incoherent. These are just some of the ways we might express ourselves in terms of tone.

In preaching, tone will likewise vary. But it must vary appropriately because tone is part of the communication process. In ordinary conversation, if we wish to confront, but speak hesitantly and weakly, that may not get the job done. If we wish to assist someone in grieving but speak with a tone that is urgent or stern, we will fail. The tone of voice must match what we're attempting to accomplish. Such is the case with preaching. Matching the tone and the purpose is important.

Unfortunately, some preachers only have one tone of voice. I attended a funeral some years ago in which the minister spoke in comforting tones throughout the entire service except during the funeral sermon. As he finished reading the text on which the sermon was based, he shifted into hyper-drive and preached with the same tone of voice he would have used (perhaps unwisely) doing street corner evangelistic preaching. It was highly inappropriate for the occasion and purpose.

Vocal Pauses
Many speakers have habits which are called vocal pauses. They consist of 'uhs' and 'ahs' and 'uhms' and even filler words like 'O.K.' and 'now listen.' Initially, they are a means of buying time while thoughts are collected and precise ways of saying things are being formulated in the mind of the speaker. It is a form of thinking out loud. Gradually, these vocal pauses become a habit that is difficult to break. They're also highly annoying to the listener! Some hearers will, in fact, become so distracted that they end up counting the vocal pauses in a sermon. Others will simply tune out assuming that the speaker is poorly prepared or has assumed a non-authoritative stance.

Recently, I listened on radio to the first 'State of the State' message given by the newly inaugurated governor of the state in which I live. It was, quite frankly, one of the worst speeches I've ever heard. In addition to a tone of voice that was far too casual for such a formal event – it didn't suit the setting – the speech (chat!) was filled with literally scores of vocal pauses. They were so distracting that the policies and viewpoints being promoted were almost totally obliterated in the process. I voted for this person and thought that his ideas, for the most part, were right on target. The speech itself, however, was a dismal failure.

Vocal pauses are speech and sermon killers! While a few may be tolerated by listeners who are patient and forgiving, an excess will severely short circuit the effectiveness of what is being said. Be forewarned: this is a habit that needs to be broken sooner rather than later.

Pronunciation

This has to do with speaking words with sounds that are correct in terms of common usage. It is to follow the verb markings in the dictionary so that short vowels are short and long vowels are long. It is to place the accent on the proper syllable. A word that is not pronounced correctly is a momentary stumbling block to listeners. Several of these in a single sermon will probably cause the preacher's credibility to be called into question. The English language is not an easy language to handle. In some languages, a given vowel always has the same sound and so do consonants. Not so in English. Phonetically speaking, the English language is a mess! I remember being told years ago that the phonetic spelling of 'fish' was 'ghoti'. I scratched my head in wonderment. Then it was explained that 'gh' has an 'f' sound in words like 'enough'; that 'o' has a short 'i' sound in the word 'women'; and that 'ti' has an 'sh' sound in words like 'vacation'. There you have it. The three sounds that make up 'fish' also make up 'ghoti'. This helps explain why non-English speakers have an extremely difficult time learning this language.

But even native speakers struggle on occasion, especially with words that are technical in nature or, related to preaching, words that have their origin in the Bible. I recently had a couple of students pronounce 'Corinth' with the accent on the second syllable instead of the first. It just did not sound right. Other words are even trickier. What is the correct pronunciation of 'Baal'? Is it a one-syllable word or a word with two syllables? The fact that it is a word borrowed from another language makes it difficult to say. How are we to pronounce 'Habakkuk'? Does the accent go on the first syllable or the second?

There is also the matter of regional and cultural standards of pronunciation. In New England, for example, words that end with 'a' often have an 'r' added, as in 'Cuba(r)'. Words that end in 'ar', on the other hand, will sometimes be pronounced without the final 'r'. So, 'car' becomes 'ca'. In the southern states, syllables are sometimes added. A word like 'declare' may become 'de-cla-yah' and 'mess' becomes 'ma-yas'. Almost anyone can recognize the sound of a native of New York City in comparison to someone from the upper mid-west. In many African-American communities, the word 'ask' is pronounced 'aks' and 'your' sounds like 'yo'. These are just a few examples of the numerous dialects one can encounter in a single English-speaking country.

At the very least, it is important to recognize that there are differences in regional and cultural dialects and to understand that these differences may impact the communication process. Not all dialects are viewed positively by others. As one popular speech book says:

> Unfortunately, dialects may produce not only misunderstandings between speakers and listeners, but they may also produce *negative judgments* – judgments which may seriously affect some auditors' perceptions of the speaker's credibility, education, reliability, responsibility, and capabilities for leadership. This happens because dialects and even professional jargon contribute heavily to what paralinguists call 'vocal stereotypes.' [42]

In the media, there is often an attempt to maintain a dialect that sounds as mid-western as possible, since this dialect seems to be a sort of middle ground and is closest to the sounds heard most widely except in the south and the east. Some have suggested that speakers need to become 'bilingual', using their own dialects when speaking to local audiences but shifting into a sound that is more mid-western when speaking elsewhere.[43] This advice strikes me as unrealistic. Speech habits cannot be changed easily after many years. It would be difficult for a Bostonian to learn to speak Georgian when preaching in Atlanta or vice versa. Furthermore, the regional dialects in the east or in the south can be divided even further. Natives of Charleston, South Carolina speak differently from natives of Greenville, South Carolina, though the cities are only two hundred miles apart. Folks in Massachusetts have a different sound than those in Maine.

While recognizing the differences of dialects, and making minor adjustments when possible, we should strive to pronounce words correctly. If you're not sure about a certain word, consult a dictionary or lexicon. If you're still uncertain, ask someone familiar with the field from which the word comes. A little extra effort may well be worth the credibility you'll retain.

Enunciation

Closely linked to pronunciation is the matter of enunciation. Whereas the former deals with the way a word should be articulated in terms of commonly preferred usage, this has to do with crispness of sound. Often, this is simply a problem of laziness. We drop an initial vowel and come up with 'lectricity', or, we drop a final consonant and end up with 'runnin' instead of 'running'. We allow our mouths to be lazy and say 'pitcher' instead of 'picture'. Or we run words together without carefully articulating each sound and the result is 'whachacallit' when we mean 'what do you call it'. The lack of careful enunciation is a learned speech pattern and it is fine in most casual conversations. In a public forum, however, where there are many people present, careful enunciation should be practiced. It will strengthen the audience's positive perception of you as a careful communicator, and it will help assure that everyone hears exactly what you are saying.

Vocal Variety

Effective preachers have learned the art of vocal variety. They understand that variation of volume, pitch, rate, and inflection helps maintain audience attention and helps communicate various parts of the sermon. A voice that is constant minute after minute after minute will lull people to sleep, mentally if not physically.

We need to speak loudly enough to be heard by the most distant person and the person with hearing difficulty. We should not constantly shout, however, as this will quickly become wearying, and possibly offensive, to most listeners. Most parts of the sermon can be spoken at an average volume while those parts requiring special emphasis can utilize a change in volume. This may be louder or it may be softer. It is the change that grabs people's attention. A soft, slow sentence or two can be just as effective as a loud fast one.

One of my seminary professors hated what was then known as public address systems. His advice to young preachers was to 'get rid of those microphones and learn to speak up!' He would not be at home in many modern church buildings! Sound systems are a fact of life most places and we need to use them effectively. A properly adjusted system will allow a whisper to be heard, yet not deafen people when the preacher is speaking loudly. Some experimentation will be required to get it right. Incidently, wireless microphones such as those worn on the lapel are wonderful tools in comparison to pulpit mounted or hand held microphones. Wireless lapel devices give a great deal of freedom for movement and hand gestures and they are usually not a distraction.

Volume (as well as other aspects of delivery) may need to be adjusted according to the physical setting. A listener sitting ten or fifteen feet away from a speaker may be overwhelmed by the volume and body language being used. Preachers who speak to large audiences will have to 'turn it down' in a smaller, more intimate setting.

Voice pitch is another area in which variety should be utilized. Everyone has a normal pitch for speaking and most voices fall within an acceptable range, acceptable in terms of audience receptivity. A few speakers have very high voices that tend to be shrill and 'grate on people ears'. These folks should consider learning to speak at a little lower pitch. A few others have very low pitched voices. While this pitch range tends to be soothing and comfortable, sounds will be more difficult to hear clearly, especially by those who have even a slight hearing impairment. While most speakers need not be concerned with their natural pitch level, a small minority may need to work at raising or lowering it slightly to a range that is more listener friendly. Even a change of half an octave can be beneficial.

Generally, the most needed improvement with pitch is to utilize purposeful variation. If we fail to do so we become monotonous, a *monotone*. This too can be tiresome to the listener and it can sometimes affect their understanding of what is being said. This change in pitch is called inflection and it can communicate mood shifts, regain attention momentarily lost, and help convey the meaning of a phrase or sentence. A declarative sentence, for example, should be inflected differently from a question or an exclamation. I've heard some speakers, especially young people, inflect their voices upward at the end of declarative sentences giving the impression they are asking questions when they're not. (Perhaps this is a sub-conscious means of expressing a fear to assert anything as factual, a by-product of our post-modern culture.) The point I'm making is that pitch, rightly or wrongly used, is part of the para-language process. It augments or diminishes that which is being communicated.

Most speakers have a pitch range of between one and two octaves. While it is unnecessary to bounce all over the scale, we can usually improve on the limited pitch range that we regularly use in public discourse without being artificial. This is part of being an effective speaker.

Another area of our speech requiring vocal variety is that of rate, also known as pace. As with a constant volume and a constant pitch, a rate that does not vary will contribute to the loss of interest and will lack the added benefit of strengthening the intent of the verbals being used. Some research has shown, for example, that a rapid speech rate helps convey feelings of fear, anger, happiness, and surprise. A slow rate strengthens the communication of sadness, disgust, or boredom.[44] A rapid rate may also communicate that the material is familiar to the listener, while a slow pace may indicate it is either unfamiliar or more difficult to grasp.

What is the optimal speech rate? Experts can't agree. Most of us speak at a rate between 120 and 160 words per minute. A safe rule of thumb is to speak slowly enough to enable everyone to understand you and enable you to increase the rate periodically without the danger of being misunderstood. At the same time, be aware that a rate that is too slow will cause boredom and eventual disinterest. The minds of our hearers can work quite quickly. If we leave too much time between words and thought, their minds will tend to wander in other directions. As with the areas of vocals previously discussed, variety is the key. Note the advice of the venerable John Broadus:

> Let there be variety – of pitch, of force, and of speed. Monotony is utterly destructive of eloquence. But variety of utterance must be gained, not by assuming it from without, but by taking care to have a real and marked variety of sentiment, and then simply uttering each particular sentiment in the most natural manner. Emphasis requires much attention. In speaking, a correct emphasis will be spontaneous whenever one is fully in sympathy with his subject.[45]

While variety in delivery is important, it must never be forced but controlled by the content.

The Effective Pause

Preachers talk! We work hard to express ourselves through the symbolism of words. This is probably why an area of para-language that seems threatening to us is that of *silence*. Many preachers are uncomfortable being quiet in the middle of a sermon. We feel uneasy and can't help but wonder what folks are thinking as they peer back at our closed mouths. If the pause is purposeful, however, we are assisting them to understand what is being said. There is effectiveness in the *sound of silence*.

Pauses, rightly placed, can be of great assistance in the communication process. They give our listeners a momentary needed break from the intensity of listening. Pauses allow them to ruminate on the choice spiritual food just distributed. They re-gather the attention of wandering listeners. They also provide that needed audible punctuation that helps clarify the arrangement of our phrases, clauses, sentences, and paragraphs.

There are some places in sermons where pauses can be extremely beneficial. Highly important statements such as propositions and main points should be vocally highlighted by means of pauses. I sometimes pause just prior to the first statement of the proposition, state it, pause, repeat it, and pause again before continuing into the next part of the sermon. This is an effective way to call attention to the pivotal statement in the message. I also pause as I conclude one main point section and prepare to announce the next, or as I finish one movement of a narrative and approach the next. I pause as I conclude the body of the sermon and prepare to transition into the conclusion. These pauses help communicate that one part of the sermon is now being finished and a new part is about to begin.

A question addressed to the listeners, whether rhetorical or applicational, demands a pause so that the hearers can consider it for a moment. A question that is not followed by a pause is a source of frustration and future questions may well be ignored.

Silence is never more golden than when it is a well-placed pause in a sermon.

Nonverbals

Effective communication includes not only well-chosen verbals and helpful vocals, it also involves appropriate nonverbals. While I question the assertion, noted previously, that the effectiveness of a speech or sermon depends more on nonverbals than verbals, I want to affirm that nonverbals are indeed extremely important. Like vocals, they are elements of para-language that can either help or hinder what we're trying to communicate. Gwyn Walters speaks of this with a word of caution:

> The congregation does not need to wait for the preacher to open his mouth and utter words before they are 'spoken' to by him.

Much in-depth study is now being undertaken in 'nonverbal communication.' . . . 'Body language' is being 'spoken' all the time preachers are in public view on platform or in pulpit. It is often unconscious, but very revealing, sometimes betraying.[46]

I concur with Walters that nonverbals are a crucial part of the communication process whose importance should not be underestimated. Let's look, then, at several issues related to nonverbal communication.

Proxemics

The first matter to consider is the use of space in the speaking situation. This is called proxemics. This can relate to the arrangement of the room in which we're speaking. The seating plan, the use or absence of a pulpit, or any barriers between the speaker and the audience are all part of this arrangement. Not every setting is equally advantageous. A long narrow room, an extremely large pulpit, or a high altar rail can be detrimental. The concept of proxemics also relates to distances. How far is the speaker from the front row? How far from the back row? What is the amount of distance between you and each listener? These matters relate not only to the physical realities present, but to the psychology of the setting as well. A wrap-around seating arrangement, for instance, communicates a sense of togetherness, while a massive pulpit ascended by a staircase conveys separation.

Sometimes we preach in settings over which we have little control. Accepting an invitation to preach in a liturgical or formal church with a pulpit that is 'high and lifted up' does not give us the freedom to alter the architecture. If a church's floor plan is long and narrow and there are pews attached to the floor, so be it. In other settings, it may not create a problem to stand beside a large pulpit instead of behind it, or even to remove it altogether. If you are the pastor of a church with some proxemics issues to deal with, exercise a little patience as you teach the church's leaders about the importance of these matters. Basically, it is helpful to be fairly close to as many of your listeners as possible and to remove physical barriers between the speaker and the hearers.

General Appearance

As you approach the moment of delivery, your audience will first take note of your appearance. This includes your clothing, neatness, and your general demeanor. Is your clothing appropriate for the setting? Does it draw unnecessary attention to itself? Are you neat in terms of the way you're dressed and your physical appearance? Do you appear to be prepared and confident without being arrogant? Like it or not, you are being evaluated before you say your first word! First impressions matter.

Clothing is an issue of great debate in many circles. American culture has become very casual and while Sunday was once considered to be a dress-up day, it is no longer thought to be such in many churches. Coats and ties and dressy dresses are scarce not only in many pews, but increasingly on some platforms as well. I think of Saddleback Church's Rick Warren, a noted figure described by *Christianity Today* as 'a regular guy who may be America's most influential pastor', [47] an opinion with which I would not disagree. He regularly wears Hawaiian shirts both in and out of the pulpit. While this may be acceptable in California's southern Orange County – one of the most laid back areas of the most laid back state in the union – it is not necessarily suitable attire in other cultural settings. The pastor of a traditional church in a conservative area may want to think long and hard before placing an on-line order with Hilo Hattie's.

I must confess that I'm a traditionalist in matters of dress. I see the gathered worship of a congregation as being a special occasion, one that requires special effort on my part. If I approach it with the same casual attitude toward dress that I have when I golf, or shop at the mall, or mow the lawn, I run the risk of making public worship just another casual activity.

Another element of appearance is our posture. Poor posture leaves a poor impression on listeners and it also affects the quality of our speaking. When we stand erect, yet natural, we show forth a suitable confidence and at the same time allow our breathing and speaking to be natural as well. Stiffness, on the other hand, betrays fear or at least a feeling of uncomfortableness.

Facial Expression

The importance of facial expressions cannot be overstated. Smiles, frowns, serious expressions, the look of fear, or the appearance of boredom all speak volumes! Litfin alerts us to this:

> The face is perhaps the most expressive part of our bodies. Some researchers estimate that the face is capable of over a quarter million different expressions, and that over half of the nonverbal messages we send to others come from the face. Moreover, certain facial expressions are common to all people (happiness, sadness, fear, etc.), while others are taught by one's culture.[48]

Before the first word is spoken, our face begins to communicate. As we speak verbally, our facial expressions will either reinforce what we're saying, contradict it, or distract the listener to consider something else.

Facial appearance must coincide with the type of truth we are presenting. A frowning face does an injustice to a message about heaven and a sermon on the realities of hell should not be accompanied with an overabundance of smiles or an appearance of lightheartedness. Our facial expressions need to reflect our sermon content.

We may sometimes need to communicate facially something other than what we are feeling inwardly. As discussed earlier for example, fear or stage fright is a common feeling even among seasoned preachers. Yet, we should not broadcast this feeling through an expression that betrays our nervousness. If we appear to be frightened, then our listeners will become uncomfortable and effectiveness will be hindered. Or consider the occasion of a difficult funeral, perhaps that of a child, a close friend, or a family member. While we may grieve deeply within ourselves, we must present the truth of the gospel in such a way that hope is communicated even through our facial expressions. We may verbally acknowledge our grief, but we must communicate the truth of the gospel with confidence both verbally and nonverbally, including our facial expressions.

In my classroom teaching of preaching, video taping is a tool often used. As students view their taped sermons and critique themselves, the single area most surprising to many of them is that of facial expression. They are often stunned by bland, changeless expressions, misplaced smiles, the look of fear, and even expressions that tend toward the appearance of anger instead of the intended look of seriousness. Young preachers especially would do well to pay special attention to their facial expressions. They communicate more than we can imagine.

Eye Contact

Another key aspect of nonverbal communication is that of establishing and maintaining consistent and well-distributed eye-contact. While there are a few cultures that avoid direct eye-contact in conversation (I've learned this from some African students), most view it as the mark of straightforwardness and honesty. A person who looks elsewhere when speaking to you may be thought of as 'shifty-eyed' and possibly untrustworthy. Establishing sincere eye-contact is an invitation to engage in conversation whether it is a one-on-one setting or a preacher speaking to a crowd of a thousand. On the other hand, looking repeatedly at the floor, the ceiling, out a window, or at one's notes makes the statement that the speaker is not really interested in conversing with the hearers.

Consistent eye-contact, at the very least, requires looking at the audience most of the time. The speaker should never look elsewhere without good reason. One good reason might be to look at one's notes. This is fine if it is not overdone. The listener will not feel disconnected if the preacher glances periodically at his notes or even reads a small excerpt. The typical preacher, however, might be dismayed to examine the number of times in a sermon in which eye-contact is broken by looking down at the pulpit. Two or three glances a minute may total between fifty and one hundred times in a given sermon. This number of interruptions is a hindrance to effective interpersonal communication.

Eye-contact is well-distributed when it includes everyone in the audience. In a small group of less than fifteen or twenty, this must be done literally. In a larger group, however, this will not be possible. Still, the preacher can help everyone to feel included. This can be done by purposely including each part of the audience within the purview of the speaker's eye-contact. Do not ignore the left side, or the right side, or the center, or the front, or the back. Good distribution also means that the eyes will not bounce quickly from person to person or area to area, but that a sense of *contact* will be made. Each person present should feel that he or she is a part of the conversation.

Body Movement

Another important aspect of nonverbal communication is gesturing. This includes simple hand gestures, the use of shoulders and arms, and even moving from one place to another. The secret of effective body movements is to be natural. Do not plan certain gestures in the style of the elocutionary movement mentioned earlier in this chapter. Rather, gesture naturally just as you would if you were engaged in animated conversation with a good friend about an important issue.

As with other nonverbals, gestures must relate appropriately to the sermon material being spoken. The content must drive the gesture, not vice versa. The old story about the line in a preacher's notes – 'weak point, pound pulpit' – is a symptom of a wrong attitude toward nonverbals in general and body movements in particular. If our content is poor, no amount of forced body language will rescue the sermon from the oblivion it deserves. If the content is rich, and we're excited about the message, helpful body language should come about naturally.

Body movements should be geared to the preaching setting. This will include the size of the audience, the nature of the audience, and the occasion of the sermon. Small hand gestures that fit a small crowd may be lost in a larger setting. On the other hand, big 'full body' gestures that are helpful in a very large crowd may overwhelm a small audience. Walking from one side of a pulpit to the other side several times during a sermon may suit an informal setting nicely, but be inappropriate in a formal situation.

Avoid body movements which are distracting or which send wrong signals. This includes things such as purposeless pacing back and forth, rocking from foot to foot, pointless arm or hand waving, hand wringing, placing hands in pockets, fidgeting with fingers or rings on fingers, and waving something around while arm gesturing, such as eye glasses or the Bible. Most of us have acquired mannerisms over the years that do not serve us well in preaching. They do not enhance what we're attempting to say and may actually prevent people from hearing what we're saying. These habits should be identified and broken.

Elevate the Public Reading of the Scriptures

One last matter needs to be considered briefly before our discussion of sermon delivery is complete. I've purposely saved this section until now for I believe it is an appropriate finale to any discussion on biblical preaching. I refer to the matter of the public reading of the Bible.

As a young seminarian, I was struck by the effective way the Bible was read by the late Kenneth Kantzer, long-time dean of Trinity Evangelical Divinity School. Particularly during chapel services, he read the Bible with a feeling and understanding that I've seldom seen or heard before or since. His pace was slow and unhurried, so as to draw attention to what was being read. His manner was dignified, reflecting the Divine source of his reading. His diction was almost flawless indicating the importance of every word. His inflection carefully pointed attention to the accurate meaning of what was being read. The entire event elevated the Scripture to a place of prominence over any event taking place in chapel or any well-known speaker.

Sadly, I've observed something quite different in many churches today. In many churches, especially those that are 'contemporary' in terms of worship style, the public reading of Scripture receives relatively little attention. Scripture verses may be interspersed here and there as a sermon is preached, but the Bible's treatment too often conveys the sentiment that what the preacher has to say is more important than the Word itself. When a passage is read, whether in a sermon or elsewhere in a service, there is often little evidence that the text was carefully thought through and rehearsed. Punctuation is sometimes ignored, pronunciation is sometimes badly handled, and the pace of the reading suggests that this is something else to finish and get out of the way. There seems to be little indication that this is the very Word of God that is being read. We must treat it with awe and respect. We must allow it to receive prominent attention. We must not allow it to be read in such a way that denigrates what it is saying.

Arguably, the most important words verbalized in a public worship service are those in the Bible. The Bible is more important than the announcements we make, the songs we sing, or the sermons we preach. The Word of God is eternal truth and should be treated accordingly.

Perhaps I should clarify that I don't want to suggest that those who read Scripture poorly are not sincerely devoted to its importance. My purpose is not to be judgmental toward pastors or worship leaders who may not handle the Word well. I am simply pleading for a more central role for the Bible in our corporate worship gatherings and a consistently careful reading of it so that its importance will not be undermined.

To consider reading the Bible well is to consider the art of oral interpretation. If this seems to suggest some kind of elitist attitude or artificial process, I would simply respond that every reading of any writing is oral interpretation. The issue is not whether we should interpret orally, but will we do it well. We will do it one way or another.

Two Processes to Effective Scripture Reading

Good oral interpretation begins with fully understanding what a writer has said and meant. When we read to ourselves, we try to make sense of what was written. If we're unsure of its meaning, we may go back and read it again until we understand it. To read the same writing aloud to someone else requires a subsequent step. Not only must I understand what I'm reading, but I must also read it orally in such a way that the hearer will grasp its meaning as well.

Understanding

Recently, I read some novels by James Fenimore Cooper: *The Deerslayer, The Last of the Mohicans, and The Pathfinder*. I chose to read the original versions, rather than more recent edited versions made to be palatable to modern readers. I was not prepared for Cooper's literary style and found myself reading some sections two or three times to grasp what was being said or even who was speaking. The thought has occurred to me numerous times that reading this out loud to another person would be a difficult, if not impossible, task. I could read the words, but some of the meaning would be lost.

This is the way it can be with the public reading of Scripture. Unless care is taken by the reader to thoroughly understand the meaning of what has been written and then to determine how this meaning can best be reflected orally, there is a possibility that the reading will not be fully grasped by the hearers. Words will be heard, but meaning may well be vague.

The first process to reading well is hermeneutical. What does the text mean? While this is not the place for a mini-course on hermeneutics, it is important to remember that oral interpretation begins with exegetical study. Answering a few basic questions will greatly assist the Scripture reader to understand the meaning of what is to be read. Who wrote or spoke it? To whom was it written? What was the historical setting? What type of literature is being used? How does this passage fit into the larger context? What is the theme of the text? What viewpoint is being taken? What is it that the writer or speaker most wanted to emphasize? What is the emotional element that is present?

Hopefully, most preachers will recognize these questions as very basic. But sometimes we assign the reading of Scripture to others who may not be aware of these hermeneutical questions. If this is the case, we should assume the responsibility of training those who assist in public services. This will help assure that the Bible is read well regardless of who reads it and that the listeners will have an accurate understanding of what the text is saying.

Interpreting

Once the reader has come to an understanding of a passage's meaning, the next step is to prepare for good oral interpretation of this meaning. There are some practical steps that can assist us in doing this.

First, note the particular words or phrases that should be accented in each sentence. This helps indicate what the author is emphasizing. In ordinary speech a given sentence can be accented in different ways depending on the intent of the speaker. For instance, I might speak the words, 'The sky is really blue' in three different ways:

The *sky* is really blue. (indicates the sky is contrast to something else)

The sky is *really* blue. (indicates the extent of the sky's blueness)

The sky is really *blue*. (indicates blueness as compared to some other color)

When I decide which word to accent, I'm engaged in helping the listener understand the precise meaning of the statement from the perspective of the original author.

The same thing needs to happen when we read the Scripture. Consider the familiar words of Psalm 23:1 in the King James Version. This verse might be read in several different ways with a variety of emphases being made.

The *Lord* is my shepherd; I shall not want. (emphasizes identity of the shepherd)

The Lord *is* my shepherd; I shall not want. (emphasizes certainty)

The Lord is *my* shepherd; I shall not want. (emphasizes personal relationship)

The Lord is my *shepherd*; I shall not want. (emphasizes the Lord's nature)

The Lord is my shepherd; *I* shall not want. (emphasizes my personal stake in this)

The Lord is my shepherd; I *shall* not want. (emphasizes certainty)

The Lord is my shepherd; I shall *not* want. (emphasizes a strong negative)

The Lord is my shepherd; I shall not *want*. (emphasizes the state being promised)

While these examples are probably exaggerated in terms of the number of options, they indicate a potential range of possibilities. The reader of this verse must first understand its meaning, in context, and then try to interpret it orally in keeping with that meaning. I would read the verse as follows: 'The Lord is my *shepherd*; I shall not *want*.' This shows that the psalm is about the nature of God's relationship to us as shepherd, with the result being the meeting of our needs.

Second, observe the punctuation in the text. This will assist the reader to use effective pauses of various lengths. David Dombek says that 'Punctuation marks are the traffic signs for oral readers. They are stop signs or yield signs.' [49] We're aware, of course, that the punctuation has been supplied by the translators. While it may not be inspired, it does reflect careful thought given to the meaning of what is being said.

Commas are the most common form of punctuation and are used in a variety of ways. They usually require only a short pause. In terms of force in reading aloud, a semi-colon suggests that a pause should be a little longer than a comma. A colon is used to introduce a long quotation, a list of particular items, or a formal explanation. Because it is used as an introductory device, in reading, it requires a strong pause. Similarly, dashes require emphasized pauses due to their use of setting off parenthetical statements. Periods, question marks, and exclamation marks all indicate the end of complete units of thought, sentences. These pauses should be fairly long. Questions and exclamations require slightly longer pauses than periods. This is because questions are best followed by a moment of reflection and exclamations are most effective if the hearer has the opportunity to have the statement make the intended impression. Pauses that are too brief defeat these purposes.

Third, emphasize certain parts of the reading by varying the speech rate. This is done by slowing down at the right places to emphasize a few key thoughts. If a constant speech rate is maintained throughout the reading, the listener assumes that everything being read carries an equal weight. The listener can also be lulled into losing attention. A few changes of rate assist the listener to keep engaged and also indicates that some ideas being read are worthy of special attention.

Fourth, in order to help you preserve your intentions regarding accents, pauses, changes of volume, and changes of rate, mark the Scripture reading to assist your oral interpretation. Devise some simple system of markings that make sense to you. This might include an underline for emphasis, a double underline for greater emphasis, a slash for a brief pause, two or three slashes for extended pauses, an 'up arrow' for higher pitch and a 'down arrow' for lower pitch, a bold font to indicate increased volume, and the use of indentation to indicate subsidiary ideas. The important thing is to keep your system simple and readily understandable to you. Don't overdo the markings in your text. In a given sentence or extended clause, not more than two or three symbols should be necessary. While these markings might be done in a Bible, it is better to print out the text in a double-space format. This prevents visual clutter and the potential confusion that might accompany it.

I might initially mark the text of Psalm 23 as follows:

(1) The LORD is my *shepherd,* // I shall *not* be in *want.* /// (2) He makes me lie down in *green pastures,* / he leads me beside *quiet waters,* / (3) he restores my *soul.* /// He guides me in paths of *righteousness* for *his* name's sake. /// (4) Even though I walk .. through the valley .. of the shadow of *death,* / / I will fear .. *no* evil, // for *you* are with me; // *your* rod // and *your* staff, // they *comfort* me. /// (5) You prepare a *table* before me in the presence of my enemies. // You anoint my head with *oil;* // my cup *overflows.* /// (6) *Surely* goodness and love will follow me *all* the days of my life, // and I will *dwell* in the house of the *LORD* / *forever.*

I would then experiment a little to try to make the marked text more reader-friendly. This might include the use of indentation to indicate main ideas and subsidiary ideas.

(1) The LORD is my *shepherd*, // I shall *not* be in *want*. ///
(2) He makes me lie down in *green pastures*, /
    he leads me beside *quiet waters*, /
    (3) he restores my *soul*. ///
    He guides me in paths of *righteousness* for *his* name's sake.//
(4) Even though I walk .. through the valley .. of the shadow of *death*, //
    I will fear .. *no* evil, //
    for *you* are with me; //
    your rod // and *your* staff, // they *comfort* me. ///
(5) You prepare a *table* before me in the presence of my enemies./
    You anoint my head with *oil*; // my cup *overflows*. ///
(6) *Surely* /
    goodness and love will follow me *all* the days of my life, //
    and I will *dwell* in the house of the *LORD* / *forever*.

Now this is admittedly a somewhat subjective exercise. Any two or three readers may mark the text a bit differently. But if the markings are based on the hermeneutical process and the same set of symbols, they should not vary a huge amount. As the oral interpreter repeats this process with various texts, a consistent method will be developed and reading a marked text will become easy to do.

Fifth, rehearse the reading aloud several times until it becomes natural and easy to do. Do not assume that you are prepared for an effective public reading just because you have a marked text.

Finally, apply good delivery techniques to your public reading. This includes posture, straightforwardness, suitable volume, eye contact, facial expression, and gestures, as appropriate. Remember, however, that this is not a performance. It is a means of good communication. Your purpose is not to 'wow' your listeners but to effectively present what the Word of God says so that each listener has the opportunity to grasp its eternal truths.

Summation
We've been reminded in this chapter that the messages we prepare are not actually *sermons* until they are preached. Furthermore, hard

work in preparation may come to nothing unless the message is presented in an effective way so that genuine communication takes place.

Various methods of delivery were discussed, some more effective than others and each having inherent strengths and weaknesses. The wise preacher will try various methods of delivery and then settle on a method that is best suited to personality and ability.

Regardless of the specific delivery method adopted, it is imperative that we preach in a natural way, not using some forced, artificial approach that reeks of pretense and performance. Listeners have the right to expect to hear preachers who are excited about the content of their messages present them in an engaging and interesting way without any sense of artificiality.

The relationship of authority and a conversational tone was discussed. While some are of the opinion that the latter precludes the former, this is not the case. The preacher's authority resides in the nature of the truth that is presented, not in the tone of voice being used. Authority is conferred, not self-generated. Further, speaking in a conversational tone doesn't mean that a lack of vocal variety. Our voice tones change regularly depending on the subject being conversed.

A variety of communication skills was discussed including verbals, vocals, and nonverbals. Preachers who are effective will be aware of these 'tools of the trade' and will constantly seek to improve good habits and toss off those that hinder the preaching process.

Finally, the importance of the public reading of Scripture was discussed. Sadly, a growing number of churches neglect what was once a traditional part of every worship gathering. Some of those who include Scripture readings do so casually without any special effort to do it well. The reading of the Word ought to be a focal point of Christian worship and it ought to be done well.

As mentioned in the outset of the chapter, there is a basic tension that is a part of the ministry of preaching. It is a tension between man's efforts and God's working in the hearts of people. Scripture teaches that God calls certain people to be preachers. At the same time, Scripture affirms that spiritual transformation occurs as the

Holy Spirit of God works in peoples hearts. As faithful stewards of the Word, preachers must work hard in sermon preparation. At the same time, we must be aware that God alone can bring about change in the lives of our hearers.

> For while one saith, I am of Paul; and another, I am of Apollos; are ye not carnal? Who then is Paul, and who is Apollos, but ministers by whom ye believed, even as the Lord gave to every man? I have planted, Apollos watered; but God gave the increase. So then neither is he that planteth any thing, neither he that watereth; but God that giveth the increase. Now he that planteth and he that watereth are one: and every man shall receive his own reward according to his own labour. For we are labourers together with God (1 Cor 3:4-9a, KJV).

Points to Ponder

1. What delivery method do you generally use in terms of the use of notes in the pulpit? Have you experimented with other approaches? Why or why not?

2. When preaching, do you speak with the same tone of voice used in ordinary conversations about various matters? Or, do you find yourself slipping into 'pulpit talk?' Have you checked this out by means of audio or video recordings?

3. How do you speak authoritatively in everyday situations? How do you preach authoritatively? Is there a difference?

4. What are your strengths in terms of the three categories of communication skills discussed: verbals, vocals, and nonverbals? What areas might require some special attention if you are to improve your effectiveness as a good communicator?

5. Do you agree with the opinion that the public reading of Scripture in corporate worship is being minimized in a growing

number of churches? Do you know of exceptions to this? What importance do you assign to the reading of the Bible in worship services?

6. How well do you read Scripture aloud? What are some of the ideas presented that might enable you to be a more effective public reader of the Bible?

APPENDIX 1

Planning an Annual Preaching Programme

Preachers tend to follow one of two approaches in the selection of preaching topics and texts. Many simply spend the first part of the work week deciding what to preach about the next Sunday. Others devote several days each year (or perhaps every six months) to plan out the preaching agenda for the next year (or six month period). It is this latter approach that is being advocated in the material that follows.[1]

Advantages of Annual Planning

1. Annual Planning Helps to Mininimize Time Waste
If sermons are planned weekly or bi-weekly, much time can be spent looking for the right topic and text for the next sermon. Instead of spending time doing this, the preacher can invest his time in study and preparation.

2. Annual Planning Anticipates Emergencies
The busy pastor or missionary knows all too well that the demands of ministry can change rapidly as the unexpected takes place. While committee meetings, weddings, and some pastoral ministry can be scheduled in advance, unforeseen circumstances can seriously encroach on sermon preparation time. A death in the flock, for example, can demand many hours of unanticipated pastoral care and funeral preparation. This kind of ministry cannot be neglected, but neither should the ministry of preaching on the next Lord's Day. Previous planning is the key to doing both tasks effectively.

3. Annual Planning Contributes to a Balanced Ministry
Short-term planning tends to result in a pulpit ministry characterized by pet topics, pet Scriptures, and pet preaching methods. The

necessity of the moment hinders personal growth on the part of the preacher for little time is allowed for that. On the other hand, when plans are being laid for six or twelve months of pulpit ministry, the preacher can make a conscious effort to broaden pulpit-fare subject-wise, Scripture-wise, and even homiletically. This will provide personal challenges to become broader and deeper, and it will also provide stimulation for the congregation to grow in its understanding of the truths of Scripture.

4. Annual Planning Promotes Church-wide Togetherness

An integrated approach to planning helps assure that the various ministries of the church are complimentary rather than competitive. There may be times, for instance, when the pastor may wish to supplement that which is happening in Sunday school, youth group, or another organization in the church. (I once taught Romans, somewhat inductively, to a youth group and at the same time preached through the book in morning worship. This was very effective.) On the other, hand, the pastor may wish to avoid subject matter or biblical material scheduled to be discussed elsewhere in the church. Without church wide advanced planning, including sermon planning, these things are left to chance.

5. Planned Thematic Worship is Aided by Long-range Sermon Plans

The persons in charge of music and other worship elements should be included in this planning process so that choir music, other musical presentations, and other worship components can compliment the sermon, and vice-versa. A service that communicates one message is usually more effective than one which sends several unrelated messages.

6. Annual Planning Facilitates Thorough Preparation

When a text and topic are chosen only a week or two before the sermon is preached, research and reading beyond exegetical considerations will tend to be minimal. On the other hand, if the preacher is aware of subjects to be dealt with weeks and weeks in advance, research can be better planned and even "casual" reading will make more of a contribution to sermons. This is particularly true regarding introductory materials and illustrations, including statistics, contemporary quotations, and relevant examples.

7. *Annual Planning Allows the Preacher to Anticipate Special Days or Other Emphases*

The preacher who looks ahead and plans sermons to coincide with calendar matters, when desirable, will be assisting the congregation to properly integrate faith with various church and community events.

Guiding Principles for the Annual Plan's Development

1. *Prayer*

The preacher who depends upon personal ingenuity only in this matter of planning will doubtless miss the mark badly in terms of devising a plan with maximum spiritual benefit for the intended hearers. While preaching is not unrelated to personal skills and human insights, it is first and foremost a spiritual activity requiring the oversight and leading of God Himself. We may perceive ourselves as knowing a great deal about the spiritual needs and shortcomings of the flock, but we see only the external. It is God who knows the heart of each one. Prayer should not only be pursued in the matter of each individual sermon, but in the matter of the annual plan as well.

2. *Congregational Input*

It is often a good idea to seek out the counsel of godly persons in the congregation regarding their understanding of the spiritual needs of the people. In what areas of doctrine are they weak or even uninformed? Where do they struggle in terms of Christian living? How are marriages and families *really* doing? Are there parts of the Scriptures about which some in the church are ignorant? These kinds of questions can provoke responses which may be better informed or more objective than the preacher's opinion. The preacher is not obligated to follow advice that is received, but it should be allowed to inform decisions concerning sermon planning.

3. Flexibility

Throughout the entire planning process as well as throughout the year which follows, the preacher must remain aware of the proper role of the annual preaching plan. This plan is not intended to be graven in stone tablets; it is not "the law of the Medes and Persians which changes not." Rather, the plan is intended to be a tool to enable the preacher to preach more effectively. As such, it must be viewed as a "living" document, one which can be revised without any sense of guilt as circumstances or events change.

Calendar Considerations for the Annual Preaching Plan

As the preacher sets out to create a workable annual preaching plan, there are many calendar events, both in the church and beyond, which need to be considered.

1. Public holidays and events

There is an expectation on the part of church-attenders that significant holidays will be acknowledged, to some extent, by the church. Days such as Mother's Day, Father's Day, Memorial Day, Independence Day, Labor Day, and Thanksgiving should be viewed as opportunities rather than obstacles. This doesn't mean that each of these deserves a special sermon each year, but that some acknowledgement of their existence is warranted. If the sermon itself does not focus on the event, perhaps other parts of the service can. This can be varied from year to year.

Some events may not be holidays, but may be worthy of notice. Community achievements or milestones (such as anniversaries), periodic athletic events (such as the World Cup or the Olympics), or political events may require or suggest notice in the preaching plan.

2. Special occasions in the local church

A church calendar should be developed each year as well as the preaching plan. The two should inform and influence one another. There are numerous events which are either required, expected, or a possibility for the local congregation. These will vary from one

denomination to another or from one church to another. They might
include:

- ◆ Evangelistic campaigns
- ◆ Mission conferences
- ◆ Bible conferences
- ◆ Communion services
- ◆ Baptismal services
- ◆ Choir programs
- ◆ Vacation Bible School rallies
- ◆ Mission trip reports

3. Denominational emphases

Most denominations or ecclesiastical associations have special
emphases during the years which will need to be considered by the
preacher as preaching plans are being formulated. These emphases
may include promotions such as missions, prayer, stewardship,
evangelism and discipleship, and Christian education. Sometimes
an emphasis may involve only one Sunday at a time, while another
emphasis may last a month.

4. Vacation and discretionary time

Time when the preacher is away from the church should also be
built into the annual preaching plan. This may be limited to vacation
time, but may also include other out-of-town assignments such as
speaking engagements or attending conferences.

5. The Church Year

Depending on one's ecclesiastical tradition and affiliation, much or
little attention may be given to the matter of the Church Year or, as it
is sometimes called, the Christian Calendar. Those with a strong
liturgical emphasis, such as Lutherans and Episcopalians, will tend
to follow the church year closely. This will often include using a
lectionary (in which Scriptures, prayers, and other worship ideas
are found) and basing the sermon on a prescribed pericope of
Scripture. Most lectionaries include three Scripture passages for
each Lord's Day (Old Testament, Gospel, and Epistle) and the

preacher is free to choose the one (or more) to be used as the sermon text. The Church Year may vary a bit from group to group.

In 'non-liturgical' churches, the choice of text and topic is left to the discretion of the preacher. While there will be relatively little pressure to closely follow the Church Year, except for Christmas and Easter, the preacher may still wish to consider this calendar when the annual preaching program is being planned. It often helps alert the preacher to certain subjects or emphases which might otherwise be overlooked.

Highlights of the Church Year

- ♦ *Advent*: Begins on the Sunday closest to November 30. It includes four Sundays and ends on the last Sunday before Christmas Day.
- ♦ *Lent*: Begins on Ash Wednesday, six and one-half weeks before Easter. It is often observed as a period of self-denial in preparation for focusing on the suffering and death of the Lord.
- ♦ *Holy Week*: The week prior to Easter, beginning on Palm Sunday, is sometimes called holy week or passion week. It includes Maundy Thursday (fr. Latin for mandate) and Good Friday.
- ♦ *Ascension Sunday*: This is celebrated the sixth Sunday after Easter.
- ♦ *Pentecost Sunday*: Also called Whitsunday, the coming of the Holy Spirit is observed the seventh Sunday following Easter.

Other Considerations in Planning and Annual Schedule

1. Pastoral needs

The effective preacher is one who recognizes and understands the life situations of the flock. The preacher needs to be aware of family situations, social pressures, ethical concerns, fears, successes, failures, and similar things faced by those to whom the Word of God will be proclaimed.

2. Current events

While pulpit ministry must be guarded from becoming a mere reaction to contemporary happenings in society, the preacher should certainly allow the truth of Scripture to inform listeners regarding society's judgments and errors in moral and spiritual matters. This is important for it allows the hearer to learn to appreciate the fact that all of life stands under the scrutiny of Almighty God.

3. Variety

As much as (most) preachers love to preach, it is well to remember that a sermon is not required in every public church meeting. The gospel can be communicated by non-sermon means as well. Drama, film, panel discussions, small groups, and other means can all be used effectively if purposes and timing are clearly understood.

4. Guest speakers

Many congregations, as well as most pastors, prefer that outside speakers be kept to a minimum while the pastor is available. A periodic pulpit guest may be a welcome change, but too many will destroy a sense of continuity and pulpit effectiveness.

5. Biblical balance

The person who desires to be a faithful preacher of the Word will strive to achieve a proper balance in sermon purposes, doctrines discussed, and behavior promoted. This will result in what is sometimes called 'preaching the whole counsel of God'. Practically, it means that subjects will be greatly varied and that texts will come from all of the major parts of Scripture.

6. Thematic Emphases

Some pastors and churches choose a theme and perhaps a special verse for a year or other extended period of time. A special series could be planned to highlight this emphasis

Appendix 2

Planning to Preach a Sermon Series

(This may be done as part of the annual preaching plan process, or the plan may leave some space for series to be added later. The former way is preferable. As with the plan itself, this process needs to be approached with prayer.)

Consider the audience

1. Where is the audience spiritually and what is their level of understanding?

    Mostly professing Christians?

    Mostly non-professing?

    Nominal or apathetic?

    What do believers and unbelievers understand about the Faith?

2. What is the audience's level of biblical familiarity?

3. What does the majority of the audience consider its need(s) to be spiritually?

4. With what other perceived needs is the audience particularly concerned at this time?

Family pressures?	Societal issues?	Particular fears?
Ethical issues?	Security needs?	Economics?
Relational Issues?	Church matters?	World affairs?

5. What, in your opinion, are some real needs of the audience to which Scripture speaks? These may or may not be the same as the audience's felt needs.

6. In view of these previous concerns, what are two or three subjects that would be most beneficial to your audience?

7. After prayerful consideration and perhaps seeking the counsel of other church leaders, tentatively decide on a series subject.

Determine the available time

1. Time limits may be determined by the calendar:

Local church calendar - The preaching schedule is only part of this.

Christian year calendar - Some series such as advent or lent are pre-determined in regard to time.

Vacation, conferences, and other commitments - Plan your vacation and other travel plans well in advance so that a series will not be interrupted.

2. Time limits may be assigned by a superior, if you are not the senior pastor.

3. Time limits may be determined by the type of subject (still to be determined).

4. The attention span of the audience must be considered. There's a lot of difference between six weeks and six months.

Select the Portion of Scripture for yor series

(Thus far you have determined the tentative subject of the series. You have also considered the probable length of time to devote to the series.)

1. Select various sections of Scripture which deal with this proposed subject.

This subject may lead you to a given book of Scripture.

This subject may lead you to one part of a given book of Scripture.

This subject may lead you to several portions of Scripture from various books.

2. Choose the two or three most likely Scripture selections and rough out an outline of each.

Study the main sections of the outline for potential sermon themes.

How do these possible themes of the broader series subject coincide with your analysis of the audience?

How do these possible themes fit the probable time limitations?

In comparing the two or three most likely Scripture selections, what are the advantages and disadvantages of each?

Which will best address felt needs?

Which will best address real needs?

Which will best contribute to the audience=s continual "growth in grace?"

3. After prayerful deliberation, select the Scripture text(s) for the series that seems to be best for you and your audience at this time.

Like an individual sermon, a series will never address everything about a given subject.

Decide what needs to be said most urgently and design your series around that.

Save unused research and materials for a future treatment of this subject.

Advantages and disadvantages of a topical series
(This refers to a series dealing with a unified subject, but whose sermon texts will come from various parts of Scripture.)

1. Advantages:

There is more flexibility in selecting suitable texts if the preacher is not tied to a given book of the Bible.

Some series subjects cannot be adequately handled from one book because the subject itself is not discussed that way in Scripture.

A topical series may be able to deal with the subject in a more in-depth way since the main text for each message is hand-picked.

This style of series can present a well-rounded series because it gives a broader view of what Scripture says. It is akin to a 'biblical theology' of a given subject.

It may be easier to title a series (for relevancy to the listener) that is more subject-oriented than book-oriented.

2. Disadvantages:

Like a topical sermon, the treatment of a topical series can be prejudicially planned and presented.

From the perspective of the audience, a topical series may appear to be disjointed.

It may be difficult for the audience to know the overall direction of the series or to be able to think ahead to "next week's" presentation. There may be less of a sense of continuity.

Advantages and disadvantages of a book series

(This refers to a series dealing with a particular subject but based on sermon texts from the same book of Scripture, or even from a smaller section from within a Bible book.)

1. Advantages:

It provides a systematic thematic study through a limited, recognizable section of the Scriptures.

This kind of series tends to impose textual limits, keeping the preacher from meandering all over the Bible to prove a point.

A thorough study of a book or portion of a book gives a sense of accomplishment to the audience and a recognition that the whole Bible is 'knowable' if studied book by book.

The audience can more easily keep track of the flow of the series. Some folks may even study ahead if they know what is happening next.

Difficult and pointed issues can be dealt with as they come along in your natural progression through a book without appearing that you specially hand-picked the text to 'get at' someone. (For instance, if you're preaching through James, you can address the problem of gossip because the text itself does.)

It is easier to acquire resource tools such as commentaries and other books if you're dealing with only one book of Scripture instead of several.

Background, contextual, and exegetical studies are cumulative if done in the same book. A topical series will require far greater preparation time.

2. Disadvantages:

A book series may not sound overly appealing to those who are unmotivated spiritually. (This can be overcome by naming the series something other than the 'book of_____.' A series in the book of James might be called 'Tough Talk for Tough Times.' In Ecclesiastes, try 'A Wise Man Looks at Life's Dilemmas.' I've done a series on 'God's New People,' based on Ephesians; and 'What Does It Mean that He's Lord?' based on the seven sign-miracles in John's Gospel and the purpose statement in John 20:30-31.)

If the series is too long, being in the same book may become tedious to the listeners.

There may be a lack of variety of literature types in a given book and this can lead to many similar presentations.

Some general comments about sermon series

1. Some general advantages of series:

They call special attention to a special subject.

They can save on planning time, for once the series is planned it is not necessary to waste time each week looking for a topic and text.

They can save preparation time, for the study done each week builds on that done previously.

Books and resources can be obtained as needed, rather than in a random fashion.

They can encourage the congregation to do some in-depth thinking about crucial matters. This is more effective than the "hit and miss" pattern of non-series preaching.

2. Some general disadvantages of series:

They can become monotonous. People get tired of long series or back-to-back series.

Irregular attenders can feel out-of-touch when they do attend.

Some subjects are important enough to require attention, but not important enough to merit a series. Don't allow a preference for series to push these subjects aside.

3. Some practical suggestions for planning series:

Keep series relatively short.

A series of 5-7 weeks may be about right in most settings. An occasional series of 10-12 weeks should generally be maximal.

Emphasize the practicality of each series and each message within a series.

Plan your series well in advance to minimize necessary interruptions.

Build variety into your series.

Vary the kind of subject from series to series.

Vary the kind of biblical material being used and vary your homiletical methods.

Use both the Old and New Testaments.

Avoid personal "hobby horses." (By definition, hobby horses don't go anywhere!)

Make certain that over the "long haul," you are declaring the whole counsel of God.

As a general rule, don't preach through a book section by section, especially a longer book. Instead, present the book on the basis of a series subject and use only those texts which relate to that subject.

Don't go from series to series, but allow a little breather in between. Many folks will appreciate the change of pace.

Make an occasional series real special by integrating it with a special emphasis in the church.

Coordinate a Sunday series with midweek small groups.

Coordinate Sunday School with morning sermons.

Do a series to prepare your people for some upcoming event such as a mission conference or an evangelistic campaign.

Plan seasonal series:

1) the candle themes of the advent wreath;

2) perspectives on the cross prior to Easter.

Plan a series around the church's theme for the year.

Appendix 3

Sermon Evaluation Form

PREACHER   EVALUATOR
DATE _____ (Underlined items that are particularly strong;
circle items which are in need of significant improvement.)

---

1. **STARTING:** Interesting beginning which led quickly and
clearly into the main thrust of the sermon. Textual background
was established. Introduction was the right length. Compelling.

( )10 ( )9 ( )8 ( )7 ( )6 ( )5 ( )4 ( )3 ( )2 ( )1

Comments:

---

2. **THE MAIN IDEA:** The theme was clear. Proposition was
stated and restated. There was thematic relevance to the audience.
Good thematic unity persisted throughout the sermon.

( )10 ( )9 ( )8 ( )7 ( )6 ( )5 ( )4 ( )3 ( )2 ( )1

Proposition/thesis statement:

---

3. **SERMON STRUCTURE:** The homiletical design, including
main points or moves, was sufficiently clear so the listener could
follow. Transitions were clearly articulated. The design was a
good fit with the text(s) and fit the purpose of the sermon.

( )10 ( )9 ( )8 ( )7 ( )6 ( )5 ( )4 ( )3 ( )2 ( )1

Main points:

4. SUPPORTING MATERIAL: The sub-points or other supporting materials were relevant and helpful to the respective main points or moves. Applications were specific. Illustrations were pertinent and clear.

( )10 ( )9 ( )8 ( )7 ( )6 ( )5 ( )4 ( )3 ( )2 ( )1

Comments:

5. STOPPING: The conclusion began with a proposition-based final transitional sentence. It was brief. It avoided new materials or tangents. It asked the listener to respond appropriately.

( )10 ( )9 ( )8 ( )7 ( )6 ( )5 ( )4 ( )3 ( )2 ( )1

Comments:

6. BIBLICAL AUTHORITY: The literary nature of the text was respected. Biblical contexts were understood and utilized. Careful exegesis was apparent. The sermon allowed the text to make its own statement. Application came from the thrust of the text. Theological implications were addressed.

( )10 ( )9 ( )8 ( )7 ( )6 ( )5 ( )4 ( )3 ( )2 ( )1

Comments:

7. APPEARANCE: Neatness; naturalness; outward composure; suitable confidence.

( )10 ( )9 ( )8 ( )7 ( )6 ( )5 ( )4 ( )3 ( )2 ( )1 ( )N/A

Comments:

8. **VOCAL PRESENTATION:** Good natural voice quality; vocal variety; pitch; volume; speech rate; clear articulation of sounds; proper pronunciation of words; vocal assertiveness; fluency.

( )10 ( )9 ( )8 ( )7 ( )6 ( )5 ( )4 ( )3 ( )2 ( )1 ( )N/A

Comments:

9. **BODY LANGUAGE:** Communicative eye contact; natural gestures appropriate to the content; varied facial expression suitable to the message; freedom to use the whole body as appropriate; enthusiasm.

( )10 ( )9 ( )8 ( )7 ( )6 ( )5 ( )4 ( )3 ( )2 ( )1 ( )N/A

Comments:

10. **PERSUASIVENESS:** The preacher was believable on a personal level. The sermon content made sense. The sermon appealed properly to the emotions. Overall, the sermon was convincing.

( )10 ( )9 ( )8 ( )7 ( )6 ( )5 ( )4 ( )3 ( )2 ( )1

Comments:

APPENDIX 4

SELF-EVALUATION OF VIDEO TAPED SERMON

TEXT_____SERMON METHOD_____
DATE

1. What pleased you most as you watched your sermon on video?

2. What displeased you most as you watched the video tape?

3. What part(s) of this sermon's preparation gave you the most problem? Did this show up in the preached sermon?

4. At what point(s) in delivery did you seem to have the greatest difficulty? Why do you think this is so and what might you do to correct or strengthen this?

5. List below at least five specific strengths in your sermon or sermon delivery.

6. List below at least five specific weaknesses in your sermon content or delivery which will require special effort on your part before you preach again.

Endnotes

Introduction
1. *Webster's II: New Riverside University Dictionary* (Boston: Houghton Mifflin Co., 1984), 510.

1. Step One. Maintain a Balance in Theological Perspective
1. R. Albert Mohler, 'A Theology of Preaching,' *Handbook of Contemporary Preaching*, ed. Michael Duduit (Nashville, TN: Broadman Press, 1992), 15.

2. Quoted in Thomas G. Long, *The Witness of Preaching* (Louisville, KY: Westminster/John Knox Press, 1989), 20.

3. O. Flender, 'Image: eikon,' *Dictionary of New Testament Theology*, vol. 2, ed. Colin Brown (Grand Rapids, MI: Zondervan Publishing House, 1977), 286.

4. Millard J. Erickson, *Christian Theology* (Grand Rapids, MI: Baker Book House, 1993 [tenth printing]), 252. Erickson includes a helpful discussion on the topic of illumination in which he first compares his own view with that of neoorthodoxy, and then discusses the somewhat representative views of Augustine, Daniel Fuller, and John Calvin (see 251-56).

5. The concept of salvation is, of course, much more complicated than the basic meaning of conversion. Yet, while an understanding of related doctrines such as election, calling, regeneration, justification, and all of the other matters often discussed in the *ordo salutis* is important, this is beyond the scope of the present discussion. Since the concepts of conversion and sanctification (apart from glorification) are most often identified with spiritual change in a person's life, the discussion here will be limited to these.

6. Long, 41.

7. J. Schattenmann, 'Koinonia,' *The New International Dictionary of New Testament Theology*, vol. 1, ed. Colin Brown (Grand Rapids, MI: Zondervan Publishing House, 1975), 639. Discussion in this paragraph is based largely on this article, found on pages 639-44.

8. Schattenmann, 642.

9. Richard N. Longenecker, 'The Acts of the Apostles,' *The Expositor's Bible Commentary*, vol. 9, gen. ed. Frank E. Gaebelein (Grand

Rapids, MI: Zondervan Publishing House, 1981), 310.

10. Maynard Matthewson, quoted in 'Wing Walkers,' *Leadership* XVII, no. 1 (Winter, 1996), 25.

11. A very helpful discussion of the exegetical nuances of this passage is found in D.A. Carson, 'Matthew,' *The Expositor's Bible Commentary*, vol. 8, gen. Ed. Frank Gaebelein (Grand Rapids, MI: Zondervan Publishing House, 1984), 595-99. See also: Robert D. Culver, 'What Is the Church's Commission?' *Bibliotheca Sacra*, vol. 125 (1968), 243-53.

12. A. Skevington Wood, 'Ephesians,' *The Expositor's Bible Commentary*, vol. 11, gen. ed. Frank E. Gaebelein (Grand Rapids: MI: Zondervan Publishing House, 1978), 31.

13. W.G.M. Martin, 'The Epistle to the Ephesians,' *The New Bible Commentary*, gen. ed. F. Davidson (Grand Rapids, MI: Wm. B. Eerdmans Publishing Co., 1965), 1019.

14. Charles Hodge, *An Exposition of Ephesians* (The Ages Digital Library [CD-ROM], Albany, OR: Ages Software, 1997), 65.

15. Matthew Henry, *Commentary on the Whole Bible* (one volume edition), ed. Leslie F. Church (Grand Rapids, MI: Zondervan Publishing House, 1961), 1849.

2. Step Two. Maintain a Balance in Personal Perspective

1. Ian Macpherson, *The Burden of the Lord* (New York/Nashville, TN: Abingdon Press, 1955), 47.

2. *Webster's II: New Riverside University Dictionary* (Boston: Houghton Mifflin Co., 1984), 634.

3. Ilion T. Jones, *Principles and Practice of Preaching* (Nashville, TN: Abingdon Press, 1956), 49.

4. Jones, 60.

5. Quoted by James S. Stewart, *Heralds of God* (New York: Charles Scribner's Sons, 1946), 56.

6. Quoted in Tony Sargent, *The Sacred Anointing* (Wheaton, IL: Crossway Books, 1994), 144.

7. Martin Copenhaver, 'Confessions of a Budding Professional,' *Leadership*, vol III, no. 4 (Fall, 1982), 109.

8. Richard Baxter, *The Reformed Pastor*, ed. John T. Wilkinson (London: Epworth Press, 1939), 157-58.

9. D. Martyn Lloyd-Jones, *Preaching and Preachers* (Grand Rapids, MI: Zondervan Publishing House, 1971), 166.

10. Lloyd-Jones, 120.

11. Helpful discussions on the divine attribute of holiness will be found in: Rudolf Otto, *The Idea of the Holy,* trans. John W. Harvey

(London: Oxford University Press, 1958); William G. T. Shedd, *Dogmatic Theology,* vol. 1 (Nashville, TN: Thomas Nelson Publishers, rep. 1980), 362ff.; and L. Berkhof, *Systematic Theology* (Grand Rapids, MI: Wm. B. Eerdmans Publishing Co., rep. 1981), 73ff.

12. Quoted by Dr. and Mrs. Howard Taylor in *Hudson Taylor's Spiritual Secret* (The Ages Digital Library [CD-ROM], Albany, OR: Ages Software, 1997), 104.

13. Andrew A. Bonar, *Memoir and Remains of the Rev. Robert Murray McCheyne* (Edinburgh: William Oliphant and Co., 1866), 366.

14. Bonar, 247.

15. E. M. Bounds, *The Preacher and Prayer* (The Ages Digital Library [CD-ROM], Albany, OR: Ages Software, 1997), 6.

16. William R. Moody, *The Life of Dwight L. Moody* (New York: Fleming H. Revell Co., 1900), 154.

17. Howard A. Snyder, *Liberating the Church: The Ecology of Church and Kingdom* (Downer's Grove, IL: Inter-Varsity Press, 1983), 204.

18. John Calvin, *Institutes of the Christian Religion*, trans. Henry Beveridge, vol. 1 (Grand Rapids, MI: Wm. B. Eerdmans Publishing Co., rep. 1966), 144.

19. *The Rhetoric of Aristotle,* trans. Lane Cooper (New York: Appleton-Century-Crofts, Inc., 1932), 8.

20. *The Rhetoric of Aristotle*, 9.

21. Paul Cedar, Kent Hughes, and Ben Patterson. *Mastering the Pastoral Role* (Portland, OR: Multnomah, 1991), 120.

22. Raymond W. McLaughlin, *The Ethics of Persuasive Preaching* (Grand Rapids, MI: Baker Book House, 1979), 134.

23. W. E. Sangster, *The Craft of Sermon Construction* (Philadelphia: The Westminster Press, 1951), 15.

24. Macpherson, 60.

25. John Henry Jowett, *The Preacher: His Life and Work* (New York: Harper, 1912), 19.

26. Frank Pollard, 'Preparing the Preacher,' *Handbook of Contemporary Preaching*, ed. Michael Duduit (Nashville, TN: Broadman Press, 1992), 137.

27. Donald L. Hamilton, *Homiletical Handbook* (Nashville, TN: Broadman Press, 1992), 17.

28. Philip Schaff, *History of the Christian Church*, vol. 3, 'Nicene and Post-Nicene Christianity' (The Theological Journal Library [CD-ROM], Garland, TX: Galaxie Software, 1998), record 9053.

29. Paul Scott Wilson, *A Concise History of Preaching* (Nashville, TN: Abingdon Press, 1992), 59.

30. Quoted in Clyde E. Fant, Jr. and William M. Pinson, Jr., *20 Centuries of Great Preaching*, vol. 1 (Waco, TX: Word Books, 1971), 54.

31. Macpherson, 65. A much fuller account of this incident and the related events is found in F.R. Webber, *A History of Preaching in Britain and America*, Part 2 (Milwaukee, WI: Northwestern Publishing House, 1955), 26-38.

32. John Bunyan, *Grace Abounding* (The Ages Digital Library [CD-ROM], Albany, OR: Ages Software, 1997), 85.

33. Quoted in Fant and Pinson, vol. 8, 133.

34. Sangster, 24.

35. Charles Bridges, *The Christian Ministry* (London: The Banner of Truth Trust, rep. 1967), 99.

36. John F. Walvoord, 'Contemporary Issues in the Doctrine of the Holy Spirit – Part IV: Spiritual Gifts Today,' *Bibliotheca Sacra*, vol. 130, no. 520, Oct–Nov, 1973 (The Theological Journal Library [CD-ROM], Garland, TX: Galaxie Software, 1998), record 44472.

37. George W. Peters, 'The Call of God,' *Bibliotheca Sacra*, vol. 120, no. 480, Oct–Nov, 1963 (The Theological Journal Library [CD-ROM], Garland, TX: Galaxie Software, 1998), record 20905.

38. Sangster, 24.

39. John Wesley, *The Works of John Wesley*, vol 1 (The Ages Digital Library [CD-ROM], Albany, OR: Ages Software, 1997), 98.

40. Wesley, 239.

41. Wayne E. Oates, 'Authentic Preaching vs. Homiletical Narcissism,' *Preaching*, vol. V, no. 2 (September-October, 1989), 7.

42. Bridges, 127.

43. James Alexander Stewart, *Robert Murray McCheyne: Scholar, Saint, Seer, Soulwinner* (Philadelphia: Revival Literature, 1964), 18.

44. Martin Lloyd-Jones, *Revival* (Wheaton, IL: Crossway Books, 1987), 295.

45. Gordon MacDonald, 'The Seven Deadly Siphons,' *Leadership*, vol xix, no. 1 (Winter, 1998), 31.

46. Sangster, 12.

47. Bill Hybels, Stuart Briscoe, and Haddon Robinson. *Mastering Contemporary Preaching* (Portland, OR: Multnomah, 1989), 145.

48. For a brief but helpful exegesis of this text, see Ralph Earle, '2 Timothy,' *The Expositor's Bible Commentary*, vol. 11, gen. ed. Frank E. Gaebelein (Grand Rapids, MI: Zondervan Publishing House, 1978), 402.

49. James S. Stewart, 196.

50. Quoted in Sargent, 136.

51. Paul Scherer, *For We Have This Treasure* (Grand Rapids, MI: Baker Book House, 1976), 39.

52. Scherer, 40.

53. Scherer, 40.

54. Lloyd-Jones, 169.

55. James S. Stewart, 204.

56. C. Welton Gaddy, *The Gift of Worship* (Nashville: Broadman Press, 1992), 75.

3. Step Three: Maintain A Balance in Biblical Foundations

1. Andrew Watterson Blackwood, *The Preparation of Sermons* (New York: Abingdon-Cokesbury Press, 1948), 47.

2. For a fuller discussion of this topic, see W. Ward Gasque, 'Marcion,' *The New International Dictionary of the Christian Church*, ed. J. D. Douglas (Grand Rapids, MI: Zondervan Publishing House, 1974), 629.

3. Elizabeth Achtemeier, 'Preaching and the Old Testament,' *Handbook of Contemporary Preaching*, ed. Michael Duduit (Nashville, TN: Broadman Press, 1992), 256.

4. Walter C. Kaiser, Jr., *Toward an Exegetical Theology* (Grand Rapids, MI: Baker Book House, 1981).

5. J. Robertson McQuilkin, *Understanding and Applying the Bible* (Chicago: Moody Press, 1983).

6. A. Berkeley Mickelsen, *Interpreting the Bible* (Grand Rapids, MI: Wm. B. Eerdmans Publishing Co., 1963).

7. Among others, see: Sidney Greidanus, *The Modern Preacher and the Ancient Text* (Grand Rapids, MI: Wm. B. Eerdmans Publishing Co., 1988); Walter C. Kaiser, Jr., *The Old Testament in Contemporary Preaching* (Grand Rapids, MI: Baker Book House, 1973); and Thomas G. Long, *Preaching and the Literary Forms of the Bible* (Philadelphia: Fortress Press, 1989).

8. Edmund P. Clowney, *Preaching and Biblical Theology* (Grand Rapids, MI: Wm. B. Eerdmans Publishing Co., 1961), 15.

9. Kaiser, *The Old Testament in Contemporary Preaching*, 11.

10. For some helpful hints for handling this kind of text, see John D. W. Watt, 'Preaching on the Narratives of the Monarchy,' in *Biblical Preaching*, James W. Cox, ed. (Philadelphia: Westminster, 1983), 72ff. Also, see Dan R. Johnson, 'Guidelines for the Application of Old Testament Narrative,' *Trinity Journal* 7 (78): 79-84; and Eugene A. Wilson, 'The Homiletical Application of Old Testament Narrative Passages,' *Trinity Journal* 7 (78): 85-92.

11. C. S. Lewis, *Reflections on the Psalms* (New York: Harcourt, Brace and World, 1958), 3.

12. Long, 45.

13. In addition to these specific wisdom books, there are also instances of the wisdom genre scattered throughout Scripture. Examples include Isaiah 28:23-29, Amos 3:3-6, Ezekiel 18:2, 1 Corinthians 15:33, 2 Corinthians 9:6, Galatians 5:9, and Galatians 6:7. See Sidney Greidanus, *The Modern Preacher and the Ancient Text* (Grand Rapids: Eerdmans, 1988), 228, 311.

14. Samuel J. Schultz, *The Old Testament Speaks* (New York: Harper, 1960), 280.

15. Leland Ryken, *The Literature of the Bible* (Grand Rapids, MI: Zondervan Publishing House, 1974), 250.

16. Ryken, 251-52.

17. R. K. Harrison, 'The Song of Songs,' volume 5 in *Zondervan Pictorial Encyclopedia of the Bible*, ed. Merrill C. Tenney (Grand Rapids, MI: Zondervan Publishing House, 1976), 486.

18. Kaiser, *The Old Testament in Contemporary Preaching*, 93ff.

19. Abraham Heschel, *The Prophets*, Vol. 1 (New York: Harper and Row, 1962), ix.

20. Heschel, 4.

21. Heschel, 13.

22. Mickelsen, 295.

23. This list is taken from my earlier work, *Homiletical Handbook* (Nashville, TN: Broadman Press, 1992), 156. Chapter 17 in that book presents more detail regarding the apocalyptic literature of the Bible than is found here.

24. For a helpful overview of various positions on the Book of Revelation, see Merrill Tenney, 'Revelation, Book of the,' *Zondervan Pictorial Encyclopedia of the Bible*, Vol. V, 89-99. Also see Merrill Tenney, *Interpreting Revelation* (Grand Rapids: Eerdmans, 1957), for a balanced and sane commentary.

25. Charles T. Cook, ed. *C. H. Spurgeon's Sermons on the Book of Revelation* (Grand Rapids: Zondervan, rep. 1964), 139.

26. D. A. Carson, 'Matthew,' *The Expositor's Bible Commentary*, Vol.11, gen. ed. Frank Gaebelein (Grand Rapids, MI: Zondervan Publishing House, 1984), 123. Carson has an extended, helpful discussion of the unity of Matthew 5–7.

27. See my earlier work, *Homiletical Handbook*, chapters 4–11, for a presentation of eight distinct homiletical approaches. Also, see chapter 19, 'Preaching from the Teachings of Jesus,' for examples of how

each of these approaches can be applied to various texts. Also, see chapter 21, 'Preaching on Parables,' for four homiletical recommendations and some examples of their application.

28. Again, see my earlier work, *Homiletical Handbook*, chapters 4–11. Also, see chapter 22, 'Preaching from the Epistles,' for specific examples of how these approaches can be applied to epistolary texts.

Step Four: Maintain a Balance in Preaching Purpose
1. J. I. Packer, AIntroduction: 'Why Preach?,' *The Preacher and Preaching*, ed. Samuel T. Logan, Jr., (Phillipsburg, NJ: Presbyterian and Reformed Publishing Co., 1986), 9.

2. Bryan Chapell, *Christ-Centered Preaching: Redeeming the Expository Sermon* (Grand Rapids, MI: Baker Books, 1994), 40.

3. Jerry Vines and Jim Shaddix, *Power in the Pulpit: How to Prepare and Deliver Expository Sermons* (Chicago: Moody Press, 1999).

4. Lloyd Merle Perry, *A Manual for Biblical Preaching* (Grand Rapids, MI: Baker Book House, 1965), 2.

5. J. Daniel Baumann, *An Introduction to Contemporary Preaching* (Grand Rapids, MI: Baker Book House, 1972), 206.

6. Donald L. Hamilton, *Homiletical Handbook* (Nashville, TN: Broadman Press, 1992), 42.

7. C. H. Dodd, *Apostolic Preaching and Its Development* (New York: Harper, 1936).

8. For further information on this subject, the reader is referred to the following books which interact with Dodd, often disagreeing with his conclusions. Robert Mounce, *The Essential Nature of New Testament Preaching* (Grand Rapids, MI: Wm. B. Eerdmans Publishing Co., 1960); and Robert C. Worley, *Preaching and Teaching in the Earliest Church* (Philadelphia: Westminster Press, 1967).

9. Wayne McDill, *The 12 Essential Skills for Great Preaching* (Nashville: Broadman and Holman, 1994).

10. Relatively few books that discuss evangelistic invitations are available. One helpful book in this area is: Alan Streett, *The Effective Invitation* (Grand Rapids: Kregel Publications, rep. 1995).

11. W. E. Sangster, *The Craft of Sermon Construction* (Philadelphia: Westminster Press, 1951), 53.

12. George E. Sweazey, *Preaching the Good News* (Englewood Cliffs, NJ: Prentice-Hall, Inc., 1976), 233.

13. Ken Hemphill, 'Preaching and Evangelism,' *Handbook of Contemporary Preaching*, ed. Michael Duduit (Nashville, TN: Broadman Press, 1992), 525.

14. Harry Emerson Fosdick, *The Living of these Days* (New York: Harper and Row Publishers, 1956), 94.

15. Fosdick, 94. There have been many studies of Fosdick's preaching philosophy and methodology. One that is especially thorough is: Edmund Holt Linn, *Preaching as Counseling: The Unique Method of Harry Emerson Fosdick* (Valley Forge, PA: Judson Press, 1966).

16. Sweazey, 263.

17. *Webster's II: New Riverside University Dictionary* (Boston: Houghton Mifflin Co., 1984), 452.

18. John R. W. Stott, *Between Two Worlds: The Art of Preaching in the Twentieth Century* (Grand Rapids, MI: William B. Eerdmans Publishing Co., 1982), 313.

19. William H. Willimon, 'Pastoral Care and Preaching,' *Concise Encyclopedia of Preaching* (Louisville, KY: Westminster John Knox Press, 1995), 363.

20. Alex Montoya, *Preaching with Passion* (Grand Rapids, MI: Kregel Publications, 2000), 89.

21. Charles Bridges, *The Christian Ministry* (London: The Banner of Truth Trust, rep 1967), 298.

22. Abraham Heschel, *The Prophets*, vol. 1 (New York: Harper and Row, 1962), 4.

23. James Montgomery Boice, 'Galatians,' *The Expositor's Bible Commentary*, vol. 10, gen. Ed. Frank E. Gaebelein (Grand Rapids: MI: Zondervan Publishing House, 1978), 504, 505.

24. Sweazey, 251.

25. William R. Moody, *The Life of Dwight L. Moody* (New York: Fleming H. Revell Co., 1900), 405.

26. Ian Macpherson, *The Burden of the Lord* (Nashville, TN: Abingdon Press, 1955), 36.

Step Five: Maintain a Balance in Sermon Variety

1. George E. Sweazey, *Preaching the Good News* (Englewood Cliffs, NJ: Prentice-Hall, 1976), 82.

2. David L. Larsen, *The Anatomy of Preaching* (Grand Rapids, MI: Kregel Publications, 1999), 84.

3. Mark Barger Elliott, *Creative Styles of Preaching* (Louisville, KY: Westminster John Knox Press, 2000), ix.

4. Sweazey, 73.

5. See Donald L. Hamilton, *Homiletical Handbook* (Nashville, TN: Broadman Press, 1992), 23-24.

6. My *Homiletical Handbook* presents eight kinds of homiletical

approaches, some of which have additional variations. (See pp 39-116.) These methods are not original with me but have been borrowed from others and somewhat refined according to my own preferences. Other books that stress variety in methodology are also available including Harold Freeman's *Variety in Biblical Preaching* (Waco, TX: Word Books, 1987), Lloyd M. Perry's *Biblical Preaching for Today's World* (Chicago: Moody Press, 1973), Mark Barger Elliotts *Creative Styles of Preaching* (Louisville, KY: Westminster John Knox Press, 2000), and Bruce Mawhinney's *Preaching with Freshness* (Grand Rapids, MI: Kregel Publications, 1997).

7. *Webster's II: New Riverside University Dictionary* (Boston: Houghton Mifflin Co., 1984), 795, 'Nihilism.'

8. Clyde E. Fant, *Preaching for Today* (New York: Harper and Row, 1975), 1.

9. Henry Grady Davis, *Design for Preaching* (Philadelphia: Muhlenberg Press, 1958), 11.

10. Typical in this regard are: Andrew Watterson Blackwood, *The Preparation of Sermons* (New York: Abingdon-Cokesbury Press, 1948), and T. Harwood Pattison, *The Making of the Sermon* (Philadelphia: The American Baptist Publication Society, 1941).

11. There is a brief discussion on this in: Warren W. Wiersbe and Lloyd M. Perry, *The Wycliffe Handbook of Preaching and Preachers* (Chicago: Moody Press, 1984), 45.

12. Davis, 32.

13. Ronald J. Allen, *Preaching the Topical Sermon* (Louisville, KY: Westminster John Knox Press, 1992), 3-4.

14. J. Daniel Baumann, *An Introduction to Contemporary Preaching* (Grand Rapids, MI: Baker Book House, 1972), 102.

15. Andrew Watterson Blackwood, *Expository Preaching for Today* (New York: Abingdon-Cokesbury Press, 1953), 13.

16. Baumann, 102.

17. See, for example, John Killinger, *Fundamentals of Preaching* (Philadelphia: Fortress Press, 1985), 53. Killinger considers expository preaching to be a 'running commentary' and makes this statement about it: 'Once a rather popular variety of preaching, especially in the more traditional and conservative churches, the expository sermon is less frequently employed today, possibly because a generation of biblically sensitive preachers is more aware of the dangers of eisogesis, or reading unwarranted meanings into the words and phrases of Scripture.'

18. Faris D. Whitesell, *Power in Expository Preaching* (Old Tappan, NJ: Fleming H. Revell Company, 1963), xv.

19. James S. Stewart, *Heralds of God* (New York: Charles Scribners's Sons, 1946), 109.

20. Stephen F. Olford and David L. Olford, *Anointed Expository Preaching* (Broadman and Holman Publishers, 1998), 69.

21. Olford and Olford, 4.

22. John R. W. Stott, *Between Two Worlds: The Art of Preaching in the Twentieth Century* (Grand Rapids, MI: William B. Eerdmans Publishing Co., 1982), 125.

23. Jerry Vines and Jim Shaddix, *Power in the Pulpit: How to Prepare and Deliver Expository Sermons* (Chicago: Moody Press, 1999), 30.

24. Elizabeth Achtemeier, *Creative Preaching: Finding the Words* (Nashville, TN: Abingdon, 1980), 17.

25. *Music of the World's Great Composers* (Readers Digest Association, 1959), 5.

26. W. E. Sangster, *The Craft of Sermon Construction* (Philadelphia: Westminster Press, 1951), 82.

27. Sangster, 84.

28. The following books, some of which have been mentioned previously in this chapter, are especially recommended to the reader who desires initial or continuing instruction in good sermon structuring: Bryan Chapell, *Christ-Centered Preaching: Redeeming the Expository Sermon* (Grand Rapids, MI: Baker Book House, 1994); Henry Grady Davis, *Design for Preaching*; Charles W. Koller, *Expository Preaching without Notes* (Grand Rapids, MI: Baker Book House, 1962); David L. Larsen, *The Anatomy of Preaching*; Wayne McDill, *The 12 Essential Skills for Great Preaching* (Nashville, TN: Broad & Holman Publishers, 1994); Lloyd M. Perry, *A Manual for Biblical Preaching* (Grand Rapids, MI: Baker Book House, 1965); Haddon W. Robinson, *Biblical Preaching: the Development and Delivery of Expository Messages* (Grand Rapids, MI: Baker Book House, 1980); Jerry Vines and Jim Shaddix, *Power in the Pulpit: How to Prepare and Deliver Expository Sermon* (Chicago: Moody Press, 1999).

29. Ralph L. Lewis and Gregg Lewis, *Inductive Preaching: Helping People Listen* (Westchester, IL: Crossway Books, 1983), 197.

30. Baumann, 80; Hamilton, 98.

31. For a detailed account of this event, see Ralph G. Nichols and Leonard A. Stevens, *Are You Listening?* (New York: McGraw Hill, 1957), 1-3.

32. Nichols and Stevens, 12.

33. Larsen, 40.

34. Fred B. Craddock, *As One without Authority* (Nashville: Abingdon Press, 1971), 58.

35. Craddock, 60.

36. Chapell, 172.

37. Ralph L. Lewis and Gregg Lewis, *Learning to Preach Like Jesus* (Westchester, IL: Crossway Books, 1989), 31.

38. Timothy S. Warren, 'A Paradigm for Preaching,' *Bibliotheca Sacra*, vol. 148, no. 592, Oct-Dec 1991 (The Theological Journal Library [CD-ROM], Garland, TX: Galaxie Software, 1999), record 119, 596.

39. Sidney Greidanus, *The Modern Preacher and the Ancient Text* (Grand Rapids, MI: Eerdmans Publishing Co., 1988), 2, 9.

40. For further helpful explanation and discussion, see: Greidanus, 175-180 and Fred B. Craddock, *Overhearing the Gospel* (Nashville: Abingdon, 1978), 112-124.

41. Kenneth E. Bickel, 'Re-Claiming the Deductive Sermon.' A paper presented to the Evangelical Homiletics Society at the 1997 annual meeting held at Gordon-Conwell Theological Seminary, 2.

42. Bickel, 3.

43. Hamilton, 76-82.

44. Freeman, 173.

45. Hamilton, 90-95.

46. This outline is found in a slightly different form in Hamilton, 100.

47. This outline is also adapted from Hamilton, 100.

48. Donald L. Hamilton, 'Behold the Lamb!' in *Come to the Banquet: Meditations for the Lord's Table*, eds. Richard Allen Bodey and Robert Leslie Holmes (Grand Rapids, MI: Baker Book House, 1998), 32.

Step Six: Maintain a Balance in Sermon Content

*Charles H. Spurgeon, *Lectures to My Students* (Fearn, Ross-Shire, Great Britain: Christian Focus Publications, rep. 1998), 79.

1. There are some kinds of sermons in which the sub-pointing related to some of the main points may not be exegetically informed. For example, a problem-solving approach (as discussed in chapter 5) will often have a first main point that explains the nature of the problem and the importance of finding a solution. The supporting material would generally not be informed by the text. The second main point will present possible solutions to the problem, some or all of which may not be biblical. Only the third main point deals with what Scripture says about a suitable solution to this problem.

2. Donald Macleod, 'Preaching and Systematic Theology,' in *The Preacher and Preaching*, ed. Samuel T. Logan, Jr. (Phillipsburg, NJ: Presbyterian and Reformed Publishing Co., 1986), 262.

3. Macleod, 263.

4. For further discussion of this process, see: Lloyd M. Perry, *Biblical Sermon Guide* (Grand Rapids, MI: Baker Book House, 1970), 35-36; and Lloyd M. Perry, *Biblical Preaching for Today's World* (Chicago: Moody Press, 1973), 55-56.

5. Keith Willhite, *Preaching with Relevance* (Grand Rapids, MI: Kregel Publications, 2001), 112.

6. Charles W. Koller, *Expository Preaching without Notes* (Grand Rapids, MI: Baker Book House, 1962), 21.

7. Bryan Chapell, *Christ-Centered Preaching: Redeeming the Expository Sermon* (Grand Rapids, MI: Baker Book House, 1994), 201.

8. Haddon W. Robinson, *Biblical Preaching: the Development and Delivery of Expository Messages* (Grand Rapids, MI: Baker Book House, 1980), 26.

9. Howard G. Hendricks and William D. Hendricks, *Living by the Book.* (Chicago: Moody Press, 1991), 283.

10. Chapell, 202.

11. David L. Larsen, *The Anotomy of Preaching* (Grand Rapids, MI: Kregel Publications, 1999), 121.

12. Andrew Watterson Blackwood, *The Preparation of Sermons* (Nashville: Abingdon-Cokesbury Press, 1948), 162.

13. John R. W. Stott, *Between Two Worlds: The Art of Preaching in the Twentieth Century* (Grand Rapids, MI: William B. Eerdmans Publishing Company, 1982).

14. Sidney Greidanus, *The Modern Preacher and the Ancient Text* (Grand Rapids, MI: William B. Eerdmans Publishing Company, 1988).

15. While working on these pages, word has come to me of the untimely death of Keith Willhite, professor of preaching and pastoral ministries at Dallas Theological Seminary. Dr. Willhite was a colleague whose friendship I have valued over a period of ten years as we participated together in various professional activities. He, along with Dr. Scott Gibson, was instrumental in the forming of the Evangelical Homiletics Society, an organization of teachers of preaching and pastors who have special academic interest in the field. Dr. Willhite was a scholar with a pastor's heart. He deeply enjoyed helping to prepare students for the ministry of the Gospel.

16. Willhite, 22.

17. Harold T. Bryson, *Expository Preaching* (Nashville, TN: Broadman & Holman Publishers, 1995), 93.

18. See Paul S. Minear, *Eyes of Faith* (London: Lutterworth Press, 1948), 181; and A. Berkeley Mickelsen, *Interpreting the Bible* (Grand

Rapids, MI: William. B. Eerdmans Publishing Company, 1963), 163.

19. Mickelsen, 164.

20. Ian Macpherson, *The Burden of the Lord* (Nashville, TN: Abingdon Press, 1955), 39.

21. J. Peter Vosteen, 'Pastoral Preaching,' in *The Preacher and Preaching*, ed. Samuel T. Logan, Jr. (Phillipsburg, NJ: Presbyterian and Reformed Publishing Co., 1986), 404.

22. David W. Henderson, *Culture Shift* (Grand Rapids, MI: Baker Books, 1998), 30.

23. Larsen, 95.

24. Clyde E. Fant, *Preaching for Today* (New York: Harper and Row Publishers, 1975), 105.

25. Ian Pitt-Watson, *A Primer for Preachers* (Grand Rapids, MI: Baker Book House, 1986), 35.

26. Spurgeon, 156.

27. Phillips Brooks, *Lectures on Preaching* (Grand Rapids, MI: Baker Book House, 1969 rep.), 220.

28. John L. Vohs and G. P. Mohrman, *Audiences, Messages, Speakers* (New York: Harcourt Brace and Jovanovich, 1975).

29. Calvin Miller, *The Empowered Communicator* (Nashville, TN: Broadman & Holman Publishers, 1994), 28.

30. Willhite, 24ff.

31. Spurgeon, 84.

32. Timothy George, 'Doctrinal Preaching,' in *Handbook of Contemporary Preaching*, ed. Michael Duduit (Nashville, TN: Broadman Press, 1992), 93.

33. Raymond Bailey, *Jesus the Preacher* (Nashville, TN: Broadman Press, 1990), 79.

34. Bailey, 80, 81.

35. Fred Craddock, *Preaching* (Nashville, TN: Abingdon Press, 1985), 79.

36. Geoffrey Thomas, 'Powerful Preaching,' in *The Preacher and Preaching*, ed. Samuel T. Logan, Jr. (Phillipsburg, NJ: Presbyterian and Reformed Publishing Co., 1986), 369.

37. James S. Stewart, *Heralds of God* (New York: Charles Scribner's Sons, 1946), 118.

38. Charles R. Brown, *The Art of Preaching* (New York: Macmillan Co., 1922), 42.

39. Henderson, 31.

40. D. Martyn Lloyd-Jones, *Preaching & Preachers* (Grand Rapids, MI: Zondervan Publishing House, 1971), 130.

Step Seven: Maintain a Balance in Sermon Delivery

1. John A. Broadus, *A Treatise on the Preparation and Delivery of Sermons* (New York: A. C. Armstrong and Son, 1893), 444.

2. H. C. Brown, Jr., H. Gordon Clinard, and Jesse J. Northcutt, *Steps to the Sermon* (Nashville, TN: Broadman Press, 1963), 164.

3. The reader is directed to the following books all of which include some detailed discussion of the anatomy of the human speaking mechanisms and their proper use: Virgil A. Anderson, *Training the Speaking Voice*, (New York: Oxford University Press, 1942); Al Fasol, *A Complete Guide to Sermon Delivery* (Nashville, TN: Broadman & Holman Publishers, 1996); G. Robert Jacks, *Getting the Word Across: Speech Communication for Pastors and Lay Leaders* (Grand Rapids, MI: William B. Eerdmans Publishing Co., 1995); Arthur Lessac, *The Use and Training of the Human Voice* (New York, DBS Publications, 1967); Wayne V. McDill, *The Moment of Truth* (Nashville, TN: Broadman & Holman Publishers, 1999); Horace G. Rahskopf, *Basic Speech Improvement* (New York: Harper and Row, 1965); Dwight E. Stevenson and Charles F. Diehl, *Reaching People from the Pulpit* (New York: Harper and Row, 1958); Jerry Vines, *A Guide to Effective Sermon Delivery* (Chicago: Moody Press, 1986); Lynn K. Wells, *The Articulate Voice: An Introduction to Voice and Diction*, 2nd ed. (Scottsdale, AZ: Gorsuch Scarisbrick, 1993).

4. Ilion T. Jones, *Principles and Practice of Preaching* (Nashville, TN: Abingdon Press, 1956), 188.

5. Jones, 188.

6. Quoted in Jones, 189.

7. Andrew W. Blackwood, *The Preparation of Sermons* (New York: Abingdon-Cokesbury Press, 1948), 198.

8. A helpful book on this subject has been written by a teacher of speech communication at Princeton Theological Seminary. See G. Robert Jacks, *Just Say the Word: Writing for the Ear* (Grand Rapids, MI: William B. Eedrmans Publishing Company, 1996).

9. Blackwood, 196.

10. James S. Stewart, *Heralds of God* (New York: Charles Scribner's Sons, 1946), 181, 182.

11. Charles W. Koller, *Expository Preaching without Notes* (Grand Rapids, MI: Baker Book House, 1962).

12. McDill, 131-148.

13. J. Daniel Baumann, *An Introduction to Contemporary Preaching* (Grand Rapids, MI: Baker Book House, 1972), 195.

14. A. Duane Litfin, *Public Speaking: A Handbook for Christians*

(Grand Rapids, MI: Baker Book House, 1981), 323. In the same year (1973), *The Bruskin Report* (No. 53) stated that public speaking is the foremost fear of Americans. See: Paul Edward Nelson and Judy Cornelia Pearson, *Confidence in Public Speaking*, 2nd ed. (Dubuque, IA: Wm. C. Brown Publishers, 1984), 4.

15. Charles H. Spurgeon, *Lectures to My Students* (Fearn, Ross-Shire, Great Britain: Christian Focus Publications, rep. 1998), 311.

16. Quoted in Milton Dickens, *Speech: Dynamic Communication* (New York: Harcourt, Brace and Company, 1954), 41.

17. Dickens, 41-42.

18. Brown, Clinard, and Northcutt, 167.

19. Litfin, 323.

20. Ian Pitt-Watson, *A Primer for Preachers* (Grand Rapids, MI: Baker Book House, 1986), 90.

21. *Encyclopedia Brittanica*, 1979 edition, 'Rhetoric,' vol. 15, 801.

22. Bryan Chapell, *Christ-Centered Preaching: Redeeming the Expository Sermon* (Grand Rapids, MI: Baker Book House, 1994), 313.

23. Blackwood, 181.

24. Arthur Clarke, 'Joseph Parker,' in *The New International Dictionary of the Christian Church* (Grand Rapids, MI: Zondervan Publishing House, 1974), 748.

25. Spurgeon,138.

26. Stephen F. Olford and David L. Olford, *Anointed Expository Preaching* (Broadman & Holman Publishers, 1998), 210.

27. Olford and Olford, 210.

28. Jim Shaddix, *The Passion Driven Sermon* (Nashville, TN: Broadman & Holman, 2003), 65.

29. Spurgeon, 341.

30. Spurgeon, 341.

31. Jerry Vines, *A Guide to Effective Sermon Delivery* (Chicago: Moody Press, 1986), 149.

32. Quoted in *2010 Popular Quotations*, Thomas W. Hanford, ed. (The Ages Digital Library [CD-ROM], Albany, OR: Ages Software, 1997), 393. Whether this quote should be attributed to Thomas Fuller (1608-1661) or to Andrew Fuller (1754-1815) is uncertain.

33. Thomas Coke, *The Duties of the Minister of the Gospel* (The Ages Digital Library [CD-ROM], Albany, OR: Ages Software, 1997), 53.

34. Ronald E. Sleeth, *Persuasive Preaching* (New York: Harper and Row, Publishers, 1956), 59.

35. Jerome, *The Nicene and Post-Nicene Fathers*, Philip Schaff,

ed., 2ⁿᵈ Series, vol. 6, (The Ages Digital Library [CD-ROM], Albany, OR: Ages Software, 1997), 245.

36. Vines, 152.

37. Clyde E. Fant, *Preaching for Today* (New York: Harper and Row, Publishers, 1975). 167.

38. Richard Baxter, *The Reformed Pastor* (The Ages Digital Library [CD-ROM], Albany, OR: Ages Software, 1997), 102.

39. McDill, 91.

40. Nelson and Pearson, 17.

41. Calvin Miller, *Spirit, Word, and Story* (Grand Rapids, MI: Baker Books, 1996), 115.

42. Douglas Ehninger et al, *Principles and Types of Speech Communication*, 9ᵗʰ ed. (Glenview, IL: Scott, Foresman and Company, 1982), 255.

43. Ehninger et al, 255.

44. Judee K. Burgoon and Thomas Saine, *The Unspoken Dialogue* (Boston: Houghton Mifflin Co., 1978), 205.

45. John A. Broadus, *On the Preparation and Delivery of Sermons*, rev. by Jesse Burton Weatherspoon (New York: Harper & Row, Publishers, 1944), 347.

46. Gwyn Walters, 'The Body in the Pulpit,' in *The Preacher and Preaching*, ed. Samuel T. Logan, Jr. (Phillipsburg, NJ: Presbyterian and Reformed Publishing Co., 1986), 454.

47. *Christianity Today*, November 18, 2002, Volume 46, No. 12, front cover.

48. Litfin, 316.

49. David Dombek, 'Reading the Word of God Aloud,' in *The Preacher and Preaching,* ed. Samuel T. Logan, Jr. (Phillipsburg, NJ: Presbyterian and Reformed Publishing Co., 1986), 438.

Appendix 1

1. A thorough treatment of this subject is found in Stephen Nelson Rummage, *Planning Your Preaching* (Grand Rapids, MI: Kregel Publications, 2002).

Selected Bibliography

Achtemeier, Elizabeth. *Creative Preaching: Finding the Words*. Nashville: Abingdon, 1980.

Adams, Jay E. *Preaching with Purpose*. Grand Rapids: Baker, 1982.

Allen, Ronald J. *Preaching the Topical Sermon*. Louisville, KY: Westminster John Knox, 1992.

Bailey, E. K. And Warren W. Wiersbe. *Preaching in Black & White*. Grand Rapids: Zondervan, 2003.

Bailey, Raymond. *Jesus the Preacher*. Nashville: Broadman, 1990.

_____. *Paul the Preacher*. Nashville: Broadman, 1991.

Baumann, J. Daniel. *An Introduction to Contemporary Preaching*. Grand Rapids: Baker, 1972, 1988.

Blackwood, Andrew W. *The Preparation of Sermons*. New York: Abingdon-Cokesbury, 1948.

_____. *Expository Preaching for Today*. New York: Abingdon-Cokesbury, 1953.

Bodey, Richard Allen, ed. *Inside the Sermon: Thirteen Preachers Discuss Their Methods of Preparing Messages*. Grand Rapids: Baker, 1990.

Broadus, John A. *A Treatise on the Preparation and Delivery of Sermons*. New York: A. C. Armstrong and Sons, 1893.

Brown, H. C., Jr., H. Gordon Clinard, and Jesse J. Northcutt. *Steps to the Sermon*. Nashville: Broadman, 1963.

Bryson, Harold T. *Expository Preaching: The Art of Preaching Through a Book of the Bible*. Nashville: Broadman and Holman, 1995.

Buttrick, David G. *Homiletic: Moves and Structures*. Philadelphia: Fortress Press, 1986.

Chapell, Bryan. *Christ-Centered Preaching: Redeeming the Expository Sermon*. Grand Rapids: Baker, 1994.

Claypool, John R. *The Preaching Event*. Waco, TX: Word Books, 1980. (Yale Lecture Series)

Clowney, Edmund P. *Preaching and Biblical Theology*. Grand Rapids: Eerdmans, 1961.

Cox, James W. ed. *Biblical Preaching: An Expositor's Treasury*. Philadelphia: Westminster Press, 1983.

Craddock, Fred B. *As One Without Authority*. Nashville: Abingdon, 1979.

_____. *Preaching*. Nashville: Abingdon, 1985.

Davis, Henry Grady. *Design for Preaching*. Philadelphia: Muhlenberg, 1958.

Demaray, Donald E. *Introduction to Homiletics*. 2nd ed. Grand Rapids: Baker, 1990.

Duduit, Michael, ed. *A Handbook of Contemporary Preaching*. Nashville: Broadman, 1992.

Eby, David. *Power Preaching for Church Growth*. Ross-Shire, Great Britain: Christian Focus Publications, 1998.

Elliott, Mark Barger. *Creative Styles of Preaching*. Louisville, KY: Westminster John Knox, 2000.

English, Donald. *An Evangelical Theology of Preaching*. Nashville: Abingdon, 1996.

Eslinger, Richard L. *A New Hearing: Living Options in Homiletic Method*. Nashville: Abingdon, 1987.

Fant, Clyde E. *Preaching for Today*. New York: Harper and Row, (Rev. ed.) 1987.

Farra, Harry. *The Sermon Doctor*. Grand Rapids: Baker, 1989.

Fasol, Al. *A Complete Guide to Sermon Delivery*. Nashville: Broadman and Holman, 1996.

Greidanus, Sidney. *The Modern Preacher and the Ancient Text*. Grand Rapids: Eerdmans, 1988.

_____. *Preaching Christ from the Old Testament*. Grand Rapids: Eerdmans, 1999.

Hamilton, Donald L. *Homiletical Handbook*. Nashville: Broadman, 1992.

Henderson, David W. *Culture Shift: Communicating God=s Truth to Our Changing World*. Grand Rapids: Baker, 1998.

Holbert, John C. and Ronald J. Allen. *Holy Root, Holy Branches: Christian Preaching from the Old Testament*. Nashville: Abingdon, 1995.

Holbert, John C. *Preaching Old Testament: Proclamation & Narrative in the Hebrew Bible*. Nashville: Abingdon, 1991.

Hostetler, Michael J. *Illustrating the Sermon*. Grand Rapids: Zondervan, 1989.

_____. *Introducing the Sermon: The Art of Compelling Beginnings*. Grand Rapids: Zondervan, 1986.

Howard, J. Grant. *Creativity in Preaching*. Zondervan, 1987.

Hybels, Bill, Stuart Briscoe, and Haddon Robinson. *Mastering Contemporary Preaching*. Portland, OR: Multnomah, 1989.

Jacks, G. Robert. *Getting the Word Across: Speech Communication for Pastors and Lay Leaders*. Grand Rapids: Eerdmans, 1995.

_____. *Just Say the Word: Writing for the Ear*. Grand Rapids: Eerdmans, 1996.

Jensen, Richard A. *Telling the Story: Variety and Imagination in*

Preaching. Minneapolis: Augsburg Press, 1979.

Jones, Ilion T. *Principles and Practice of Preaching*. Nashville: Abingdon, 1955.

Kaiser, Walter C. Jr. *Toward an Exegetical Theology*. Grand Rapids: Baker, 1981.

Killinger, John. *Fundamentals of Preaching*. Philadelphia: Fortress Press, 1985.

Klein, George L., ed. *Reclaiming the Prophetic Mantle: Preaching the Old Testament Faithfully*. Nashville: Broadman, 1992.

Koller, Charles W. *Expository Preaching without Notes*. Grand Rapids: Baker, 1962.

Larsen, David L. *The Anatomy of Preaching*. Grand Rapids: Kregel, 1999.

Lewis, Ralph L. and Lewis, Gregg. *Inductive Preaching: Helping People Listen*. Westchester, IL: Crossway Books, 1983.

_____. *Learning to Preach Like Jesus*. Westchester, IL: Crossway Books, 1989.

Liefeld, Walter L. *New Testament Exposition: From Text to Sermon*. Grand Rapids: Zondervan, 1984.

Lischer, Richard, ed. *Theories of Preaching: Selected Readings in the Homiletical Tradition*. Wheaton, IL:, Richard Owens Roberts Publishers.

Lloyd-Jones, D. Martyn, *Preaching and Preachers*. Grand Rapids: Zondervan, 1971.

Logan, Samuel T. Jr. ed. *The Preacher and Preaching: Reviving the Art in the Twentieth Century*. Phillipsburg, NJ: Presbyterian and Reformed, 1986.

Long, Thomas G. *Preaching and the Literary Forms of the Bible*. Philadelphia: Fortress Press, 1989.

_____. *The Witness of Preaching*. Louisville, KY: Westminster/John Knox Press, 1989.

Loscalzo, Craig A. *Evangelistic Preaching that Connects*. Downers Grove, IL: InterVarsity Press, 1995.

_____. *Preaching Sermons that Connect*. Downers Grove, IL: InterVarsity Press, 1992.

Lowry, Eugene L. *How to Preach a Parable: Designs for Narrative Sermons*. Nashville: Abingdon, 1989.

_____. *The Homiletical Plot*. Atlanta: John Knox Press, 1980.

MacArthur, Jr., John, *et al. Rediscovering Expository Preaching*. Dallas: Word, 1992.

Macpherson, Ian. *The Burden of the Lord*. Nashville: Abingdon, 1955.

Markquart, Edward F. *Quest for Better Preaching: Resources for Renewal in the Pulpit*. Minneapolis: Augsburg, 1985.

Massey, James Earl. *The Burdensome Joy of Preaching*. Nashville: Abingdon, 1996.

McClure, John S. *The Four Codes of Preaching: Rhetorical Strategies*. Minneapolis: Augsburg Fortress, 1991.

McDill, Wayne. *The 12 Essential Skills for Great Preaching*. Nashville: Broadman & Holman, 1994.

Miller, Calvin. *Marketplace Preaching*. Grand Rapids: Baker Books, 1995.

_____. *Spirit, Word, and Story*. Grand Rapids: Baker, 1996.

_____. *The Empowered Communicator: 7 Keys to Unlocking an Audience*. Nashville: Broadman & Holman, 1994.

Mitchell, Henry H. *Black Preaching: An Analysis of the Black Homiletic Tradition*. San Francisco, Harper and Row, 1979.

_____. *Celebration and Experience in Preaching*. Nashville: Abingdon, 1990.

Montoya, Alex. *Preaching with Passion*. Grand Rapids: Kregel, 2000.

Olford, Stephen F. and David L. Olford. *Anointed Expository Preaching*. Nashville: Broadman & Holman, 1998.

Pattison, T. Harwood. *The Making of the Sermon*. Philadelphia: American Baptist Publication Society, 1941.

Perry, Lloyd M. *A Manual for Biblical Preaching*. Grand Rapids: Baker, 1965.

_____. *Biblical Preaching for Today=s World*. Chicago: Moody Press, 1973.

_____. *Biblical Sermon Guide*. Grand Rapids: Baker, 1970.

Piper, John. *The Supremacy of God in Preaching*. Grand Rapids: Baker, 1990.

Pitt-Watson, Ian. *A Primer for Preachers*. Grand Rapids: Baker, 1986.

Robinson, Haddon W. *Biblical Preaching*. Grand Rapids: Baker, 1980.

Rummage, Stephen Nelson. *Planning Your Preaching*. Grand Rapids: Kregel, 2002.

Sangster, W. E. *The Craft of Sermon Construction*. Philadelphia: Westminster, 1951.

Scherer, *For We Have This Treasure*. Grand Rapids: Baker, 1976.

Shaddix, Jim. *The Passion Driven Sermon*. Nashville: Broadman & Holman, 2003.

Skinner, Craig. *The Teaching Ministry of the Pulpit*. Lanham, MD: University Press of America, (Rep.) 1988.

Sleeth, Ronald E. *Persuasive Preaching*. New York: Harper and Row, 1956.

Spurgeon, Charles H. *Lectures to My Students*. Ross-Shire, Great Britain: Christian Focus Publications, rep. 1998.

Stewart, James S. *Heralds of God*. New York: Charles Scribner's Sons, 1946.

Stott, John R. W. *Between Two Worlds*. Eerdmans, 1982.

Sweazey, George E. *Preaching the Good News*. Englewood Cliffs, NJ: Prentice-Hall, 1976.

Troeger, Thomas H. *Ten Strategies for Preaching in a Multi-Media Culture*. Nashville: Abingdon, 1996.

Van Harn, Roger E. *Pew Rights: For People Who Listen to Sermons*. Grand Rapids: Eerdmans, 1992.

Vines, Jerry. *A Guide to Effective Sermon Delivery*. Chicago: Moody Press, 1986.

Vines, Jerry and Jim Shaddix. *Power in the Pulpit: How to Prepare and Deliver Expository Sermons*. Chicago: Moody, 1999.

Ward, James and Christine Ward. *Preaching from the Prophets*. Nashville: Abingdon, 1995.

Wiersbe, Warren W. *The Dynamics of Preaching*. Grand Rapids: Baker, 1999.

_____. *Preaching and Teaching with Imagination: the Quest for Biblical Ministry*. Wheaton, IL: Victor Books, 1994.

Willhite, Keith and Scott M. Gibson, eds. *The Big Idea of Biblical Preaching*. Grand Rapids: Baker, 1998.

Willhite, Keith. *Preaching with Relevance: Without Dumbing Down*. Grand Rapids: Kregel, 2001.

Willimon, William H. *The Intrusive Word: Preaching to the Unbaptized*. Grand Rapids: Eerdmans, 1994.

_____. *Peculiar Speech: Preaching to the Baptized*. Grand Rapids: Eerdmans, 1992.

Christian Focus Publications
publishes books for all ages

Our mission statement –

STAYING FAITHFUL

In dependence upon God we seek to help make His infallible Word, the Bible, relevant. Our aim is to ensure that the Lord Jesus Christ is presented as the only hope to obtain forgiveness of sin, live a useful life and look forward to heaven with Him.

REACHING OUT

Christ's last command requires us to reach out to our world with His gospel. We seek to help fulfil that by publishing books that point people towards Jesus and help them develop a Christ-like maturity. We aim to equip all levels of readers for life, work, ministry and mission.

Books in our adult range are published in three imprints.

Christian Focus contains popular works including biographies, commentaries, basic doctrine and Christian living. Our children's books are also published in this imprint.

Mentor focuses on books written at a level suitable for Bible College and seminary students, pastors, and other serious readers. The imprint includes commentaries, doctrinal studies, examination of current issues and church history.

Christian Heritage contains classic writings from the past.

Christian Focus Publications, Ltd
Geanies House, Fearn,
Ross-shire, IV20 1TW, Scotland, United Kingdom
info@christianfocus.com